K·I·S·S

The Only Guides You'll Ever Need!

THIS SERIES IS YOUR TRUSTED GUIDE through all of life's stages and situations. Want to learn how to surf the Internet or care for your new dog? Or maybe you'd like to become a wine connoisseur or an expert gardener? The solution is simple: just pick up a K.I.S.S. Guide and turn to the first page.

Expert authors will walk you through the subject from start to finish, using simple blocks of knowledge to build your skills one step at a time. Build upon these learning blocks and by the end of the book, you'll be an expert yourself! Or, if you are familiar with the topic but want to learn more, it's easy to dive in and pick up where you left off.

The K.I.S.S. Guides deliver what they promise: simple access to all the information you'll need on one subject. Other titles you might want to check out include: Playing Guitar, Playing Golf, Living With a Dog, Microsoft Windows, and Astrology.

GUIDE TO THE

Internet

WILLIE LUBKA
& NANCY HOLDEN

Foreword by **Barry Golson**

Editor in Chief, Yahoo! Internet Life

A Dorling Kindersley Book

Dorling **DK** Kindersley

LONDON, NEW YORK, SYDNEY, DELHI, PARIS,
MUNICH AND JOHANNESBURG

Dorling Kindersley Limited
Editorial Director Valerie Buckingham
Senior Editor Bridget Hopkinson

Managing Art Editor Stephen Knowlden
Jacket Designer Neal Cobourne

Dorling Kindersley Publishing, Inc.
Editorial Director LaVonne Carlson
Series Editor Beth Adelman
Editor Matthew Kiernan
Copyeditor Wendy Christensen

Created and produced for Dorling Kindersley by
THE FOUNDRY, part of The Foundry Creative Media Company Ltd,
Crabtree Hall, Crabtree Lane, Fulham, London SW6 6TY

The Foundry project team
Frances Banfield, Lucy Bradbury, Josephine Cutts, Sue Evans, Douglas Hall,
Sasha Heseltine, Dave Jones, Jennifer Kenna, Lee Matthews, Ian Powling, Bridget Tily,
Karen Villabona, Nick Wells, and Polly Willis. Special thanks to Karen Fitzpatrick.

Published in the United States by
Dorling Kindersley Publishing, Inc.
95 Madison Avenue
New York, New York 10016

Published in Great Britain by
Dorling Kindersley Limited,
9 Henrietta Street,
London WC2E 8PS

A CIP catalogue record for this book is available from the British Library

ISBN 0-7513-2738-7

Colour reproduction by Kingswood Steele, Modern Age and The Foundry
Printed and bound by Printer Industria Grafica, S.A., Barcelona, Spain

For our complete catalogue visit
www.dk.com

Contents at a Glance

CONTENTS

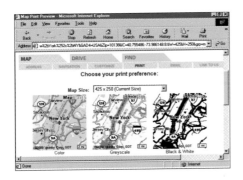

PART THREE *Finding the Good Stuff* 206

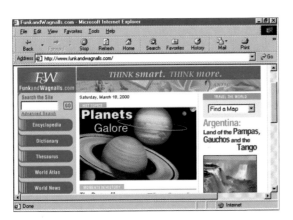

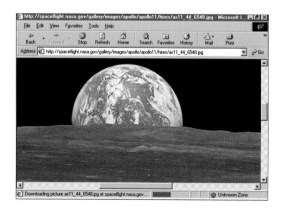

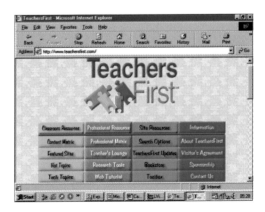

Foreword

The magazine I edit, Yahoo! Internet Life, is generally aimed at a sophisticated (though nontechnical) web user. Yet we, too, believe passionately in the art of keeping it simple. From the beginning, I always felt it was important to cover the creative chaos that is the Internet in an orderly, common-sense way. To be confused by this brash new digital world does not mean you're a dummy or an idiot, as some would have it. On the contrary, most bright and educated people know how important it is to master the essentials of the Internet. But most of us have lives, too. We may be lawyers or doctors or candlestick makers, but what we don't have is the time to decipher the obscure, technical, and ever-changing instructions of the computer and Internet worlds.

I fell hard for this new world in the mid-80s. Though I was always more a klutz than a geek when it came to software and hardware, I was thrilled by what these new machines could do, especially when they began to be connected to each other. It seemed as if every few months there were dazzling new tricks they could perform. But I was astonished at how poorly the inventors of these tricks explained themselves. Manuals – when they could be called that – were unreadable. Screens popped up without instructions. You didn't know how to start, what to do, how to exit. Exciting new programs were created that promised you could write more efficiently, balance your budget, send messages, pay your bills. But the task of telling you how to do these things seemed to be the last thing on the inventors' minds, and was often assigned to non-English speakers. At least it wasn't any language I understood.

In this Internet era, with a new web site going up every second, with the nonstop avalanche of new programs, new services, new browsers, new hardware, and new ways of accessing the Net, it's even more important to try to explain things clearly, basically, and directly. It's worth noting that some of the biggest names on the Internet – America Online, Yahoo!, Amazon – owe much of their multibillion dollar successes to keeping things simple. But that's still not the rule in cyberspace.

As the rest of the Internet keeps growing, with such issues as privacy, security, search techniques, multimedia, kids online, education, and the prospects of nearly everything we know being affected by the onrushing Information Highway, it's vital to step back and review the rules of the road. That applies to new "drivers" and old alike. Because that's almost everyone's guilty little secret: We don't know as much as the technical people think we do. Not because it's so terribly difficult, but because it's often explained so badly.

And that's why it's worth supporting those who, like the authors of this book, are putting up road signs you can read clearly and get you where you want to go. Have a good trip!

Barry Golson

BARRY GOLSON
Editor in Chief, Yahoo! Internet Life

Introduction

UP UNTIL THE MID-1990s, most of the people connecting to the Internet for the first time were experienced computer users. They knew all about hardware, software, and computer networks. Many already used their home computers for word processing and financial record-keeping. Going online was fairly easy – an extension of skills they already knew.

Along with these experienced users, there was another group that took to the Internet very naturally – youngsters who had grown up with computers. The generation who are now students, from elementary school through college, have likely used computers most of their lives.

If you've never been a computer nerd and you're not a kid anymore, you may have a vague feeling that the world is passing you by. In the United States and the rest of the industrialized world, the Internet is becoming a top-to-bottom cultural phenomenon. We're moving toward a time when not being on the Net will be like not having a telephone or a television. So even though you're still finding your way around your computer, you probably want to get online as soon as possible.

Approaching cyberspace for the first time can be both exciting and intimidating. But it's really a lot simpler than it looks. Set aside some time to play around, to practice. You'll be glad you did. At first, when it's slow going, you may be tempted to think there's something wrong with your computer – or with you. By the time you finish this book you'll know it isn't either!

When we told people we were writing a book introducing the Internet, many were skeptical. They asked questions like, "Will it be in English?" So, we knew there were a few barriers to overcome. We've carefully studied many other books, and we think we know what those barriers are. We also know because we've been there. We struggled ourselves. And we want to share our experience by writing a new kind of book. In this book, we intend to keep it simple.

Learning to use the Net isn't hard. And once you get up to speed, you'll relish your feeling of greater power, access to an almost limitless world of information, new opportunities to connect with other people near and far, and more options for enjoying life and learning. It may even boost your career. This book will tear down the barriers and give you the confidence and knowledge you really need.

In this book, we'll use ordinary language, and define a few important new terms along the way. Once you understand the basics, you won't have to hack your way through a thicket of technological hype. You'll learn to navigate the World Wide Web by actually doing it, with your own computer and programs. There are oceans of ideas and practical help readily available online. We'll help you learn how to find them.

You won't find step-by-step instructions about specific types of computers, software, or web sites in this book – for a good reason. This type of information will likely be outdated before you ever read it. The pace of change in cyberspace is so rapid that specific information could be wrong by the time this book hits a bookstore. Web sites are updated monthly, weekly, daily – even hourly. New sites come into being and old ones disappear so rapidly that it's impossible to keep the lists current. The Internet is on the cutting edge of modern technology, where change and development occur at their fastest.

Technology will keep changing the landscape of the Internet. An amazing variety of new ideas are just coming over the horizon. The good news for Internet users is that the trend is toward increasing variety and decreasing complexity, making the Internet faster, simpler, and more useful to the average consumer – people like us.

We recommend you start by reading this book straight through once. Take your time and have fun discovering the Internet along with us. Then, leave it near your computer and consult it as you work.

The Internet is a huge subject, and no book could cover all the details. New users often think they need to start by learning specific how-tos – where to point, when to click. But weighty books with page after page of click-by-click instructions can just bog you down and make the Internet seem complicated, obscure, and forbidding. This book is intended to give you an easy-to-read foundation in everyday language that will help you get up to speed, competent, and confident in cyberspace, as quickly, simply, and enjoyably as possible. You won't find masses of tedious, mind-numbing details here. And you won't find yourself painfully trying to pry the few nuggets of useful information out of endless procedures. What you will find is a straightforward, simple, friendly, and enjoyable path into the exciting new online world.

What about those so-called experts who treat you as if you're really dumb because you don't know as much as they do? These folks often try to wow or intimidate you with lots of high-tech jargon, unfamiliar acronyms and cyber-slang. Don't let that keep you offline! The secret? Ignore them. Use this book, start with the basics, learn and explore at your own pace.

We believe that just about anybody can become a confident citizen of cyberspace. We know we can't possibly cover the whole subject. We can't teach you every specific – there are just too many options, and that's not what you need most anyway! What we will do is give you the basics – the understanding you'll need to master the details. Before you know it, you'll be ready for those details, and we'll show you how and where to learn them. But for now, we want this book to empower you so you'll become comfortable and competent online. You can do the rest yourself.

WILLIE LUBKA & NANCY HOLDEN

What's Inside?

THE INFORMATION IN *the K.I.S.S. Guide to the Internet is arranged from the basic to the more advanced, making it most effective if you start from the beginning and slowly work your way to the more involved chapters.*

PART ONE

In Part One we'll give you information on what the Internet is, its history, and reasons why it has become so popular. We'll discuss the advantages and disadvantages of the Internet and explain why you should use it.

PART TWO

In Part Two we'll concentrate on the growing range of communication options that are available to Internet users, from one-to-one contact of e-mail, to group communication and chat, to ways of reaching out to the whole Internet community.

PART THREE

In Part Three we will advise you how to search and thus find useful information on the Internet. Once you find what you are looking for, we shall discuss more specific ways of searching and of course will inform you how to download the information you find.

PART FOUR

Part Four looks closely at the ways the Internet affects family life and suggests ways that your family can get the most from the Internet.

PART FIVE

In Part Five we will tour the realm of e-commerce and online shopping. We also consider the endless opportunities that are available and suggest some powerful software to help organize your balance sheets.

The Extras

THROUGHOUT THE BOOK, *you will notice a number of boxes and symbols. They are there to emphasize certain points we want you to pay special attention to, because they are important to your understanding of computers and the Internet. You'll find:*

Very Important Point

This symbol points out a topic we believe deserves careful attention. You really need to know this information before continuing.

Complete No-No

This is a warning, something we want to advise you not to do or to be aware of.

Getting Technical

When the information is about to get a bit technical, we'll let you know so that you can read carefully.

Inside Scoop

These are special suggestions that come from our own personal experience and may prove to be useful.

You'll also find some little boxes that include information we think is important, useful, or just plain fun.

Trivia...

These are simply fun facts that will give you an extra appreciation of the Internet in general.

DEFINITION

Here we'll define words and terms for you in an easy-to-understand style. You'll also find a glossary at the back of the book with all Internet-related lingo.

INTERNET

www.internet.com

We think the Internet is a great resource for information, so we've scouted out some web sites that will add to your enjoyment and understanding.

PART ONE

GETTING STARTED ON THE INTERNET IS AS EASY AS ABC

WELCOME TO THE INTERNET

O F THE MILLIONS of people who've joined the Internet community in the past few years, most have probably gone through the stages of slowly growing interest, overcoming doubts, and finally taking the plunge. It's easier now than it's ever been. Computers are rapidly becoming more *user-friendly* and the Internet is becoming simpler to use all the time.

We hope this first Part will fan the *spark* of your interest and make you eager to read on. We're excited about the *power* of the Internet, and we believe you'll be too, as soon as you see what awaits you online. So, fasten your seatbelt! You're about to learn how to "drive" your computer on the Internet highway!

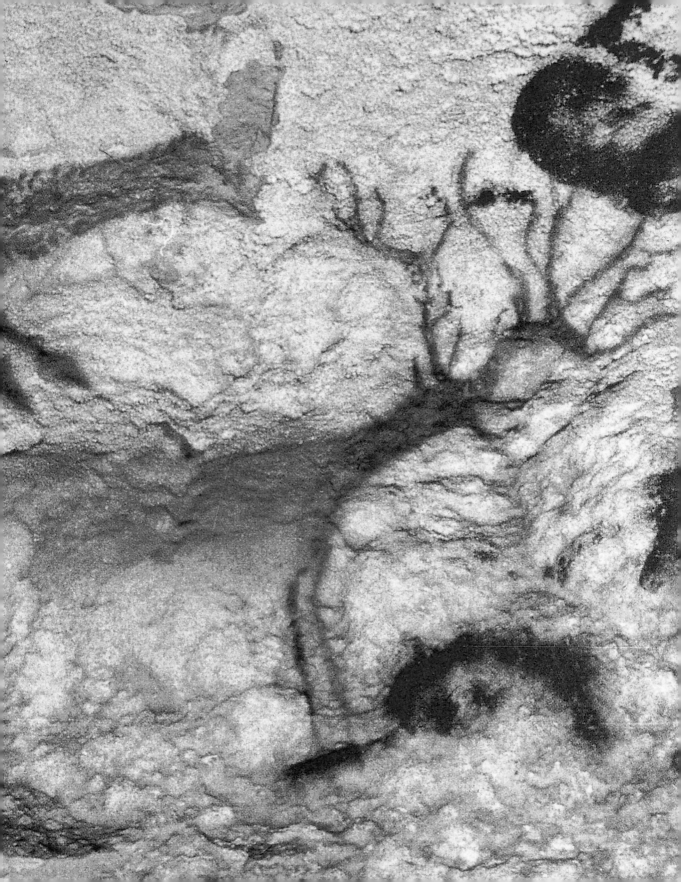

Chapter 1
Getting a Handle on the Internet

THE INTERNET is the focus of so much attention that it's bound to make you curious. Now that your interest has led you to buy this book, we want to answer some basic questions: Just exactly what is the Internet? Where did it come from? How big is it? How can someone get started? In addition, we want to take an honest look at some of the dangers you've heard about. We believe that you can handle those concerns without much problem, and that you'll decide to plunge ahead and get connected. We're going to give you some great reasons why and show you the way!

In this chapter...

✓ What is the Internet?

✓ In the beginning

✓ The global shopping mall

✓ Just how worldwide is it?

✓ The good and the bad

✓ Why use the Internet?

FROM CAVE PAINTINGS TO THE INTERNET: HUMANS HAVE ALWAYS LOVED TO COMMUNICATE

What is the Internet?

THE INTERNET IS THE WORLD'S BIGGEST *computer network, connecting millions of people and organizations in our "global information society." It's really a "network of networks." Although the lion's share of participants are still in North America, international use is growing fast and every continent is now on the Net – even Antarctica.*

Behind the scenes on the Internet, there's hardware sending data from place to place and software that glues the system together and lets you join in the action.

■ **Email is** *connecting people even in the most distant of places.*

What is a network?

A network is a set of connected people or things.
Networks come in all shapes and sizes, from webs to circles to lines. The size and shape of a network is determined by the number of items to be connected, their relative locations, the needs of the users, and the available technology.

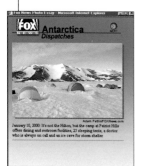

Telephone systems are good examples of communication networks – systems in which a sender can transmit a message across some kind of channel to a receiver. Once communication is established, the sender and receiver can exchange information in both directions. Early telephones carried only audible voice messages Today, all kinds of information – voice messages, video, music, digitally-encoded information and pictorial images – routinely traverse simple telephone lines. In fact, most people access the Internet through a telephone system.

■ **The Internet** *opens up the extremes of Antarctica for virtual travelers.*

Another type of communication network is the kind built by the major radio and television networks – CBS, ABC, and NBC. These broadcast networks carry information in one direction, sending the same programs to many distant points, but are not designed for interactive (that is, two-way) communication. Cable and satellite systems, originally designed to bring improved television reception into homes, are now being modified to allow two-way communication. Today, it's possible to access the Internet through these systems.

You've probably heard the Internet referred to as the "information superhighway." Like the Internet, the Interstate Highway System in the United States is a complex network of corridors with no central hub. Millions of individual vehicles can travel from coast to coast or to any state or local network within the larger interstate network without ever exiting – just like the millions of individual messages exchanged by users of the Internet.

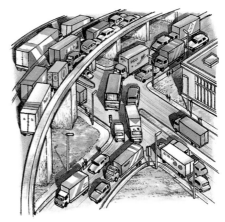

■ **The "information superhighway"** *allows you to "travel" anywhere.*

As a traveler on the Internet, though, you can "surf" from a cozy bed-and-breakfast on the California coast directly to the latest show at the Metropolitan Museum of Art in New York City – with just a simple click of your mouse. It's simple, convenient, and blindingly fast. No heavy traffic, no wasted gasoline, and no tedious days of driving through those endless Midwest cornfields.

As an Internet user, you have at your fingertips the ability to access this network of networks and enter a universe of boundless information and communication.

Computer networks

A single stand-alone computer is not a network, but as soon as two computers are connected and able to exchange data, they form a network.

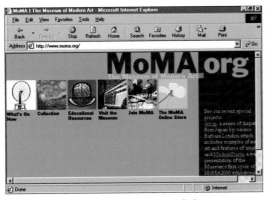

■ **The latest show** *is just a mouse click away.*

Back in the 1960s and 1970s, networks linked large, powerful mainframe computers with varying numbers of dumb terminals. The central mainframe stored all the data and did all the processing. The individual terminals had little or no processing power or data storage space themselves, but merely served as access ports for users to send requests and data to the mainframe and to receive replies. You've probably used such a system when you looked up books in the card catalog at the public library.

More modern networks use desktop computers, each with its own powerful processing capabilities and data storage facilities. Most of these desktop computers are far more powerful, economical and speedy than the giant mainframes of past years. (We'll explain more about desktop computers in Chapter 2). These newer networks include computers that provide common services such as e-mail, and access to shared resources such as network printers. These computers are called servers. Other computers on the network might be individual users' desktop computers that provide local processing power, plus access to the servers. These are called clients. Together, this type of network is called a client-server network.

The Internet is an example of the client-server approach to computer network systems. This relationship is like the pharmacist-customer relationship at the corner drugstore. Many customers come to have their prescriptions filled by the same pharmacist. In the Internet world, the network's server computer software is the pharmacist. Your personal desktop computer's client software is the customer. The pharmacist-server will fill many customer/client prescriptions, including yours.

The network of networks

The Internet is one giant connected system made up of many millions of smaller networks. A mixture of media carry Internet communications, including copper telephone wires, coaxial cable (the same kind of cable that's used to carry cable television signals), fiber optic cable (cables made of glass threads that are also used for some telephone lines), microwaves, and satellite transmissions.

■ **Home networking** is the current craze as the digital home gets wired.

If you plan to connect to the Internet from your home computer, you'll need the services of a computer network. In Chapter 2, we'll talk more about the kinds of Internet service providers (sometimes called ISPs) available, how to select the right one, and how to connect to your provider's network and then to the Internet.

Not all types of computing and network systems are compatible. To provide universal accessibility, early Internet engineers created an open set of protocols for using the Internet – a kind of common language. In computer terms, a protocol works something like the rules of etiquette, but is much more rigid and formal.

On the Internet, protocols are how networks and computers that speak different languages successfully shake hands. You may have noticed that addresses on the World Wide Web begin with the letters "http." This acronym stands for Hypertext Transfer Protocol, which is a set of rules and procedures that allow web sites to work for any visitors, regardless of what type of computer or network they're using.

In the beginning

■ **The language** *of computers knows no international boundaries.*

TO FIND PEOPLE *who were born before the Internet existed, you don't have to visit senior citizens' centers. In fact, the very earliest elements of the Net date back only to the 1960s. During the Cold War, the U.S. Department of Defense thought it might be a good idea for the government, military, research institutions, and corporations to be able to communicate quickly via electronic messages and to share resources and information on a computer network. Like the Interstate Highway System (originally called the National Defense Interstate Highway System, designed to move military cargoes and personnel quickly and efficiently over long distances), such a project would also obviously be useful for national security. In case of hostilities, maintaining communication between military command and control centers, and preserving the integrity of computer records and logistical information might become a matter of life and death. The resulting telecommunications network was created within the Advanced Research Projects Agency (ARPA).*

■ **When Buzz Aldrin** *stepped on the Moon in 1969 scientists had invented the framework for the Internet.*

This network enabled the computers in far-flung military and government installations to talk to one another, and ensured their ability to sound warnings and manage counter-attacks.

Happily, the ARPAnet was never subjected to the ultimate performance test of operational survival during a nuclear attack. Instead, it served as a highly successful prototype for other computer networks. Because the U.S. government provided the funding to develop the network, it continued to control progress at this early stage. But as the Cold War thawed, academic and computer research communities saw the expanding possibilities for the ARPAnet networking model. Networks with e-mail and other communication and information tools began springing up at institutions such as the University of California at Los Angeles (UCLA) and the University of Michigan, in non-military government agencies such as NASA, and in other countries.

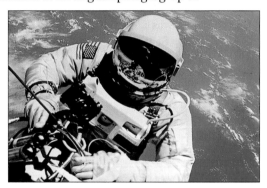

The academics join in

Most of the scientists who developed the ARPAnet worked at universities and research institutions. During the early 1970s, institutions that had government contracts were invited to join the network. The National Science Foundation (NSF)

■ **NASA** *used its technological expertise to make progress in cyberspace as well as in outer space.*

wanted to expand the network to include the whole scientific and educational community. In 1979, NSF established the Computer Science Net (CSnet). ARPAnet and CSnet joined in 1982, when the Department of Defense and the National Science Foundation established a pathway for direct communication between their networks.

Was that the birth of the Internet? People disagree. Some date the beginning of the Internet to 1969, when four major universities established telephone interconnections

between their computer systems. Others say the Internet was born in 1979 when the ARPAnet and CSnet networks were connected. By the mid-80s, many other fledgling

■ **Many networks** *were at the "fledgling" stage by the middle of the 1980s, which made access more extensive.*

networks were on board, access became more widespread, and thousands of individuals were using the Net. A seemingly endless stream of new tools and interactive opportunities appeared, and rapid expansion began.

THE HISTORY OF THE INTERNET

To see the development of the Internet in its historical context, it's interesting to consider what else was going on in the world during the years when computer science was still the province of experts and gurus. For instance, in 1963 the idea of the Internet was nothing more than that – an idea in the minds of the scientists. In that year the Beatles played for the Queen of England. In 1964, the movie, *Doctor Strangelove* made entertaining satire out of the mindset of the Cold War. In 1965 ARPA began research on a "cooperative network of time-sharing computers." In 1966 the United States Surveyor probe landed on the moon. To read more deeply into this early history, see www.isoc.org/Internet/history.

The world online

By the end of 1984 over 1,000 participants had joined the rapidly growing Internet. An organizational system was needed, and this led to the creation of the Domain Name System. You've noticed that internet addresses end with three-letter combinations such as .com, .gov., .org, and others. Theses "domains" became even more helpful to internet users as the number of participating networks grew to over 10,000 in 1987 and more than 100,000 just two years later.

By 1990 the government dropped its restrictive membership policy, opening the door to any organization with the technology and desire to join the Net. The floodgates opened! The world at large started to come online. World.std.com set up shop as the first commercial provider of Internet dial-up access. The private sector moved in at an astronomical pace, creating new businesses and bringing vast changes and challenges to established industries of all kinds.

■ **The first** *commercial Internet Service Provider (ISP) is still going strong in Massachusetts.*

Your interface looks familiar

In the 1980s, people began buying computers for their homes. They were still a novelty, relatively expensive, and often maddeningly difficult to use. When you "booted up" (turned on) your new computer, you'd see a dark screen with just a few enigmatic characters in the top left corner, usually "C:>". Then, you were on your own. What did the computer want? Usually, it was expecting a cryptic collection of letters, numbers, and abbreviations called a command line string, in which an extra space or misplaced comma could mean disaster. While those tricky command lines and the so-called DOS C-prompt were no problem for the experienced programmer or hard-core computer hobbyist, they held a world of terror for the ordinary consumer. And reading the manual was usually not much help; the manuals assumed you already know an awful lot about this strange new beast on your desk. No, computers were not yet conceived or designed as tools for the average person. That C-prompt was a formidable barrier!

The graphical user interface

Enter the GUI. It was the advent of the graphical user interface (GUI, pronounced "gooey"), a much more intuitive and user-friendly type of software made popular with Apple's Macintosh and Microsoft's Windows operating systems, that finally opened the doors to cyberspace for the average consumer. GUI interfaces use little pictures called icons to help you operate your computer. The trash can, an hourglass, and file folders are all examples of icons. With a pointing device (usually a mouse), even a beginning computer user could direct the progress of a blinking indicator, called a cursor, around the computer screen. The user could now convey instructions and data, start and stop program operations, find stored data and perform many other useful tasks quickly and easily. No need to encode his wishes into arcane command strings, and no need to interpret terse and usually uninformative (if not downright misleading) error messages. Just point to an icon, then click the mouse button, and you're off and running.

■ **In the 1980s,** *computers became fashionable and more obtainable enabling anyone to bring a computer into their home.*

The GUI led to a new mass market for personal computers and software for the new machines. Personal computer ownership skyrocketed from 8 percent of American households in 1983 to 43 percent in 1997. Software quickly became a multi-billion dollar business.

■ **Going all gooey.** *The Apple Macintosh with its GUI (graphical user interface) is more user friendly.*

The global shopping mall

UNTIL 1991, though, the Internet was still just a network of networks. Yes, it was incredibly powerful and promising, but still (even with the early GUIs) mostly accessible to experienced computer professionals and researchers. Two innovations changed all that.

In March, 1989, Tim Berners-Lee of CERN (a collective of European high-energy physics researchers, also known as the European Laboratory for Particle Physics) proposed a project that had been evolving in his mind for many years – the notion of being able to link random bits of information with other bits. This kind of complex cross-linking is often referred to as hypertext, and had been explored by previous researchers. But Berners-Lee was the first to join the hypertext concept together with the burgeoning Internet. He called his first web-like software program "Enquire," seeing it as a spare-time project for his personal use.

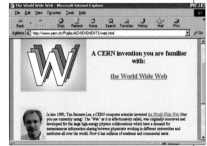

■ **Pioneer of the Web,** *Tim Berners-Lee.*

Berners-Lee tinkered with Enquire, finding that its interconnected network of links helped him and his colleagues keep track of the thousands of researchers, projects, and computers within CERN. Enquire, with its important notions of URL (Uniform Resource Locator, or web address), pages and links, went on to become the foundation for the World Wide Web as we know it today. The web itself was born in 1991, when Berners-Lee's creation was released by CERN.

DOUGLAS ENGELBART

Remember those all-but-forgotten e-mail pioneers? Well, they're famous compared to Douglas C. Engelbart, the brilliant engineer who was so far ahead of his time he was actually ridiculed for years for developing such innovations as the computer mouse, graphical user interfaces, on-screen windows, a browser-style interface, text-editing, on-line video conferencing, and personal desktop computers networked for "groupware," or collaborative problem solving. Yes, one man was largely responsible for all these groundbreaking concepts! Take the mouse, for example. Engelbart designed and hand-built the first mouse around 1963, while he was working at the Stanford Research Institute. Although Douglas Engelbart has finally received the recognition he long deserved as an Internet visionary, he never became even modestly wealthy from his many revolutionary innovations.

The other major barrier to easy Internet access was torn down shortly thereafter, with the advent of Mosaic, the first GUI web browser program, in 1993. Before Mosaic, the brand new World Wide Web was uncharted territory – hard for the average person to access at all, and even harder to navigate. But with the ease of learning and ease of use offered by Mosaic, the stage was set for the Internet gold rush. Commercial Internet service providers soon began offering GUI browsers and other software, and the commercialization of the Net began in earnest.

E-commerce

With the online community growing every day, commercial interests have transformed the Internet, and especially the web, into a huge new global marketplace, open 24 hours a day, seven days a week. It offers avenues for advertising, direct sales, price discounting and many other business opportunities. Collectively, all this Internet business is known as e-commerce.

■ **Shopping is less** *wearisome thanks to the computerized checkout.*

Most of the business world had computerized before the Internet. Remember typewriters and carbon paper? Remember grocery store check-outs where clerks picked up each item, read the price, and punched it into a cash register? People under 30 do not remember any of that.

Today computers are incorporated into everything we do, and almost everything that can be put on computer is going online. New sites on the World Wide Web are being created by the thousands, and are becoming ever more innovative and interactive. In the early 1990s, an Internet web site address (or URL, the now-familiar "http://"), marked a commercial enterprise as up to date. By the late 90s, not having an Internet address had become a real handicap.

Online advertising in 1998 totaled $2 billion. Direct sales over the Internet have begun to take away business from malls and retail stores. In the fall of 1999, more than 14 percent of parents polled said they would be doing back-to-school shopping via the Net. While the growth rate for online shopping declined slightly in early 1999, the range of products offered continues to expand.

■ **It's the fashion** – *online advertising is a big money business.*

U.S. businesses already report billions of dollars of sales and cost savings through e-commerce. That translates into a major shift in the national economy, with old jobs lost and new ones created. Internet business is gradually eliminating many intermediaries, or wholesalers, and the ripples from that change are spreading throughout society.

For instance, travel agents are worried, and have argued that being able to make travel arrangements directly through the Net discriminates against the unconnected. They cited a study by the U.S. Commerce Department that outlines a widening digital divide between those with Internet access and those without, many of whom are members of minority groups. More such disputes are sure to arise.

Just as the telephone affected more than communications and jet planes affected more than travel, the Internet is affecting every aspect of life.

Just how worldwide is it?

THE INTERNET HAS GONE MAINSTREAM. Millions of people have learned to depend on it. The online virtual world is filled with a universe of information and a rich array of communities, business activities, and a staggering wealth and variety of sites and sounds. There is no map to this virtual world, and even if there were, it would change every day – even every minute – as new sites are launched and old ones abandoned.

■ **Travel** is just one aspect of life changed by the Internet.

> ### Trivia...
> How big is the Net? Worldwide, there were nearly 200 million Internet users when we wrote this sentence. North America accounts for more than 100 million of those and Europe another 40 to 50 million.

Another way to measure the growth of the Net is by the amount of time the average user spends online. During August, 1999, the average user went online six times a week, for a total of two hours and 43 minutes.

Television use is gradually decreasing as Internet use goes up. Web sites measure their popularity by the number of "page views," which translates roughly into number of visitors to the site.

Thousands of new users

New users are joining the action at the rate of many thousands a day. While most of these new users are individuals, more and more schools are also getting online.

In education, the Internet supplies both the form and the content — computers have become a primary teaching method and Internet skills are seen as part of the curriculum, like the 3 Rs.

Sales of computers on the global market continue to increase. Nations currently set to greatly expand their Internet usage include Germany, Ireland, several of the new democracies in Eastern Europe, and some Middle Eastern countries.

The U.S. is far ahead of the rest of the world in individual computer ownership, but the other industrialized nations are quickly catching up. However, the Third World lags far behind in all forms of communications and computer technology, making terms like "World Wide Web" somewhat misleading.

■ **Developing countries** *are a long way behind the rest of the world when it comes to technology.*

Still some barriers

Within the U.S. the demographics of Internet use have expanded from a core of highly educated, white, male, English-speaking, technologically-savvy early users to include a more diverse population. But there are still barriers for many groups. Black Educational

■ **The Internet** *helped build the craze for the film* The Blair Witch Project.

Television (BET) Holdings is expanding a web site it launched in 1995. The NAACP, the United Negro College Fund, and other Black leadership organizations will use the BET site to try to reverse the trend that has skewed Internet usage to a white audience.

INTERNET

www.BET.com

Black Entertainment Television's web site represents a significant addition to existing web sites aimed at particular minority audiences, such as www.netnoir.com for African-Americans and www.latinolink.com for Hispanic-Americans.

Who's in charge?

There is no central governing authority with power over the Internet. Each of the computer networks that make up the Net is run by the owners and managers of that particular piece in the overall framework.

For instance, the U.S. government, which once controlled the whole computer development program, now runs only its own computer networks. Many of these networks have sites with addresses on the web that generally end with ".gov" rather than ".com." Anyone can visit them there, just as you might visit the Post Office or the U.S. Capitol Building. On those sites, Uncle Sam makes the rules and provides the material that visitors can access. But that control doesn't extend to any other part of the Net.

■ **Visit The White House** *online.*

WHERE TO FIND THE GOVERNMENT ON THE INTERNET

DEPARTMENT OR AGENCY	WEB ADDRESS
President	www.whitehouse.gov
Senate	www.senate.gov
House of Representatives	www.house.gov
Department of Commerce	www.doc.gov
Department of Education	www.ed.gov
Department of Energy	www.doe.gov
Social Security Administration	www.ssa.gov
Veterans Administration	www.va.gov
National Transportation Safety Board	www.ntsb.gov
Postal Service	www.usps.gov

■ **The U.S. government** *has a range of sites accessible on the web.*

The Internet basically runs on an honor system, and is no more free of opportunities for crime and fraud than any other system created by humans. Many people who have used the Internet and the web to perpetrate criminal activities have been arrested, prosecuted and punished; others have not.

INTERNET

www.gksoft.com/govt

This site offers a full listing of U.S. government sites on the web. Links within government sites will take you to the offices of individual members of Congress and other government leaders. Web sites exist for all Cabinet departments, most Federal agencies, courts, and embassies in foreign countries.

A good rule of thumb regarding legal and ethical conduct in the Internet is that if something would be illegal or unethical to do in some other place or way, it's likely to be illegal or unethical on the Internet as well.

If you decide to create your own web site, it will be up to you what goes into it. Standards come not from any governing authority, but from the technology (remember the protocols we mentioned earlier in this chapter) and some mostly unwritten etiquette, or "netiquette."

Sites on the web originate from places all over the world, use different languages and reflect many different cultures. Society benefits from this free flow of ideas, and it's reassuring to know that governments have little power over the Internet.

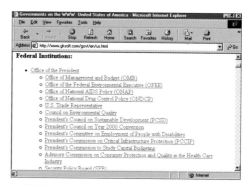

■ **U.S. Government sites** *are listed on the web.*

That doesn't mean, of course, that governments can't find ways to block free Internet access. Some have done so by regulating the providers, and some have attempted to censor certain kinds of information or materials. The freedoms offered by the Internet – rapid, global communications, instant access to all kinds of information and images – have naturally raised many questions about what limits, if any, might be needed.

The good and the bad

WORLD-CHANGING *advances in technology always bring some predictions of doom, but no one can stop progress. When you have a tiger by the tail, you need to watch out for its teeth and claws! The good, bad, and ugly of the Internet is us, the human beings who use it. On the Net we display our best – and our worst.*

■ **Finding the right** *CD to buy is easy.*

While the Net offers new ways to locate and access existing information, it's also contributing its own wealth of new knowledge, information, and opportunities. The Internet and the web are creating dozens of brand new careers – webmasters, animation designers, content editors, page designers – as well as fueling myriad career tracks in e-commerce, computer technology, education, research, information brokering, and thousands of other related specialties. The lure of the Net is feeding the huge demand for home computers, just as the information superhighway at our fingertips is changing the definition of education.

Traveling on the net

When you begin to travel on the Net, you may feel a gradual but pretty thorough change taking place in your lifestyle. Over time, you'll discover that your phone bill goes down due to e-mail, your Christmas shopping no longer requires you to lug big packages through the mall, and you'll be able to quickly locate the exact book or CD you want rather than settling for whatever you can find at the corner store. It's a sense of empowerment, and it feels good!

But you may also find things that may disturb you. From neo-Nazis to advocates of violence to jailed criminals to pornographers, you're sure to run into images, information, and ideas that you don't like on the Internet. Free speech includes the freedom to say things other people may not like.

Trivia...

You're going to hear more and more in the news about convergence. Convergence is changing the way we receive different media. Instead of having separate appliances for TV, telephone, Internet, fax, music, and other electronic functions, full convergence might mean one central home, office, or mobile access point bringing a number of information and entertainment streams into one one multifunctional, highly networked, appliance. We'll talk some more about these exciting changes in detail in Chapter 15, "Multimedia."

Name any human weakness and you can find it on the Net. For instance, of the millions of Internet users who've applied for a credit card or a loan online, some have found themselves in debt or taken in by scams – just like in offline life. And, you might be horrified to find yourself talking to others in a way you'd never do in person.

In short, the same rules of behavior that guide you everywhere else in life should also pertain when you're online. But because online we're all invisible, the old-fashioned rules, etiquette, and courtesies are sometimes overlooked. Seize the Internet opportunity, but take care!

Cooperation and competition

An amazing era of cooperation brought the Internet into existence. Since then, flurries of competitive skirmishing have sometimes placed that cooperation, and the seamless integration of the Internet, in jeopardy. Consumers benefit from cooperation, since universal, common standards keep the Net working. On the other hand, while competition can cause fragmentation and restrict access to services and information, it also fuels innovation and improvement. In 1999, the U.S. government brought anti-trust charges against Microsoft, Microsoft's Chairman William "Bill" Gates was messily socked with a pie in the face, and a fight broke out over instant messaging. Expect many future controversies. Fortunately, people are working together to meet the challenges in ways that keep the Internet integrated and growing.

As a new Internet user, you're about to join a global cooperative venture that will let you offer your personal resources to the pool of collective thinking, as well as enable you to make use of the ideas and resources provided by your millions of fellow "netizens."

Keeping your balance

The Internet offers an unparalleled and ever-growing world of opportunities. But keep a healthy balance in your life, and keep your Internet explorations in perspective. More than a few divorces have been attributed to "Internet addiction!" "He has no time for me anymore," she said. "She threw the budget out the window and ordered all this stuff over the Net," he said. Then there's carpal tunnel syndrome and other so-called repetitive stress injuries, blurred eyesight, and a strange sense of withdrawal from the real world.

■ A pie in the *face for Microsoft's Chairman Bill Gates is replayed in a screen saver.*

Just as television can take over all our leisure time and turn us into couch potatoes, so can too much time spent online.

It can turn us into hunched, squinting creatures of the night. Even if you've never before felt any hint of addiction to anything, watch out for the warning signs. Don't push aside the family and friends you love just to surf the Net. If you gamble or find online romance, remember the hazards of unlimited access and keep your balance.

Why use the Internet?

IF YOU'VE EVER LOOKED *over someone's shoulder as they surfed the Net, you probably heard yourself saying "Wow!" Page after page of colorful graphics flashes by and you want to say, "Stop! I want to see that!" If you are absolutely convinced, ready and eager to get online right now, go directly to Chapter 2.*

■ **Some people** *meet their partners through work but an increasing number nowadays meet on the Net.*

■ **Young children** *can restrict your movements but with the Net you are still connected to the big picture.*

The big picture

Are you disabled and unable to get out of the house? Are you tied to home by the needs of your children or others who depend upon you? Do you live in a remote area where there's no place to go? If so, life can feel pretty restricted. But with the Internet, you can now enjoy easy access to the big picture, the world outside your own territory, whether that territory is restricted to a wheelchair, a small apartment or a tiny rural community.

■ **The Internet** *has visual appeal.*

Unlike television, which is passive — the only interaction is between you and the remote control — the Internet stimulates your curiosity and requires your active participation, putting you into intimate, lively contact with the world. And it's so simple to get started!

You don't have to be able-bodied to get up to speed quickly and easily on the Net. Online, no one knows who you are, how old you are, or what you look like – unless you tell them. You could be six or 60, in bed in a hospital or a nursing home, or out on the patio outside a posh apartment. Professional people can contact colleagues far beyond their own area, bringing the big picture to bear on their own businesses or other activities. Hobbyists can easily contact fellow enthusiasts half a world away.

Reaching out to learn what other people think, feel, and know is a time-honored, gratifying and deeply worthwhile human pursuit. No matter who you are or what you know, there's always more to discover and learn!

Your busy life

There's no need to say much here! Busy is the theme song of our time. At the end of that long day when you realize the kids haven't even started their homework, you can point them to kid-friendly encyclopedias online. If it's too late to call your important client or your Aunt Sue, there's always e-mail. Forget your anniversary? No problem. Just visit the web site of the local florist or chocolate shop – even at two in the morning – to ensure that crucial delivery. It's all pretty simple – as well as quick, convenient, and fun.

■ **Forgotten that** *important occasion? No need to panic, flowers can be ordered online.*

Our shrinking world

In the 19th century, the educated, sophisticated "man of the world" spoke flawless French, knew his Latin and Greek, and could quote classical poetry by the yard. In the 20th century, the humanities, though still prized, yielded pride of place to mathematics, physics, biology, and computer science. We admired the inventors and scientists who gave humanity electricity and antibiotics, and propelled us gloriously into space. It's clear that in the 21st century, being an educated, sophisticated "person of the world" will mean just that, literally. We are truly becoming global citizens, active participants in the global community. Products from anywhere are marketed everywhere. Business is global. Increasingly, so are social relationships. From Olympic athletes to oil magnates on the news, all the people of the world seem like next-door neighbors.

Trivia...

Wes Keizer, an aeronautical maintenance man whose home is in North Dakota, is online wherever he may be. Currently working in Greece, he represents an outpost of the U.S., communicating via the Internet with his home office. Many, if not most of the Internet users in the Third World today are actually expatriates from industrialized nations.

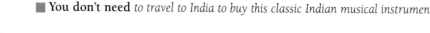

■ **You don't need** *to travel to India to buy this classic Indian musical instrument.*

Any time of *day or night you can order chocolates to make up for that forgotten anniversary.*

Yes, it does take time and practice to learn to use the Internet. Even after you've learned the basics and are up and running online, you're likely to find time racing by. There's so much to see, do, and discover! But don't overdo it. Occasionally, you may glance at the clock and discover, to your surprise, that you've been online for many hours. Then, take just a moment to consider how else you might have used those hours. With a bit of experience, you'll discover how to make the most of every online minute. You'll learn to say goodnight and disconnect, knowing that your time on the Net was time well spent.

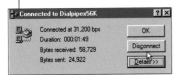

When you *disconnect from the web you can see how long you have been online.*

A simple summary

✓ The Internet joins separate computer networks from all over the world into the biggest computer network on Earth.

✓ It was born about 1969, when government and academia in the United States pooled their resources and expertise.

✓ Every continent is now on the Internet, with North America far ahead in numbers of people online. Business on the web, called e-commerce, is growing rapidly.

✓ There's no governing authority – nobody controls the entire Internet.

✓ Good and bad can be found online. Opportunities are there, but also temptation. It's up to each user to strike the balance.

✓ Busy people like you can get things done quickly on the Internet. You can overcome geographic and personal limitations, and communicate with the world.

Chapter 2

Getting Started

YOU MAY ASK YOURSELF: How much do I need to know to get started? A better question may be: What do I most need to know? In this chapter, we'll take the first steps towards answering that question. We'll start with something you already have – a computer. Probably the most important thing to realize is that you don't need to understand absolutely everything about your computer in order to use the Internet. This chapter will help you build confidence in the basics. Yes, we'll even explain about those two kinds of "ware" that you've heard so much about – hardware and software. We're going to cover the essential things you'll need to connect you to the wired-up world that's out there for you. So what are you waiting for...?

In this chapter...

✓ Driving your computer

✓ Gearing up to go online

✓ Introduction to Internet software

GETTING STARTED REQUIRES CAREFUL PREPARATION

Driving your computer

PEOPLE BEHIND THE STEERING WHEELS *of cars, vans, and trucks usually don't know much about the complex machinery under their vehicles' hoods. But they do know enough to be competent, independent drivers. They know basics like how to start the engine, steer, accelerate, and brake. They know how to use turn signals, speedometers, headlights, and fuel gauges. They also (should) know the rules of the road, how to drive safely, how to read traffic signs and signals, how to handle rain or ice on the road, and what to do (or who to call) in case of a breakdown.*

■ **Your computer** *will soon become as familiar as the controls of your car.*

THREE BASIC FUNCTIONS

You're getting ready to drive your computer on the information superhighway. A computer, like an automobile, is a "system." A system is a collection of interrelated parts organized into a unified whole. Most systems share three basic functions:

1 Receiving some kind of input
2 Processing that material or information
3 Transforming the inputs into a new kind of output or result

Your computer is a system with four types of components: 1) human resources (that's you), 2) hardware (physical parts), 3) software (instructions and programs), and 4) data (words, images, numbers, etc.).

As the "driver," you don't have to know very much about the technology under the hood, but you should have a basic knowledge of your system, its purposes, and how to use it. This section will help you become comfortable and competent "behind the wheel" of your computer. The average computer user probably doesn't know all the things the computer can do.

That's OK, because some of the more obscure functions are probably not very useful very often.

But remember, it's easy to get into a rut! Keep exploring and learning all the time, and you are likely to discover many quicker, better and simpler ways to do familiar tasks.

Hardware

Hardware is the part of your computer that you can see and touch. Your computer's main box contains its Central Processing Unit (CPU), sometimes called its "brain" or "engine," plus its memory (RAM), and its main storage device or "hard disk." You most likely have a floppy drive and a CD-ROM or DVD drive, built right into your computer's main box, and you may have other storage devices built in as well.

■ **The CPU is** *the engine of your computer.*

The main box

The main box also houses a number of printed circuit boards that control various peripheral hardware devices. Peripheral devices include input devices such as your keyboard, mouse or other pointing device, microphone, and scanner, and output devices such as your monitor (screen), printer, and speakers. One of the most important circuit cards, at least for purposes of getting online, is your modem. We'll talk more about your modem later in the chapter.

The CPU is the engine that runs your computer system. Like an auto engine, it may be more or less powerful. Its power is measured in several ways, including the speed and number of processors, and the amount of Random Access Memory (RAM). The greater the speed, number of processors, and RAM, the quicker you can process information – and the quicker you can interact with the Internet.

CPUs also contain hard drives that store software and data; these days new computers typically come with at least 6gb (gigabytes) of hard drive storage capacity.

You may not realize that you have some control over how your monitor displays things. Try changing the settings to see what suits you best. There are several screen resolution options as well as color and appearance settings that have a major impact on how things look and how large things are on your screen. The way your monitor was set when you bought the computer may not be best for your eyesight and your personal preferences.

Controlling your monitor's display is sort of like sliding your driver's seat forward or back to make you comfortable in your car. Take charge, you're the driver!

49

The keyboard is a lot like the typewriter keyboard of old, but with more keys. The "F" keys along the top are called function keys. Function keys are not necessary for Internet use, but they can add lots of convenience to using your computer. To learn more about them, we recommend *KISS: Windows 98* or your software manuals.

The mouse, speakers, and microphone are the fun part of the system. Surfing the Internet really means clicking your mouse to jump from one site to another. The mouse is a powerful convenience tool. Master your mouse — not by emulating your cat, but by reading the books we mentioned above.

Good speakers are more and more useful, not only for listening to music, but for news and even for hearing greetings and messages from your e-mail pen pals. You can answer those messages by using your microphone to send your own recorded voice messages out to family and friends. The printer comes in handy when you find things on the Internet that you want to download to hard copy (print on paper).

ONE EXAMPLE

Let's say you have an interest in genealogy and have recently taken on the project of researching your family tree. You could set up a folder called "Jones Family" and within that have a subfolder for each major branch of the family. In each of those subfolders you could create records for each nuclear family or even for each individual. If information arrives via e-mail, you could immediately save it, right in the appropriate folder. When you want to check that information, you'd open the directory where these files are stored, click on the folder labeled "Jones Family," and select from among the subfolders labeled "John," "Mary," "Sue," and so on.

Fun with files and folders

Computer files are organized in much the same way we used to file all those papers. An electronic filing cabinet is a hierarchy, starting at the top level with a drive, which contains directories. Directories contain subdirectories, (also called folders), and as many "nested" subdirectories (or subfolders) as you want.

Eventually all these directories contain individual files, which may be letters, spreadsheets, pictures, or other varieties of files. Take time to get acquainted with the process of moving around in your computer's storage system.

■ **Computer files** *need to be organized just as paper files do.*

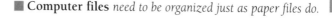

On most computers, the main place where things are stored is named "C," which refers to the computer's hard drive. The A drive is usually the floppy disk drive. Many systems do not have a B drive. (In some computers, B is used for a second floppy disk drive). CD-ROM and DVD drives are commonly known as the E drive; you may have others as well. For example, some computers partition the hard drive into C and D drives.

■ **Folders, sub-folders,** *and files are organized in a tree-like structure, just like a family tree.*

Regardless of particulars, drives and directories are very simple once you understand the basic logic of the structure. Your main requirement, in order to get your Internet driver's license, is to understand the hierarchy of directories on your computer. Set up your own folders and subfolders according to the projects for which you'll be using your computer and the Internet. Give each folder a clear, descriptive name. Then ensure that you'll be able to store and find things, and navigate your drives and directories quickly and easily. This basic skill is important on the Internet as well. Many web sites and online resources use a similar hierarchical organization.

Software

Hardware is "hard" because it has a physical form, while software is "soft" because it consists of electronic programming instructions – you can't actually see it or touch it. There are two main kinds of software. Your computer uses both system software (such as an operating system like Windows 98), and applications software (programs for word processing, managing databases, financial calculations, or manipulating graphic images).

■ **Graphics software** *has the power to make the ordinary appear extraordinary.*

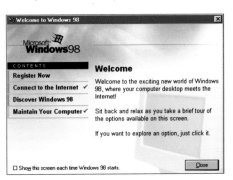

Applications software is what you use for getting things done. There are thousands of software applications addressing almost every imaginable purpose or interest.

They all have an interface of some kind, and many use similar toolbars and menus to provide control over their functions. For instance, almost all computer users have some kind of word processing software because almost everything we do involves the use of language.

■ **Windows 98** *is an operating system.*

Software options

Whatever your interests or needs, there are software options available to make your tasks easy. Choosing the right programs can be confusing. Before you invest a lot of money at the local computer store, first be sure you know what you already have. Read the specifications that came with your computer. If you do buy additional programs, they will come on CDs or floppies, complete with instructions.

Later, you'll learn how to download software programs directly from the Internet. If you decide that you don't like some of this software, you can always uninstall it. In Chapter 5, you'll learn how to uninstall software you don't like or no longer want.

Staying out of ruts

Intending to make computer work convenient, engineers have provided many different ways to do almost any task. This should not cause you confusion if you understand what you're doing. Experiment! While learning the best ways to get the result you want, you're certain to discover new functions hidden behind the icons. You'll come to regard trouble or temporary confusion as a problem to solve and an opportunity to learn something new – not a cause for frustration or panic.

When you consult help menus or manuals, try to think like a computer. You may have all kinds of complicated work underway, but the computer thinks of all your work in terms of specific computer tasks. You'll find help under the words that describe the task you are asking the computer to do.

Computers are logical. Solving problems and correcting mistakes, we learn to follow the logic and not to skip any steps. Pay close attention to any messages that appear on the screen – remembering what they said can help you solve the problem sooner.

Computer crashes

Almost all computers occasionally "crash" or "freeze" while working. You may be barreling along and suddenly notice that nothing is happening on the screen. You try different keys but everything is locked in place. This happens for several reasons and usually does not

■ **Troubleshooters** *like these take you through the logical steps that can help solve some problems, provided, of course, your computer has not crashed completely, in which case you will need to reboot it.*

represent a major system failure. To help reduce your headaches when these occasional glitches occur, good practices include frequent saving of your work in progress, backing up important materials regularly, and not having too many programs open at once. There are also software programs available to reduce the frequency of crashes. These programs allow you to save work and even safely close the file or program that froze.

Finally, if trouble persists and you just can't figure out what the problem is, don't be afraid to call for help. However, it's not a good idea to call techie "Uncle Jed" for detailed advice, or to hop around from one self-styled expert to another trying different things.

■ **Have a note pad** *ready when calling a customer helpline.*

Many well-intentioned people can give advice that causes disaster. When you call a software or hardware company's customer support help line, always document the dates of your calls, reference and ticket numbers, and actions taken, in case you have to retrace your steps. Always be ready to tell the support person exactly what you were doing when you encountered the problem, exactly what happened, and the exact text of any messages that appeared on the screen.

Gearing up to go online

NOW WE'RE GETTING CLOSER *to the moment of truth. We've been going slow, and that continues to be a wise policy, but some things can only happen all at once, like flipping a light switch.*

Modems

The modem is the gizmo that forms a connection, via telephone or cable-TV lines, between your computer and a computer network that provides Internet access. Your modem may be external (a separate box connected to your CPU), or internal (built into the CPU so you don't see it). Either way, the wires that carry information between your computer and the outside world are plugged into your modem, which in turn allows your computer system to connect to the Internet. Modems require software that will enable you to control the modem, set it up with dial-up numbers for your Internet Service Provider (ISP), and start online sessions.

■ **Your modem software** *must be configured to dial your ISP's access number.*

The speed at which a modem can transmit data is measured as baud rate, also called bits per second (bps). The greater the baud rate, the faster your modem will function. Online connection capacity is often referred to as bandwidth or as your "pipeline" to the Internet.

Most new PCs now come with 56Kbps modems ("56K" in common parlance), which is the minimum speed we recommend for web surfing. Locating a phone jack as close as possible to your computer will give the best performance. You may wonder how important this is, and maybe you cannot yet picture yourself complaining "my modem is too slow!" Trust us – it could happen!

Modems typically connect at speeds up to their top baud rate, which means even though you have a 56K modem, your actual connection speeds will fluctuate, and may often be below 56K. Connection speeds are dictated by a number of conditions, including your ISP's bandwidth, and the number of simultaneous users. Most modem software will tell you your actual speed while you're online. If it often seems a bit slow, check the clock! Many ISPs have their heaviest traffic during business hours, so it may help to avoid using the Internet then. On the other hand, if you connect through a university system, daytime hours may be fastest, since student use increases in the evening. If nothing seems to help, you may need to change ISPs.

If your computer shares the household telephone line, remember that calls cannot go in or out when someone is online unless you have a second line. We'll discuss that some more in a moment. If you have call waiting on your household phone, you should disable it while online, since it can disrupt your Internet service.

■ **Your modem** *may slow down during the Internet rush hour.*

Broadband

Finally, a word about a new area of technology called broadband. Among the many new Internet businesses and technologies arriving, faster access for consumers and businesses is a primary objective. Faster speed allows for richer content, such as audio and video, and makes Internet use more convenient.

The term broadband has become a popular buzzword for a variety of technologies that deliver higher access speeds (far faster than 56K), and allow perpetual connections, which means the computer is always connected to the Internet and the user never has to dial up to gain access. We'll talk about some of the leading broadband options.

■ **Modem software** *will tell you the speed of your connection while you are online.*

Connection options

You have several options for obtaining Internet access. You have a modem, but to get on the Internet, you have to use the modem to connect to a network. Looking for Internet access means finding a network through which your modem can connect you to the Internet. Chances are you'll have to pay for this service. Each type of Internet access service has advantages and disadvantages, and many seasoned Internet users hold strong opinions on the subject of what kind is best. Making the right choice can seem confusing. We'll try to make it easier by explaining your options and giving you some common-sense guidelines.

Online services such as America Online (AOL) provide access to their own exclusive content and resources, available only to members, plus access to the Internet.

These services have the advantage of software that is usually easy to install and use. Signing up with them provides access to their exclusive content. One disadvantage is their competitive orientation – they want to steer users to their exclusive content, and often do not provide the best or easiest access to the Internet. Internet Service Providers (ISPs) provide direct connections to the Internet and typically do not require proprietary software like the online services do. ISPs come in many forms, including big, well-known companies like AT&T and IBM, most local telephone companies, national Internet companies like Earthlink and Mindspring, and dozens of regional and local providers.

Free Internet access

Free Internet access may be available if you're a student or otherwise part of a college campus. Call your alma mater to check if they offer free Internet service and if you qualify to use it. If you're a member of the Armed Forces, your base may have a dialup network to access the Internet. A new type of provider offers free access in return for requiring users to view online advertisements. Many areas also have non-profit organizations called FreeNets, which are primarily geared toward building local communities and enabling low income people to enjoy the benefits of online services. Some FreeNets restrict access to certain kinds of Internet materials, while others allow full access. Free access is also available at many local libraries – a good way for Internet beginners to explore the Net before buying their own computers.

■ **Some Internet Service Providers** *like AOL also provide exclusive content for members.*

WebTV

WebTV is one more way to access the Internet. This involves using your television rather than a computer. WebTV equipment costs less than a home computer and you don't have to find space in your home for a new appliance. But, many web sites are not formatted to appear properly on WebTV and without a computer you lose all the additional benefits a computer brings, such as the ability to use applications software like word processors.

You can check out WebTV at many major electronics outlets.

If you happen to live where there are no local ISP numbers, there may be few affordable choices available. Make sure the ISP you choose has a toll-free number for your connection, as telephone bills can be more costly than the monthly charge for Internet service.

Broadband access is a growing option across the nation. Among the several flavors of broadband, the primary competitors are currently cable access and DSL (Digital Subscriber Line) service. Broadband is much faster and more convenient, but also costs more. The rush to sell broadband has led to an intense series of regulatory skirmishes among telephone companies, cable operators, regulatory agencies, and others. The jury is still out on which type of broadband provides the best performance and which will eventually win in the marketplace. To find out if broadband is available in your neighborhood, check with both your telephone company and your cable television company. Also, keep an eye on new technologies such as wireless and satellite Internet delivery. These may be better options as they reach the mainstream, especially if you don't live in a major metropolitan area.

■ **The Internet** *is making it possible to view video online.*

If you haven't yet purchased your computer, be sure to gather detailed information about ISPs and other connection options available to you before deciding which computer components and options to buy.

■ **Teenager in the house?** *You might need that second phone line!*

Do you need a second phone line?

If there are more than two people living in your home, especially if there are any high school or college students in the family, a second phone line might save your sanity. You probably know people who've put in a second line just to support their teenagers' social life. If there's already conflict, it will get much worse when you install that Internet connection. Should you decide to invest in a second computer and maybe even consider a home computer network, the second phone line will be essential.

Even if you live alone a second line can be very useful. Most people find that they spend a lot more time online than they ever expected. If you enjoy real time chat groups, for instance, it can mean that your phone is tied up for long periods. A second line will also allow you to do two things at once – place and receive phone calls, and navigate the Net.

COLLABORATION

Producing this book called for constant contact between two authors, one in New York City and one in far-off North Dakota. The New York author has a second phone line in his office, which enabled him to access the Internet during phone conversations. As a result of this experience, author number two has decided to get a second line installed!

Making your choice

Now that you're ready to sign up with someone for Internet access, we suggest you test at least a couple of options. Many providers offer trial periods free of charge or for low introductory rates.

It's decision time. Knowing yourself and your family members and what your Internet habits are likely to be, think about which of the following factors are most important in this decision. This is just a partial listing of things to consider:

✓ What will it cost? Is this a monthly fee for unlimited time, or a per-minute fee? Does a per-minute fee kick in if I exceed a certain number of hours per month?

✓ How easy is the set-up? Good providers make it relatively painless for you to configure your software to connect to their network.

✓ How reliable is access? During your trial period, did you get a lot of busy signals? Were connection speeds dependably good?

✓ Do they allow multiple e-mail addresses in case more than one family member will be using the Internet? How much do additional e-mail addresses cost?

✓ Have the customer representatives been available, polite, and helpful?

✓ Do they offer 24-hour customer support, or only during business hours?

✓ Do they provide up-to-date tools and software?

✓ Does the provider offer space for your own web site?

✓ Do they have a solid privacy policy?

✓ Will they assist you in how to filter undesirable content?

✓ Does the provider offer access numbers in many places in case you travel a lot?

■ **Some ISPs give** *you space to build your own web site.*

When you sign up with a provider, you'll get a user ID and a password. (Ordinarily, you'll be permitted to select your own password, and change it at will.) The provider will set up an account in your full name, but you'll be identified online by your user ID. When you dial up with your modem to connect to the Internet, you'll always enter your user ID and password to gain access to the provider's network. (Some operating systems will give you the option of remembering your password for you, so you don't have to type it in every time you log on.) You'll also use your user ID and password to retrieve e-mail messages.

■ **Remember to** *keep your ID and password secure.*

Your user ID

Many people use their names for their user IDs, but you can also get cute and use a less obvious nickname, occupation, or fun word. For instance, our list of e-mail pen pals includes redbaron, metaworld, ruralpreacher, and champ.

Your e-mail address will be your user ID, followed by @, then the address which identifies your service provider, a dot, and finally the domain. If you are connecting through a campus computer network, the domain that ends your address will probably be ".edu." Most others end with ".com" or ".net" or ".co.uk" or ".au." It usually doesn't matter whether you use lower case or upper case. For instance, if our cat, Wookie, became an AOL customer, his e-mail address might be Wookie@aol.com.

No spaces are allowed within the e-mail address, though you can indicate a space by using an underscore (Wookie_cat@aol.com).

Online time

Only a few steps remain between you and cyberspace. Now that you have an Internet access provider, an account, a user ID, and a password, it's time to install or configure your computer's modem and dial-up software.

This should be straightforward. Just follow your provider's instructions. But don't be surprised if you need a bit of patient, step-by-step assistance from your provider's customer service representative. When you're all done, your modem will dial up the provider, send the magic signals, and make a successful connection. Congratulations! You're online!

■ **To log on to** *some services you need a user ID and a password.*

Introduction to Internet software

THERE ARE LITERALLY *thousands of software applications available for using the Internet. Don't worry; you don't need them all! In fact, all you really need, especially at first, are a web browser and an e-mail client. We'll discuss lots of other software as we go along, but for now let's get started with these two most important ones.*

Your computer may well have come pre-loaded with a web browser and e-mail client. But you can also go to any software outlet and choose from a wide variety of software packages, usually on CDs, and install them yourself. And once you're online, you'll also be able to download all the software you could ever need or want right from the Internet; some of it for free.

Each one of the following sites has some specialty, and there are also many others.

✓ www.winsite.com
✓ www.shareware.com
✓ www.tucows.com
✓ www.nonags.com

Once you're online, you can download software called freeware or shareware. There are enormous libraries full of this software, and you'll learn a lot just looking through all of the lists of available programs.

See an application, font, game, or other tantalizing goodie you'd like to try? Downloading is easy, and each site will walk you through the simple process. Freeware is just that – free. For shareware, you'll be invited to use the software for a specified period of time to see if you really like it. Then, if you decide to keep it, you'll be asked, on your honor, to send a (usually nominal) fee to the software's developer.

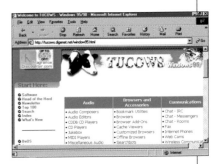

■ **You can download** *both shareware and freeware from sites such as tucows.digenet.net.*

E-mail programs

E-mail means "electronic mail." E-mail is just like old-fashioned mail but without the paper, the envelope, or the stamp. In Chapter 6, you'll find all the details about e-mail; here we just want to get you started on your new Internet journey.

Getting e-mail software in place is the first step in learning a whole new way of communicating.

There are many e-mail programs available. Most of them perform a similar set of simple tasks geared around sending and receiving e-mail messages, although their appearance and advanced features may vary. Among the most popular e-mail programs are Eudora, Netscape Messenger, and Microsoft Outlook. For Apple Mac users, Claris e-mailer remains one of the most popular choices. Corporate systems may use a business-oriented e-mail program, such as Lotus Notes. Online services such as AOL provide their own e-mail programs, which you must use if you're a member of that service.

After you've gained some experience sending and receiving e-mail, you may want to compare a couple of different e-mail clients.

Initially though, just making sure you have some tool for e-mail installed will prepare you to get your feet wet.

E-mail is the most popular use of the Internet, and at least three-fourths of all Internet users report sending and receiving e-mail daily. In Chapter 6, we'll turn you into an e-mail expert. For now, though, get someone's e-mail address, and give it a try!

Web browsers

A web browser lets you view the pictures and words, and, often, hear the sounds and see the animations or videos, that make up web sites, and to click on the hyperlinks (more on those in Chapter 3) that allow you to surf from one

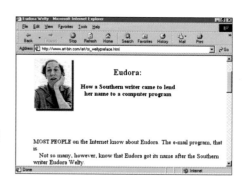

■ **What's in a name?** *The e-mail software Eudora is named after American author Eudora Welty.*

page to another. Two web browser applications dominate the Internet – Netscape Navigator and Microsoft Internet Explorer. New computers usually have one or both already installed. Both browsers are updated frequently, and are available free to individual, non-commercial users. Online services also usually provide their users with Netscape Navigator or Internet Explorer.

Both browsers perform similar functions, while each has some unique qualities, we recommend trying them both and using whichever one you find most congenial.

■ **ISPs** *are like pharmacies – every customer has a special prescription and the ISP will get each one right.*

You may remember the analogy we made back in Chapter 1 between an Internet Service Provider and the local drugstore pharmacist. If you want to work with e-mail, the server fills that prescription – if you want to surf the Internet, the server fills a different prescription, but the process is similar. Once your browser is installed, you're ready to rock and roll on the World Wide Web. Chapter 3 is your guide to the web, with lots of definitions and explanations.

INTERNET

home.netscape.com

Netscape's home page for Netscape Navigator.

www.microsoft.com

Microsoft's home page for Internet Explorer.

■ **Microsoft's home page** *for Internet Explorer.*

■ **Netscape's home page** *for Netscape Navigator.*

YOU DON'T NEED TO KNOW THIS, BUT...

Telecommunications lines, whether phone lines, cable, fiber optic, or satellite links, don't carry your e-mail messages or Internet requests in complete chunks. Instead, based on the discoveries of Leonard Kleinrock and Paul Baran, each transmission is broken up into multiple, fairly small packets of data. Each packet is sent through the Internet by a different, unpredictable, route, and the packets are then reassembled at their intended destination. This packet-switching strategy is one of the foundations of the fail-safe nature of the original ARPAnet, and it's what was so attractive to the U.S. Defense Department in the first place. This doesn't at all affect the sending and receiving of your e-mail messages, but it may help explain all the rapidly-changing numbers and indicators on, for example, your browser's status bar. Look for more details on this in the next chapter!

Other stuff

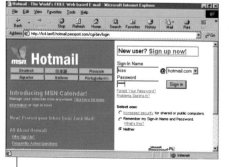

When you visit the software store or the online shareware libraries, you'll likely be tempted to sample everything! You may feel like a kid in a toy store, where everything looks shiny and new and promises to make your life better.

■ **Resist the temptation** *to sample all the goodies you see offered.*

We recommend you exercise your willpower, though, hard as it may seem. Wait until you've worked with the basics for a while and know exactly what's already available on your computer.

E-mail and web sites are just the beginning. There are many other Internet resources we haven't even considered yet. You may be hearing terms like MPEG, instant messaging, newsgroups, FTP, telnet, IRC, search engines, portals, and gopher. Some of these are growing in popularity (you'll hear more about these in later chapters) while others are disappearing and being replaced by newer resources and services.

Just briefly, though, each kind of Internet activity requires a particular kind of software, and in most cases there are several choices available. By the time you finish this book, you'll know what all of these terms mean, you'll have a good idea as to whether or not they matter to you, and, if they do, you'll know how to go about mastering them. You'll become a good steward of this personal resource called your computer system.

■ **Services such** *as Hotmail let you access your e-mail via the web.*

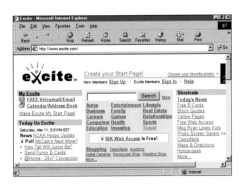

Getting started is exciting. Your computer had already earned a place in your heart, but now it comes to life in a new way, as your portal to the Internet world.

■ **"Excite" is just** *one of the many entry points to the web.*

A simple summary

✓ You don't have to know everything about your computer, but understanding and feeling confident about computer basics will make it easier to use the Internet.

✓ You need a modem and a telephone line, or TV cable access.

■ **You need** *your basic tools to get started on the Internet.*

✓ You need an account with a network to access the Internet. This can be an ISP, an online service, a community FreeNet, or possibly a campus provider.

✓ Certain kinds of software are necessary for using the Internet. The software you need may already be installed on your computer, or it may be provided by the online service or ISP you choose.

✓ E-mail is the most popular of all Internet services. You will get your own e-mail address when you sign up and get connected.

✓ The second major use of the Internet is the World Wide Web; to access the web you need web browser software.

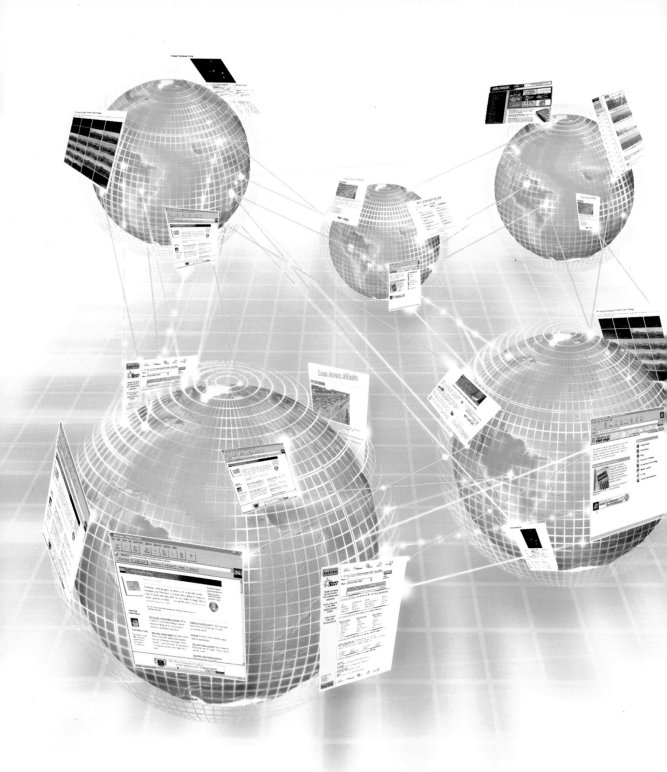

Chapter 3

The World Wide Web

THE WORLD WIDE WEB, or web for short, dates from 1989, when Tim Berners-Lee first released his Enquire software within CERN. It was late 1991 before the web became well known outside CERN, and 1993 when its phenomenal growth began. Before the web, the Internet was known and used mainly by computer experts, academics and researchers, not the general public. In this chapter we'll cover everything you've ever wanted to know about the web, whether it's where the web was born, or how web pages are constructed. You'll learn the basic skills on how to operate Netscape Navigator, on caching pages and much, much more...

In this chapter...

✓ What makes up the web?

✓ At home with your browser

✓ Surf's up!

✓ Common problems

THE WEB MAKES WORLD-WIDE COMMUNICATION A REALITY FOR MILLIONS

What makes up the web?

MANY WORDS USED to describe the web, such as web pages, are based on analogies to more familiar terrain, such as books, libraries, and offices. These analogies are useful as long as you remember that computers and the Internet are dealing with electronic data, which is more dynamic than anything printed on paper.

■ **The Internet** *is a very different medium to pen and paper, but just as easy to use.*

Web pages

In the simplest terms, a web page is a single screen of information, which may contain text, images, animation, and perhaps sound and video. Web users view pages through their web browser software. You can view some web pages in their entirety on your monitor, but most require you to scroll to see the entire page from top to bottom.

Various simple coding schemes allow a web page's designer to specify what text and which images and other features will appear on that page. The designer can also specify how large and where each element will appear, and how each will be linked with other information and other web sites. The most commonly-used of these coding schemes is called Hypertext Markup Language (HTML). With HTML (and similar universally-understood coding languages), different web browsers and other software programs can read the same web page and display it for users more or less as the web page the designer intended.

■ **Star-studded**. *Even the Oscars has its own web page.*

Static or dynamic?

Many web pages are static. That is, the page always looks the same unless an editor or administrator changes the page content. Other web pages are dynamic and may be created or changed as you interact with them. A web page can be flashy and glamorous, or it can be as simple as a plain typed sheet.

Every web page has a distinct Uniform Resource Locator (URL). The most important thing to know about a URL is that a single typo will usually result in failure to get what you're looking for, so precise typing is very important. The good news is that if you find a web page you're interested in visiting again, your web browser makes it easy for you to avoid re-typing the URL. This is especially useful when trying to remember or type long URLs. We'll tell you about that and other browser tricks shortly.

Some people still don't quite realize that the Internet and the World Wide Web are not the same thing. The confusion is understandable, since "www" seems to appear everywhere these days and even non-computer users know it refers, somehow, to the Internet. Remember, the Internet itself is the underlying communications framework, a massive network of hardware and software. The World Wide Web, like e-mail, is an application — a specific use built atop the communications facilities provided by the Internet.

WHERE THE WEB WAS BORN

The Internet came into being in 1969 when the U.S. government and the academic community created a set of unifying protocols and tools that allowed them to interlink computer networks.

As the Internet evolved, before the web's advent, virtually everyone involved in the computer and telecommunications industries began to see the potential that could be realized through cooperation and standards. Early confusion and competition gradually gave way to a universally-accepted set of communications and data transfer protocols.

Great conceptual leap

The stage was then set for Tim Berners-Lee to unleash his invention on the world. Although Berners-Lee had been tinkering with web-like and hypertext concepts for years, it was his appreciation of the power of the Internet that sparked his world-changing innovation. Berners-Lee's great conceptual leap was to marry the power of hypertext – dense cross-linking of millions of individual pieces of information – with

■ **Where it all began.** *CERN – where the web was born.*

the power of the Internet – instant communications among densely interlinked computers and networks. Thanks to Berners-Lee's work, CERN now proudly calls itself "where the web was born" (Visit CERN at www.cern.ch/Public). In this chapter, we'll see how the web is organized, how it works, and just what web surfing is all about.

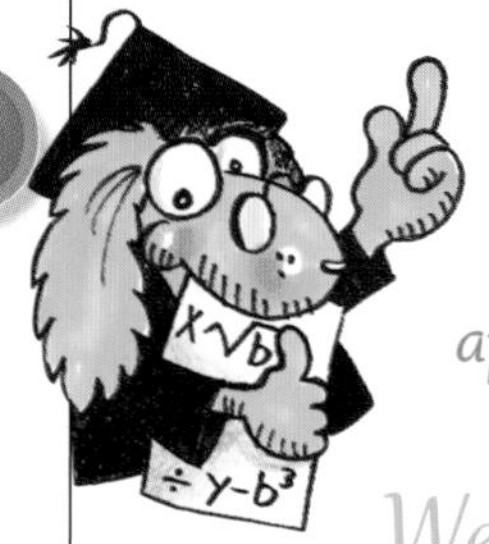

TIP: does case matter? No – and yes. When typing in a URL or other Internet address, use of upper or lower case often doesn't matter. However, for some servers, case does matter and using the appropriate case is necessary to make a successful connection.

Web sites

A web site is a collection of web pages, which may include anywhere from a handful up to millions of pages, published as one interconnected entity. Web sites generally share a common base, or home, URL. For example, web pages that are part of the Dorling Kindersley web site start with www.dk.com. Most web sites have a home page that provides an introduction and lists the site's main content areas. Large web sites often provide site maps, similar to tables of contents, as well as search engines, which allow you to enter keywords and search for pages within the site that contain those words.

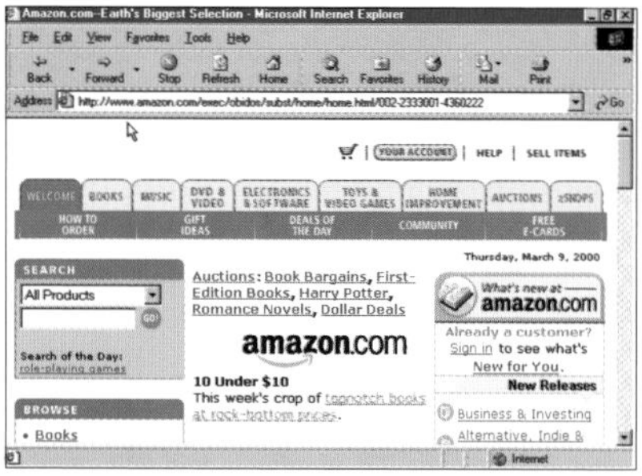

■ **For most sites** *you don't have to type in "www".*

ANATOMY OF A WEB ADDRESS

Protocol: *Web URLs begin with **http** protocol.*

Country: *There are over 2000 national TLDs, such as ".uk" for the United Kingdom or ".ca" for Canada.*

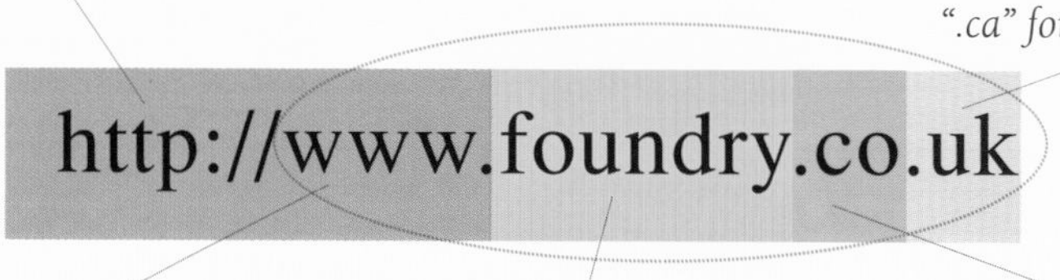

http://www.foundry.co.uk

WWW: *Many URLs begin with "www".*

Domain Name: *The middle term or domain is the place where it is appropriate for your name or business to appear, see page 180.*

Top Level Domain (TLD): *The combination of letters at the end can indicate the type of site, e.g., ".com" is commercial, ".gov" is government.*

Links

To get from one web page to another within a web site, or to another site altogether, you have to find hypertext or hypergraphics on the page you're viewing. Hypertext works a little like the time machine fantasy from science fiction. The imaginary time machine served as a portal between the present, past, and future. When someone passed through the portal, they were transported in the wink of an eye into another time. Hypertext in a web page transports the Internet traveler from that page to a different page or site in seconds.

Hot links

Hypertext links, or "hot links," on a web page usually appear in a different color than ordinary text, and are usually underlined. Point your cursor at a hypertext link, and it will change visually. (On Microsoft Windows systems, you'll usually see a little hand with a pointing finger.) Click, and the hot link will take you away – you'll actually be activating a hyperlink, and opening a new web page that's cross-referenced or "linked" to the page you started from. Hypertext is really what makes the web so much fun.

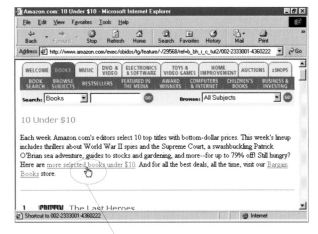

■ **On MS Windows** *systems, the cursor turns into a hand when it is positioned over a hyperlink. Click and you will get a new web page.*

The owner of a web site is responsible for choosing the links that appear on his or her site's pages. Each site you visit will supply its own links. As you follow these leads, it may feel like tracking through a maze, but don't worry it's easier than you may think!

The ability to link a word or image to other web pages or web sites makes the web a dynamic, fast-moving, interactive environment, vastly different from print or television. When you click from link to link to link, you're surfing the net.

At home with your browser

THE WORD BROWSER *conjures up images of libraries, where readers browse through endless stacks of books, or of department stores, where shoppers browse through aisles of clothing and other goods. The software applications called web browsers are somewhat similar. Your web browser is the tool that lets you dig into the stores of information and images on the web, to have a look-see, and then to move on and continue digging and looking – as long as you stay interested.*

Two browsers, Netscape Navigator and Microsoft Internet Explorer, dominate the market as of this writing. Most computers come with one or both already installed, and both can be downloaded for free from the Internet.

Experienced Internet users, as well as web site designers and engineers, have their preferences. Both of the leading browsers are powerful and effective, each does things the other doesn't do, and each does some of the same things in slightly different ways.

AOL, the owner of Netscape, and Microsoft work very hard to remain competitive, which results in lots of enhancements and new versions of each browser. We recommend loading both onto your computer and trying them out until you get a feel for which browser you're most comfortable using.

Browsing basics

When the web first came into existence, Internet users typically needed a variety of software applications to accommodate each unique Internet activity. Modern web browsers have largely replaced this motley collection of software.

While a browser's main duty is to present hypertext pages (the ones starting with "http"), they also have many other capabilities, including the ability to view material formatted in older Internet protocols such as "gopher" (a hierarchical system invented at the University of Minnesota and named after their team mascot); "ftp" (File Transfer Protocol, usually used for transferring software or large files); and Telnet, a remote terminal emulation program still used by thousands of libraries and organizations.

■ **Browsing the Internet** *is as easy as this.*

Try alternative Internet protocols yourself with the following URLs:

✓ The Panix Gopher Server: gopher://gopher.panix.com
✓ The Dartmouth University FTP Server: ftp://www.dartmouth.edu
✓ FedWorld via Telnet: telnet://fedworld.gov

On most browsers, you don't need to type in the protocol indicator "http://" when looking for an ordinary web page. The browser assumes you're looking for a hypertext page and automatically adds it when you request a URL.

In fact, more and more commonly, web sites are referred to without including "http://". In this book, we don't include the protocol indicator when referring to URLs unless it's something other than "http://".

Starting up your browser

Starting up, or "launching" your browser is just like starting up any other type of software you use. However, you have to be connected to the Internet to access web pages. Some computers are configured so that launching a web browser causes the modem to dial up and connect to the Internet, while other computers require connecting first, before launching the browser.

■ **Home is where** *the house is.*

The web page that appears in your browser window when you first log onto the Internet is called your home page. Most computers and browsers come with a pre-set home page, usually a computer or software's company's web site. Many ISPs program your computer to default to their home page when you dial up. But you can change this default home page to any other page you want. We'll show you how in Chapter 5, "Guidelines for Smoother Sailing." To return to your home page anytime you're online, just click the home button, or the little picture of a house, on the tool bar along the top edge of your browser window.

In addition to the actual web pages that appear in its main content window, your browser window also includes a number of useful and important navigation and control features. We'll go through the main tools and features of each of the major browsers below.

At first, it's fun just to walk through the web with this eager dog on a leash. But your browser can do much more than this, and you'll soon discover the need for its other abilities. For instance, when you find a web site that seems useful, you may wonder how to remember the URL so you can visit there again. Newcomers to web surfing sometimes keep a handwritten log to jot down special web addresses, but the browser gives you a much easier way.

Blaze trails

Browsers blaze trails during Internet travels by making copies of pages you have most recently visited in a temporary storage area called the cache. If you want to go back to a page you just left, hit the Back button on the tool bar, and that page will appear more quickly than it did before.

That's because the computer simply reached into its own internal cache instead of going back out on the web and requesting that the page be downloaded to your computer again. Likewise, hitting the Forward button will move the browser up a notch in the cache. You can customize the size of your computer's browser cache.

Caching pages

Caching pages you refer to frequently can save you a lot of time, especially if the contents of those pages don't change very rapidly. For quickly changing data, such as breaking news or sports scores, you're better off re-loading the latest version of the page from the web, rather than relying on possibly obsolete cached data.

For a more lasting list of the URLs of sites you've visited, take a look at your browser's history list. That's why you don't need the handwritten log. You can change the settings in your browser to keep a short history list, or to save the history for a very long time. It's also a good idea to take control of this process by going through the history list now and then, turning some of those URLs into bookmarks and deleting others. We'll tell you more about bookmarks shortly.

Sometimes you may encounter web pages that have elements such as sound recordings, special animation, or image types your browser is not equipped to display. You'll then see a message box, stating the need for an additional, specialized program, and often offering you the option of downloading that program immediately. These extra, special-purpose programs that complement the basic abilities of

■ **Plug-ins** *enhance the capability of your browser.*

your browser are called plug-ins. Video and some audio files often require special plug-ins. As browsers increase in power and sophistication, though, the need for plug-ins is likely to decline. Modern browsers have been enhanced to automatically handle many types of web data that used to require plug-ins.

Netscape Navigator

At the top of Navigator's window you'll see a title bar, menu bar, and tool bar. A status bar runs along the lower edge. Navigator provides lots of user-friendly features, such as excellent help and product information resources. For descriptions of toolbar elements, just hold your cursor over the toolbar; explanatory labels will appear on screen.

2 Reload: Updates the page in case there have been any changes since it was last loaded.

4 Search: One click to start searching the Internet.

1 Back: Click this and you go back one page. Click forward and you move to the next page.

3 Home: Takes you to your usual start page.

5 Print: To print the current web page.

6 Stop: Click to stop loading a web page.

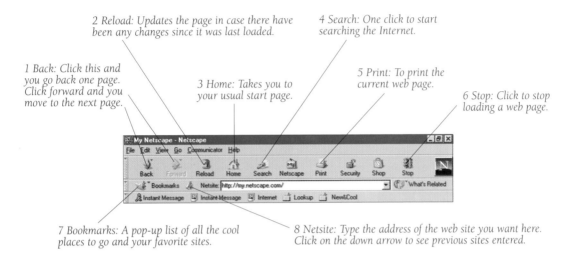

7 Bookmarks: A pop-up list of all the cool places to go and your favorite sites.

8 Netsite: Type the address of the web site you want here. Click on the down arrow to see previous sites entered.

■ **Navigator's** *Toolbar and Address bar.*

Requesting a web page

There are several ways to request a web page with Navigator. You can type a URL in a window called Location in the toolbar and hit Enter. Or, you can click on the File menu, select Open Page and key in the URL. On Windows systems, you can also press the Control (Ctrl) and letter O keys at the same time, and then type the URL you want.

Once you have a web page visible in your browser's window, the easiest way to begin navigating is simply by clicking on links. (Hint: Look for underlined text that's displayed in a different color than the main body of text.)

The status bar appears at the bottom of your screen; it shows information about operations that are underway. Navigator also shows a security indicator on the status bar – an icon of a chain, a key, or a padlock. Most of the time, the padlock will be open or the key broken, but when you're transmitting secure information (such as a credit card number), you'll see the key intact or the padlock closed. If you click on the padlock, Navigator's security feature will check to see that the web page you are communicating with is what you think it is. You'll learn more about this important topic in Chapter 4, "Privacy, Safety, and Security."

We've mentioned how tricky it can be to type a long URL correctly. Navigator offers a shortcut. If you've typed the URL before, you can simply type the first few letters and Navigator will "guess" the rest and complete it for you. If the browser's guess is wrong, just type another letter or two and let Navigator try again. This is a little like an old game called "Name that Tune," which you could win by guessing the tune after hearing only a few notes.

■ **As with** *"Name That Tune", Navigator will attempt to "guess" your web site's name.*

Navigator offers clear and simple Help. We've just touched on a few of the topics you'll find under Navigator's Help menu.

When you have some spare time, you can learn a lot by reading through the entries in Navigator's online Help. It will answer questions you would never have thought to ask, so it's much like sitting with a top-notch tutor and practicing as you learn.

Microsoft Internet Explorer

Although much is made of competition between the two major browsers, they are essentially very similar. Microsoft Internet Explorer offers the same basic capabilities as Navigator, though sometimes using different terms. In Chapter 5 we'll do some fine tuning of the skills you're learning, and everything said there about browsers applies equally to both Navigator and Explorer.

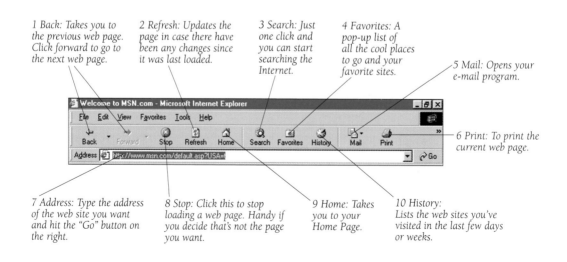

1 Back: Takes you to the previous web page. Click forward to go to the next web page.

2 Refresh: Updates the page in case there have been any changes since it was last loaded.

3 Search: Just one click and you can start searching the Internet.

4 Favorites: A pop-up list of all the cool places to go and your favorite sites.

5 Mail: Opens your e-mail program.

6 Print: To print the current web page.

7 Address: Type the address of the web site you want and hit the "Go" button on the right.

8 Stop: Click this to stop loading a web page. Handy if you decide that's not the page you want.

9 Home: Takes you to your Home Page.

10 History: Lists the web sites you've visited in the last few days or weeks.

■ **Internet Explorer** *Toolbar and Address bar.*

With either of these browsers, you see a similar starting screen – at the top are the page title, menus, location, and tool bars, and at the bottom a status bar. Many of the buttons have the same names; for instance, Stop, Back, and Forward. A few are different; for example, the spot for entering a URL, called Location by Navigator, is called Address in Explorer. Navigator's Bookmarks are Explorer's Favorites. The three ways to enter URLs and access web sites outlined above also apply in Explorer. Navigator's ability to complete a URL for you so you don't have to type in the whole thing is called, in Explorer, AutoComplete. The two browsers' cache, history, and security features are very similar.

Channels

In Explorer, you'll notice a sidebar called Channels. A channel is a web site that has established a relationship with Microsoft, making the contents of its web site immediately and directly available to Explorer users. You can add your own Favorites to the Channel bar, so you can jump directly to them without any additional steps. We'll show you how a bit later.

Within the Help listings in Explorer, hyperlinks provide cross-referencing among related subjects. The Help menu also offers Microsoft on the web, followed by a listing of options for requesting special types of help available from Microsoft's home office.

Finding web sites and information through search engines and directories is an important subject we'll cover in Chapters 11, 12, and 13.

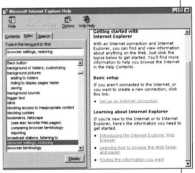

■ **Help is at hand.**
Internet Explorer's Help file has hyperlinks to enable you to move easily between related subjects.

Internet Explorer recommends its All-In-One page, a so-called meta-search engine, which sends a search to all the popular search providers at once.

Other browsers

Because most new computers have Netscape Navigator or Internet Explorer pre-installed, other browsers are much less common. However, there are other good choices available, including several browsers for specific operating systems, as well as a variety of alternatives to the two most popular packages.

The popular web search portal Yahoo (www.yahoo.com) lists more than three dozen available web browsers. A word of caution, though: Many of them come with no product support.

Surf's up!

REMEMBER OUR ANALOGY *with driving a vehicle? At first, it's slow-going and everything requires effort, but soon it starts to come naturally and you get into the flow. The same process of growing mastery happens with computer skills. Suddenly, you'll find you feel quite comfortable surfing the World Wide Web!*

■ **Internet surfing** *can be just as much fun as the real thing.*

Just as drivers have to deal with bad weather, road construction, and other hazards, Internet travelers also experience a few annoyances and difficulties. The Internet is sometimes overloaded and suffers latency — that is, slowing and bogging down of the delivery of data.

Occasionally, major system problems occur in specific geographic areas. For instance, when MCI WorldCom, one of the largest Internet service providers in the world, suffered a system breakdown, service was disrupted to thousands of customers. Barring such major problems, local glitches and the occasional busy signal from your service provider may cause you some occasional inconvenience. But generally, the Internet is highly reliable. You'll soon find that surfing the web becomes a pleasant part of your day. You should, however, note the common problems that can occur.

Common problems

IN THIS CHAPTER, *we've already mentioned many of the problems people encounter while surfing the web. Everyone who uses the web encounters the common pitfalls, such as URLs not working due to typos, dead links, slow-loading graphics, and telecommunication breakdowns. In addition, there will be times, especially at first, when your problems stem from inexperience. Just give yourself a break — you'll figure it out!*

Trivia...
Many people consider the term Error Message a poor choice of words because it implies that you, the end user, did something wrong. Quite often you did nothing wrong at all and the problem is on the other end. Some error messages are delivered to your screen from web servers on the Internet, others are produced by your browser.

Don't jump to the conclusion that something has gone wrong with your computer. Of course, that's possible, but don't even think of it until you've ruled out every other possible cause.

Error codes

There are a number of standard, three-digit http errors used by most types of web servers. These codes are sometimes accompanied by helpful information that provides a clue as to what went awry, but more often they appear as pure techno-babble.

COMMON ERROR CODES

✓ 404 (File not found): there is no web page at the URL you just attempted
✓ 403 (Forbidden): the web page exists but can only be viewed by authorized users
✓ 401 (Unauthorized): you did not submit the required, valid user ID and password
✓ 400 (Bad request): usually means the server was unable to process a database lookup
✓ 500 (Server Error): the server is malfunctioning
✓ 503 (server unavailable): too many concurrent users are trying to see the same web site you are

■ **If you see** *a message like this, don't panic – take a break and you'll figure it out.*

Other error messages include:
✓ File Not Found, or Page cannot be found: if you typed in the URL yourself, chances are you may have made a tiny mistake somewhere. Check carefully for typos, and try again. This type of error also may mean a page has been moved or deleted, or that a hypertext link you clicked contained a typo.
✓ Service not responding: often just a temporary situation such as overloaded lines. You may be able reach the site with no trouble later.
✓ Connection Refused: usually means you need a password to access the information you requested.

■ **The "Error 404 File Not Found"** *message can be because of a mistyped address – or because the web page has been removed.*

✓ Unable to locate server: usually means there is no such web site. This may occur because a site has been deactivated and no longer exists, or because of a bad or mistyped URL.

✓ Unsupported Media Type: one of several error messages which you'll get if a page or link you requested includes content formatted for a special viewer or player that you don't have installed. To see the formatted content, you'll need a special software application called a browser plug-in or helper application.

✓ Under construction: sometimes links are provided to pages or sites that are planned but not yet ready. Look to see if there's a date when they expect to be online, and try again then.

Other problems

You're likely to come across a variety of other error messages now and then. Remember, the error may have occurred at any point in the long chain between your computer and the Internet: your computer itself, your modem, the telephone or cable that connects you to the ISP, your ISP's server computer, the lines that connect your ISP to bigger networks, and so on. Error messages give clues to the problem, but it often takes detective work to uncover the real cause. If you get a series of error messages, or cannot seem to reach any web sites, including reliable ones you visit frequently, chances are good that either your ISP is having trouble, or your modem has lost its connection.

One day while writing this book, we encountered the message, "404 Not Found" repeatedly when looking for a number of familiar web sites. Knowing there was something wrong, we tried to reach the home page of a large local university which had never failed to be up and running.

When the same message appeared, we called the customer support line at our ISP, and learned that the Internet backbone — a main data transmission trunk — was out in a crucial spot, stopping all online traffic in our region.

You, too, should keep note of a few reliably fast, dependable web sites to check when things seem bogged down. This will help you quickly determine whether a problem lies out there in cyberspace, or if the trouble is at your end.

Slow web pages

The most common cause of slow-loading web pages is the use of large graphic images. Pictures and designs enhance web pages with attractive visual richness, but also require

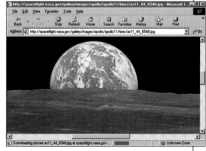

■ **Large images,** *such as this view of Earth taken from the Apollo 11 spacecraft, are very slow to download.*

more data to be transmitted, making web pages "heavier," or slower to load and display. Sometimes, for example when you're doing research, all you're interested in is the text on web pages – the graphics just slow you down.

To speed up your surfing when you just want to tour a number of sites in a hurry, you can temporarily disable the display of graphics. You'll find that the pages load much faster. To disable or re-enable the display of graphics, look at the "Advanced" section under your browser's Options or Preferences menu.

Another trick which sometimes helps speed up slow pages is to use your browser's Refresh or Reload button. Web content is delivered in "packets" which travel on the Internet in bits and are then reorganized on your browser. Sometimes a packet gets lost and delays the whole page. Reloading sometimes speeds-up delivery the second time.

Be patient

Another key resource for dealing with slow web pages is patience. There are lots of reasons for slowness on the web (a wise guy once called it the "World Wide Wait"). Big web sites get overloaded with traffic; small ones may use relatively low-powered servers. As demand for Internet services keeps growing, faster content delivery is a top priority for companies who provide the services and technology. Hang in there: Broadband is coming soon to a modem near you!

A simple summary

✓ Each web page is identified by a unique label or address called a Uniform Resource Locator (URL).

✓ Web sites are collections of related web pages, and links are clickable hypertext connections to other pages and sites.

✓ A browser enables you to view web pages, but also provides many other valuable services.

Netscape Navigator and Internet Explorer are the two most popular browsers.

✓ Surfing means clicking from one web page to another, following a self-directed path of hypertext links.

✓ The problems you encounter are usually not your fault and errors are usually not yours.

Chapter 4

Privacy, Safety, and Security

SURVEYS OF NEW and prospective Internet users have shown over and over that privacy, safety, and security are major concerns for millions of people. These concerns reflect very real, and serious, underlying issues. In this crucial chapter, we'll tell you about some of the potential threats to privacy and security represented by the Internet, and what you can do to counteract them. The number one priority is protecting children from harm. Other vital issues are maintaining control over information you consider private, and securing your personal financial information, such as credit card numbers, against possible fraud and misuse.

In this chapter...

✓ Privacy

✓ Interacting and communicating

✓ Keeping it safe and secure

✓ System security

SECURITY IS ONE OF THE MOST IMPORTANT INTERNET ISSUES

Privacy

■ **One argument for** *the storage of our personal details on the Net is to help the police catch criminals quickly.*

IN THE PAST FEW YEARS, we've been increasingly concerned about the gradual erosion of personal privacy. The advent of the Internet has only intensified this concern. New technologies that make it easier for our personal data to be collected, tracked, and stored, have created an uneasy sense that privacy itself is at risk. Most of us are routinely recorded by video surveillance cameras at supermarkets, parking lots, ATMs, and even on city streets. Giant databases of detailed personal information have proliferated in credit card companies, banks, direct marketing companies, government bureaus, pharmacies, and health care institutions. Telemarketers invade our dinner hours; junk mail fills our mailboxes. Phones are tapped and cell phone calls are intercepted. Photographers lurk outside the homes of famous people.

Concerns

Numerous surveys have shown that preservation of personal privacy is a top concern among Internet users. Privacy advocates have suggested that we need tougher laws to prevent unauthorized collection and disclosure of personal information. Others point out the ways sensible and sensitive collection of personal information can benefit society, for example, police can more quickly and easily find criminals. As might be expected, privacy issues in relation to the Internet are receiving intense and increasing scrutiny from business organizations, government, and citizen advocacy groups.

■ **Some people** *are happy to expose their daily lives through webcams.*

If you use the Internet, we strongly suggest that you follow a few practical guidelines to protect your family, your privacy, and your financial assets.

We'll help you understand the privacy issues involved in Internet participation. When you're done reading this chapter, you'll be a safer, better-informed participant in the marketplace of public opinion.

To learn more about Internet privacy issues and policies, take a look at these web sites:

✓Electronic Privacy Information Center: www.epic.org
✓Electronic Frontier Foundation: www.eff.org

✓ Privacy Rights Clearinghouse: www.privacyrights.org
✓ Online Privacy Alliance: www.privacyalliance.org
✓ Federal Trade Commission: www.ftc.gov/privacy

Passive surfing

At the most passive level, web surfing is just clicking and looking. This kind of web surfing, in which you never actively submit information, seems like a safely anonymous activity – and often is. However, as you surf around the Internet you're not quite as invisible as you may think.

■ **"Visiting" a web site** *involves no physical travel.*

Whenever you request a web page for viewing in your browser's window, the server which sends you that page can detect certain pieces of information about you.

Those bits of information typically do not include anything as personal as your name, but they do include what kind of computer system and which browser you're using, and which ISP you use. The server also keeps track of each page you view, exactly when and how often you visited, and if you were referred by a link.

We say request a web page rather than visit a web page because it's more accurate. If you were really "visiting" somewhere, you'd have to take a car or an aircraft. What actually happens when you go to a web site?

You enter a URL or click on a hypertext link. Your browser software sends a request out to the Internet. Then, the requested page is retrieved and transmitted back to your browser, which displays the requested page on your screen. So, it may be more accurate to say that the page has visited you, rather than that you have visited the page!

FINDING THE FAMOUS

We were once looking for the lyrics to a song we remembered from some time back. Our search led to the publisher of the song, and the name of the artist who had composed and recorded it. The recording artist's personal web page told us he lived in California. We found the address and phone number of his agent in a telephone directory. A call to the agent yielded paydirt – the recording artist's home phone number. Next thing we knew, the composer was singing the song for us over the phone while we copied down the lyrics. To us, this forcefully demonstrated how increasingly hard it is for anyone to remain anonymous in the Internet era.

Hiding yourself through proxies

Most Internet users don't mind the fact that external web servers can track technical variables such as browser type and ISP address. And, in fact, its pretty harmless, because most web publishers simply analyze this kind of data in aggregate form, to track site traffic and assess page popularity. But some people prefer not to let strangers know even the smallest bits of information about themselves. If you feel strongly about this, you can use an intermediary or proxy service that reveals to external servers its characteristics as you view web pages, rather than your own.

You also can use the Internet from one of the growing number of cyber cafés, or other public terminals sprouting in places like libraries, schools, even airports.

■ **Cyber cafes** *are a popular choice.*

To surf anonymously, check out these sites:

✓ Anonymizer: www.anonymizer.com
✓ ProxyMate: www proxymate.com
✓ Rewebber: www.rewebber.de
✓ Aixs.net: www.aixs.net

■ **Surf anonymously** *on the web through intermediary services such as Anonymizer.*

Cookies

There's another footprint sometimes left behind when you visit a web page, but this footprint is actually left on your own computer. It's called a cookie. Internet cookies don't come in chocolate chip or peanut

THE FAVORED CUSTOMER TREATMENT

We have a friend who's an avid gardener. Her favorite web site shows her gardening information specifically tailored to her climate, and to her preferences in flowers. Cookies enable her web server to customize web pages for her. Without cookies, she'd have to re-enter her climate zone and plant preferences over and over again. Another friend visits an online music archive, where cookies allow him to go directly to the kind of music he likes best. One of our relatives regularly checks a sports site for news about his favorite teams. Cookies help him to get the specific scores and statistics he wants quickly and conveniently. In short, cookies remember your preferences and requests, reducing your need to tediously retype them.

butter. They're actually snippets of data that web servers drop off on your hard drive when they deliver web pages to your browser. Cookies serve a number of purposes. For example, they allow web publishers to recognize you when you return to a web page. One major publishing company shows a pop-up window to first-time visitors, but uses cookies to prevent people from seeing it twice. Cookies also allow web pages to be strung together, so, for example, you can use shopping carts in online stores.

On the other hand, many people object to cookies because of concerns about privacy. They are aware that cookies can be used by advertisers to target potential buyers.

If you visit several web pages about golf, you may begin to notice more advertising banners for golf products popping up in your browser window. Now, you may indeed be interested in finding out about new golfing products. But the targeted advertising you see is evidence that cookies have been placed on your computer without your direct knowledge or control. You have, in effect, unwittingly revealed your tastes and preferences. This may well make you uncomfortable.

Privacy advocates also point out that data trails can follow your online searches for such information as treatments for diseases. These hidden footprints could lead to assumptions about health concerns of you and your family.

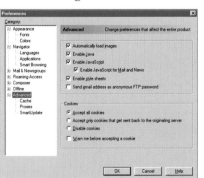

It's even conceivable that these data trails could be used to deny you insurance coverage or employment.

The pros and cons of cookies

The debate on the pros and cons of cookies will continue to rage. But you do have more than a little control. You can set your browser preferences not to accept any cookies. (This option may prevent some web sites from functioning as intended). For Internet Explorer, click the Tools menu, then Internet Options, Advanced, and Security – then select High. For Netscape Navigator, click the Edit menu, select Preferences, then Advanced. There you can elect to be alerted before a cookie is deposited, or to disable all cookies.

■ **Cookie control** – *you choose whether to accept cookies or not.*

■ **Your browser** *provides you with options regarding your acceptance of cookies.*

Interacting and communicating

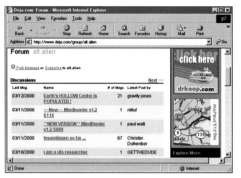

■ **Online bulletin** *boards can produce some heated debates.*

SO FAR, WE'VE TALKED *mostly about simply viewing the words and images offered by web sites. But many web sites are interactive. That is, they offer services, activities, communities, and other applications which call for your active participation. Frequently, these interactive opportunities are available only if you register at the site. Registering may be as simple as creating a user name and password, or may require submitting more information, such as your e-mail and home addresses. Interactivity makes the web more interesting and useful, but also brings new opportunities for others to gather information about you.*

We don't suggest there's anything wrong or dangerous in taking part in interactive web sites, but we want to remind you to be deliberate and thoughtful about any information you submit. Online bulletin boards, for example, are famous for message exchanges so incendiary or uninhibited, you'll wonder if the writers ever thought much about who might be reading. We'll talk more about bulletin boards and other public or group online communication channels in Chapter 7, "Group Communication."

Pressing the Send button is much easier than filling out and returning a response card to an advertiser or charitable organization, or waiting for an operator on a toll-free telephone line, but it can have the same effect.

Your name and address may be put on a mailing list, sometimes an e-mailing list. You may continue getting solicitations and newsletters for years. Your name, address, and e-mail address may even be rented to advertisers and direct marketers.

Most reputable businesses doing e-commerce will not deliberately abuse your privacy. It does them no good to send you solicitations if you don't want them. In fact, most companies and organizations want you to feel secure visiting their sites and doing business with them. They usually explain their policies for using any information you submit online, and offer relevant cautions about taking part in interactive web sites, such as message boards.

Homes and castles

The idea that your home is your castle implies complete ownership and autonomy, an image hard to maintain in modern society, much less in the Internet world. But there are some ways to build a moat around your computer castle. The more concerned you feel about maintaining privacy, the more important it is to educate yourself about the protection options available. If you're a parent, we also suggest you closely review Chapter 17, "Children Online," where we cover essential privacy and safety concerns for online kids.

Before you consider submitting personal information to a web site, whether to become a member, to enter a sweepstakes, to request product information, or for any other reason, we suggest looking for their privacy policy.

If they don't have one, ask them for one. (Just drop them an e-mail.) It might prompt them to formulate a policy for the future. If they do have one, make sure it clearly promises to promptly disclose any and all ways in which they intend to use the information you give them.

■ **Many health** *and medical web sites maintain a high standard of consumer privacy.*

PRIVACY SEALS

Several organizations have begun issuing privacy seals. A privacy seal shows that a web site's privacy policies and practices have been carefully scrutinized by third parties who maintain rigorous standards for consumer privacy. The two leading privacy seals are TRUSTe (www.TRUSTe.org) and BBBOnline (www.bbbonline.org). A few specialized privacy seals have also emerged, notably the HON code of conduct for health/medical web sites, provided by the Health On the Net Foundation (www.hon.ch).

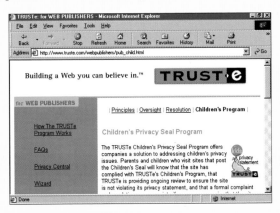

■ **Seal of Approval** – *organizations like TRUSTe issue privacy seals to web sites that follow their guidelines.*

On the job

Never forget that anything you do on the Internet at your workplace, using your employer's computer, belongs to your employer. Whether you're browsing, sending e-mail, or chatting, everything you do is open to examination. When you close out your session of personal work, your footprints are still there, and your employer has every right to follow the track. If you're chattering away in chat rooms during working hours, playing online bingo games, viewing sexually explicit material, trading stocks, keeping up with the latest collectible auctions, or just surfing travel destinations and daydreaming about far-off places, your employer can, and likely will, find out.

■ **Booking** *your next vacation on the Internet during work hours is not advised.*

It's amazing how many people look for new jobs while sitting at their current employer's computer. Maybe the boss is too busy to investigate your Internet log, but if he or she does, the message is loud and clear. Our advice? Learn to be more productive with the Internet at work, and save your personal pursuits for your home computer.

Keeping it safe and secure

CONSUMERS INDICATE THAT PRIVACY WORRIES *are more important than cost, or any other factor, in keeping people from going online. A Business Week poll showed that almost two-thirds of non-Internet users would be more likely to go online if they were not worried about possible violations of their privacy. The biggest concern is the undisclosed use of personal information.*

Keeping your personal information safe and secure involves common sense, as well as taking advantage of the security measures available on the Internet.

Shopping safely online

Online shopping carries a small risk. If you follow a few basic guidelines, though, it's as safe as handing over your credit card to a waiter in a restaurant – probably safer. It's now possible to purchase almost any type of product online. Mail order houses and major retailers have put their catalogs online.

You can get your prescriptions refilled online, stock up on art supplies, and even purchase big-ticket items like cars, fine art, jewelry, and homes.

At the incredibly popular and fast-growing auction sites, you can buy (and sell) almost anything you can imagine. In a third of all online households, someone makes an online purchase about once a week – and this trend is accelerating rapidly.

Recent surveys asked online shoppers whether their experience was satisfactory. 88 percent replied that it was. Of those with complaints, the problem most often mentioned was poor customer service, especially items ordered arriving very late or not at all.

A few basic ground rules will help you be a safe and secure online shopper. Most of these are guidelines any responsible shopper follows before buying anything, anywhere!

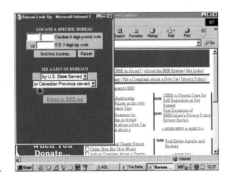

■ **The Better Business Bureau's** *national home page can link you to the nearest local office.*

SOME GROUND RULES

✓ Know who you're dealing with. Check out the seller before giving your credit card number. You'll be safer if the seller has, at least, a physical address, and, preferably, a track record of legitimacy and reliability. Contact the Better Business Bureau or a state consumer protection agency to check on a vendor's license or record of consumer complaints. Be wary of buying from individuals rather than businesses. They may be harder to track down if your goods never arrive.

✓ Know what you're buying. Make sure you understand all the details before you agree to a purchase, including exactly what the product is, any specifications, the price, any additional charges (don't forget shipping and handling charges, which can add up), return policies, shipping time, and the like.

✓ Keep records (preferably printed records) of any transaction, including order confirmations.

✓ Provide only the minimum information required for the transaction. Always be wary of providing vital personal information, especially when it doesn't seem vital to the transaction at hand. Most purchases require only your name, shipping address, phone number, and credit card number (with expiration date).

BE CAUTIOUS

■ **Sending credit card** *details via e-mail is a gamble that should be avoided.*

✓ Beware of unsolicited e-mails, especially if they have deceptive subjects designed to trick you into reading them, if they request you to make phone calls, or ask that you open e-mail attachments.

✓ Beware of get-rich-quick money-making schemes, easy-money loan deals, or investment tips from strangers. Get sound advice from a financial advisor before spending your money in risky endeavors. Remember, anything that sounds too good to be true, probably is!

✓ Don't order anything over the Internet which may be illegal, such as devices to steal cable television signals.

✓ Report any theft or fraud to your credit card company immediately.

✓ Don't use e-mail to send confidential information, such as a credit card number. E-mail can be intercepted. Submit such information through a secure web site, by telephone or fax, or through the mail.

✓ Keep your browsers up-to-date. Newer versions of browser software tend to have improved security features, and include fixes for any security holes that have come to light.

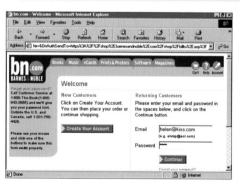

■ **If a web site** *is secure, there's a closed lock in the status bar at the foot of the screen.*

Secure web sites

When you're ready to place an order or submit sensitive information such as your credit card number, reputable online shopping sites go into secure mode. In secure mode, the information you transmit is encrypted before it's sent across the Internet. *Encryption* scrambles your data in a special way that can be accurately unscrambled only by using the correct decryption key. Each e-commerce site has its own unique key. These kinds of encryption keys have been mathematically shown to be quite safe and secure. It's a good idea to restrict your online shopping to sites that offer these safe, and secure, encrypted transactions.

DEFINITION

Encryption *converts plain text into ciphertext so unauthorized agents, whether people or software programs, can't read your message. Only those with the proper decryption key can decipher the text.*

Secure sockets layer

Secure Sockets Layer (SSL) is the technical name for the secure encryption method most often provided on the web. When SSL is in effect, the http in the web site address is followed by an "s". Your can also tell you're on a secure page by the closed lock (or unbroken key, in Netscape Navigator) icon that appears on the status bar of your browser.

Secure mode provides three forms of protection:

1 encryption, or coding which prevents eavesdropping.
2 data integrity, which assures that communications are not tampered with.
3 authentication, which verifies that the party receiving information really is who he says he is.

Breaches of security can still happen online. But telephone conversations are also subject to tapping and eavesdropping, and in old-fashioned brick-and-mortar retail stores, credit card numbers can be easily stolen. Even the U.S. Mail can't promise infallible security. In general, security risks on the Internet are certainly no higher than in other shopping environments.

■ **Telephone**
Conversations are subject to eavesdropping.

Account numbers and passwords

Account numbers and passwords have become a bane of the computer age; many of us feel like we're drowning in personal identification numbers (PINs), passwords, and account codes. Internet users need a whole new batch of passwords to get online, to retrieve e-mail, to log in to web sites, to manage accounts online, and for subscriptions.

Don't be careless with your passwords and codes, especially those which provide access to your private information and accounts.

INTERNET

**www.home.netscape.
com/security**

This is a good site for more information about SSL and other security topics.

www.scambusters.org

Scambusters discusses general security issues.

■ **Frauds, scams,
and myths** – *check out
the truth at sites like
Scambusters.*

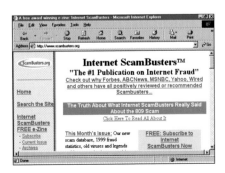

■ **Shareware password** *software at sites such as tucows.com can help you keep track of passwords.*

Finding a practical system to remember important passwords is a challenge. For example, if you choose to write them all down in the margins of this book, what are you going to do if you accidentally leave the book on the cross-town bus? We aren't going to tell you how to keep track of passwords, because personal organization and memory tricks are a matter of what works for you. Several new computer-based password management tools are available, but they're still too new for us to recommend any specific application.

If you want to learn more about password managers, use a search engine to find product reviews and information.

However you keep track of your passwords, here are several practices we strongly suggest you use to protect yourself.

✓ Don't make a password easy or obvious, such as your name or birth date.
✓ Change passwords every now and then. Many administrators recommend every three months.
✓ Don't post them in public view on bulletin boards or sticky pads at your office.
✓ Don't e-mail passwords. More people than you intend might see in transit.
✓ Make sure to log off when you're finished using a site that required a password.
✓ Don't use the same password for everything. Don't use sensitive ones, such as your ATM Personal Identification Number, for relatively trivial purposes.
✓ Change shared passwords immediately, no matter how well you trust the other person.

System security

IT'S AMAZING HOW QUICKLY *your computer becomes your trusted servant. We start to take this servant for granted, when, in fact, it does have limitations and is vulnerable to harm. You may have heard that stories about computer viruses are generally hoaxes. That's often true, but there are some serious threats every computer user must be aware of. A good precaution is to update your browser software frequently, as each new version usually includes protection against the latest viruses.*

■ **Viruses don't only** *attack the human body, they can also cause problems for your computer.*

Viruses

A virus is one type of program that can be classified as mal-ware, malicious software intended to damage or create mischief on your system. Types of viruses include the worm or the dropper. We'll give you some web sites to visit if you want to know what each of these are.

The most common potential source of a virus is a file that gains access to your system as an attachment to an e-mail message. Your computer can also catch a virus through a download, as well as through infected floppy disks you get from friends or from your office.

INTERNET

www.datafellows.com/ virus-info

On this site, you'll find a lot of background information on the subject of viruses, current concerns, and descriptions of known viruses. They also publish an e-mailed virus information newsletter.

There are hundreds of known viruses, and new ones continue to spring up. Some viruses affect only certain systems. CIH, a very damaging virus that can overwrite the hard disk and cause complete loss of data, affects only systems running Windows 95 or Windows 98. A malicious e-mail virus called Melissa (Mailissa) enters a Microsoft Word document and secretly adds a new macro module called Melissa. This causes mass mailings from your Microsoft Outlook e-mail software, tying up programs as well as phone lines.

We strongly recommend that you make sure a good anti-virus package is installed on your computer before you begin heavy e-mailing and web surfing.

Antivirus software

We also encourage you to subscribe to services that regularly issue updated anti-virus software to protect against the newest viruses. The risk of viruses, which can never be completely eliminated, also points out the importance of frequently backing up your data. In a worst-case scenario, a virus could wipe out all the data on your hard drive. If your data is backed up, you'd be back in business relatively quickly.

■ **Try Mcafee.com** *for virus advice.*

Some excellent sources of information are:

✓ Symantec's Anti-Virus Research Center: www.symantec.com/avcenter
✓ McAfee's Anti-Virus Center: www.mcafee.com/centers/anti-virus
✓ IBM's Anti-Virus home page: www.av.ibm.com

DEFINITION

Internet veterans make a big distinction between hackers and crackers. A hacker is a person who enjoys computer technology and is highly capable at working directly on coding, programming, and system problems. Hackers consider the term a compliment. Crackers, on the other hand, are those who seek access to private systems or to intercept data they are not authorized to have, sometimes with malicious intent.

Crackers, hackers and intruders

The language and lore of the *hacker* culture is rich with fascinating history and terminology, much of which has become part of today's Internet lingo. Several hacker lexicons have been created. You can see one example online at www.netmeg.net/jargon.

■ **Intruders favor** *cracking into large business and governmental networks.*

Computer networks in businesses, large organizations, and government are the usual targets of crackers and intruders. Networks permanently connected to the Internet, such as your ISP, are more vulnerable than your desktop computer, especially if you connect to the Internet through a dial-up modem. Therefore, your data, when it resides at your ISP, is more vulnerable than information on your home computer.

If your ISP hosts a web site or e-commerce business on your behalf, you should really inquire about "firewalls" and other measures implemented by your ISP to prevent security breaches.

Your own computer is at much greater risk of intrusion if you have broadband service. Cable modems and DSL allow the home computer to remain continuously connected to the Internet, but this great convenience also represents vulnerability. If proper precautions are taken, unwelcome incursions onto your computer are unlikely.

A variety of relatively inexpensive firewall products are available to lock down your system against intrusion. Ask your cable or DSL provider, or your ISP, for recommendations.

Trivia...

A martyr figure in the hacker culture is Kevin Mitnick, who was arrested in 1995 for breaking into high-level government networks and stealing secrets. He was imprisoned for years, but exactly what harm he did, to whom, or how much it cost, has yet to be clearly established. A FREE KEVIN movement was a major cause in the community of hackers, and endless articles about the case appear in their pages.

System hazards

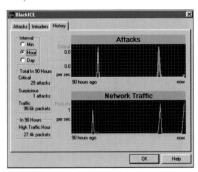

■ **Personal firewalls** *such as BlackICE can help protect your system against intruders.*

Through simple carelessness and ignorance, Internet users can become security risks to their own computers. For instance, installing too much new software can create a risk of system overload or internal conflicts. To maintain the integrity of your system, don't go overboard with software. Be especially careful regarding beta versions, pre-release versions of software that a manufacturer is using consumers to test, to tease out the bugs and work out the kinks. Any new application software you install takes up space on your hard drive, and, if you're not careful you could exceed your system's storage capacity. New software may also be redundant, duplicating something you actually already have.

Most people, especially beginners, use only a small part of the software already installed on their computers.

This chapter has outlined, in a general way, some of the major Internet safety and security issues. In later chapters, we'll take in-depth looks at some of the more complex security issues: e-mail, protection of children, and financial questions. We've offered some sensible rules, and tried to reassure you that the risks in using the Internet are not as big and scary as you may have heard.

A simple summary

✓ Remaining anonymous online is difficult – but not impossible.

✓ Maintaining privacy is a high priority for most people, and there are many ways to assure privacy.

✓ Shopping online is very popular. It's easy, and just as safe as doing business over the phone – as long as you follow basic safety guidelines.

✓ System security is an important concern. The more you know about your hardware and software, the better you can protect your system from viruses, hackers, and operator error.

Chapter 5

Guidelines for Smoother Sailing

Y OU'VE DECIDED TO GET ONLINE, and learned that it's really pretty simple – you can do it! Now, it's time to learn to do it well. If you've taken all the steps outlined so far, you're probably online already, but you may still feel a bit uncertain and shaky, like a new driver still getting used to that feeling of speed, control, and power. In fact, you have much more power than you might realize. This chapter will help you exercise some of your newfound power. And, we'll go into a little more depth about support services and self-education.

In this chapter...

✓ Tender loving hardware care

✓ Tender loving software care

✓ The monitor

✓ Experimentation

✓ Geting help and confidence

Tender loving hardware care

THESE BASIC GUIDELINES *will help your computer system operate reliably and safely so you can surf unworried. All electrical plug-in connections and related equipment should be grounded. To prevent equipment damage and data loss that can occur due to weather conditions or power fluctuations, use surge protectors (available from any electronics, computer supply, hardware, or office supply store) between all your computer equipment and your home power source.*

Your computer and its peripheral devices have vents that allow air to flow and help dissipate the heat produced naturally by the operating electronics. Don't block these vents by placing the computer in an overly crowded location, or by placing objects on top of, or too close, to any piece of equipment. (Sometimes computer vents get clogged with pet hair. Cats, in particular, like to rest on top of warm computers – probably not a good idea!)

■ **Pets should be** *kept away from the computer.*

The system should not be subject to extreme heat, cold, moisture, or wind from fans or air conditioners. It's also important not to place the computer close to other appliances with magnetic fields, such as radios.

Tender loving software care

THE QUALITY OF YOUR INTERNET EXPERIENCE *will be strongly influenced by how well you take care of your computer system and your software. That includes not just your browser and e-mail software, but all your software. We've used several analogies in this book, comparing your computer to older office systems with filing cabinets and typewriters, and with driving a vehicle. Let's try a new one!*

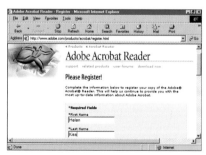

■ **Registering software** *gives you access to support, updates, and new versions.*

Managing your software is a little like organizing your kitchen for efficient operation. Your microwave oven, blender, and refrigerator should be registered in case they need service; pots and pans, dishes, and utensils must be well organized for handy access; and adjustments in the organization must be made now and then as your experience, usage, or needs indicate.

Registering commercial software

Registering commercially-produced software that you buy, or that's pre-installed on a new computer system, entitles you to support services, information about upgraded versions as they become available, and access to patches (fixes) that correct small problems ("bugs") in the application. Registration provides documentation in case you ever need to prove where and when you bought the software – and that you actually did buy it. Using pirated or copied versions of someone else's software is against the law, and it's also unwise, since it leaves you without support services or access to upgrades and patches. (It's also unfair to the developers of the software.)

Always find out how to obtain any support services that may be provided for any software, even if you don't expect to ever need help. Just knowing help is available can be quite reassuring and empowering.

Shareware

Shareware is software that you can download free and try out. If you decide to continue using it, you can ■ **When you download** *a file you can choose where to save it.*

send a registration fee to the software's developer. Most shareware is distributed on the honor system, and the registration fees are usually much less than licenses for commercial software. Shareware producers are often small companies or individual programmers whose work benefits thousands of Internet users, and contributes to the improvement of the Internet experience for all. Using their software without paying the registration or licensing fee is really a form of thievery, so we hope you will uphold the honor code.

Freeware

Freeware is just that – free. Shareware and freeware can be found in many repositories on the Internet, some of them containing hundreds of applications. Some of these sites were listed back in Chapter 2 in the section "Introduction to Internet Software." Before downloading software from a web site, create a folder to put it in, such as a new download folder on your C drive. Click the link for the file you want to download, and then follow the directions for saving the file in the download folder you created. (If you don't create such a folder yourself, your computer will create one in a place it deems appropriate and ask if that's okay with you.) The file will be copied from the Internet site to your computer, and you'll usually see a progress report showing how much of the file has been transferred and how much remains.

When the progress reaches 100 percent, the download is complete. You may then navigate to the folder where the file was placed and double-click on it to begin installing the new application. Most downloadable programs send an installer file, which installs the full program and can be deleted after the installation is complete.Shareware and freeware can be wonderful low-cost or no-cost resources for web surfers, but we recommend a conservative approach to downloading and installing them. Support may be limited or non-existent. Some freeware programs are older and less functional versions of commercial applications that have been "decommissioned" as more up-to-date successor programs have been released. Others may be buggy. In addition, these programs take up space on your hard drive, which can slow down your computer's operation. Too many gizmos and gadgets can clog up your system and cause performance problems. Some new users are tempted to behave like kids in a candy store upon finding archives of free software online.

We suggest you download and try out new programs one by one, rather than en masse. You can also read reviews of programs from reputable sources before installing them, or talk to other Internet users you know for suggestions.

We do hope you'll read the section on safe uninstalling before you begin adding new software you've downloaded from the Internet. Removing software after you've installed it can be tricky, even if you do it correctly. In fact, there's a whole category of commercial software with the sole purpose of helping you to completely remove the remnants of software applications.

Plug-ins

Plug-ins are software programs that extend the functionality and capabilities of web browsers. Some come already built in when you install your browser, but others must be downloaded and installed. They're almost always free, and usually very easy to install. Sometimes the software maker requests that you register and agree to their terms and conditions for use of the product. You'll know you need a plug-in when you arrive at a web page that requires one, and your browser gives you a message asking if you want to install the plug-in. Usually, if you say yes, you'll be transferred to a download page with instructions. Plug-ins often add a great deal to the web browsing experience, such as audio and video, interactivity, and other enhancements and effects.

■ **Some plug-ins** *will install themselves automatically into your browser.*

DEFINITION

Beta software *is software that is not yet officially released. It's offered conditionally, strictly for testing and experimentation. It probably has bugs, and is not yet stable enough to be released to the general public.*

Software manufacturers make *Beta software* available, often for free, hoping that consumers will do the testing for them and find all the bugs. But beta testing is not for beginners. Some experienced computer users enjoy downloading beta software just to have the satisfaction of finding and reporting bugs to the software's developers. But remember, beta software is not supported, and not guaranteed. For now, we suggest letting the experts do the testing first, and wait for that software to be released as a completed product.

Evaluation or demo software

Evaluation or demo software is like a sample. It often provides only limited functionality, or has a temporary usage period programmed in so that, if you don't pay for a license, it will cease to function after a certain date. If you use it, pay attention as you install it to directions about uninstalling. A common problem with demo software is that it looks interesting, you install it thinking you'll take time later to learn what it can do, and before you know it, the period of time allowed for free trial has gone by.

■ **Flash is a technology** *that will enable you to see animation in your browser.*

Test it, use it, and decide whether or not to keep it as soon as possible. Otherwise, you'll end up deciding by default, and you'll start piling up useless, disabled software in your computer.

Keeping current

Why do you need a new version when the software you have is working just fine? Upgraded versions are never just new – they're always new and improved. If you don't upgrade, over time your ability to do things with your present software will be slowly eroded. New programs will be tailored to the upgraded versions and your older software may not function completely.

When you attempt to perform some action for which your software is not prepared, you may get an error message. Sometimes these messages will tell you what software upgrades you need.

For example, the newest versions of web browsers come loaded with a plug-in that allows you to view and experience a popular technology called Flash. Flash is used to create high-impact web sites, with animation and action-oriented graphics. If your browser is out of date, you may not be able to enjoy presentation technologies like Flash, and you may miss out on the full effect of these high-impact web sites.

Read the friendly manual

Internet users sometimes have a flippant attitude about instructions on paper. Eager to get online, we want to just do it, not read about it. But even a toaster or an electric mixer comes with instructions, and it does make sense to read them. If you take the time early on to read about the software you're going to be using, you can avoid mistakes and gain a good understanding of the capabilities of that software. Don't wait until you have a problem to look at the manual. Read it first. Then, if a problem arises, you won't have to search for answers at a time when you're busy with some project.

The rest of this chapter is really a little supplement to your software manuals. If you've at least skimmed through your own manuals, the topics raised here may ring a bell. Go back to those manuals and read more carefully. We feel sure you'll learn a lot about how to customize your software and take better advantage of all its features.

Bookstores now offer third-party manuals for popular software packages. These are books written by someone other than the software manufacturer, and often go into much greater detail about how to get the most from that software. There are usually loads of examples, samples, and illustrations, which most users find very helpful.

If you like to read, and plan to use a particular software product quite extensively, this kind of book is a good investment and a worthwhile addition to your personal reference library.

Configurations

Most software programs are initially set up with certain default settings. Launch the software, and look for menu options with names like Preferences, Options, or Settings. Here, you'll find all kinds of choices for adjusting the software to fit your own likes and dislikes. If you don't make any choices, the original default settings will prevail, when some other configuration might actually suit you better. Allowing the default settings to remain in place without examining other options is like getting into a car you never drove before, and failing to adjust the driver's seat or mirrors. The basics are there, but you might drive more comfortably and safely if you moved the seat back or tilted the mirror. For instance, if your vision is not the best, you might find that surfing the web is a little stressful because you're straining and squinting just to see.

■ **You can change** *formatting as well as fonts and colors, in Internet Explorer Options.*

The text and pictures can be enlarged just by choosing a larger type size from the Options menu. With one more step, you can make that option the default setting, so it's not necessary to change it each time.

The monitor

AMERICANS SPEND *a lot of time looking at movie, television, and computer screens. We know that the quality of the picture makes all the difference in the viewing experience. In customizing your screen settings, you need to address practical questions such as readability, esthetic concerns such as your ability to appreciate beautiful graphics in full color, and your personal likes and dislikes.*

■ **Avoid hurting** *your neck by lowering your computer screen.*

On a Windows computer system, click on the Start button at the lower left corner of your monitor. You'll see a menu that includes Settings. A click on Settings reveals another menu; one of the choices there is Control Panel. A click there reveals a grid of computer components — some hardware and some software.

Choose Display. You'll have opened an array of choices controlling the appearance of visual elements on your monitor. This is where the fun starts! Try a few options to see what they do. You may laugh, or groan. But you'll probably find some settings you like, and you'll know where to return if you ever want to do some more fine-tuning.

A CRICK IN THE NECK

A few lucky people have the ideal computer work center, ergonomically engineered to fit their body shape and size. But many of us are using some old desk or table and a straight chair out of the kitchen. In addition, we may be wearing bifocals, and can't read the monitor through the top lens, so we tilt our heads back to see through the bottom lens. This is a recipe for a crick in the neck. The more time you spend online, the more you may wonder if you're going to need a cervical collar. Find some way to lower the level on which the monitor rests, or raise the level of your seat. Or, look into getting progressive lenses with a middle range ideal for computer work. Likewise, if your mouse is located where you have to reach, you'll increase the risk of uncomfortable wrist and arm strain. Even if you have to buy or build some new furniture, be good to your body and make sure you have an ergonomic work center. For more information on ergonomics, see pages 297–300.

Resolution

You can also set your monitor's Resolution control. The best way to choose a resolution settings is by experimentation. *Pixel* rates of 640, 800, or 1024 will result in small, smaller, and smallest as well as sharp, sharper, and sharpest images on your screen. The quality and size of your monitor are also important. On a bigger screen, the smaller images of higher pixel rates are more acceptable than they might appear on a smaller monitor.

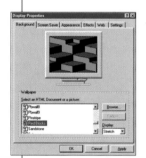

■ **Choose from a** *range of backgrounds for your Windows desktop.*

The Pattern and Wallpaper options determine the default appearance of your monitor screen background. If you choose "none," the monitor maintains a plain, solid color background. You can also change the color without introducing any pattern, or you can choose a variety of visuals from geometric blocks to blue sky and clouds.

Color

Behind the same series of buttons on a Windows system, (Start, Settings, Control Panel, Display, Settings) you'll see a palette of colors. The dropdown menu from that button will offer ranges of color starting with the bare minimum "16 color," and moving on to a maximum setting of "true color." If you don't see those other choices and are limited to "16 color," the appeal and appearance of many web sites will suffer greatly. (Unless your computer is more than five years old, it's not likely to have this limitation.)

You can test the effect of the "16 color" limitation and the other options by trying each of them in turn. Without at least "256 color," everything looks faded and washed-out. If you see the "true color" option, that's probably the default setting for your monitor.

Fonts etc.

Word processing software offers a wide selection of print styles and sizes of type. You may have already had some fun producing greeting cards, posters, or other documents that use different options for special effects. All those same choices are available for customizing your online communications. Look for the lists of options available in your browser under Edit, Preferences, or Options.

There are also many other kinds of settings you can choose. For instance, a setting for language is generally included – if English is the only option offered, Spanish or other languages can be added and then chosen as the default.

PRACTICE PRACTICE

An elderly woman who lives in a nursing home has gone online from the computer station in her room. She was a music teacher during her working years, and firmly believes that practice is the key to success with any skill. So, she's developed the habit of learning one new thing every day. Before beginning any e-mail or other online activity, she tries out some new option and learns what it can do. She reports that you shouldn't expect to remember all these little exercises, but it demystifies the system. And generally, some details do stay in the memory to be used when needed. She believes it's good training for your memory – at any age.

Experimentation

WHEN MICROSOFT'S Windows 95 *came on the market, software stores were swamped with long lines of customers. The pre-sale publicity had convinced millions of people that this was something they really, really needed. Few software applications since then have hit the market quite so strongly, but there is a rush now and then when the latest "must-have" application arrives on the scene. Deciding whether to join the crowd can be hard.*

■ **As you have** *the option to upgrade your car, you can upgrade your computer software when it suits you.*

There's an old maxim from an earlier time: "If it ain't broke, don't fix it." Software is hardly ever "broke" and in need of fixing, but when a brand new package becomes available, the old version will eventually start to feel as if it's broke. There are ways to strike the balance between stampeding to the new just because it's new, and clinging to the old because it still works. While we don't suggest you upgrade every program you have the minute a new version becomes available, we do suggest, especially for the applications you use most often, that you not get too far behind the latest version.

■ **Computer operating sysems** *offer a setting for your language of preference.*

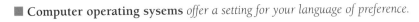

Priorities

Software takes up space on your hard drive. If it contributes to your work, it earns that space, but if not, it becomes excess baggage. When setting priorities for the addition of new software, consider your needs. When a need develops, do some research about new software that could fill the need. But be conservative. Remember that new software will cost you, not only in money, but also in the time you'll spend learning it. It may change your experience with the existing software in your computer, causing a ripple effect in the way you approach your day-to-day work.

There's always the danger of incompatibility between new software, and software you're already using. The more you know about what you already have, the better prepared you'll be to avoid that problem.

Installing new goodies

When you've found new software that fills a real need, follow these good practices for installing:

✓ Close all other applications before installing the new application to help reduce the possibility of conflict between the new and the existing software.

✓ Install slowly and carefully, following the step-by-step instructions of the "installation wizard."

✓ Note the location of the new program on your hard drive; take charge of where the new software goes.

✓ After the installation is complete, always read any supplied "Readme" or other documentation.

✓ If the new software is on a CD-ROM or floppy, be sure to keep it, and store it in a safe place. If it's downloaded software, print out any important information, such as registration codes, phone numbers, and the like.

✓ When the installation is complete, shut down and then restart your computer.

✓ If you're interrupted in the middle of an installation, cancel it and try it again later.

■ **The installation wizard** *will help you to set up new software.*

If you adhere to this conservative approach, your inventory of software will become ever more valuable, and you'll never find yourself feeling confused about what software you have, and what to do with it.

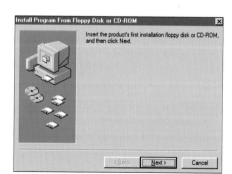

■ **Wizards help you** *install programs correctly.*

Safe uninstalling

No matter how carefully you choose and install new software, you're likely to run into some problems sooner or later. Other members of your family might have installed some software that you have no use for. When the kids go off to college, or when you lose interest in your online trivia game, you may want to remove some of those space-hogs that once seemed so nifty.

On Windows systems, the best way to uninstall software is to click on Start, select Control Panel, then choose Add/Remove Programs.

Follow the directions step by step from there. Do not try to remove a program by simply deleting its folder on the C drive; that will not remove the program at all. This is a common mistake that even some experienced computer and Internet users make.

Getting help and confidence

JUST WHEN WE'VE CONVINCED YOU it's important to read the manuals for all your software, now we're going to say that the newest software on the market doesn't come with any manuals – at least on paper. The manuals are still there, but they've gone electronic. These electronic manuals give you all the same vital, detailed information that used to come bound in a book. Sometimes, this documentation is provided on CD-ROM, but more often, software manufacturers are including electronic manuals as part of the program itself, often accessible through the Help menu. In addition, most software companies post complete software manuals (often in Adobe Acrobat format), updated information, and access to assistance on their web sites.

Software help online

Electronic manuals have several significant advantages over the traditional paper kind. A manual published at a web site can be updated immediately, as software changes are made, without the work, expense, and delay of publishing and distributing new editions on paper. The manual can be updated more often, giving you a much better chance of finding the latest information each time you go to the web site to look something up. And although paper ("hard copy") manuals do have indexes, an online hypertext index is much easier to work with. One click will take you directly from the index to the information you want.

If you just can't find the answer to some particular question, many software makers' web sites will offer to find the answer and e-mail it back to you, especially if you can document that you are a registered user. FAQs (frequently asked questions) and message boards are also included in most of these web sites. It's common to find that other people have asked the same question, and that the answer is already there somewhere. If you're still stumped, though, don't hesitate to e-mail your question. This is part of the learning experience.

When we arrive at Chapter 7, "Group Communication," we'll tell you how to post messages to other Internet users who are working with the same software you use. Some people find this helpful. When reading messages posted in online message boards and newsgroups, keep in mind that those messages were created by individuals, with all their opinions, prejudices, and blind spots, and therefore may not be entirely reliable. On the other hand, many Internet communities enjoy a genuine grassroots, people-helping-people spirit, with recognized experts jumping in willingly and generously to help out beginners. These user groups can be a great source of assistance, information, ideas, and experience.

Another way to assure yourself smooth computer sailing is to pay attention to the way you turn off your computer. This is extremely important!

■ **Some web pages** *are slower than others to load.*

Get in the habit of always first shutting down all your software applications, and then powering off the computer properly. To properly shut down a Windows system, first close all applications. Then, click the Start menu, then Shut Down. Then, select the Shut Down option, and click OK. Finally, remember to turn off your monitor and any peripherals still running, such as your printer. Shutting down your computer improperly can cause data loss and software corruption.

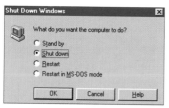

■ **It is recommended** *that you shut down your Windows system properly.*

Software help offline

Getting through on the telephone to a software manufacturer's help line can be extremely frustrating. They're usually swamped with calls, virtually around the clock. When you finally get an answer, the customer service representative will probably be able to advise you, but the process will likely call for tremendous patience. You'll soon realize why the help lines are always so busy: the investigation of your trouble may well take a long time. Be as specific, clear, accurate, and informative as you can in describing your specific problem. And before doing anything to your computer, be sure you understand precisely what the support rep is suggesting that you do.

Before calling the support help line, always try shutting down (properly!) and restarting your computer first. Restarting is often the first suggestion the support rep will make anyway, and, surprisingly often, it resolves the problem.

When you call a support help line, remember you're talking to a fellow computer user. Ask for his name, and tell him yours. A little rapport goes a long way in these stressful situations!

We also encourage you to use software manuals, third-party reference books, and general books like this one. Periodicals can be helpful, and there are many of these on the market. Many computer-related periodicals are available online, too.

Internet service

As we've already discussed, web pages sometimes load slowly or fail to finish loading at all. Sometimes, a simple way to speed up a page that seems to be taking forever is to click the browser's Stop button, and then click Refresh or Reload. If this doesn't help, the problem may just be a slow page and you may want to try a different web site altogether. If all your web pages seem slow, your modem's connection to your ISP may be below its optimal speed. It may help to disconnect and re-dial to get a fresh connection. Having too many software applications running at once, or too many browser windows open at a time, will also slow down performance, sometimes significantly. Closing a few programs and using fewer simultaneous windows might speed things up nicely.

Web browsers maintain a special storage area, called the cache, on your hard disk. Caching a web page lets it load much faster after your first visit.

As you surf, though, your cache tends to fill up fairly quickly. A too-full cache can cause the browser to perform poorly. Cache sizes can be set larger or smaller, but regardless of size, the cache should be regularly cleared.

To clear the cache in Netscape Navigator, open the Edit menu and select Preferences. Click on Advanced and then choose Cache. Click both the Clear Memory Cache and Clear Disk Cache buttons. The cache for Internet Explorer is called the Temporary Internet Files folder. To clear it, go to the Tools menu and select Internet Options. Under the General tab, look for Temporary Internet Files and click Delete Files.

■ **Periodically, caches** *need to be cleared out.*

When you're experiencing slow access to even usually speedy sites, and the problem persists more than a few moments, contact your ISP's customer service line. When you suffer a disruption of service, you probably won't have any way of knowing the cause. If it's something general the ISP may be able to tell you all about it. If not, the next help line you call will probably be the manufacturer from whom you purchased your computer. When there's a problem with hardware, that help line is a good place to start.

Continuing education

There really is a language of computerese – with lots of new terms and acronyms to learn. But it's never wrong or inappropriate to say, "Would you please put that into plain language?"

Don't ever miss out on the help you need because you don't understand the terminology. This is like leaving a doctor's office not understanding your diagnosis because the doctor failed to explain it in terms you could understand.

Most customer service representatives are careful about this, but during an average day they may speak with all kinds of Internet users, from beginners to experts. They're usually pros at adjusting their vocabulary for each customer, but sometimes the adjustment doesn't come fast enough. You're actually helping them by asking for clarification.

You might occasionally encounter a customer service representative who insists on talking in jargon, or seems impatient with your questions. Don't be intimidated. Even the knottiest technical subject can be explained. Don't ever start thinking of yourself as slow to catch on – stand up for your right to a clear presentation. If you want to learn more of those technical terms, jot them down and look them up later. Finally, be careful with your own language. If you use terms you're not absolutely sure about in an effort to sound confident, you might inadvertently mislead those you're calling on for help. Do unto others as you'd like them to do to you!

You're never too old to learn

The teachers among us always say that education is a lifelong adventure. People of all ages are adventuring on the Internet, and most are eager to learn as much as possible. Back in the first chapter of this book, we pointed out that the Internet is becoming both the form and content of education in many schools, as children learn about computers and the Internet, and also learn through this wonderful teaching medium. The same is true for adults.

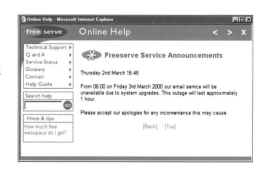

■ **Some ISPs give** *service status reports with news of any problems affecting their networks.*

You can learn through the Internet about almost any subject. Every web site will educate you about its particular topic, and every chapter in this book supplies you with some helpful web sites where you can explore and learn.

Wherever your interests lie, there are online courses available. Many colleges and universities now offer coursework online.

Visit their web sites and look for Internet courses under continuing education or off-campus courses. At www.zdu.com, you'll find a web site that exists just to provide online learning experiences. Their home page invites you to search for instructor-led courses or self-study on any subject you choose. To test this offer, we asked for a wide variety of subjects. Interestingly, we found no courses

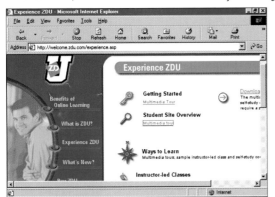

offered in such traditional subjects as psychology or poetry, while the entry computers showed six courses. A request for music brought two courses, and cooking brought one. There are several other online businesses like ZDU for all kinds of online learning. We'll list a few more in Chapter 20, "Education on the Internet."

■ **There are online** *courses available in every subject under the sun.*

A simple summary

✓ Manage your software carefully. Get it registered, keep it current, read the manuals provided, and configure it to your own needs. Question default settings, and test other possibilities.

✓ Delve into the settings that determine how the monitor looks. Choose resolution, color, fonts to your pleasing.

✓ Experiment with new software, but set priorities for things you really want. Install carefully and know how to uninstall properly if new software doesn't work out.

✓ Take all the help you can get, online and offline.

✓ Continue gaining confidence by continuing to learn.

PART TWO

THE INTERNET IS ALL ABOUT INTERACTING

COMMUNICATION ONLINE

THIS PART OF THE BOOK is all about the *ever-expanding* range of communication options available to Internet users. We'll talk about the one-to-one contact of e-mail, as well as group communication, as well as ways of reaching out to the whole Internet community.

Studies show that of the many things we can do online, e-mail is the most *popular*. E-mail is *easy*, puts us in closer touch with family and friends, and is a whole new way to communicate. It's not quite like the personal letters we used to write, and it's not quite like a phone call – it's something new that incorporates features of both. Once you have it and get used to it, we believe you'll wonder how you ever managed without it.

Chapter 6

E-mail

THE INTERNET now handles more communications per day than the U.S. Postal Service. In this chapter, we'll define e-mail, explain the parts of an e-mail message, and outline the process of sending and receiving e-mail. We'll also discuss filing and storage issues, safety and privacy, netiquette, free e-mail, and some advanced techniques and tricks.

In this chapter...

✓ What it is

✓ E-mail ABCs

✓ Netiquette

✓ Free-mail

✓ Advanced e-mailing

✓ Moving and multiple addresses

E-MAIL: THINK OF THE TREES YOU'LL SAVE

What it is

THE "E" IN E-MAIL *stands for electronic. Any kind of electronic mail is e-mail, whether or not it's transmitted on the Internet. For instance, large offices often have interoffice e-mail systems that enable employees to communicate within the office computer network, partly replacing interoffice telephone communications. In general, e-mail has reduced both snail mail and telephone traffic for vast numbers of businesses and households. E-mail is used as a verb, a noun, and as a collective noun. So, you can e-mail someone, you can send and receive a piece of e-mail, or you might be asked, "Do you have e-mail?" Most mail still being carried by the old postal system consists of bulk commercial mailings, and bills.*

The huge impact of e-mail on the postal system will be even greater as the submission and payment of bills also moves online. This is already happening.

A personal network

E-mail is a relatively new form of communication. It's like snail mail in that it's written (actually typed), and that it's asynchronous – that is, it's composed and sent at any time convenient to the sender, and received and read at any time convenient to the receiver. But it's also like a telephone call – it's so easy that most people get in the habit of sending many short, casual messages to members of their personal network, rather than composing long, carefully thought-out letters. With regular correspondents, you'll probably find yourself dashing off lots of replies, which entails simply tacking a short response on an e-mail you've received, and shooting it back to the sender. This can feel much like a phone conversation, especially if both sender and receiver are online simultaneously while tossing e-mails back and forth.

■ **Weave a web** *of communication with e-mail.*

Even when the members of your personal network are only a local phone call away, you may find yourself turning to e-mail instead of calling – especially when you know you may encounter an answering machine or voice mail.

(These "face" emoticons have a long Internet history, and originated when all e-mail was strictly plain text. Early e-mailers, searching for a short-hand to replace facial expressions and body language, invented literally dozens of these text emoticons. Only a few are still commonly used, though.) These little quirks make e-mail a unique kind of expression – written, but with the feel of casual conversation. Some people have decried e-mail as "dumbing down" the quality of writing in general, but others have noted that e-mail has prompted lots of people – even those who may have virtually stopped writing, and only used the phone – to take up writing once again.

			From	Subject
✉			TheSt...	The Industry Standard's Daily News - ...
✉			Last ...	7 nights of Winter Sun in Egypt for 325 ...
✉			TheSt...	TheStreet.co.uk's AFTERNOON BULLETI...
			Jesse ...	Has Intel Fallen Behind? / Security Goes Ope...
✉			Red H...	Whole hog - Red Herring Catch of the D...
✉			Individ...	Individual.com Insider -- February 2000 Edition
✉			the sh...	Photo Greetings + E-mail Chess = Stay...
✉			Jesse ...	Grammy Winners on Your PC? / Why th...
✉			nytdir...	Technology
✉			nytdir...	Business
✉			Fred L...	[langalist] 24-Feb-00 LangaList
✉			Allaire...	Allaire DevCenter News, February 2000

■ **It's easy** *to store e-mail messages on your computer, to read again and again.*

An electronic message can be sent any time, and will be there for the receiver to open and read any time, so it doesn't matter how different your schedules are, or how often their phone line is busy.

You can also send copies of the same message to many people at the same time. This is almost as good as a conference call, but without the cost. Over time, most people find that they've drawn much closer to their personal network of friends and family members because of e-mail. While you won't have those piles and file folders of personal letters written by each individual, you can easily store e-mail messages right in your computer, ready to be pulled out and read again any time. And if you really want to keep certain e-mail messages on paper, you can print out a hard copy.

Lifelines

E-mail is one of the big factors contributing to our feeling that the world seems to be shrinking. No matter where the members of your personal or business network may be, it's possible to stay in close touch.

The sense of isolation that people once experienced when living in remote areas or traveling far from home is becoming a thing of the past.

In crisis situations, maintaining communications has always been a challenge. In war zones and at disaster scenes, relief workers struggle to maintain contact with base camps and support services. News from the front can often be sent by e-mail, enabling people to stay in touch under extreme stress. For instance, while Belgrade was being bombed during the crisis in Kosovo, many Serbian and Kosovar nationals in the U.S. received regular e-mail from families in their homelands. This high level of direct contact also helps dispel the suspicion some people feel toward news media reports – it's the next best thing to being there and seeing for yourself.

The convenience of laptops

With portable laptop computers and satellite data transmission, people in transit, whether in automobiles, ships at sea, planes, or trains, can now communicate with anyone online, easily and instantly. Laptop computers, just the right size to balance on your lap, are increasingly lightweight, powerful and inexpensive. They came on the market around 1989, and were first used primarily for offline computer functions; the connections necessary for online work were not readily available.

Laptops have now become so common that motels and hotels, airports, train stations, and other travel accommodations provide data ports for modem connections, and the traveler can send and receive e-mail virtually anywhere.

E-mail ABCs

WHETHER YOU HAVE *an account with a dial-up ISP, or use an online service such as AOL, sending or receiving e-mail requires an online connection.*

If you pay by the minute for your online connection, you'll be glad to know that you can read your e-mail and compose messages offline – we'll tell you more about that, too.

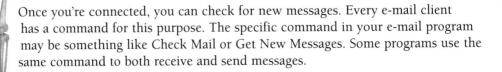

Once you're connected, you can check for new messages. Every e-mail client has a command for this purpose. The specific command in your e-mail program may be something like Check Mail or Get New Messages. Some programs use the same command to both receive and send messages.

■ **An e-mail** *is made up of different parts.*

Anatomy

The body of an e-mail contains the message itself. The message may be made up exclusively of plain text, or it may be formatted with special characteristics such as bold, italic, underlining, or graphics. On your receiver's screen, your message may appear differently-formatted than it looked on your screen. Different e-mail programs vary in their capacity to display formatted information, or because the receiver has asked his e-mail program to suppress some or all special formatting.

COMMON HEADER ELEMENTS

✓ TO: Here, you must enter the e-mail address to which you are sending your message. Remember, all e-mail addresses have three elements – the recipient's name, the @ sign, and the recipient's domain (as in "john@dot.com" or "jane@dot.org").

✓ FROM: Here, your e-mail software will enter your address.

✓ SUBJECT: It's not mandatory to enter something here, but it generally helps. If you leave it blank, the recipient will have to open your message to know what it's all about.

✓ CC: stands for carbon copy – an anachronism, since there's no carbon paper involved. The term comes from the time when a typist, to make extra copies, had to put carbon paper and tissue behind the sheet of paper in the typewriter.

✓ BCC: stands for blind carbon copy, meaning a copy of your message is sent to an extra address, without any indication of that action appearing in the main recipient's copy of the message.

✓ DATE: the date and time the message was sent.

✓ MAILER: the e-mail program used to send the message.

✓ ATTACHMENTS: the name and location of any file you may be sending along with the message.

Some e-mail programs will allow a URL for a web site to be clickable. That is, clicking the link will launch a browser and bring up the web page the URL points to. With other e-mail programs, the user must copy and paste the URL into his browser window to view the referenced page. A message's page width may be different, causing messages to show long lines followed by lines of only one or two words, and various other cosmetic differences may occur. Despite these differences, your message will be transmitted, word for word, just as you created it.

Depending on where the message is going, it will usually be delivered in anywhere from a few minutes to within a maximum of a day or so.

At the foot of an e-mail message, a signature is often used as a standard sign-off to mark the end of a message, as in a personal letter. Most e-mail programs offer an option or preference that allows you to create or modify your customized signature. You may also be allowed to choose whether to append your signature to all outgoing e-mail, or select whether to append it to each individual message. And some e-mail clients let you specify more than one personal signature – for you to use with different types of e-mail you send, at your discretion.

When an e-mail message is printed, a runner or extra line will appear above the header, giving vital information such as the date and time it was sent. At the bottom of the e-mail a similar runner, or footer, entered automatically, tells who sent the message and how many pages there are.

■ **Information** *such as the time and date of sending can be printed out with the e-mail message itself.*

Receiving and reading e-mail messages

When someone sends you an e-mail message, it doesn't come directly to your computer, but arrives at the mail server of your online service or ISP. This is very much like having a post office box at the old Post Office building, where all the old-fashioned mail was gathered and sorted. The postal clerks would put mail into stacks for home delivery, or would place it into the boxes within the building rented by individuals and businesses. To get mail from your box, you had to visit the post office and use a key to open the box. In fact, Internet standards for e-mail require mail servers to maintain a "postmaster" address; any mail directed to the postmaster usually goes directly to whoever serves as the e-mail system administrator. Once the new incoming messages have been delivered into your mailbox, you can go offline, if you wish, while reading them. The first thing you'll see is a list of the new messages in your e-mail program's Inbox. Most programs have a way of showing whether a message has been read yet.

Replying to your e-mail

Saving, deleting, and thoughtful filing of messages is an important part of good e-mail practice – we'll talk about that shortly. Since the address of the sender is an integral part of every message, there's an easy way to quickly and easily send a return message if you wish – just click on

■ **You can** *sign-off your e-mails with your own customized signature.*

Reply on the Toolbar. This automatically reverses the TO and FROM, and enables you to supply your answer before or after the original message, or even to intersperse comments throughout the message, perhaps answering point by point. Finally, you send the reply as if it were a new message, by clicking on Send.

It's also possible to forward a message to someone else. If you click on Forward, you must fill in the address of the person to whom you want that mail to go, and then click Send. If you've gone offline while reading and replying, your e-mail software can automatically re-establish your connection.

Composing and sending

To create a new e-mail message, use whatever "new message" command your software provides. With Eudora, Messenger, or Outlook, the command is called New Message. Other e-mail programs use a variety of other words. For example with AOL's e-mail client, click on Write; with Lotus Notes, use New Memo; and with Pine, select Compose. Next, fill in the blank sections of the message header.

Most important is the e-mail address of your recipient. Add a message subject. Click or tab down to the body, and begin typing your message.

Remember, the biggest attraction of e-mail for busy people is its speed. Therefore, short, snappy messages are usually best. On the other hand, e-mail can also be a way for family members and old friends to keep in touch, so long, flowing messages may also be appropriate. It's up to you.

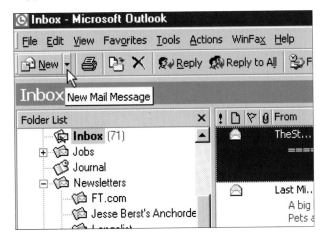

■ **To create a** *new message you simply click here.*

If you have a long message to send, or perhaps a series of messages, it's best to do your composing offline, even if the charge you pay for online service is not time-related. It's even possible to compose messages and set them aside in a queue for a while, just in case you change your mind about the content, or need to finish the message later.

When you need to send many e-mail messages, it can be much more efficient to do all your composing at once, and then send all the messages in one batch. Different browsers handle e-mail in different ways. The most common is to send your mail to an Outbox once you click Send. From the Outbox, you have a variety of options. Your Outbox can deliver your mail immediately, hold it for a set amount of time, or hold it until you click on Send-and-Receive. Once your browser sends your messages, they travel from your computer to your ISP or online service provider, and from there out through the Internet to the host computer specified in the TO address. The message is then placed in the recipient's e-mail account, ready for retrieval.

Outgoing messages

Most e-mail programs can be configured to retain copies of your outgoing messages. Some programs store them in the Outgoing Mail file, while others use similar terms, such as the Sent or Sent Mail file.

Your e-mail program may offer you an option to ask for a confirmation of delivery, like the receipt the post office supplies for Registered Mail. If you request a confirmation of delivery for a particular e-mail, you'll receive an automatic message when that e-mail has been delivered.

However, this receipt message doesn't always mean your message has actually been opened by the recipient – it may just mean the receiving e-mail system has logged the incoming message. To be sure someone has seen an e-mail message, ask the person to e-mail you an acknowledgement, or ask them directly.

If, for some reason, an e-mail message can't be delivered, it will come back to you with a notation such as "undeliverable." A message can be undeliverable if the recipient's address is incorrect or out of date, but sometimes it just indicates some kind of temporary system glitch.

Keeping up and keeping track

At first, your incoming e-mail will probably be light, but over time it's sure to increase and diversify. If you're away from home and don't keep up remotely, your e-mail will stack up – just like the snail mail on your desk. Some e-mail programs allow you to set up an autoresponder, a sort of pre-recorded message, to inform correspondents of your temporary absence.

■ **As your volume** *of incoming e-mail increases, you may need to create storage files for them.*

It helps greatly to organize your mail by creating folders for regular correspondents, topics, projects, or newsletters. If you don't create folders, all your e-mail will pile up in the Inbox, creating a disorganized hodgepodge that's hard to manage and keep track of. Many e-mail applications provide a way to automatically file messages into the appropriate folders, as they download to your computer.

Your e-mail program also probably provides some choices as to how your mail is listed: chronologically, by subject, or by the sender's name, for example. As with every type of software discussed in this book, we encourage you to find your e-mail program's Preferences, Options, or Settings menu. Learn what choices will make your program serve you best, and set it up to suit your personal style and needs.

As time goes on, the number of commercial and other unsolicited e-mail messages you receive will probably grow. Some of these messages may contain legitimate information from online marketers, with product news and special offers you want to know about.

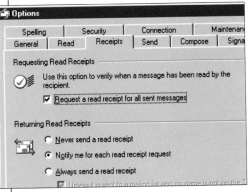

■ **You can get** *an automatic receipt sent to you when your e-mail has been read.*

You can create a folder for this type of e-mail, so you can choose to open that folder and read the latest messages, or put it aside till you have spare time. Legitimate businesses don't want to send you e-mail without your permission, and will provide easy ways to stop such e-mail. For example, you can send them an e-mail requesting that your address be removed from their list.

Then there are those unsolicited messages, commonly referred to as spam. *Spam* pushes every kind of product and service, often in gray areas of semi-legality. Spammers often "harvest" people's e-mail addresses through a variety of surreptitious methods, then send their solicitations and come-ons to complete strangers, probably soon to include you. Spammers use a variety of tricky practices, such as deceptive subject lines. For example, you may see a message with a subject like, "Hey John, here's the answer to your question!" But when you open the message, it may urge you to visit a web site about a get-rich-quick scheme, a miracle weight-loss program, a cable television descrambler device, or any number of other dubious ventures.

■ **Not all e-mail** *is welcome. Some people refer to unsolicited messages as "spam."*

Unfortunately, especially when children are involved, UCE may contain offensive and explicit advertisements for hardcore pornography. Another potentially dangerous variety of spam urges you to make a telephone call for more information. Calling may result in huge telephone charges. Several states are implementing laws to reduce the heinous types of UCE. For example, Washington requires senders of commercial e-mail messages to always include valid return addresses, and not to use deliberately deceptive subject lines.

If you feel a message is abusive or possibly illegal, send a complaint to your state attorney general's office or equivalent. All U.S. state attorneys general now have web sites; a national directory is available at www.naag.org.

Wait a minute! We also want to be sure you don't get the wrong idea. We don't intend to alarm you about the dangers lurking in your Inbox. Surprise e-mails may not be spam at all, but may be messages from relatives, old friends, Alumni associations, clubs, organizations, or any number of other perfectly innocent sources. We've talked about some of the bad side of e-mail because it's part of the reality of the Internet, but we certainly don't want to overshadow the good parts.

FILTERING YOUR EMAILS

To filter your e-mail, there are three main avenues to pursue.

✓ Many e-mail programs offer Preferences for customized screening criteria.
✓ Your ISP probably also has tools to assist customers in filtering out undesirable e-mail.
✓ There are a number of software applications that can be helpful, especially for parents. (We'll talk more about kids and the Internet in Chapter 14.)

Get in the habit of checking your e-mail every day. E-mail is such a quick, easy way to communicate that senders often expect you to respond more or less instantly. Important news may be waiting in your Inbox; the sender may assume a phone call isn't necessary, because he sent the e-mail! Organizers of business meetings often send e-mail messages to the list of all persons expected to attend some meeting, giving dates, places, and agendas. If you are on such an e-mail list, that may be the only notice you'll receive of scheduled meetings. It can be a bit of a shock to read that message – and discover that the meeting has already taken place.

■ **Make sure** *you delete your old e-mails regularly.*

Copied e-mail messages

Sometimes, copies of your e-mail messages are kept by your ISP, where they'll stack up indefinitely, possibly overflowing your mailbox at your ISP and thus blocking incoming new messages.

Look for an option in your e-mail program called something like, Do not leave mail on server, or call your ISP to check how to delete old copies of your messages from the ISP's mail server.

Also, check to see if your e-mail program has a "trash" folder. If it does, you may be simply piling up messages there that you thought you had deleted. If your trash folder doesn't automatically empty when you exit your e-mail program, remember to empty it periodically.

■ **Netiquette** *is the etiquette for good behavior online.*

Netiquette

MOST OF THE RULES *and practices for e-mail etiquette also prevail in other Internet activity – that's why this section is called netiquette. Netiquette is just common courtesy online. It's mostly a matter of practicing good manners, while contributing to a safe and pleasant online experience for everyone.*

Two important rules should govern everything you do online: follow the same standards of behavior you use everywhere else; and remember that you are not visible online, so you must make yourself as clear as possible with words alone. It's also true that the more educated you are about the way the Internet functions, the less likely you'll be to unintentionally offend.

Sometimes, people feel a little too anonymous online. They'll write things in e-mail they'd never say in person, especially if they're writing to some anonymous recipient such as a customer service department or technical assistance line. Failing to remember that there's a human being at the other end, some people cut loose with angry retorts, which can generate "flame wars" of escalating abusive talk – the online version of what athletes call "trash talking."

Needless to say, the original purpose of the contact gets lost. Consider the effect if such "flaming" exchanges ever became public.

INTERNET

www.albion.com/ netiquette

www.jade.wabash.edu/wabnet /info/netiquet.htm
These web sites provide information on netiquette.

125

Free-mail

FREE E-MAIL *is widely available via web-based e-mail accounts. Most of the major portals, as well as hundreds of other sites, offer free e-mail. Free, web-based e-mail accounts allow you to create a new e-mail address, and send and receive e-mail through that address via a web page you access with a user name and password. These accounts are free in the sense that you don't have to pay a fee for them, but most of them display paid advertisements along the edges of the screen while you're reading or writing e-mail messages.*

You create and send web-based e-mail through your browser, so you don't have an additional piece of software to deal with. And with web-based e-mail, you can use graphics and hyperlinks in your e-mail messages. But remember, the actual messages don't reside on your computer, but on the free e-mail provider's server.

When you log off the free e-mail site, your messages are not kept on your computer. To see them again, you have return to the free e-mail account web site.

These accounts provide the convenience of being accessible from any Internet connection, so you don't have to be connected via your ISP. However, some advanced e-mail features aren't available with web-based e-mail, and you must tolerate viewing those advertisements. Also, you can't access these accounts unless you're connected to the Internet, so you still have to have an ISP or some other method of getting online.

A few companies have created free e-mail systems that don't require Internet accounts. Instead, the user installs a piece of software that automatically connects and disconnects from these companies' mail servers to send or receive messages.

Again, the user must view advertising, but doesn't need to have an ISP. The most popular free e-mail program of this type is Juno (www.juno.com).

Advanced e-mailing

THE WORD ADVANCED *in this section doesn't mean complicated or technical – it means more possibilities, beyond the sending of original messages and replies. Many of these so-called advanced features will become second nature to you with just a little practice.*

Attachments

Sometime you might want to e-mail someone a document, picture, or even a sound file such as a music clip or recordings of your own voice. Say a document you've created in a word-processing program contains formatting you want to keep, and you'd like to e-mail it in exactly that form. But if you paste the text into an e-mail message, your formatting will be lost. The answer is to create an e-mail message, and then attach that document file.

■ **It's easy to** *send family photographs via e-mail.*

All e-mail software provides ways to accomplish this. For instance, the message menu might offer the option Attach file. Click there, and specify the exact location and label of the file you want to attached. Many programs have a paper clip icon on the toolbar,

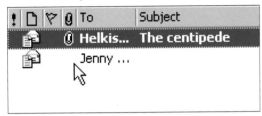

■ **With some e-mail clients,** *a paper clip icon shows there is a file attached to an e-mail.*

which can be used as a shortcut command to attach a document. After the file is attached, sending the message will send a copy of the file along with it.

Attachments sent to you are generally stored automatically in a folder called Attachments, separate from your incoming mail file. Sometimes, you might find that you can't read some of the files sent to you as attachments. This usually means that either you don't have the software in which the file was created, or that you have an earlier version of the software. It also may mean you are simply trying to view the attachment with the wrong software. Find out what kind of file it is, and open it with the correct program. (If all else fails, you can always ask the sender what type of file it is.) Sending family photos via e-mail holds a big attraction for many people. Basically, any file can be attached to an e-mail message, including images such as photographs you've previously downloaded into a file.

Very large files, whether image files, sound files, presentations, spreadsheets with graphs and charts, or very long word processing documents, are sometimes too big to be sent as e-mail attachments. Trying to send such large files may take a very long time over a modem, and may result in the file being corrupted, or intercepted by ISPs with attachment size restrictions.

Larger documents are often "zipped" with compression utility software that "squeezes" the original file into a much smaller, so-called archive file that can travel more quickly as an attachment.

Web page links in e-mail messages

More and more e-mail messages contain links to web pages. For example, many web sites now offer an option to "send this page to a friend." When you choose this option, an e-mail message is sent to whatever address you specify, usually with a link back to the web page you want to share. Another popular web activity is sending web-based greeting cards. When you send one of these, your designated recipient receives an e-mail saying something like, "You've received an electronic greeting card. Click on the following URL to access your card," accompanied by the URL (often a live link) of the web page where the greeting card is. Or, a sender may just type a URL in a personal e-mail message to tell you about an interesting web site. Each e-mail program handles URLs in its own way.

Some allow "hot" or "live" links. With these, you just click on the URL, and your browser automatically launches and brings up that page.

Some e-mail readers don't provide hot links; in these cases, you have to highlight the URL, and copy and paste it in your browser to see the page, or retype the URL by hand.

INTERNET

www.winzip.com
www.zipmagic.com
www.pkware.com
www.aladdin.com (Stuffit)

Compression programs are easy to use, both for zipping large files you want to send and for unzipping compressed files you may receive. These are web sites for some of the most popular compression programs.

Encryption

When we talked about safety and security back in Chapter 4, we noted that secure web sites use encryption for protecting privacy of information. In that context, the ability to scramble information so it can't be read without exactly the right de-scrambling program makes good sense.

Most people never feel the need for such a system of secret coding in e-mail messages, but if you feel the need, it's possible to encrypt your e-mail messages, too.

■ **If you don't** *want your e-mails to be read by all, "wrap" them using an encryption program.*

Address books

Setting up an address book in your e-mail program, listing the names and e-mail addresses of regular correspondents, will save you a lot of time and effort. You'll be able to send messages without having to remember or look up the recipient's e-mail address every time you send.

■ **E-mail address books** *will become as indispensable to you as the old-fashioned sort.*

Under Tools, Options, or Preferences, your software will offer you the opportunity to set up a personal address book. Once your address book is set up, one click on a name automatically enters that person's entire e-mail address for you. Every time you correspond with someone new, it's helpful to ask yourself whether this person is likely to become a regular correspondent. If so, enter that name and address in your address book. Changing addresses, deleting names, and adding new contact information is also as easy as a mouse click.

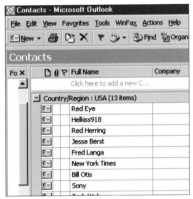

■ **Setting up an** *address book with your contacts in it saves a lot of time.*

Many e-mail programs let you use your address book to create distribution lists, so you can broadcast a message to a number of recipients all at once. For example, you may want to create a family distribution list, so you can send updates and news to everyone in the family — with a single keystroke.

INTERNET

www.pgp.com

Pretty Good Privacy (PGP) is a program that can encrypt a message so solidly it's virtually tamper-proof. You can install your own version of PGP and use encrypted e-mail fairly easily, especially if you use a common, recent version of a major e-mail program.

■ **Electronic** *greeting cards come in handy when you've forgotten an anniversary.*

Moving and multiple addresses

FOR A NUMBER OF REASONS, *you might end up with more than one e-mail account, and, therefore, with multiple e-mail addresses. You may have one address at home, and a different one at work. Or, you might decide to try many different services, including some of the free mail options, just to see which one you like best. Many people set up an account with a national or regional online service in addition to their local ISP dial-up account. It can be a little confusing to those who are trying to contact you, but it can also serve to channel personal mail away from business correspondence. The important thing is to make sure everyone knows the right address.*

■ **Reach out** *in all directions with multiple e-mail addresses.*

If you move, your e-mail address might have to change too. If your account is with a national on-line service, the existing address will move right along with your computer – no problem. But if your e-mail dial-up connection is with a local or regional ISP, moving out of the area may necessitate a change. However, you may be able to continue accessing your old local mail account remotely, and many ISPs will forward mail to a new address for some period of time, much as the postal service does. Call your ISP to find out what services are available if you move.

To be able to receive forwarded e-mail, you obviously must establish an account in your new location. And be sure to give your new e-mail address to all your correspondents as soon as possible.

INTERNET

www.relaymail.net
www.bigfoot.com
www.pobox.com

There are many services on the web that will forward your e-mail, as well as perform other helpful functions. Check out these sites.

Finally, it's possible to establish your own domain name, which will remain the same no matter where or how often you move. We'll explain more about this in Chapter 9, "Your Own Web site."

In this chapter, we've surveyed the subject of e-mail, the most heavily used Internet service of all. By now, you're probably discovering the joys of this new form of communication for yourself. As with web browsers, e-mail software is going to be a big part of your life, so it might be wise to purchase a book that outlines in depth the ins and outs and features of your e-mail software.

Customizing these programs is just as helpful as customizing your browser. And be sure to give yourself time to develop a good filing system — you'll need it!

A simple summary

✓ Electronic mail doesn't have to be Internet-based. Any form of electronic mail is e-mail, while snail mail is the new term for the post office's old paper-based type of correspondence.

✓ An e-mail message has a basic anatomy, including a header and a body. By filling in the proper information in the header of a message, you can send copies of an e-mail message to any number of people, forward a message from one source to another, or reply to any incoming message.

✓ Encrypting, or coding of messages to prevent loss of privacy, is possible by using a program like PGP.

✓ In the e-mail world, there are clear rules of "netiquette" that you should follow. Ordinary courtesy applies to all Internet activities.

✓ Free forms of e-mail are available, including web-based services.

✓ Files of any kind, including text, images, audio files, and programs, can be attached to an e-mail message. All e-mail programs provide a way to do this.

✓ You can automatically file incoming mail in folders that will help you keep messages organized; you can also filter out at least some unwanted e-mail.

✓ Newer e-mail software may offer clickable hot links that allow you to jump directly from an e-mail message to a web page.

✓ You can have more than one e-mail address if you so desire. If you move, a locally-based address may have to change, while web-based addresses and accounts with national online services can remain the same.

Chapter 7

Group Communication

WHEN YOU SEND E-MAIL TO, and receive e-mail from, an individual, you're communicating one-to-one. In this chapter, you'll learn how to communicate and interact one-to-many. The Internet provides many different ways to connect with others. We'll look at three of the most popular methods, web-based message boards, mailing lists and newsgroups. These three terms have definitions in relation to the Internet that are slightly different from their customary meanings. After looking at these three group communications options, we'll consider how anyone can set up their own virtual community, focused on whatever mutual concern draws people together.

In this chapter...

✓ Message boards

✓ Mailing lists

✓ Newsgroups

✓ Setting up your own group

COMMUNICATION IS MADE EASY ON THE INTERNET

Message boards

ALL THE TYPES OF *group communications covered in this chapter are* asynchronous. *Chapter 8 covers synchronous, or "real time," communications, such as online chat rooms.*

What it is

■ **Internet notice boards** *enable your information to reach a global audience.*

Message boards, discussions, and forums function like public bulletin boards, where people tack up messages and others post responses, and responses to responses, underneath. But unlike public bulletin boards, message boards on the Internet are easy to access from any computer connected to the Internet, anywhere in the world, any time of day or night. Message boards are found all over the web, and have become very popular. Sometimes elaborate and sometimes simple, they represent a public environment where people can place messages and respond to the messages of others.

Millions of news-oriented web sites, search engine and directory sites, virtual communities, and niche interest sites now provide bulletin boards. Many software companies also offer them, enlarging the scope of your opportunities to share.

Bulletin boards

Creators of bulletin boards use a variety of software, and the various packages operate in slightly different ways. Most of them provide guided tours, help pages, and message board indexes. Many offer search tools to enable you to search through large volumes of messages for specific words or topics. These amenities help show newcomers how the board works and what it's like, so they can decide whether or not to participate. Many bulletin boards will ask you to register before posting a message, but this is usually free and easy.

Despite a variety of visual presentations and operational variations, the underlying structures and functions of message boards tend to be very similar and easy to navigate, once you've tried it a few times.

■ **Message boards** *are found all over the web.*

On message boards, threads connect related messages. The concept of threads is really quite simple. For instance, you might see a message on a subject that interests you, and want to respond or ask questions of the sender of that particular message. The message board will show you how to indicate exactly which message you're responding to; then your own message will appear, threaded to that one and to other incoming responses to the same message. If other people respond directly to what you've said, those messages will be threaded to your message, and so on. Some original parent messages spawn several threads, which in turn lead to new threads and subthreads.

Remember that most bulletin boards are open to the world. If you attach your name and e-mail address to a message, any Internet user in the world will know who posted it and how to reach you.

For this reason, many users choose not to reveal their real names or e-mail addresses, using pen names instead.

Many message boards provide statements of their online policies and terms of use. We suggest you always read these before participating. They may say the publisher disclaims the veracity of information posted, which may be very important to know, if, for example, the board addresses health and medical issues. Some policies state that posts become the property of the publisher, which means your post may be recycled somewhere else. Wouldn't you be surprised to see your message board post in a magazine! Message boards often mention how to complain if someone is abusive or otherwise in violation of the board's standards of behavior.

Trivia...

The term "bulletin board," which comes from the BBS realm, remains popular to describe web-based message board services. We'll use the term "message boards" as a generic description for web-based boards, but as you surf from web site to web site, you'll frequently see the term bulletin board.

■ **Threads connect** *related messages.*

TOO MUCH TRUST

We know a woman who, when pregnant, posted a message to a message board, asking other pregnant women to contact her to share experiences and questions. She received many responses and actually made some good friends among the group. These friendships continued from pregnancy through birth and early child care. One day, someone who had found her address sent her an e-mail, asking if she might want to sample new products for lactating mothers. It sounded legitimate, but turned out to be a man with a fetish for nude photographs of nursing mothers. She felt so violated by this experience that she stopped using the Internet for a long time. Finally, she set up an anonymous e-mail address with a pen name.

Bulletin boards can produce great personal rewards, but always remember that everything on them is public, and your messages may have a much longer life on the Internet than you had ever expected.

Where it is

To access and begin navigating a message board, start from the web site that provides it, and click on a link into the message boards area. The link may have any number of labels, such as "boards," "member-to-member," or "join the debate."

Topics

At most boards, beyond any introductory information pages, you'll notice a list of major topics, appearing rather like folders in a hierarchical filing structure. Each of these will lead to sub-topics or sub-folders covering certain points. Within these are individual messages and threads of responses and also follow-up messages.

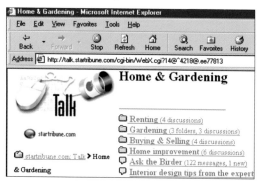

■ **The Minneapolis Star-Tribune**, *like many other newspapers, has its own message board.*

INTERNET

www.startribune.com

The Minneapolis Star-Tribune newspaper web site provides a message board entitled "Talk."

www.aqualink.com

Aqualink, a web site for fishkeepers, calls their boards area the WebForum.

www.thirdage.com

At Third Age, a web site for active older adults, the link "community" leads you to the message boards.

Some message boards provide overview information, such as a list of all topics under discussion, the number of sub-groups and their subjects, and the number of messages actually posted to each one.

To see how this works, visit www.cnn.com. On their home page, click Messageboard. (You might have to scroll down the page to find it.) You'll be offered a guided tour, the right to register and post messages, and a list of all the ongoing topics. Like many large message boards, CNN has created various topical sub-lists such as issues, health, entertainment, nature, books, travel, and many others.

While message boards can be a great source of information, and a pleasant way to communicate, never assume that people are who they say they are – some may misrepresent themselves. For example, commercial interests sometimes post messages under false names. Claiming to be consumers, they will lavish glowing praise on some product, or criticize a competitor's product.

They hope these seeds will convince readers to try their products. Just be aware that on message boards, people are not always who they say they are.

■ **People on** *message boards can be chameleon-like, and not what they seem.*

Posting a message

Most boards make it easy to figure out how to post a message. There's usually a form, which asks for a subject line, a name, an e-mail address, and your message (similar to the items you fill out for an e-mail message). Some boards let you preview your message and then edit it, in case you see a typo or want to fine-tune your words. Others may not offer a preview, so always type carefully. You may want to write your message outside the online form, perhaps using a word processor, so you can review it, spell-check it, and assure yourself it's ready to publish. Then, copy and paste the text into the message board's posting form.

Once a message is out there, there's usually no turning back! It can be fun and exciting to check back later to see what kind of responses your message will bring. It can also be unpleasant if you get "flamed" (a visceral and often vituperative negative response), but don't despair – most message board users have been flamed at least once. It's not that much different from being yelled or gestured at by an irate driver.

Type your comments in the box below. Just click Send It! and they will instantly be part of the discussion! To format your message add HTML to your comments.

Hi Bobbie,
Try tofu with alittle bit of cheese mixed together and warmed in the microwave. Very delicious. Try rice cheese or a low fat brand. I love it! It only takes about a minute. Fruit is really great too. Pick lower carb ones like tangerines, peaches, oranges, or grapefruit.

Send It! When you click Send It!, your comments will appear. You will have thirty minutes to edit or delete them if you so choose. If not, you're all done!

■ **Most message boards** *make it easy to post a message.*

Remember your netiquette. Those who violate netiquette on a message board are likely to be buried under a tide of flames and objections. It's OK to speak directly to the writer of one particular message if you want to respond, but do so with carefully considered, courteous language.

Be aware that many message boards have low tolerance levels for certain kinds of messages. For example, posting a message that asks for basic technical help – especially on a board frequented by experts – often produces more sarcasm than help. Always read any online help or Frequently Asked Question (FAQs) pages before posting a technical question – you'll often find the answer to your question there. Many message

■ **Protect yourself** *from barbed comments by thinking carefully about the questions you post on online message boards.*

board veterans bristle at "me too" messages – from people who read an opinion or comment and post a message saying nothing more than, "I agree." Try, instead, to add something original to the discussion.

Private messages

If your message is really intended as a private communication to an individual, it doesn't really belong on a message board at all – use e-mail, if possible, instead. Clearly private communications posted to boards annoy veteran board users, and you probably don't want thousands of people to read your private message anyway. Off-topic messages are also likely to produce a bit of negative feedback. But the type of message board posting most likely to result in intense flaming is a commercial advertisement, especially one the writer attempts to disguise. For example, the person who posts, "Here's a really great product, click over to my web site for more information," had better be ready to don his asbestos union suit.

■ **FAQs are** *helpful on message boards like communities.msn.com.*

Starting a new discussion

Suppose you have a deep personal interest in some issue or question, or a specific problem you need help with. After looking through the index of discussion groups at several web sites, you don't find that topic being discussed anywhere. Pick a bulletin board where the overall tone and subject matter seems to fit your interest.

We suggest using a board that seems well-organized, and where the postings on other topics seem to be relevant and of good quality If your chosen board requires that you be a registered user, sign up and log in.

Then, find the option for starting a new discussion, which might be called something like New Message, Post, Add a Topic, or Create New Discussion. If you can't find it, review the message board help page. You'll probably be asked to include your name, address, and e-mail address with your message, but you can use pen names and external, web-based e-mail addresses if you prefer. (For more information on getting a free web-based e-mail address, see Chapter 6.) Some boards will allow you to request that your name and e-mail address not appear on the bulletin board.

Receiving replies

There are a few boards that allow you to click a box to be automatically informed, via e-mail, when someone else replies to your message. Otherwise, you'll have to check back occasionally to find out if any related messages have been posted. If you've included an e-mail address, you're also likely to get replies to your message via e-mail.

Sometimes, this leads to a private exchange of e-mail messages with someone else who shares your interest. For example, a friend of ours collects certain types of rare paperback science fiction books. Through message boards, he has begun ongoing e-mail relationships with several other collectors and dealers of these esoteric collectibles.

Each web site has a policy about how long a message stays in the active lists. Sometimes, after the time for active listing expires, a summary of earlier messages will still be available. To access an earlier message, you may need its message number, or other specific information about it. In other cases, expired messages are erased and not retrievable. So, if you see some bit of information you may need, it's a good idea to print it, or copy it onto your hard disk, for later reference.

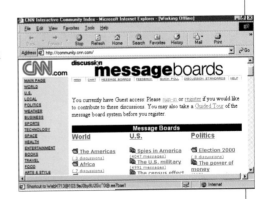

■ **Some message** *boards, for example community.cnn.com, require you to register.*

Mailing lists

■ **Whatever your** *interest, try diving into mailing lists of like-minded people.*

IN OFFICE TERMINOLOGY, a "mailing list," or distribution, is a list of names and addresses to which periodic mailings of snail mail or e-mail are routed. In Internet group communications, the meaning is related but significantly different. Internet mailing lists have been in use since the mid-1970s, and they remain a thriving arena for online communication. Among the mailing list programs in popular use are Listserv, Listproc, and Majordomo. Lists also have human administrators, but users rarely need to interact directly with the administrators, as the process is highly automated.

What it is

A mailing list is a grass-roots network, operating through e-mail, organized for the purpose of putting people who share some interest in touch with one another. A mailing list has the advantage, in most cases, of being almost completely non-commercial. Most lists are generated by universities, organizations, and individuals, rather than by businesses. Those who participate in a mailing list are self-selected. The quality of the input tends to be fairly high, as everyone has a real interest in the subject. The disadvantage can be a tremendous volume of mail.

The types of messages that are not condoned in message boards and other types of one-to-many online communications are even more unwelcome on mailing lists.

Each list member receives each message in their e-mail Inbox, imposing on their time, resources, and attention. When inappropriate messages are sent to mailing lists, a playful member may comment, "I hope that person is wearing fireproof underwear." Mailing lists are potentially some of the most useful, valuable resources you'll find on the Internet. When you're new to a list, just read without posting for a while (called "lurking"), and get the feel and tenor of the group's dynamics. When you're ready, send a message introducing yourself.

Lively Discussions

Witness Against Lawless Logging
Eco-activists share news and resources on forest conservation.

Reef List
Phish fans? No, fish fans! Aquarists talk about their hobby.

NRG
Raving discussion for DJs, producers, and fans of this electronica genre.

More Discussions

Informative Newsletters

John Marks Recommends
Top critic rates the finest music, books, videos, and wine around.

Internet Insider
Marketing know-how and e-commerce news from the online experts.

Gramma Dean's Ezine
Family-oriented fun for parents and kids. Gramma knows best!

More Newsletters

Moderated mailing lists

Some mailing lists are moderated – that is, all messages are routed through one person who reads everything and decides whether it's appropriate for

■ **Mailing lists** *are great for communicating shared interests.*

that mailing list. If something is too tangential, redundant, or provocative to contribute to the discussion, the moderator can choose to not post that message.

This may sound like censorship, but it does provide a way to weed out inappropriate or objectionable material from the flood of mail.

Where it is

Mailing lists are operated by countless sources, and you may learn of them in any number of ways. If you're a member of a professional organization or club, you may hear of mailing lists from a newsletter or journal, or from a colleague. Several web sites also provide directories of mailing lists, searchable by keywords, or browsable by topic.

At these and other sites maintaining mailing list directories, you'll also find information on using mailing lists, and on filtering your incoming mail so you won't be burdened by excessive e-mails that aren't directly related to your needs or interests.

INTERNET

www.Liszt.com

At Liszt.com, almost 100,000 different lists are catalogued as of this writing. Additional resources include eScribe (www.escribe.com), Topica (www.topica.com), and Tile Net (www.tile.net). As with all types of online searching, it's often a good idea to try multiple searching tools when you're looking for something that's important to you.

How it works

Mailing lists offer basic commands you can execute by sending specific e-mail messages to the list manager's

■ **Like lists?** *You'll love Liszt.com – it's a catalog of mailing lists.*

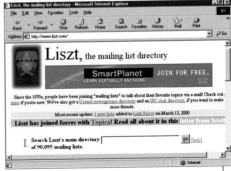

e-mail address. These special-purpose messages usually contain a single line in the body or subject line. For example, some mailing lists provide an "INFO" command, which will automatically cause an e-mail message describing the list to be sent to you.

The New American Folk Music mailing list provides a typical assortment of mail list command options. First is the INFO command, activated by sending an e-mail message addressed to: Majordomo@nysernet.org, with the single line, info folk_music, in the body of the message. Minutes after sending this command, a new e-mail message arrives with a subject line that says, "Majordomo results." The e-mail message contains a useful description of the group, its purposes and its membership. It says that the list is moderated, and that an online archive of list messages is available at the designated web site address.

Many mailing lists offer, as a subscription option, a digest version of the ongoing discussion. This gives you each day's messages in a single, large digest message, rather than sending you each individual message. Digest versions save time, but delay the transmission of each message and make it slightly more cumbersome to reply to a particular message.

Subscribing to a mailing list

The mailing list directories mentioned above, and other similar web sites, give step-by-step instructions for subscribing and unsubscribing to any mailing list. Locate a list you want to try, and follow the instructions. Every mailing list has two addresses – a list command address, and a list distribution address. You'll be directed to send an e-mail message to the list command address, saying certain, exact words in the body of the message, usually "subscribe," followed by the name of the list, and then your own first name and last name – nothing else. This enables the software maintaining the list to add you and welcome you to that list.

If you add anything else in the message, your attempt to subscribe won't be accepted, and you'll probably get an e-mail containing an error message. That's because the list sign-up process is done automatically, and the software recognizes only correctly formulated messages.

You'll then begin receiving e-mail from the other people on that mailing list. All this mail, including your replies, goes through the list distribution address. If you later decide to unsubscribe, that request must be sent to the list command address, not to all of your e-mail pen pals at the list distribution address.

If you try to unsubscribe by e-mailing your request to the list distribution address, that message will go to all the people on your mailing list, who cannot do anything about your request and will likely be annoyed.

If you accidentally do this, and especially if you accidentally do it twice, it might be wise to quickly don your flameproof skivvies. You get off a list in the same way you got on the list, through the list command address.

Who does it

Who creates all these lists on all these different interesting, curious, or esoteric subjects? We do – we the ordinary Internet surfers.

This is a database listing at Tile.net/Lists: The Reference to Internet Discussion Lists	
Listname:	**Blondie Mailing List**
Description:	List dedicated to band Blondie and singer Debbie Harry.
You can join this group by sending the message "blondie-subscribe@list.tdce.com.au" to blondie-subscribe@list.tdce.com.au	

■ **To join a list,** *send an e-mail to the list command address.*

AT THE CITY GATES

Ancient history gives many examples of settings where people got together to discuss news, politics, and other shared concerns. From these gatherings of the elders or the citizens, a consensus of opinion sometimes emerged, helping set the direction of society. In Greece, men met at the gymnasium; in Rome, it happened at the forum; and in ancient Israel, the elders met every day at the gates of cities such as Jerusalem. Sometimes, they actually settled disputes and passed judgement on those who had violated the written or unwritten laws. This tradition of pooling knowledge and experience carried over into the town meetings of colonial America. It's now alive and well on the Internet, but the circle of those able to speak up includes a much wider range of people, in every corner of the world.

■ **People have** *gathered in forums to share ideas since ancient times.*

Not all mailing lists are open to the general online public. Many are set up for specialized groups of people, and open only by invitation or on the basis of certain criteria.

Many mailing list subscribers never actively participate, but become permanent lurkers. In all the types of one-to-many communications discussed in this chapter, lurking has the same definition – reading and observing, but not posting. As with face-to-face conversations, some people really like to talk, and others say little or nothing. Estimates indicate that only about ten percent of mailing list subscribers make up the vocal majority, responsible for most of the message traffic. Some lists are set up so you can respond to just one member of the list, while others will automatically send every response to every subscriber. If you do want to post a message, it must be from the e-mail address with which you subscribed. You won't be recognized by the list if you use some other return address, and your message won't make it to the list.

However, some lists offer ways for non-subscribers to post. For example, the HTML Writer's Guild maintains a list called HWG-jobs, which sends its subscribers information about job openings in the Internet industry. Employers who have openings can send descriptions of open positions to the list manager, who then forwards the job descriptions to the list.

■ **The HTML** *Writer's Guild lists job vacancies on their web site hwg.org.*

Newsgroups

■ **Whatever your** *interest, you can chat about it on the web.*

LIKE E-MAIL *and mailing lists, newsgroups have been around much longer than the web, having first appeared at Duke University around 1979. Like e-mail, newsgroups are text-based, but instead of using e-mail readers to view and transmit messages, the first newsgroups were based on a new protocol which required a special piece of software called a newsreader. An advantage of a newsgroup over e-mail is that it presents messages in hierarchical, threaded lists, and allows posting and reading in a single environment, rather than via fragmented individual e-mail messages.*

Like mailing lists and web-based message boards, newsgroups are asynchronous. However, newsgroups are a step closer to synchronous communication. While e-mail messages remain until you deal with them, postings in newsgroups must be dealt with quickly or be lost, because the group automatically updates itself frequently. The dialog in newsgroups is more like an ongoing conversation. This is really the roots of the grass roots, as it's not web-based, contains little commercial input, and is responsive to individual needs, quirks, and preferences. It's also the place where you'll find a lot of the more far out material online.

Though newsgroups are text-based, images and other types of files can be attached, just as in e-mail. Modern newsreader software can display this multi-media content inline.

Trivia...

Newsgroups existed long before the web, and are especially popular with long-time computer users. If there are any real geeks among your family and friends, just bring up the subject of newsgroups, or USENET, and watch them come to life! One member of our family lives alone in an isolated place, and spends almost all his spare time online. When he visits our home, we know where to find him – at our computer, looking up newsgroups and comparing them with the ones he belongs to at home.

What it is

The realm of newsgroups is called USENET. Finding appropriate newsgroups is much easier than finding mailing lists, because newsgroups are catalogued and indexed in a strict hierarchy by USENET databases, which you can find with search engines.

🖳 Deja.com's Usenet Discussion Service - Microsoft Internet Explorer

File   Edit   View   Favorites   Tools   Help

Back   Forward   Stop   Refresh   Home   Search   Favorite

Address 🔍 http://www.deja.com/usenet/

Welcome to Deja.com's Usenet Discussion Service, the largest such archive on the Net, which includes Usenet

BROWSE DISCUSSIONS

alt. (alternative) Anything-goes type discussions covering every conceivable topic from aliens to Zen.

■ **Deja.com gives** *you access to USENET news groups and other forums.*

These indexes are comprehensive and up-to-date, so the search for just the right group can be straightforward.

You might want to begin with the USENET Info Center Launch Pad at sunsite.unc.edu/usenet-i, Tile Net at www.tile.net, or www.cyberfiber.com.

When searching for a newsgroup, begin with keywords. For instance, if you want to find a newsgroup of people interested in discussing Shakespeare, a search would reveal the newsgroup called humanities.lit.authors.shakespeare. Finding what you want may take patience, but the overall realm of USENET is organized logically. If the group exists, you'll find it eventually. For example, the Shakespeare group uses a typical newsgroup naming convention, lying under a top level category of humanities, which contains sub-sets for lit (literature) as well as music, language, classics, philosophy, design, and others. Under lit, there are more than 80 newsgroups devoted to specific authors, including Shakespeare.

■ **There are newsgroups** *on the net dedicated to discussing Shakespeare.*

INTERNET

www.deja.com

This useful site allows you to search or browse, either to find newsgroups dealing with specific subjects, or to find postings containing specific keywords. We did a search for posts by our friend, the "early adopter," and found more than 700 messages containing his name – these included both his own messages and replies to those messages from others.

Newsreaders

Newsgroups are neither web-based nor e-mail based, so using them has traditionally required a type of software called a newsreader. There are dozens of newsreaders available, most of them for free. Both Internet Explorer and Netscape Navigator have newsreader tools built right in.

Using a newsreader software program has advantages, though, as these specialized programs usually include more sophisticated, customizable, and functional options.

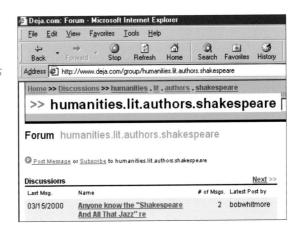

■ **The Shakespeare** *newsgroup has a typical name: humanities.lit.authors.shakespeare.*

To activate the newsreader software in Internet Explorer, go to Tools, Mail, and New, and then Read News. With the Netscape Navigator browser, click Communicator, then Newsgroups.

Whatever software you use for newsgroups, you may have to go through a bit of set-up to point it at the proper news server location at your ISP. Contact your ISP for the name of their news server, and for assistance in setting up your newsreader.

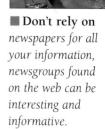

■ **Don't rely on** *newspapers for all your information, newsgroups found on the web can be interesting and informative.*

There are literally thousands and thousands of newsgroups. ISPs generally don't offer every possible newsgroup in existence, because newsgroups tend to require significant resources on the part of the ISP. You can learn which newsgroups are already available through your ISP by using your newsreader to access their current list. The command you need will probably be something like, "show all newsgroups." The groups you're most interested in may not be there, but most ISPs will add additional groups at your request. There also are a number of new, web-based systems that let you access and participate in newsgroups directly through your web browser. Deja.com is probably the most popular of these services.

Ready for a little adventure? Check out the category of newsgroups under the alt heading.

Alt means "alternative." The alt sphere of USENET contains many fascinating and interesting discussions, but also tends to be the repository of some of the weirder and more disturbing topics, including some of the extremist groups you may have heard of, as well as just about anything wild, wacky, or kinky. Some ISPs will not subscribe to some of the more objectionable alt groups. On the other hand, they may. If you have children at home, you might want to implement your own filter against inappropriate material. More on that in Chapter 17.

How to do it

Navigating in newsgroups is very similar to using bulletin boards, and similar cautions prevail. Protect your privacy, observe all the rules and customs of netiquette, and don't assume that everyone is who, or what, they say they are. Most newsgroups provide a FAQ file, which is always worth reading before leaping in with your own postings.

The first level of participation comes when you select a newsgroup and click on it. The next window will display the current article headers (which show the message subjects) for that group. From this list, click on a header to read the message. To post a reply or new message, find your newsreader's New Message command. A good newsgroup message follows basic netiquette, and should have a clear and concise subject line.

Get in the driver's seat

There are many possibilities for customizing the way you read and take part in newsgroups. Your newsreader software's preferences hold the key to putting you in the driver's seat. Want to filter out some of the spam that inevitably invades most newsgroups? Use your message filters.

Newsgroups also provide an avenue for special help, such as problem-solving and needle-in-a-haystack searching. People have been known to turn to newsgroups for locating rare toys, retired versions of hot collectibles, or out-of-print software manuals. Newsgroups are also places to share common interests, debate issues, or learn how to troubleshoot an obscure technical problem. You might be able to help someone else as well, which reinforces that atmosphere of grass roots, people-to-people communication.

Setting up your own group

LET'S SAY YOU'VE LEARNED to use all three types of group communication described here. After a while, you discover you have a unique idea for a group that doesn't yet exist. Maybe the mailing list you chose is good, but would suit you better if it had a different focus. Maybe the newsgroup that seemed perfect goes off on tangents that just don't interest you. Many of the groups now in existence began just this way, when someone felt the need to overcome these limitations. Maybe you're part of a highly-focused special-interest group that has no online group communication vehicle.

Starting a list or group of your own is an intriguing possibility. And you can do it! The technology isn't very complicated. The process can be short and sweet or lengthy and time-consuming — that's up to you. In part, it depends on you, and how elaborate your idea is.

Perhaps you'd prefer a private, tightly-controlled, mailing list. You'll be the moderator, retaining the right to pass approval on every message. On the other hand, if you're too busy to screen all that e-mail, or if your group is not likely to produce inappropriate messages, having an unmoderated group is an easier choice. Whether to choose a web-based message board, a mailing list, or a newsgroup depends on your purpose.

Implementing web-based message boards

We've already mentioned the possibility that you might want to create your own web site. (In Chapter 9, we'll tell you just how to do that.) On your own site, you could establish your own bulletin board and start it off with one or more topics important to you. Several options are available in message board software for your own web site, including a number of free programs as well as commercial applications with more robust options and power. Most of these programs come with straightforward instructions. But before you select a package, check which packages are compatible with your ISP's server platforms, and whether your ISP supports or recommends specific applications.

If you don't particularly want to establish your own web site, but would still like your own bulletin board, there are some web sites that will let you log on and set up your own board as part of their space.

SOFTWARE REVIEWS

A growing number of web sites provide amazing services to help people create robust virtual communities, including message boards. Here are just a few good ones:

✓ www.forumone.com/build.htm
✓ www.myfamily.com
✓ www.familypoint.com
✓ www.anexa.com
✓ realdiscussions.com
✓ my.deja.com
✓ clubs.yahoo.com

■ **Forumone.com** *helps people create online communities.*

A sense of community

Surfing the web is a solitary activity, while group communication, by definition, can never be truly solitary.

The ability to reach out for a sense of community is the main reason many people want to get online.

Even as we write, the dividing lines between the three types of group communication discussed in this chapter are blurring. The sites just mentioned, for instance, offer combinations of bulletin boards, mailing lists, and chat rooms. To take it a step further, the lines between all media are blurring. New services such as OneBox, (www.onebox.com), combine telephone, fax, and e-mail into a single application.

Knowing the audience

If you want to draw a specific type of people into your group, you must decide exactly who they should be. Even in a family group, questions will arise about extended family, in-laws, friends that are almost family, and so on. If it's a professional group you want to create, consider the purpose carefully. Is it a meant to be a think tank, a place to share information, a support group, or an attempt to network or build friendships?

■ **Your group** *could be a catalyst for intellectual debate.*

Alumni associations of many universities maintain mailing lists specifically to share news about fellow alumni. These lists are also used to get groups together for telecasts of games from the alma mater. If you want to start a list like this, suggest it to your campus alumni association, and offer to help set it up.

Starting a mailing list

A mailing list is often the best option for a narrowly targeted group. To start a mailing list, you need a provider who will operate it for you. Check with your ISP about mailing list services they may offer. There are also many web sites that offer opportunities to create mailing lists. A group offers free support, and a host is also available to manage mailing lists for a fee. Some examples are listed below:

✓ www.onelist.com
✓ www.egroups.com
✓ www.coollist.com
✓ www.topica.com
✓ engage.webpromote.com

■ **Some web sites,** *for example onelist.com, help you create your own mailing list.*

Starting a newsgroup

Starting a new newsgroup is more time-consuming and difficult than starting a message board or mailing list. Why? Before anyone on the Internet can access your new newsgroup, that person's ISP or online service provider must add your newsgroup to their "newsfeed," and store your group's messages on their news server. That means that every new newsgroup potentially affects many people and takes a lot of resources. For example, if you felt the Shakespeare newsgroup we found above wasn't specific enough, and a new group was needed just to discuss Shakespeare's sonnets, here's what you'd have to do.

SETTING UP A SPECIFIC NEWS GROUP

✓ First, post a formal Request for Discussion (RFD) to the newsgroup called news.announce.newgroup, as well as to any newsgroups related to your topic, such as the existing group.

✓ Then, interested people will discuss your idea for 30 days and try to reach conclusions on the need for the new group, what it should be called, and where it would be placed in the USENET hierarchy.

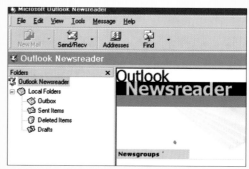

■ **There are** *myriad fascinating news groups to explore.*

✓ When these issues are decided, a Call for Votes (CFV) is posted. Votes are sent via e-mail to a list moderator, and then the results are posted to news.announce.newgroup. If there are no major objections, and at least 100 more "yes" votes were cast than "no" votes, and if at least two-thirds of the total number of votes were "yes" votes, the new group will be created.

In this chapter we've stepped into the world of asynchronous group communications, and explored the advantages and disadvantages of bulletin boards, mailing lists, and newsgroups. Having already learned that the Internet is much more than just the World Wide Web, we've now seen a little more of some of its other aspects.

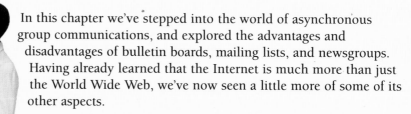

■ **You could** *set up a newsgroup which serves a supporting function.*

A simple summary

✓ Message boards are web-based, available at many web sites, and offer ongoing discussions on a wide variety of subjects. Related messages are linked together by a system called threads. Boards go by many names, but operate in similar ways.

✓ Messages posted on boards are open to the whole online community around the world, so it's wise to consider the public nature of message boards when posting messages.

✓ Mailing lists are e-mail based, and consist of self-selected groups of people who communicate about some specified topic, with messages from all the participants e-mailed to everyone in the group.

✓ Directories of mailing lists are available on the web, giving current information about what lists exist.

✓ Subscribing and unsubscribing to a mailing list may be done through e-mail. It's important to follow the exact directions.

✓ Newsgroups are not web-based or e-mail based, but rather require special software, generally called newsreaders. Newsgroups have existed since long before the web, in an Internet realm called USENET. Some web sites now allow users to read and post to newsgroups without newsreader software.

✓ Newsgroups are accessed through your ISP, which can provide a list of all the groups currently available. If the ones you want aren't offered, you can request them, and most ISPs will fill your request.

✓ Setting up your own bulletin board, mailing list, or newsgroup is always an option.

✓ If you create your own web site, a bulletin board can be part of it. If not, some web sites will provide space for your personal message board.

Chapter 8

Can we talk?

THE INTERNET HAS given rise to a new mode of communication, where text is the currency for expression, but where the leisurely pace of old-fashioned letters has given way to flurries of quickly-typed bytes flying across the global network. But e-mail, newsgroups, and message boards still allow you to fine-tune your message.

Online chatting and instant messaging combine elements of a telephone conversation and letter writing. The conversation is still typed, but the person you "talk" to is online at the same time you are.

In this chapter...

✓ What is real time?

✓ Chat technology tried and true

✓ Chat technology: new and newer

✓ Etiquette and common sense

✓ Internet Telephony

INSTANT MESSAGING CAN BRING YOU CLOSER

What is real time?

REAL TIME IS WHAT TICKS by on the clock. The opposite of real time isn't unreal time, but rather, different, or asynchronous time, as when you send e-mail in the morning and the receiver opens it in the evening. Real time passes when people are in direct contact – they may be in different time zones, so their clocks will not show the same hour, but all their clocks will show the same passage of time. It might take you twenty minutes to compose an e-mail message that the receiver reads in twenty seconds, but when you're chatting, a minute is a minute for both or all involved.

What is chat?

In the telegraph era, Morse code provided a real-time link between people. An operator at a distant station would receive a message clicked out in dots and dashes, and would click back an answer. Newcomers to the Internet sometimes think a chat is actual voice contact, but, in fact, it's more like a streamlined version of telegraphy – without the dots and dashes. Conversations are typed, but the rhythm of chatting can seem very much like live discussion.

Groups of online chatters are often called "chat rooms." Web sites that offer chat usually provide lists of rooms available, as well as the opportunity to create a new chat room and invite others to join.

Most chat rooms have maximum capacities, and will spawn new rooms when existing rooms get full. If a chat room begins to get too crowded (more than 12 to 15 people), it not only tends to become more chaotic, but it also often begins to suffer a performance drag. The delivery of messages slows down, causing the discussion to proceed in a conversation-inhibiting "herky-jerky" manner. If you find the performance of your chat software is erratic, switching to a less-busy chat room might help.

Chat messages

Chat messages are generally brief, especially in chat rooms where many people are all talking at once. To help make tiny bits of text more meaningful, and keep up with the fast

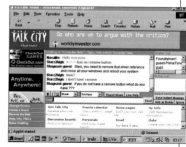

■ **Online chatters** *gather in chat rooms.*

pace, many chat room messages contain shorthand and acronyms that a newcomer may find unintelligible. We advise listening without entering into the discussion for awhile (called lurking). When you've got the hang of it, you're ready to join in.

We also suggest reading the site FAQ or help page before trying to participate in a chat. Those who interrupt the flow of conversation by sending lengthy messages, or asking "how do I..." questions, may find themselves excluded by other participants.

It's not that anyone wants to be rude or fails to care about your problems as a newcomer, it's just that veteran chatters know you can find the answers yourself – if you really try.

What good is it?

To some people, the word "chat" implies wasting time. Images arise of neighbors leaning across the back fence to gossip, or teenagers hanging out and exchanging jokes. But in fact, chat can facilitate group planning, study, support, discussion of common interests, community-building, and staying in touch with friends and family.

If your family is trying to plan a summer reunion or a Christmas homecoming, especially if you have many family members spread out in different parts of the country, try getting them all together in a chat room. You'll save phone bills and cut down on confusion.

■ **Reading the** *site's FAQ list will help you learn how to chat online.*

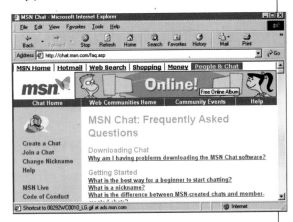

Companies with representatives in different locations sometimes hold meetings in chat rooms. Colleges put teachers in rooms where they're available to students for study help. Several real-time software "collaboration" tools have been developed for business users, allowing common "white boards" to be deployed right on users' screens, much as a blackboard might be used in a conference room.

You've doubtless heard stories about offensive, hard-core sex talk in chat rooms, and frightening tales of attempts by predators to lure people to personal meetings.

Unfortunately, those things have happened. We'll outline some sensible ways to protect yourself and your family from this type of thing. But don't let that stop you from trying online chat.

It's now possible to get an idea of what chatting is like with very little effort. Although many chat room discussions do end up slanting toward frivolous or lewd subject matter, there are lots of others that address subjects like health, culture, politics, sports, hobbies, travel, religion, parenting, and almost any other subject you can think of. Many others are interesting because of their timeliness, such as online chats that take place concurrently with television or radio shows.

Chat technology tried and true

THE EARLIEST FORMS *of synchronous communication existed long before the web. Like newsgroups, the earlier systems remain popular with dedicated computer geeks, who got used to them in the old days. More modern, web-based methods are easier to use though, and may not even require special software. It makes sense to sample chat with the most convenient methods, and then, if you like it, to look into the possibility of acquiring more specialized software.*

Some of the early forms of Internet-based real-time activities were highly creative online games or "virtual worlds," known by names like MUDs, MOOs, MUXes, MUSEs, and MUSHes.

These names refer to various forms of "Multiple User" environments, which usually involve participants assuming personae or characters, and engaging in extemporaneous role-playing. MUing has remained popular at many universities and with individual Internet users around the world. Many teachers have adapted MUing as an educational tool.

Multiple User Domains continue to thrive, and some have migrated from their original text-based environments to graphical versions, accessible from the web. There are numerous web sites devoted to the Multiple User realm, and to getting started with MUDs, MOOs, and the like. Here are a few:

✓ MUing for Beginners: www.cwrl.utexas.edu/moo/
✓ MOO links: ebbs.english.vt.edu/moo.html
✓ MUD Connector: www.mudconnector.com
✓ MUD Central: www.mudcentral.com
✓ MOO Cows FAQ: www.moo.mud.org/moo-faq/

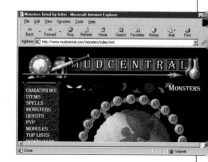

■ **Online games** *or virtual worlds known as MUDs continue to thrive.*

Internet relay chat (IRC)

Although IRC is an older form of chatting, it's still used by many people, and the needed software is still available as shareware or freeware. IRC enables chatting for people who don't care to surf the web (it's not accessed through a browser), but through an IRC server. Most of the features available in online and web-based chatting are available in IRC, too, along with the means to participate in multiple groups at the same time.

If you really enjoy chatting, and might want to spend a lot of time doing it, look at some of the IRC software and check out, in detail, what it offers. Bear in mind that you would be able to communicate only with others who also have IRC.

AOL

The popularity of chatting exploded in the mid-1990s, largely as a result of AOL's growth and their public, well-publicized online "events." AOL would announce that a public figure or celebrity would be present at a certain time in a chat room, available to answer questions and talk with people. This led to explosive growth in chatting, and also to rapid growth for AOL itself. Internet users jumped at the chance to converse, in real time, with Michael Jordan or Buzz Aldrin. To visit an AOL chat room, you must be an AOL subscriber.

Open the chat access by clicking the People button, and then People Connection, or, in some cases, the keyword Chat. Choosing the option List Chats gives you a list of all available chat rooms, arranged by category. Click on one chat room, and then choose the option Who, or People Here, to see mini-profiles of the individuals currently in that room.

In the earlier days of AOL and the Internet, many people were charged by the minute for their Internet access. This became a huge problem for some parents, whose teenagers spent hours and hours in chat rooms, resulting in staggering charges on the parents' credit cards. While "metered" online service is less common now, it's still extremely important for parents to supervise their kids' chatting experiences. (We'll talk more about this a little later.) If your online account has time limits, you might also want to establish your own personal usage policies, to make sure you don't unwittingly run up massive fees.

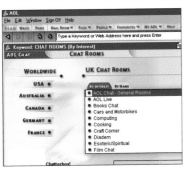

■ **AOL has** *chat rooms.*

Web-based chatting

Along with the explosive popularity of AOL chat and live events, many pioneering community, portal, and e-commerce sites, such as The Well, IVillage, Women.com, Garden.com, and Yahoo, helped to bring chat to wider audiences of web users. New online communities, such as TalkCity and the Webchat Broadcasting System (now owned by Disney), sprang up, centered on topic-oriented chatting.

Web-based chats have proliferated at an astounding rate, and are available on thousands of web sites. Sometimes, television town meetings or forums provide real-time participation opportunities, and this feedback then becomes part of the telecast. Some examples include CNN's "Talkback Live" and ABC's "Nightline." Sports-oriented channels may open chat lines for viewers to discuss games in progress, or to comment on current issues.

■ **Flower lovers** – *go to garden.com to indulge your passion.*

Chat clients

■ **Right click on** *the name of a chatter to see their profile.*

Web-based chatting often requires some kind of chat client. A chat client is, simply, a program that allows you to participate in online chats. The client connects to a chat server that manages and routes the messages to the users who are participating in a particular chat.

Chat clients may be browser plug-ins, which must be downloaded and installed to function automatically. They also may be external clients that "float" on your screen, on top of your browser window. Another type of chat client appears and is used inline, right inside a web page.

Like many other software programs for the Internet we discuss in this book, chat clients come in several varieties, but all of them perform essentially similar tasks. Chat clients have a window where messages appear, a smaller window for typing messages, and some kind of Send Message button. Clicking this button causes your message to be transmitted to the main window where it will be visible to everyone in the room. Any of them may then respond.

Chat clients generally provide ways to send public messages for the whole group to see, or private messages to an individual who is also in the chat room. You'll usually be able to review a list of everyone who's currently in a particular chat room, and you'll be able to click on the names of other chatters and see their profiles. You'll have your own profile, too – which you may choose to leave empty, or fill with non-essential information.

Like other types of software, chat clients generally offer several options or preferences that allow you to control how the software works for you. There are usually help pages, too.

Anonymity and impersonation

Remember, people may not be who or what they say they are! Anonymity and impersonation are part of the chat room scene. The individual who uses a "handle" like Bluto or Terminator may be a frail teenager, an aging geek, or a gray-haired grandma. "SweetGirl" may really be a sour guy. Habitués of chat rooms often chuckle when selecting their screen names, and may change them often, on a whim.

Select a handle of your own. You may notice some welcome messages appearing, as folks who want to be friendly see that you've entered the room. As we've said before, it's a good idea to simply listen for a while before beginning to contribute to the discussion. There's nothing sinister about lurking – in fact, it's exactly what you'd do in person if you walked into a room where a conversation was already underway.

By clicking on certain commands, you can exercise some control over the chatting environment. For instance, the command Ignore or Squelch enables you to exclude the messages from a specific particular speaker.

If there's a real loudmouth in the chat room, many people may tune him out until he realizes nobody's listening to him. The command profile will bring up whatever information has been provided by an individual member of the ongoing chat. Usually, this will be very little, as most people are too cautious to provide their real names and addresses.

Private rooms

When a chat room is nearly full, it can get to be a confused babble, as there is no moderator to keep the conversation focused. Your attempts to participate may be delayed as the messages of others elbow in before yours. The conversation becomes disjointed. Meanwhile, you might have noticed the messages of one chatter in particular, and want to explore ideas with him or her without the interruptions of other speakers.

■ **People rarely** *use their real name in a chat room.*

Obtain the profile of any member from the Who's Here list. Then, you can respond specifically to that person amid the babble. This then becomes a one-on-one conversation, but still carried on against the background noise of the group. To suggest a private conversation, use a command with a name like Invite to send a message directly to another person in the room. If the receiver of your invitation is willing to talk privately with you, the two of you will then move to a Private Chat or Private Room for one-on-one messaging.

Unexpected invitations

If you ever receive such an invitation unexpectedly from someone you don't know, check their profile. If there isn't one, we suggest caution. You can refuse, accept, or ignore an invitation.

It's never a good idea to give out personal information about yourself, or any member of your family, in a chat setting, public or private. This can be especially dangerous for minors. If anyone ever asks for your password, no matter what reason they give, never reveal it.

But do tell your service provider about the request. If you ever decide you'd like to meet an online friend in person, be sure to observe the safety precautions we outline later in this Chapter.

■ **As in real life**, *kids should be careful when chatting to strangers online and ideally parents should be present.*

Chat technology: new and newer

LET'S TALK *about some slightly newer forms of chatting, both with groups and one-on-one. Some of the software starts to sound a bit like science fiction, but don't be scared by the addition of visual components, or terms beginning with the word virtual. Remember the definition of communication we started with? Adding other components to text communication adds variety to your Internet experience.*

Instant Messaging

One-to-one, real-time chatting is usually called "Instant Messaging" (or "IMing," which rhymes with "timing"). Some software programs call the invitation from a chat room to a private room an "instant message," but here, we're talking about simple, one-to-one communication – independent of chat rooms. There are many reasons why one-to-one chatting may be more appealing than using public chat rooms. One-on-one conversation can be more focused and personal, and avoids the distraction of messages that don't really interest or concern you.

Instant Messaging is ideal for casually keeping up with friends, relatives, and co-workers.

Instant Messaging is a relatively new technique that resembles a very old one. Before the web, UNIX users had one-on-one chats through programs called talk and ntalk. Messages went directly from one person to another, not through a chat room. Instant Messaging, introduced via software such as ICQ, and by major Internet companies like AOL and Excite, is now widely available on the web.

Unfortunately, Instant Messaging has not benefited from a set of universally-accepted protocols, like the web and e-mail have – even though virtually all IM applications do essentially the same things. Software differences among IM packages keep users of different software from exchanging messages. If you want to exchange Instant Messages with someone, they have to use the same software you do. If you have many friends or family members who use IM, you may need to install more than one IM software product to be able to talk to everyone. You can use AOL's IM software, one of the most widely-used packages, whether or not you're an AOL member.

Here are some of the URLs where you can download the most popular Instant Messengers:

✓ ICQ: www.icq.com
✓ Microsoft: messenger.msn.com
✓ Excite: pal.excite.com
✓ Yahoo pager: pager.yahoo.com

■ **Use an** *invitation to send a message directly to another person.*

Invitation	✕
MillenniuM 2000 invites you to join: italia_scambio_di_tutto	
Choose to accept or reject the invitation by using the buttons below. You may also choose to ignore future invitations and messages from this user.	
☐ Ignore user	
Accept	Reject

Some people use IM to break into the Internet activity of busy people, like an emergency phone call cutting through. If you know the person you need to reach is probably online, you can use IM to reach them instantly.

However, this can be extremely annoying to the person you're interrupting, especially if you disturb their work for non-emergency or trivial reasons.

On the other hand, IM is a great way to keep in touch with family and friends when you know what time of day they're likely to be online. Many IM programs leave the IM icon on the receiver's screen; when the receiver comes online, the picture of the little running man tells them someone's been trying to make contact.

Visual chat rooms

In a visual chat room, each person assumes a sort of mask or persona called an *avatar*. Avatars appear in "virtual worlds," where chatting takes place along with sound effects and animation. Sometimes, the text you type appears in "balloons" on screen, just like in a comic strip. Visual chat rooms, like many advanced web experiences, generally require a browser plug-in.

■ **Avatars are** *characters that represent the people in a visual chat room.*

If your browser is up-to-date, you should be able to easily download and install the correct plug-in. One of the best-known visual chat applications is The Palace, at www.thepalace.com.

Live customer service

Banks, retailers, online catalog companies, software and technology vendors, auto companies, and many other businesses provide links on their web sites that let you interact directly, in real time, with service representatives, salespeople, or other experts. You can ask questions, order merchandise, and get assistance. Chat programs are also becoming prominent in online learning applications. We'll discuss that more in Chapter 20.

Webcams

Webcams, digital cameras connected to web servers, deliver continuously-updated photographic images to web sites. Many of the earliest webcams were clever but trivial, such as one that continuously updated images of a soft drink vending machine at a university.

Countless webcams are now available on the web, offering views of thousands of indoor and outdoor locations, interesting and mundane.

■ **How's the** *traffic in Manhattan? Take a look through the webcam.*

Some webcams serve useful purposes. For example, visit the Washington State Department of Transportation's web site at www.wsdot.wa.gov to see webcam views of mountain passes commonly affected by snow and hazardous road conditions.

Some webcam presentations require plug-ins, and some send "streaming" video, rather than simple updates of static image frames. Here are some sites where you can find lists of webcams to check out:

✓ Earthcam: www.earthcam.com
✓ The Discovery Channel's Live Cams page: www.discovery.com/cams/cams.html
✓ AllCam: www.allcam.com
✓ Cammunity: www.cammunity.com
✓ Web Cams of the World: www.livewebcam.com
✓ OnTap's SpyCams: www.ontap.com/spy-cams

Emerging technology for delivery of streaming video over the web has enabled real-time chat with video, using digital video cameras connected to computers. Tools like iVisit, Cu-SeeMe, and VDO allow both video-enhanced, one-to-one and multiparty chat via the Internet. These applications require a digital camera connected to your computer.

LIVE CHATS

Radio talk shows sometimes set up portable studios in public places and host live chats with passersby or visitors to a store, mall, restaurant, or other location. These broadcasts never fail to attract a crowd, and there are usually plenty of people ready and willing to join the discussion.

If the subject happens to be a local college or professional sports team, there's never a shortage of strong opinions.

An animated, entertaining, and often unpredictable chat line discussion goes out to the public over the radio. Most people find it enormously fun to sound off in a lively, dynamic conversation, whatever the medium.

Roving chat rooms

A new category of chat software lets users chat while visiting a web site, rather like a roving reporter with a live connection. You can roam around the web, chatting with people on any site you visit – as long as they also have the software. The site's publishers will have no record or knowledge of the chats taking place at their sites.

These external chat tools are generally available as free downloads, and many offer lists of links to sites with active user groups. Web surfers armed with this capability can roam from one site to another, carrying on chats with other visitors and making the web itself much more of a community experience. Here are examples of these interesting options:

✓ Gooey: www.gooey.com
✓ Odigo: www.odigo.com
✓ ThirdVoice: www.thirdvoice.com.

Etiquette and common sense

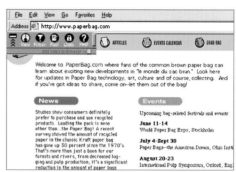

■ **ThirdVoice software** *lets you post your thoughts on any web page, such as the one above.*

IN CHATTING, as in other online communications, remember your netiquette. You should always strive to follow the same ethical and behavior guidelines online that apply anywhere else. Just to make sure basic rules are clear, here are a few of the important ones.

✓ The people with those funny handles are still real people. Don't say anything to hurt them.
✓ You have no idea who they really are, so don't take personal information anyone gives at face value.
✓ Don't begin talking immediately when you join a chat; listen (lurk) for a while until you can contribute something relevant.
✓ Read the help and FAQ pages to help you make the most of your participation
✓ Keep messages short, and refrain from bad language and flaming.
✓ If the tone of conversation in a chat room is unpleasant or too dull, just leave the room and try another.

■ **There are** *chat rooms created specially for children.*

INTERNET

www.utok.com

Utok works much like regular roving chat rooms, but functions more like a roaming message board, overlaid on web sites as you visit them.

DIVERSITY IN ACTION

■ **Women** *may prefer to converse with other women.*

One woman we know much prefers chatting with other women, and will read messages carefully, lurking for a long time, sifting names and words, searching for other women to converse with. This often works well for her, and she reports receiving much personal affirmation from other women in the chat room setting. Occasionally, though, her gender guesses turn out to be wrong. Her previously hostile attitude towards men has mellowed after two pleasant exchanges with like-minded "women" who turned out to be sensitive men. Both men were using feminine names in the chat room because they had learned from experience that the tone of responses are greatly influenced by a sender's perception of the recipient's gender.

Remember the human

Feelings do get stirred up when people engage each other in conversation. Many online chatters use emoticons, little faces made with punctuation marks, to supplement their words. The meaning of most emoticons is obvious, while some of them require a little thought. Even if you don't care for this embellishment, remember, there are all kinds of people out there. Among them are sure to be some who really enjoy these little faces.

Here are some favorites. Explore or ask around--you'll find more!	
☺	:-) or :)
☹	:-(or :(or :-< or :<
☺	:-O or :O or :-o or :o
☂	(D) or (d)
✉	(E) or (e)
♡	(K) or (k)

■ **Emoticons** *show your feelings as you chat.*

Safety and security

The opportunity to spend time in chat rooms, posing as adults and engaging in adult talk, or lurking and listening to the adults, can seem exciting to young people, but we believe it's a bad idea. Not all chat rooms are R-rated, and not all teenagers are searching for R-rated material. Sometimes, interesting knowledge and opinions may be aired on subjects of interest to young people. We do suggest that parents always remain near by if youngsters are allowed to participate. Minors should never chat unsupervised. In Chapter 17, we'll tell you how find chat rooms specifically for children. These chats are actively monitored and supervised by responsible adults dedicated to providing kid-friendly, safe environments.

If you're a child or teenager reading our book, please don't accept an invitation to a private chat room with anyone unless a parent is with you. Parents, this is one of the reasons you should stay close by. It's up to you to prevent your young person from accepting such an invitation on his or her own.

Some relationships that develop through chatting do lead to the desire to meet in person. Don't take this step until you've talked by telephone as well as online, and have received some kind of confirmation that this individual really is who he or she says. Bring someone else along to the first meeting if possible, or, at least, let someone responsible know exactly where you're going. Arrange to call immediately after the meeting, just to let them know everything is OK. Meet in a well-lit, public place. Never leave with the person you've just met. If you travel a long distance for the meeting, stay in a hotel. Never give information about your location to your new friend. We don't want make you needlessly fearful. In fact, we have several friends who are happily married to people they met through the Internet. We do want to urge you to use the same kinds of common-sense safeguards you'd use to protect yourself if you were meeting someone through a newspaper ad.

■ **You never know** *where your new Internet friendships might lead!*

For your own well-being, be on guard against addiction to chatting. Like many activities, chatting and other cyber-activity can become obsessive and compulsive behaviors. There are support groups to help those who've formed harmful habits.

■ **Internet telephone software** *lets you make calls via the web.*

If you, or any member of your family, stays up all night, chatting away in public chat rooms or in Instant Message conversations with strangers, we suggest you shut off the computer for a while.

Internet telephony

ALL THE FORMS OF *synchronous communication outlined in this Chapter are computer functions, and offer alternatives to conference or one-on-one telephone calls. Real-time communications now also include Internet telephony, the ability to make telephone calls via the Internet. Internet telephony is another form of convergence, or the merging of telecommunications media – in this case, the Internet and the telephone – previously separate and distinct.*

To use the Internet for phone calls, you need to get a microphone for your computer (an inexpensive peripheral that simply plugs in to most newer PCs), and to install Internet telephone software. As with any other software you download, try it out immediately. If you decide to keep and use it, register the software and pay the fee.

Several new web businesses combine Internet telephony, e-mail, traditional telephones, voice-mail, and facsimile transmission into powerful new "unified messaging" services.

Ready to find out more about these new ways the Internet and telephones are converging, and how these services might be useful to you? Check out these web sites, where information, software, and new services are available:

✓ Virtual Voice: www.virtual-voice.com.
✓ Net2Phone: www.net2phone.com
✓ WebPhone: www.webphone.com
✓ VocalTec: www.vocaltec.com
✓ Pagoo: www.pagoo.com
✓ Getmessage.com: www.getmessage.com
✓ ShoutMail: www.shoutmail.com
✓ UReach: www.ureach.com

■ **Chatting** **is** *easy and popular.*

If your computer is relatively up-to-date, you can probably install an Internet telephony software package that will let you make long-distance phone calls through your computer and Internet connection – free from the usual long-distance charges. The more RAM your computer has, and the faster and more capable your modem, the better sound quality you'll enjoy on these calls.

A simple summary

✓ Real time communications are synchronous.

✓ The software programs that enable chatting are provided by online services such as AOL, through web sites, Internet Relay Chat, and Instant Messaging (IM) software.

✓ Internet users can make long-distance phone calls via their computers.

✓ People can talk one-on-one in a private room.

✓ Don't do online what you wouldn't do somewhere else.

✓ Chatting means talking with others through typed messages in a setting called a chat room.

✓ Remember the dangers of meeting strangers, and observe safety and security precautions.

Chapter 9

Your Own Web Site

YOU'VE ALREADY LEARNED about e-mail, message boards, mailing lists, newsgroups, and chat rooms, all of which put you in touch with a few or a lot of other people – known or unknown. But there's something enticing about the idea of communicating to the whole Internet community by publishing your own web page. This chapter will help you decide whether you want to construct your own web page. If you decide you do it, Chapter 10, " Do It Right," will tell you exactly how to go about it. If you decide not to create your own web page, you can skip Chapter 10.

In this chapter...

✓ Why, what, and how

✓ Basic HTML

✓ Creating web pages

✓ Your own dot.com

✓ Web site hosts

YOUR WEB SITE WILL BRING OUT THE DESIGNER IN YOU

Why, what, and how

ONE OF THE MOST EXCITING things about the
Internet is its invitation to the user to take an active role.
Radio, television, and film are passive activities for the
viewer, while the Internet can't function without active user
involvement. The Internet is "interactive." It beckons,
urging us to participate in the new power of expression
offered by online communication. The Internet can take
whatever we publish and give it instant, worldwide
distribution. You don't need lots of money, or a famous name –
the Internet invites ordinary people to become publishers.

■ **Surfing the**
Internet is much more
active than sitting
back watching a film.

Why the web beckons

Publishing on hard copy (paper), which is, and probably will remain, a vast industry,
requires a large investment for materials, expertise, and distribution costs. Small-
scale publishing, in the form of newsletters and small-press periodicals, still
requires an outlay for materials and expenses. Only a finite number of copies
of anything can be printed, distributed, sold, and mailed. Online publishing,
on the other hand, reaches millions of people right where they live.

*And unlike hard copy, which can't be changed once the ink dries,
online publishing allows for frequent, instant updates of information.*

At first, you might consider creating your own web page for the enjoyment of family
and friends who are also online. It's a way to share news, pictures, jokes, creative
products such as art, poetry or cartoons, and possibly to provide a message board or
chat room. To be accessible to your personal
online circle, you must have a Uniform
Resource Locator (URL) or address on the web
– and this makes your site accessible to any
surfer or searcher. So, it makes sense to think
through just what the real purpose of your web
site is, and to prepare for the possibility of
visitors from far and wide.

■ **Your own web site** *can be
shared with friends and family.*

YOUR BUSINESS

If you're in business for yourself and think a web presence would help (as it almost certainly would), be sure to read Chapter 10. One of the toughest jobs for professional and commercial web sites is getting the word out. Once people find you on the web, you can expect increased business. But what can you do to help them find your site among the millions of pages on the Internet? This is where traditional merchandising methods and computer technology shake hands and work together. We'll describe this in more detail in Chapters 12 and 13, when we discuss searching. And in Chapter 24, "Making Money Online," we'll provide lots of ideas for doing business on the Internet.

In your travels around the Internet, you'll encounter many web pages published by individuals and small businesses. Pay attention to these – you may begin thinking, "I could do better than that!"

Your purpose

Artists and social activists often publish web pages to share their creative compositions or promote their causes. But even if you don't see yourself in this light, chances are you do have some significant interest that could be a prominent theme of your web site. If your site gets included in the listings accessed by major search engines, the theme you choose will determine the category in which your site is listed.

Keywords

If people looking for your site are likely to search for certain words related to the content of your site, be sure to include those words – referred to as keywords – within the page. This will make it more likely that search engines will show your page in a list of sites when someone searches for that word. If you choose your keywords carefully, people searching for information and sites like yours will be more likely to find your site. For instance, say you love chili. You've collected a hundred recipes, put them all on your web site, and have given your site a name in which the word "chili" appears. You can expect a lot of visits by chili-lovers. Or your site could be dedicated to a particular author perhaps. Including the titles of major works will help searchers find your site.

Before you start publishing, be sure to read about the copyright issues we discuss in Chapters 14 and 15. You must be sure not to violate anyone else's copyrights, or use anyone's work without permission. If you're publishing your own work, be sure you understand your own rights to copyright protection.

In short, web publishing is not just a new kind of "vanity press," but a way to share your knowledge, beliefs, and values with the online world. In all the other forms of communication we've discussed – sending and receiving e-mail, posting and reading messages, or engaging in chat – you must be actively involved to make communication happen.

But when you publish a web site (with some reservations and conditions), you can sit back and let interested people seek you out.

Cooking versus recipes

There are some easy ways to set up a web page, and we'll be sharing those, but we hope you won't be too quick to take the line of least resistance. A little basic knowledge about Hypertext Markup Language (HTML) and the structure of web sites will spell the difference between well-founded confidence in the kitchen, versus blindly following a recipe. A bit of fundamental understanding of what you're doing gives you a lot more flexibility to control what you're producing.

This is like using a calculator – if you know how to add and subtract, you'll get the same answer from the calculator as someone who just pushes buttons with no understanding. But it ain't the same!

As we discussed in Chapter 3, a web page is a single electronic document of information, which may contain text, images, forms, and various other objects such as animations. Web pages are created with HTML and viewed via web browsers. A single web page can be visible on your monitor in its entirety, or may require you to scroll to see the whole page. A web site is a collection of related pages. There are many free reference sources on the web that offer tutorials and excellent help on HTML and web page design. We believe a little time spent at some of these how-to-do-it sites will convince you that technical know-how is not a big concern. If you want to do it, you can!

Trivia...

We know a Lutheran pastor who had a helpful-message-of-the-day telephone line called The Warmline. Anyone who picked up the phone and dialed the Warmline number would hear a recorded message of his loving voice reading a few lines of poetry or scripture, and wishing the caller a really happy day. He now serves a church with its own web site, where the Warmline can be opened with one mouse click. The same loving, recorded voice offers the same kind of message, but through an online connection.

■ **Kids can** *learn about HTML at lissaexplains.com.*

■ **As in the** *kitchen, a little confidence goes a long way.*

OUR FAVORITES

Here are a few of our favorites pages on HTML and web site design. Some of them have strange or funny names, but that just reflects the creative and often irreverent nature of the web. Some are basic, while others offer more advanced information, as well as resources and links to many other useful sites.

✓ W3C: www.w3.org/Markup
✓ Getting Started: www.gettingstarted.net/
✓ HTML Help: www.htmlhelp.com
✓ Web Monkey: www.webmonkey.com
✓ Web Builder: www.builder.com,
✓ HTML Writer's Guild: www.hwg.org
✓ Web Developer: www.webdeveloper.com
✓ Yale Style Manual: info.med.yale.edu/caim/manual
✓ Web Pages That Suck: www.webpagesthatsuck.com

Basic HTML

HYPERTEXT MARKUP LANGUAGE is the coding system used to make web pages. Every web page contains HTML tags (special coded commands) which tell browsers where and how to present the text, graphic images, links, and other web page components. You should compose your HTML documents carefully and slowly as you implement your ideas, perfect the look and flow of your page, check for errors, and test to make sure it's going to work for people who will access your site through different browsers. When your pages are ready for "prime time," you'll put them where they can be viewed by the online community. Part of what makes it fun is that you can always change your site to improve it over time.

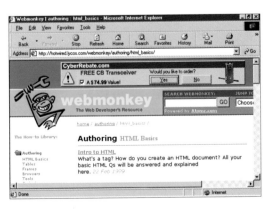

■ **Plenty of sites** offer help with web site design. This one is at webmonkey.com.

Codes and commands

You've probably been using a word processor for a while, and gotten used to the keystroke commands and menu choices that enable you to format text. In a Microsoft Word document, for instance, you can use endless formatting variables to give your documents a special appearance with options such as bold, italic, different fonts, sizes and colors, tables, charts, and graphs.

It's possible to create a web page in a word processor, but this may not produce very satisfying results. For your page to appear on the web, it must be translated from the word processor's format into HTML, and some of your formatting may be lost. Web pages must be more "elastic" than word processing documents

■ **Your chosen** *web page colors might vary in different browsers.*

because of the many browsers, platforms, monitors, configurations, and other variables in play on the web. That means that the web page you create will probably look a little (or a lot) different on different systems.

HTML commands

HTML commands are bracketed by tags, inserted between "less than" and "more than" symbols (< >). These symbols usually come in pairs, "<" signaling the start of a command and ">" signaling the end. Let's say we're constructing a web page right now, and we want to entitle our page, "Home Sweet Home." The coding to accomplish this would look like: <TITLE>Home Sweet Home</TITLE>. Notice that the tag which closes the command is just like the code at the beginning, except for the forward

■ **To entitle** *a page "Home Sweet Home" use the < title > tags.*

```
Untitled - Notepad
File  Edit  Search  Help
<!DOCTYPE HTML PUBLIC "-//W3C//DTD HTML

<html>
<head>
        <title>Home Sweet Home</title>
</head>

<body>


</body>
</html>
```

slash. The "/" in an HTML command indicates that it's a closing command. This pairing of tags tells the browser loading the page that everything after the opening tag and before the closing tag is the page's title.

The genius of HTML is that it's simple to use and highly portable. Computer users on almost any kind of system, from Macs to PCs to UNIX workstations, can view documents created with HTML. These documents travel quickly via telecommunication lines across great distances, and are delivered to users' computer screens around the world in seconds, at the click of a mouse. And users can surf from one web page to another with ease. When you first became computer literate, it probably took you quite a while to learn word-processing software. But with practice, what once seemed difficult is now second nature.

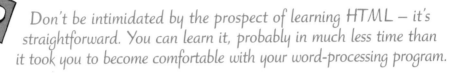

Don't be intimidated by the prospect of learning HTML – it's straightforward. You can learn it, probably in much less time than it took you to become comfortable with your word-processing program.

Links

We introduced you to links in Chapter 3, but let's review here. HTML coding can also create links to other locations on the web, right within your HTML documents. Links are the clickable bits of text or graphic images that let web users jump from one web page to another. Because these bits of text or graphics link a web page to other web pages, they're called hypertext or hypergraphics. This linking ability is what the term hypertext refers in the name Hypertext Markup Language. The HTML command for inserting links into a document requires a URL that points to the document you're linking to.

It usually takes this form: protocol://domain.name/directory/document.name. Web browsers often display hypertext in a different color from regular text. For example, regular text is usually black, while hypertext is usually blue.

You may wonder at first how important links will be in your potential future web page. We believe that even a little thought in envisioning that future site will answer this question. For instance, where did you get all those chili recipes? Are there web sites with other recipes by the same cook, or sites about the place or culture from which each recipe came? Are you interested in the history of the dish – where and when was it created and first enjoyed?

You could expand your own web site by creating additional pages with all this other information, or if you know of other places on the web where it already exists, you could simply provide links to those other sites. A web page that doesn't offer visitors any hypertext to take them further along in their surfing feels like a dead end.

So, once you've picked a theme or focus for your own site, your next logical step is locating links to include.

■ **Hypertext** *links usually appear in a different color.*

Creating web pages

THE HTML CODE *used to create web pages consists of simple, raw, unformatted text. That means it's completely possible to make web pages with primitive text editors such as Notepad on the PC, SimpleText on the Mac, and Pico on a UNIX system. Many sophisticated web sites have been created with these basic tools.*

In fact, advanced text editors such as WordPerfect and Microsoft Word are sometimes less effective for HTML than a basic tool like Notepad, because advanced word processors tend to create formatting in documents that interferes with HTML coding.

Trivia...

One of the most popular and successful online businesses, Yahoo, started back in 1994 as a project by a couple of students at Stanford University who began collecting and indexing links to web sites they found personally interesting. When they put their collection on the web, it proved to be a popular, much-sought-after service for web surfers. Today, Yahoo.com gets upwards of 40 million visitors each month, and enjoys a market cap of over US$47 billion.

There are dozens of products and methods you can use to make a web page – far too many for any one book to cover. We'll walk you through the various approaches available, and tell you what your options are. We're going to list these from the easiest to the somewhat more challenging. Knowing how HTML works will enable you to do a better job and be more in control of any web page you create. The good news is that making a web page is really simple, and any of these options will work for you!

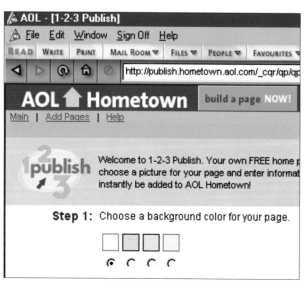

Online wizards

Probably the easiest way to make your own web page and web site is through a step-by-step, online process. More and more of these are now available. Many are available through ISPs.

■ **AOL members** *can make their own web page using 1-2-3 Publish.*

For example, Earthlink, one of the largest national ISPs, offers its members an online tool called "Click-n-Build" which lets you make your web site in minutes without learning a thing. AOL members can use a similar tool called 1-2-3 Publish. Similar tools are provided by ATT WorldNet, Microsoft Network, and many other ISPs.

To find out if your ISP offers such tools and opportunities, check the ISP's web site or call customer service. These online site-building tools are usually free if you're an ISP subscriber. If you develop a site this way, your site's URL will start with the ISP's name. For example, one of this book's authors created a test page with AOL's 1-2-3 Publish tool that can be viewed at hometown.aol.com/wlubka/myhomepage/index.html. These tools are fast and easy, but provide little flexibility, and often include branding and promotional information from the ISP.

Beyond the realm of ISP member page-building tools, lots of other free, easy-to-use web page builders are advertised and promoted on the Internet. We'll talk more about web site hosting and various free hosting services below. In general, though, we caution you to exercise discretion in using anything advertised as "free." Read the fine print first – there may be strings attached!

Standard applications software

Perhaps the next easiest method for making a web page is to use whatever software you're already familiar with. Many modern software packages let you create a new web document as easily as you can create any other document. For example, WordPerfect includes the Internet Publisher tool, which lets you create a new web page from scratch, or turn an existing WordPerfect document into a web page.

Microsoft Word and Excel now both include Save as HTML options, which automatically insert HTML tags into a document and make it web-ready.

These tools are easy because there's nothing much to learn. But they require one step the ISP tools don't – transferring the HTML file you've created to a web host on the Internet so people can see it. In a bit, we'll explain the role of "web hosts." Transferring files to a host is easy, but not as easy as the ISP process, which is usually automatic. It all depends on how much control you want over your pages. Using standard application software gives you a little more flexibility than an online wizard, but still provides a relatively limited range of control.

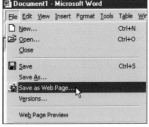

■ **Software like** *Word will let you save your documents as web pages.*

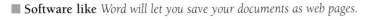

WYSIWYG authoring tools

If you want to go a little further into creating your own unique web site, another option is to use a software package called a WYSIWYG authoring tool. WYSIWYG (pronounced "wizz-ee-wig") stands for "what you see is what you get." It's called that because what you see on the screen as you build a web page with a WYSIWYG tool is what will actually appear in the finished product. The software automatically inserts the HTML tags into the document. You just drag things into position with your mouse. WYSIWYG HTML software is sometimes referred to as a "visual development environment."

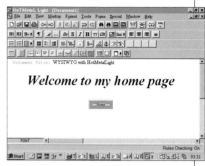

■ **What You See Is What You Get** *(WYSIWYG) in SoftQuad's Hotmetal.*

WYSIWYG authoring tools are popular because they eliminate the need to work with HTML commands, making web page development faster and easier. WYSIWYG authoring tools range widely in cost and power. Some are meant more for beginners, while others combine powerful feature sets and are used by professionals.

Some of the best-known WYSIWYG HTML authoring tools include Microsoft FrontPage, Netscape Composer, Adobe PageMill, Claris HomePage, Macromedia DreamWeaver, and SoftQuad's HoTMetaL Pro. These tools offer templates and simple, user-friendly commands for inserting graphics and links, and for formatting text. The two most popular web browsers, Netscape Navigator and Microsoft Internet Explorer, are both bundled with WSYSIWYG editors. These WYSIWYG tools are convenient because they're integrated with your browser, but they're not as feature-rich as some of the other HTML authoring products. Some WSYSIWYG tools include options to work in a raw code environment, or in a visual environment.

If you learn HTML and then elect to use a WSYSIWYG editor, it's a good idea to select one with this option so you can fine-tune and perfect your pages by working directly with the HTML code.

Text-based HTML tools

As we mentioned before, learning HTML is simple and will give you greater knowledge and flexibility in making and modifying your web pages. But it does take a bit more time. Chapter 10 includes an easy-to-follow tutorial on HTML that will have you building your first web page before you even close this book.

■ **You no longer** *need to use primitive web authoring tools.*

Before trying any of the methods discussed above, we recommend that you experiment, at least briefly, with creating HTML by hand.

Many tools are available for working directly with HTML. Notepad (or its equivalent, if you're not using Windows) is an excellent tool to start with. However, creating HTML documents with primitive text editors like Notepad is laborious, and increases the likelihood of errors. A host of text editors made specifically for HTML are available. Many professionals prefer Allaire's HomeSite, or BBEdit from BareBones Software. Dozens of other options are available, including many freeware and shareware products. By this time, you may be getting the impression that it's really easy to build a web page, and you may be tempted to move too quickly. But, while the actual creation of your page is pretty simple, deciding what your page will contain, and what it should look like, takes time and careful thought.

Don't rush ahead as soon as you know the rudiments — you'll do better by "making haste slowly!"

Your own dot.com

■ **Is your name** *Jane Smith? Sorry, that domain name is taken.*

HAVE YOU EVER WONDERED who makes up web site addresses? They often seem to contain some form of the name of the host or company represented by that site, or some reference to their primary purpose, activity, or product. In fact, you can usually make a guess at the nature of a business from their web site address. Remember, these web addresses are generally in the form, www.domain. extension. If your name is Jane Smith, and you're ready to put your first web page online, you might want the address: www.janesmith.com. That would make it easy for people to find you. Unfortunately, if your name is Jane Smith, it's too late. The domain has already been registered and is currently being used by a New Mexico company that sells Jane Smith sweaters.

You can use any of several easy-to-use online search services to see if a domain name you're interested in has already been registered. You can also check to see who registered it. Here are three sites you can use to research a domain:

✓ Register.com: www.register.com
✓ Names4Ever: www.names4ever.com
✓ Network Solutions: www.networksolutions.com/cgi-bin/whois/whois
✓ Domain Bank: ru.domainbank.net/whois.cfm

SOFTWARE REVIEWS

The combination of letters at the end of a domain is called its Top Level Domain, or TLD. Here's a list of the most common TLDs:

✓ .com (commercial sites)   ✓ .edu (educational institutions)
✓ .net (network-related sites) ✓ .gov (government agencies)
✓ .org (non-profit organizations) ✓ .mil (military sites)

There are also more than 200 national TLDs, such as ".fr" for France, ".uk" for the United Kingdom, ".ca" for Canada, and ".jp" for Japan.

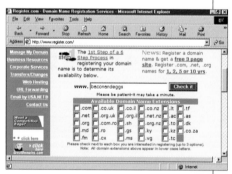

The middle term, or domain, is the spot where it's appropriate for your name or business to appear. There are considerable advantages to having your own domain. It makes it easier for people to find you, easier to get listed by search engines and directories, and it means that your web site address doesn't have to change if you move or change ISPs. To register your own domain, you must pay a modest fee to an accredited Domain Name Registrar, such as one of the companies listed above that provide domain searches.

■ **There are many** *search sites where you can check if a domain name is available.*

When you register a domain on your own, you'll be asked for technical information about web site hosting service. We'll talk more about web site hosting in the next section. If you don't yet have a host, some registrars offer a "holding service" that allows you to register without a host for an extra fee.

■ **You are likely** *to get stung by companies offering free domain registration.*

We also caution you not to be misled by tempting advertisements to "Register your own domain free!"

There are a number of companies who claim to offer free domain registration, and we know of several people who were "sucked in" by such claims. These folks rediscovered, the hard way, the old adage, "Anything that seems too good to be true, probably is."

Web site hosts

THERE ARE MANY *different kinds of web site hosts. Costs for web site hosting services range anywhere from zero to millions of dollars. The top of that range represents huge web sites for big commercial interests, while free hosting is more for individuals who don't expect to ask much from the host. But even for an individual, this can be a difficult choice.*

There are a number of factors you need to consider. When looking for a host, you're not limited to your own current service provider, and you might find that you'd rather pay a little for better conditions and service. On the other hand, if your ISP provides free web site space for its members, and you don't expect a lot of traffic or require your own "dot.com," then your ISP's options might be perfect for your needs.

■ **You will have** *to weigh many factors in deciding whether to use a free ISP or pay for a better service.*

INTERNET

www.iana.org/cctld.html

Go to this web site to find out more about registering international TLDs. Registration policies and costs in each country vary.

If you want to host a web page with your own personal domain, you'll probably have to pay a fee. The cheapest kind of hosting takes place on "shared servers," where many web sites are served from the same computer. Hundreds of web hosting services offer this kind of service monthly.

■ **The costs and** *services offered by web hosting companies vary enormously.*

If you're looking for such a web site host, investigate the range of software supported, service options, and technical help resources offered. Always keep backup copies of your web site in case something happens to your data at the server, or if you need to recreate your site again with a new host. Costs for web site hosting go up when your needs grow to include complex e-commerce operations, databases, massive amounts of server space, and greater bandwidth to support high traffic volume. High-end corporate hosting services support dedicated servers and server farms with huge amounts of bandwidth.

When you register your own dot.com, part of the required information for registration must be provided by your web host. Several sites provide useful, searchable listings of web site hosts such as The List: thelist.internet.com, Top Hosts: www.tophosts.com, and BudgetWeb: www.budgetweb.com/. You can also check your local yellow pages for a local host.

But because web hosting occurs in the environment of cyberspace, it's just as easy to use a host hundreds of miles away as one across the street.

■ **Online wizards** *are used by many "community sites."*

Free web site hosting

There are several ways to get free web site hosting. We already talked about using your ISP. Another option is to use any of the "community sites" on the Internet that encourage people to create free web sites within their domains, in return for displaying their advertising and promotional messages. Many of these sites use "online wizard" processes such as the ones offered by EarthLink and AOL.

Community web sites offering free web publishing opportunities have proliferated, and you're likely to see many such offerings as you surf the web.

Some of the best-known include GeoCities, HomeStead, Xoom, Tripod, TheGlobe, Fortune City, and Nettaxi. A crop of "niche-oriented" free web page services has also arisen, focused on particular populations or interest groups. Examples include CampusWest, AnimalHouse, ChickPages, The Digs, AllSports, Artists-in-Residence, TrainWeb, Acme City, and AudioGalaxy.

Free hosting for non-profit and charitable organizations

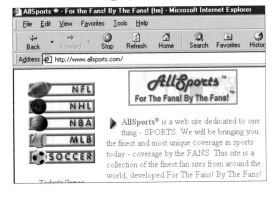

A variety of free hosting options are available for non-profit and charitable organizations. Some ISPs provide a certain amount of "pro bono" service to community organizations and non-profits, so one option for your organization is to inquire with local ISPs. If your needs are modest and your cause worthy, you may find a receptive response. Some organizations that are chapters of major national organizations may find that the national office provides free web site hosting.

■ **Allsports.com** *is a collection of sports fans' sites.*

Visit your national office

For example, one of the authors of this book happens be a pastor of a local church. When her district conference of ministers decided to set up their own web page, they discovered the national board offered web site hosting to any church or organization throughout the denomination. Another friend, who was active in the local Audubon Society chapter, learned that the National Audubon Society office provides free hosting for any chapter that wants to post information about its activities. This saved them the cost and hassle of hosting their site independently.

So, if your local chapter of an organization is planning a site, check with your national office first.

Several web sites provide useful resources for assistance for non-profits seeking to use the Internet to promote their causes, and to increase access to the Internet among their constituencies. Here are some starting points:

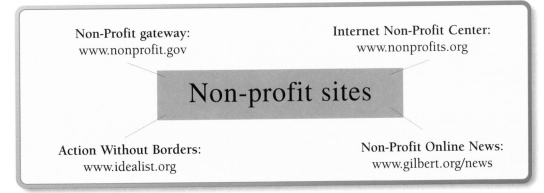

| Non-Profit gateway: | Internet Non-Profit Center: |
| www.nonprofit.gov | www.nonprofits.org |

Non-profit sites

| Action Without Borders: | Non-Profit Online News: |
| www.idealist.org | www.gilbert.org/news |

www.helping.org

Want to help some worthy cause? At Helping.org, you can search for exactly the right place to volunteer. Just click on "volunteers." You'll be asked where you live, how far you're willing to travel, when you're available, what you're interested in, and whether you have in mind a specific organization you'd like to help.

You can make donations online there, too, as well as register your own charitable organization if it's not already there. Additional resources for assisting non-profit groups are available at this and similar sites.

Many organizations have individual members or local chapters who published web pages before the parent organization learned how to create its own site. Sometimes, the initiative of these "early adopters" has resulted in some local outposts being represented on the web out of all proportion to their size and importance. The Boondocks club or church shows up because they happened to have a member who's a computer geek or gung-ho surfer. For example, take a look at www.ymca.org. Thought you'd see the national YMCA web site? Nope, it's just the San Diego County, CA, chapter.

For fun, have a peek at www.holidayinn.com. Welcome to the web site of the Niagara Falls Holiday Inn!

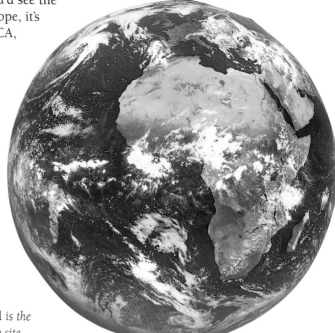

■ **The whole world** *is the audience for your web site.*

In this chapter, we've introduced you to the wide-open audience you can reach online – namely, the entire World Wide Web. Millions of Internet users have constructed personal web pages. Now you've seen how simple it really is, and that you can do it, too.

■ **Some URLs** *with company names don't always take you to the top.*

A simple summary

✓ The web offers everyone the opportunity to publish, and will give worldwide distribution to your creation.

✓ It's important to think through the purpose of your web site, and possibly to pick a theme or focus to emphasize.

✓ Software applications are available to create a web page without your really learning much about the behind-the-scenes coding steps, but it's better to gain a basic understanding of HTML, the language of the web.

✓ HTML works through software called text editors; codes must be inserted in the text to create formatting commands.

✓ Microsoft Internet Explorer includes a text editor called Front Page Express. Netscape Navigator's text editor is called Composer. AOL also provides a simple program that works similarly.

✓ If you want to have a web address that's the same as or similar to your e-mail address, you can purchase your own domain or your own dot.com.

✓ Many ISPs offer free web hosting. Or, for fairly small fees, you can select from among hundreds of hosts.

✓ Sometimes, space for your web page might be provided within the site of an organization or campus you're part of.

Chapter 10

Do It Right

I F YOU'RE READING this chapter, chances are you've decided to learn how to build your own web page. Congratulations! After learning HTML, you may elect to use WYSIWYG tools (see Chapter 9), which is fine. But this chapter will give you an understanding of what underlies "what you see," so you'll know why you get "what you get" – and how to fix boo-boos and make improvements when you want to. We'll get you started, and give you enough information to create simple web pages on your own. In addition to deciding your web site's purpose, message, and tone, it's also necessary to think about how it will look. If you catch the HTML bug, you'll want to learn more than this book offers, so we'll point the way to lots of resources for learning more.

In this chapter...

✓ Hypertext Markup Language

✓ HTML learning resources

✓ Tables, frames, and forms

✓ Mistakes to avoid

IT'S WORTH TAKING YOUR TIME TO CONSIDER HOW YOU WANT YOUR WEB SITE TO LOOK

Hypertext Markup Language

IN CHAPTER 9, *we discussed the rudiments of HTML, but we'll review them here. HTML is a type of coding used to create web pages. HTML coding is made up of raw, unformatted text that you can create easily with any text editor, such as Notepad on a PC, SimpleText on a Mac, or Pico on a UNIX system. An HTML document or HTML file is what a browser loads when you view a web page.*

The browser doesn't show the HTML; rather, the HTML tells the browser what to show, where to show it, and where to display clickable hypertext links and input forms.

HTML documents

HTML documents are files, just like word processing files or spreadsheets you might create and save in folders within directories on your hard drive, or on diskettes. If you create HTML and save it locally, you have to "upload" it to a web server before it can be visible at a URL for others to see. (If you use an automated online web page creation service such as AOL's 1-2-3 Publish, the web pages you create don't have to be uploaded because they are created remotely with input from your computer.) This Chapter tells you how to make your web page, rather than how to upload it from your computer to an ISP's

■ **Underlying every** *web page is an HTML file that tells the browser what to show.*

web server. We'll explain uploading in Chapter 14. Don't worry – it's simple. If you can make your own pages, transferring them to the host will be a snap!

Remember that people will view your page with different browsers, so it's a good idea to pre-test it on several browsers and platforms, and fashion it to provide the greatest convenience and accessibility to everyone. Keep in mind that graphics will slow down your page's loading time, and flashy animations may distract visitors, rather than help communicate your message. Resolve that visitors to your site will never be disappointed.

HTML commands

HTML commands, usually called tags, begin with the left angle, or "less than," symbol (<), and end with the right angle, or "more than," symbol (>). Most HTML commands appear in a pattern of opening and closing pairs. The two commands in each pair are the same, except that the closing command includes a forward slash (/). In Chapter 9, we saw that the title command, which surrounds the text designated as the document's title, starts with <title> and ends with </title>.

Some tags don't require opening and closing pairs because there's no intervening text. For example, the tag used to insert a line break, <br>, is used all by itself. HTML tags are almost never case-sensitive.

White space and carriage returns are generally ignored in an HTML document. Leaving a blank line in your HTML document will generally not create a blank line when the document is displayed by a browser. However, many HTML authors leave plenty of space in their original documents to make them easier to edit in the future.

Not all HTML tags are supported by all browsers. If a browser sees a tag it doesn't recognize (which could be either a tag it doesn't support, or a tag which contains an error), in most cases the browser simply ignores it. There are two main reasons some tags aren't recognized by some browsers. First, HTML continues to evolve, so many older browsers may not have been programmed to recognize newer HTML tags. Also, the competing browser companies have developed certain proprietary tags that fall outside formal HTML standards. These "browser-exclusive" tags work only with specific browsers, such as Microsoft Internet Explorer.

A proper HTML document identifies itself as such. So, an HTML document normally has the <html> command at the top of the document, and the closing command, </html>, at the end of the document.

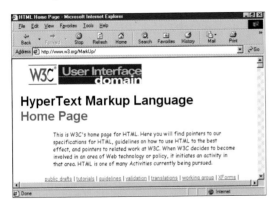

The World Wide Web Consortium (WC3) is the organization responsible for determining the formal standards of HTML. HTML has evolved through several versions. At this writing, the most current version is HTML 4.0.

■ **The World Wide Web**
Consortium (WC3) determines the way HTML evolves.

Head and body basics

HTML documents have two parts – the head and the body. The head is the first part of the document, and is bracketed by the <head> and </head> commands. The head includes the document's title, bracketed by the <title> and </title> commands. The title is displayed in the Title Bar area of a web browser window, usually at the very top, above the toolbar. The title is also what most browsers record when saving the document into the user's "Bookmarks" or "Favorites" list. Therefore, it's important that the title be descriptive and short enough to fit comfortably on one line.

The document head can also include a variety of "meta data," and is used for certain advanced purposes such as JavaScript. (You can learn more about JavaScript from the online technical and design resources we list below.)

■ **Like us**, *every HTML document has a head and a body.*

The body of the document begins after the head, and is bracketed by the <body> and </body> commands. The body contains all the elements displayed in a web browser's viewing window.

Using these basics, here's a formatted bare minimum web document:

```
<html>
<head>
<title>This is the title!</title>
</head>
<body>
Hello, World!
</body>
</html>
```

■ **This HTML** *document will look like this when viewed in a browser.*

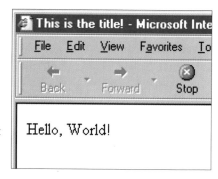

You can write an HTML document as a long single line – (<html><head><title>This is the title</title></head><body>Hello World!</body></html>) – but we suggest writing it as an orderly list, as we did above, to make it easier for you to see and work with.

Tags and more tags

Now, we'll present a series of simple sets of HTML tags. We suggest you replicate each one yourself. You'll be amazed how easy it is to start making web pages! We won't present a complete list of HTML tags here; there are too many and we don't recommend that you try to memorize them all. What's most important in becoming adept at making web pages is to understand the basics of how HTML works. Once you have the basics down pat, it's simple to learn more advanced techniques, try new innovations, and use new HTML tags. The web makes it easy for you to learn from the masters. Every web page is built with HTML, and you can take an inside peek at the underlying code for any page you visit.

While viewing a page, simply use your browser's View Source command, or use the Save As command to save a copy of the page's HTML code in a file on your own computer, for later study and reference.

Structuring headings

HTML provides easy, excellent tools for documents structured with headings, subheadings, and lists. You can specify six heading levels. Your most important heading should be a "level 1" heading; subheadings range from "level 2" through "level 6." Level 6 usually appears in a text size smaller than the regular text on a web page. The heading commands are <hX> and </hX>, where "X" indicates the heading level. In most documents on the web, the first heading is a duplicate of the document's title. After we added the first heading, our skeletal web document would look like this:

```
<html>
<head>
<title>This is the title!</title>
</head>
<body>
<h1>This is the main heading</h1>
</body>
</html>
```

Structuring paragraphs

Within the body, you must use tags to denote the beginning and ending of paragraphs. Most existing HTML documents use the <p> command without an ending </p>. However, the latest HTML specifications require paragraphs to begin with <p> and end with </p>.

■ **The heading** *looks like this in a browser.*

So even though most browsers will display paragraphs correctly without the </p>, it's more technically correct to include the ending command.

Here's our sample document after we add paragraphs and a subheading:

```
<html>
<head>
<title>This is the title!</title>
</head>
<body>
<h1>This is the main heading</h1>
<p>This is a sample paragraph. </p>
<h2>This is a second-level subheading</h2>
<p>Here's another paragraph.</p>
</body>
</html>
```

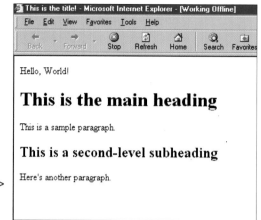

Hello, World!

This is the main heading

This is a sample paragraph.

This is a second-level subheading

Here's another paragraph.

■ **Paragraphs** *and subheadings add a bit more detail.*

Lists

HTML supports three kinds of lists: ordered lists, unordered lists, and definition lists. In ordered lists, browsers insert a number in front of each item in the list.

This is convenient, because you don't have to worry about renumbering sorted list elements by hand if you insert or delete items. The browser just does it automatically. An ordered list begins with <ol> and ends with </ol>.

Ordered and unordered lists

Unordered lists, which begin with <ul> and end with </ul>, are displayed with bullets (or whatever similar symbols the browser uses to indicate list items, e.g., asterisks).

In both ordered and unordered lists, you designate individual list elements with an <li> command. For an outline effect, you can also nest lists. Here's a sample document with lists:

```
<html>
<head>
<title>This is the title!</title>
</head>
<body>
```

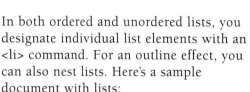

■ **HTML may look** *like hard work, but don't give up.*

```
<h2>This is a second-level
subheading</h2>
<p> Here's another paragraph.</p>
<p> Here's an ordered list:</p>
<ol>
<li> first item.
<li> second item.
<li> third item
</ol>
<p> Here's an unordered list:</p>
<ul>
<li> an item.
<li> another item.
<li> here's a nested unordered list
<ul>
<li> a nested item
<li> another nested item
</ul>
<li> the last item in list two
</ul>
</body>
</html>
```

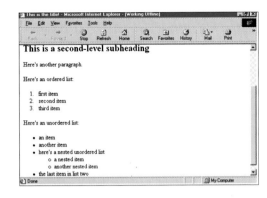

■ **An ordered** *list appears like this in a web page.*

Definition lists

A definition list starts with a <dl> command and closes with a </dl> command. This structure is useful for lists where you want to include a bit of explanatory text along with each item. Each item in a definition list has two parts: a term (indicated with the <dt> command), and a definition (indicated with the <dd> command). Here's a sample definition list:

```
<html>
<head>
<title>This is the title!</title>
</head>
<body>
<dl>
<dt> First Term
<dd> First term's definition.
<dt> Second term (or title, or whatever)
<dd> Text that explains or expands on the
second term.
</dl>
</body>
</html>
```

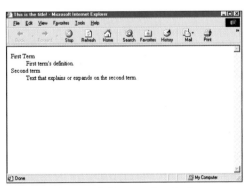

■ **This is how a definition list** *looks in a web page.*

Hypertext and hyperimage links

The HTML command for putting a link into a document takes this form:

<a href="URL">clickable text or graphic</a>

The URL (web site address) you're pointing to is placed inside the double quotation marks shown above; the clickable text or graphic for the link goes after <a href="URL">, and before the </a>.

■ **JPEGs begin** *as photographs or non-digitized graphic images.*

So, here's our sample document with links. Remember that web browsers usually display the hypertext in a different color from regular text.

```
<html>
<head>
<title>This is my title</title>
</head>
<body>
<h1>This is my title</h1>
<p> This is a sample paragraph. A link to
the Public Broadcasting Service web site is
coded into the document and the user can
<a href="http://www.pbs.org"> click here
</a> to call up their web site.</p>
<h2>This is a subheading</h2>
<p>This paragraph includes another link.
<a href="http://www.unodostres.com">
click here </a> to call up the Uno Dos Tres
web site.</p>
</body>
</html>
```

■ **Hypertext links** *will show up in a different color to normal text.*

Images

Most web browsers will display only two types of graphic file formats, .GIF and .JPEG (a.k.a. "JPG"). There are dozens of graphic image software applications that can create files in these formats, or convert other digital image files to these formats.

Depending on the skills and needs of the designers and illustrators working on a web site, the programs used range from relatively primitive freeware applications to expensive, top-of-the-line professional tools.

Web browsers display images at a far lower resolution than is possible with ink on paper, or on television or film. The higher the resolution of a web image, the greater the chances are that it will download slowly.

One of the primary challenges for professional web site producers is mastering the techniques to make web images clear and crisp, while still downloading as quickly as possible.

Inserting an image

The HTML command for inserting an image takes this form:

<img src="imagefile.gif">

This command tells web browsers to display the indicated image file in the position you've specified on your web page.

You can augment both image and text HTML commands with a variety of "attributes" such as alignment, positioning, and spacing commands. Here are a couple of examples:

<img align="top" src="image.gif"> Text. This command aligns the top of an image with the text that appears next to it.

<img align="middle" src="image.gif"> Text. This command positions an image so its center point is aligned with the text.

<img align="right" src="image.gif"> This command places an image on the right side of the page.

text <img src="image.gif"> Text and images within the centering tags are centered in the browser window.

■ **This image** *has been positioned on the right side of the page using HTML commands.*

Alternate text

Another useful option is to provide "alternate text" for an image. The "alt" directive is used like this:

<img alt="[photo]" src="image.gif">

Alternate, or Alt, text serves several useful purposes. The text is displayed while the image is downloading, helping your visitor know what's coming, lessening the sense of waiting. Alt text can also be displayed when the viewer moves the cursor over the image, so it's another way to communicate with your visitor. Alt text is perhaps most important for viewers with text-only browsers. These users see the alt text in the space where the image would have appeared on your page.

■ **Decorate your** *web site with graphics from online archives such as iconbazaar.com.*

Remember, there are still a lot of people, including many visually impaired users, who use text-only web browsers. Therefore, it's a good practice to provide "alt text" with every image.

To keep your web page data well organized, keep your image files in the same folder or directory as your HTML document. Or, use a special folder inside your HTML folder with a name like "images" or "graphics."

There are many archives of free "clip art" images available on the web, from which you can select from thousands of icons and other free, public-domain images to use on your web site.

Before you use anyone else's images, though, whatever the source, check first to make sure there are no copyright restrictions on the material!

Online image archives

Here are a few examples of online image archives from which you can access and download graphics for your own personal web site:

✓ Icon Bazaar: www.iconbazaar.com
✓ Clip Art Connection: www.clipartconnection.com
✓ Xoom ClipArt Archive: xoom.com/clipart
✓ Image Paradise: desktoppublishing.com/cliplist.html
At all of these sites, you can review topic-oriented folders full of free, downloadable images.

■ **Why not** *give your web page a floral background image?*

Professional web designers usually don't use these free archives. They go to stock image sources, which charge a fee but offer greater selection and higher quality. By using these sources, professionals minimize the risk that a particular piece of art will appear on another site.

Leading examples of professional stock image sources are Photodisc (www.photodisc.com), Stock Market (www.tsmphoto.com), Image Bank (www.theimagebank.com), and Tony Stone Images (www.tonystone.com).

Backgrounds, colors, fonts

To specify a background image for your web page, use the <body background="image.gif"> command. (As you can see, it appears within the <body> tag.) You can use a GIF or JPEG image as your page's background; the chosen image will automatically be tiled (that is, repeated like bricks or tiles on a wall) behind the entire page.

If you don't want your viewers to wait for a background GIF or JPEG to download, you can specify a solid background color for your page simply by using a hexadecimal color code.

The command is <body bgcolor="xxxxxx">, where the x's stand for the color code. You can choose from 216 web-safe colors. (Web safe colors remain true across all browsers and platforms.) For example, the following HTML document uses the code "808080" to create a gray background.
Try it – you'll see how simple it is!

```
<html>
<head>
<title>This is the title</title>
</head>
<body bgcolor="808080">
Hello World!
</body>
</html>
```

■ **It's easy to** *give the text some color.*

Specifying colors

You can specify colors for many other elements of an HTML document, too. For example, watch what happens with the last document when we use the value FFFF00 to change the font color.

```
<html>
<head>
<title>This is the title</title>
</head>
<body bgcolor="808080">
<font color="FFFF00"> Hello World! </font>
</body>
</html>
```

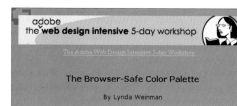

■ **There are** *specific sites where you can learn more about color on the web.*

To learn more about color on the web and about hexadecimal values, see these sites:
✓ www.lynda.com/hex.html
✓ www.upenn.edu/computing/group/dmp/technical/colors/curious.html
✓ www.infi.net/wwwimages/colorindex.html
✓ www.lightsphere.com/colors

There are several HTML tags you can use to modify the appearance of text. For example, to make a word or series of words bold, enclose that text in the <b> bold text </b> tag pair. For italics, use <i> italic text</i>.

The <hr> command inserts a nifty horizontal rule across your page. The <hr> command can also be modified with attributes. For example, <hr width="50%"> will make the rule 50 percent as wide as the page. You can control the size of the rule with the <hr size="xx"> command, making the rule as small or as enormous as you want.

HTML *learning resources*

THIS INTRODUCTION TO HTML *provides only a starting point into the universe of web page authoring. Booksellers offer many excellent volumes on the subject, but you can also find almost any information imaginable on the subject of HTML and web design right on the web itself. Here are several wonderful online resources. These and similar online resources will also lead you to information about cutting-edge extensions to basic HTML, including JavaScript, Dynamic HTML, Cascading Style Sheets, and XML.*

✓WebMonkey: www.webmonkey.com
✓Library of Congress HTML page: lcweb.loc.gov/global/html.html
✓HTML Goodies: www.htmlgoodies.com
✓HTML Help: www.htmlhelp.com
✓Ask Dr. Web: www.zeldman.com/askdrweb/
✓The HTML Writer's Guild: www.hwg.org
✓Index Dot HTML: www.blooberry.com/indexdot/html/index.html
✓HTML Tips & Tricks: www.tips-tricks.com
✓How do they do that with HTML?: www.nashville.net/~carl/htmlguide/index.html
✓Web Developer: www.webdeveloper.com
✓Project Cool Developer's Zone: www.projectcool.com/developer/

HTML is fun! Want to know more? There are many more possibilities and skills you can explore. The following is just a very brief summary of some advanced skills, with definitions and possibilities, to whet your appetite.

Tables, frames, and forms

MOST HTML GUIDES AND TUTORIALS *include entire sections on tables, frames, and forms. Web page authors almost always need to learn these skills. Tables, frames, and forms are important, but each involves a bit of learning and patience.*

We're going to describe each of these HTML elements, but leave it to you, dear reader, to run with the ball from there. If you do, we refer you again to the web authoring resources listed above.

Remember, you'll find almost everything and anything you need to know about creating web pages and advanced HTML – right on the web.

■ **Plenty of sites** *offer advice on HTML – htmlgoodies.com, for example.*

Organizing your web pages

You can use HTML tables to organize the layouts of your web pages. The basic tags are <table> and </table>. Within tables, headers are contained in <th> </th> tag pairs; rows are coded with <tr> </tr> pairs; and columns are marked up with <td> </td> tags. A variety of attributes control alignment, borders, and other table elements. Mastering tables takes most HTML writers a lot of practice, but this part of HTML is essential for controlling exactly where the various elements will appear on your web pages.

Several of the online web authoring resources mentioned above include tables tutorials. Practice makes perfect!

HTML frames let you divide the browser window into multiple, smaller windows. Each of the windows actually contains an HTML document. If you've surfed around much, you've probably seen lots of pages which use frames.

Some implementations of frames are helpful for navigation or presentation, but, in other cases, the frames tend to cause confusion.

■ **Frames can** *make it easier to navigate around a site.*

Frames sometimes create unpleasant complexities while using Back or Forward buttons, in printing documents, and in saving bookmarks or favorites.

HTML forms use a family of tags that enable interactive elements and user input. Forms are created within <form> and </form> tags. Forms include text boxes on web pages, where users type information and then click a Submit button; as well as radio buttons, checkboxes, and pull-down menus (a.k.a drop-down menus). A radio button is a round button you click on to make a choice. When a radio button appears on a form, you can pick only one selection. Checkboxes on a form let you pick multiple choices. It's actually quite simple to add forms to your web page.

Responding to a form

After a user responds to a form on a web page, for example, by clicking on a radio button or checkbox to answer a question, the form must execute a script.

This starts to add just a bit of complexity, as form actions often require the use of a Common Gateway Interface (CGI), Active Server Page (ASP), or a JavaScript (JS).

Writing these scripts requires the use of programming tools more complex than HTML. These tools vary, depending on the specific server set-up where your web pages are hosted. Many ISPs provide support and documentation on how to incorporate and configure forms into web pages hosted on their server platforms. Once you've made your first few successful, working forms, you'll find that mastering this part of web page authoring is really as fun and easy as HTML. And, as with HTML, you'll find a treasure trove of helpful resources right on the web, covering CGI, ASP, JS, and any other requirement you'll encounter when you start coding forms and writing scripts.

Mistakes to avoid

SOME PEOPLE *find HTML so interesting they get too fancy! Others lose patience with the detailed work of getting it just right, and resort to building web pages heavy with large, slow-loading graphic images, or elements that can be viewed by only one browser. These approaches may result in web documents that look terrible, take forever to*

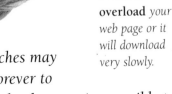

■ **Don't overload** *your web page or it will download very slowly.*

download, or are inaccessible to many people. No web site is perfect, and even the best are vulnerable to poor maintenance. Overleaf are just a few common mistakes to watch out for.

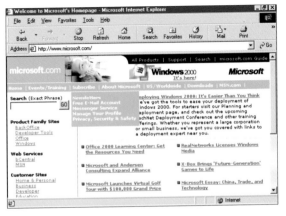

■ **Microsoft.com** *has scripts added to the HTML to make it a highly interactive site.*

Design

Design seems subjective, but there are some well-defined criteria for what's pleasing to the eye. Simple is generally better. The web is filled with pages that sport ornate script against deep-colored background, lettering that blinks like neon signs, and space cut up into boxes for no good reason except to keep the viewer's eyes moving.

Restraint, balance, and good taste should prevail over lurid, attention-getting tactics.

■ **Avoid garish,** *over the top designs when creating your web site.*

Here are some of our favorite web sites devoted to promoting top-quality web design (and preventing poor design).

✓ Efuse: www.efuse.com
✓ The Yale Web Style Guide: info.med.yale.edu/caim/manual
✓ Sun Computer's Style Guide: www.sun.com/styleguide
✓ HighFive.com: www.highfive.com
✓ Web sites That Suck: www.websitesthatsuck.com
✓ Design for Designers: www.wpdfd.com
✓ Bandwidth Conservation Society: www.infohiway.com/faster

Too much of anything lessens its effectiveness. Use bold, italics, underlining, and even combinations of all three, but not to excess. Use pictures and graphics, but not too many. Check over and over again for typos and inaccurate grammar. Nothing spoils a beautiful page more quickly than a glaring, avoidable error.

INTERNET

www.word-detective.com

This web site has been reviewed and recommended by all sorts of publications and named "Cool Site of the Day" by Apple Computer and People magazine. The site is the online version of a newspaper column by Evan Morris called "The Word Detective." It's so appealing to the eye that it invites leisurely exploration. Against a plain white background, with plenty of calming white space, colorful letters spell out the contents of the site. Surrounding the text are Sir John Tenniel's illustrations for Lewis Carroll's Alice in Wonderland. *This site is an example of the successful union of form and content that spell truly excellent design.*

Technical

HTML code requires precision. Any typo, accidental omission, or tiny boo-boo can cause errors and unexpected results in your pages. Even if you've relied on a software template rather than creating the HTML tags yourself, errors and mistakes can happen.

That's one reason why basic knowledge of HTML is so helpful — it will enable you to quickly find problems and fix them. You should also know about several excellent online sources for help in perfecting and improving your web site.

We recommend our well-used collection of online resources to provide help in assuring the quality of your site. These are some of our favorites; we suggest you look over each one and then save it in your bookmarks or favorites list.

- ✓ Dr. HTML: www2.imagiware.com/RxHTML
- ✓ Dr. Watson: watson.addy.com
- ✓ Net Mechanic: www.netmechanic.com
- ✓ Web site Garage: websitegarage.netscape.com
- ✓ Bobby: www.cast.org/bobby
- ✓ WebLint: www.weblint.org

Once your site is up and running, several other technical aspects will become important to you. You'll want to have a way of knowing for sure that your site is active, available, and online, or if there's a problem causing your site to be inaccessible to the Internet community. You should have a way to assure that backup copies of your site are maintained in case a catastrophic failure occurs to the server or the data center. There should also be a "firewall" in place at the ISP to prevent intruders from gaining unauthorized access to your site data.

Server logs register visits to your site, and can usually provide interesting information about where your visitors are coming from, the times of day they visit your site, which browsers and operating systems they use, and if they came to your site by clicking a hyperlink from another site.

■ **Form and content** *work well together on this web site.*

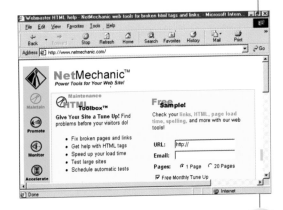

■ **Check your site** *for problems using online resources such as NetMechanic.com.*

If your site offers any kind of business transactions or includes personal information, you'll want the ability to invoke a secure server state. These and other technical issues are beyond this book's scope, but we raise them here to remind you to cover these bases with your host ISP, before your web site launches for the world to see.

Don't abandon your web site. If you start to think of it as an interesting experiment, but not something you want to stick with, take the necessary steps to remove the web site.

The web is filled with abandoned, forgotten sites, and poorly maintained sites, with links that no longer work and "what's new" areas that haven't changed in years. While no specifically measurable harm is done by these stale sites, they increase the overall clutter of the web, and certainly can cause frustration when people actually come to them looking for something of relevance or value.

■ **Don't let** *your web site become stale or old-fashioned!*

Reconceptualizing

Over time, your needs and interests may change. Your business grows or develops a new product, your creative energy takes a new twist, there's something new and different you want to publish.

Reconstruct your page to reflect the changes. This may mean establishing different links, or maybe even a different word or two in the address.

Or, expand your site by adding new pages that address your new interests and activities. Web sites are living entities, unlike printed matter that's static once the ink dries.

In this chapter we've explored HTML, outlined how to go about setting up a new web site, and offered lots of suggestions for where to turn if you get more serious about web site creation and production.

■ **Like a living thing,** *your web site should grow and change.*

Internet publishing is a powerful way to communicate to countless people near and far. It's well worth the effort of putting your web site together well, and taking good care of it.

A simple summary

✓ HTML commands follow an orderly and logical pattern. Web pages have two parts, the head and body.

✓ HTML tags are contained inside left and right angles, easily created on any computer keyboard, using plain text. HTML is used to create text, page headings, lists, and other page elements and formatting.

✓ Images and hyperlinks are inserted into web pages with HTML tags, and they can be sized, formatted, and positioned with HTML.

✓ Tables, frames, and forms are used for a variety of more advanced web page layout and functional purposes. Forms require scripting, which your ISP can help you learn to configure in ways which best suit your web server environment.

✓ Web page publishers should be alert to mistakes in design, technical execution, and maintenance, so the end result will be an attractive and effective site. Testing is important to assure a functional web site.

✓ There are several technical requirements and issues related to operating a web site that you should discuss with your ISP.

✓ When needs change or new information arises, your site can be modified and/or expanded.

PART THREE

THERE'S A WORLD OF INFORMATION OUT THERE

FINDING THE GOOD STUFF

LET'S TALK ABOUT looking for information – the sort of thing that used to call for a trip to the library. Now, those books, and thousands more, are online, *constantly* updated, and always *available*.

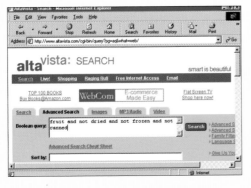

We call the first chapter in this Part, "Searching and finding," just to make it clear that your searching will lead to *finding*, whether your objective is simple or complex.

Chapter 11

Searching and Finding

WHILE IT'S TRUE the Internet is often described as somewhat chaotic, online technologies have actually made the process of finding (and distributing) many kinds of information faster and easier than ever. An important concept to understand when approaching a web search is that the Internet is decentralized. That is, the structure and distribution of information are not managed or controlled by any person, government, or organization. The Internet is not finite; it's a dynamic network. New web sites, and new additions to old web sites, spring up every day, while other sites disappear or change. Finding certain things, such as the web site of a well-known corporation, is relatively easy, but tracking down many other kinds of information takes skill and smarts.

In this chapter...

✓ The online research library

✓ Search engines and directories

✓ Portals

✓ Boolean logic

YOU'LL SOON BECOME PROFICIENT AT SEARCHING THE WEB

The online research library

SEARCHING THE INTERNET *is a lot like going to the library. At one time or another, you've probably gone to the library to explore ideas to use on the job, research topics for a class paper, browse through a few cookbooks, find plans for a woodworking project, or maybe just to seek out something fun or interesting. If you don't have a particular book or piece of information in mind, though, you just browse the shelves devoted to a particular topic, occasionally pulling down a book for a quick scan of its table of contents or introduction. After a while, you discover that different aspects of the subject are shelved together, so you narrow your attention to just one or two shelves.*

You may also find that a related topic, located near your original starting point, catches your attention, drawing you off in another direction. Eventually, you'll probably take a few volumes off the shelf, look more closely at their contents, decide which specific topics really interest you, and select a few books to check out and take home. By starting out with a general idea of what you want, exploring where your initial efforts lead, and eventually narrowing your focus through a process of discovery, you've gone from browsing to searching for specific information. This process carries over to the Internet in many ways, as you'll soon discover. Your own mind, learning style, and common sense will play major roles, so we won't try to tell you how to think as you search for information.

Rather, we'll introduce you to the main tools and web sites available for web searching. We'll talk about how they work, outline some useful techniques, and point out a few important issues to be mindful of when searching on the web.

Try a variety of tools

Some online search tools are geared towards database searching, while others are more oriented to browsing through subjects and topical listings. We recommend you try a variety of tools, and develop your own preferences and savvy in finding what interests you in cyberspace.

■ **Searching the** *Internet can be compared to looking up information in a book.*

There's no magic or high-tech knowledge needed; just a computer system connected to the web, and an active, curious mind.

Of course, you don't always go to the library to browse. Sometimes, you want very specific information: a telephone number, a word definition, a map, a source for replacement parts, sports scores, movie showtimes, currency exchange rates, the date of an event, or the text of a poem. The Internet provides a panoply of ready avenues for these types of searches.

Search engines and directories

■ **Explore the** *British Library's web site at bl.uk.*

ONLINE SEARCHING SERVICES are often grouped under the term search engine, regardless of how they work. We'll break the main types of searching sites into two categories: search engines and directories. Search engines are automated systems that use "spiders" or "webcrawlers," specialized bits of software that automatically search the web far and wide, copying all the information they find into huge databases. Then, end users (that's you and me) can enter keyword queries, and get back listings of web pages where those keywords appear. Lycos, AltaVista, Excite, and Northern Light are examples of search engines.

One criticism of search engines is that queries often return thousands of listings, many of which are not relevant or useful.

Directories are listings of web sites, selected and classified into subject-tree hierarchies by human editors. Leading examples include Yahoo, LookSmart, About, and Snap. Search engines can cover a lot more ground because they're automated, while directories can only cover a relatively limited expanse of the web because they're managed manually. This means directories can't provide such extensive results for all searches, and may miss some useful online resources. On the other hand, directory searches almost always produce fewer irrelevant or useless results.

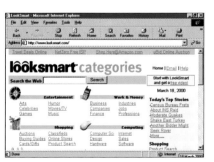

■ **A directory like** *LookSmart employs editors to select and classify web sites.*

The two types of searching tools described above are distinct and different from each other. However, they've become blended; the top search engines now offer directories, and the major directories have augmented their own web site listings with search engines that extend their results. Search engines and directories offer two ways to "drill down" to find information — by submitting keyword queries, and by clicking through subject hierarchies. And even as they become more and more similar, there are still very profound differences between them. A search engine is an automated, computer-driven database function, while a directory is selected and edited by humans.

You can drill *through layers of information with a search engine.*

The search engine casts a wider net, but lacks the unique added value of intelligent selection by experienced human editors. Human-edited directories have a higher quality of relevance, but a smaller universe of total data.

Along with an overview of search engines and directories, we'll also tell you about some newer, cutting-edge search applications that are helping to overcome some of the drawbacks and limitations of traditional web search systems.

When you're not sure what you want

Exploration on the web can help to bring a fuzzy idea into focus.

If the information you need isn't clearly defined, you have a fuzzy query. In this case, browsing through categories of information while mulling over your fuzzy question may be the best way to begin. While browsing, you'll think about web sites that might contain helpful information, visit a few of them, and either get what you want, or refine the focus of your search in response to what you did or didn't find. Sometimes, workers in the same office browse the Internet separately, mulling over the same fuzzy query, and call a brainstorming session when someone thinks they've found an insight. Ten people searching the same general topic might find ten different, but equally valuable, pools of information.

Selecting the right category

Let's take a simple example. Suppose you're planning to entertain the boss in your home for the evening, and would like to serve a very special dinner. It's not at all clear what that should be, so you begin with a fuzzy query. Now that you've become an Internet user, online

resources, may pop into your mind right away – for instance, web site addresses for famous chefs, sites you learned of from television or magazines, or recipe archives you heard about from a friend.

If you don't have those addresses at hand, you could easily find them, and similar ones. Browsing toward the right "shelf" translates, in Internet terms, into selecting the right category.

■ **You can find** *over 3,000 recipes under Food and Drink on the Netscape site.*

For instance, in its web directory, the Netscape home page (www.netscape.com) lists "Lifestyles" as a subject category. One of the choices in that category is "Food and Drink." Under that heading you'll find the "Recipe Center," listing over 3,000 recipes. (Multiply that easily-located store of information by many thousands, and you'll start to get some idea of the resources available on the web – in just this one subject area.)

There are many ways to look for most answers, and many possible approaches. For instance, if you know the boss loves Chinese food, you might browse in categories devoted to the culture of China, where a subcategory on cuisine would be likely to contain Chinese recipes. You may find, though, that too broad a strategy takes you off the track. For example, you might get a list of Chinese restaurants rather than recipes.

Narrow your line of querying to screen out what's not helpful. It doesn't matter how you do it as long as it works. Any route to the information is fine, as long as you end up with the perfect Mu Shu Pork!

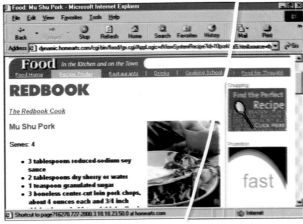

■ **Find that** *recipe for the perfect Mu Shu Pork.*

At the beginning of this information retrieval process, a directory may be more useful than an index. Directories are like the table of contents in a book, providing subject trees with big branches dividing into smaller branches, and each of those into still smaller twigs, and so on, as your search becomes more focused.

When you know what you want

Searching is a little different when you're looking for a single, clearly-defined piece of information. If you're searching in a library with such a question, you might look for encyclopedias or dictionaries. These kinds of resources are plentiful online. Here are a few examples, but keep in mind that there are thousands of more specialized and niche-interest sites, with loads of reference information on almost any subject imaginable.

✓ Information Please: www.infoplease.com
✓ Encyclopaedia Britannica: www.britannica.com
✓ Funk & Wagnalls: www.funkandwagnalls.com
✓ Columbia Electronic Encyclopedia: www.encyclopedia.com
✓ Encarta: www.encarta.msn.com
✓ Oxford English Dictionary: www.oed.com
✓ Merriam-Webster: www.m-w.com
✓ Internet Reference Desk: www.refdesk.com

■ **Online encyclopedias** *offer interactive and multimedia options not possible in printed editions.*

A more specific pursuit

■ **Looking for** *that perfect recipe? It's probably on the web.*

Let's return to our example of dinner for the boss. When you've seen lots and lots of possibilities, your visions of the right dinner will start to focus on a particular main dish. Then, you can start a more specific pursuit of the information you need. Instead of just browsing web sites devoted to cooking, you can stop at one of those sites and look for the exact recipe you're considering. You've now moved from browsing to focused searching. Further elements of your search may entail discovering which dishes go well together, which recipes can be prepared ahead of time, or which ones seem closest to the one your mother used to make.

Once you know the question to ask, where is the best place to ask it? Search engines are only one avenue you can pursue. There are also many web sites with their own on-site searching services, indexing all the material on those individual sites.

For example, if you're seeking recipes, the Internet gives you access to several searchable archives. Here are a few worth checking out, both to find great recipes and also to try out site-specific search engines:

✓ Epicurious: www.epicurious.com
✓ Betty Crocker: www.bettycrocker.com
✓ My Meals: www.my-meals.com
✓ Food @ Women.com: women.com/foodchannel
✓ The Culinary Connection: www.culinary.com
✓ UCook: www.ucook.com

■ **The web has** *healthy diet sites on the menu today.*

Sometimes, these stores of topic-specific data are a better place to start than a general search engine, since the selection of the web site is itself a step in the process.

For instance, if you have a health question to ask or want information about a particular medical problem, it would make sense to find one of the many excellent health-related web sites and access its on-site search engine.

Starting from the general search engines, you might accomplish the same goal by choosing health care from the list of categories, but this path may take you to the specialized site anyway.

When you can't find it

New Internet users sometimes expect miracles, and get frustrated when their searches aren't successful, or when the results are overwhelming. Search engines provide helpful suggestions for improving your results.

For example, Infoseek gives a mini-tutorial under the heading, "How to Search," and a selection of ideas on "Where to Search."

AltaVista offers to search several different forms of data, including newsgroups, discussions, and audio and video files. Northern Light's "Help Center" describes how to get more relevant search results. Excite offers a feature called "Search Voyeur" that lets you look in on live searches other people have underway, so you can observe the methodology others use. Enhanced functions, helpful tips, and guidance have become standard services at most search engine and directory sites. Modern search engines also routinely let you sort your search results by date or by domain, as well as let you search for web sites in different languages.

■ **Most search engines** *offer helpful hints for improving your search results.*

The following is a list of the major search engines, with a little information about each one. We're putting it here so that we can use this information for examples, and so that you can test them yourself online.

Seach engines – a selected list

www.altavista.com

One of the largest databases in existence, AltaVista indexes more sites in the .com domain, but not as many in the .edu domain, as other engines. The simple search option here will show "term counts" for each word in a query – that is, how many times a given term occurs in each document returned by a search.

If you're trying to narrow your focus but getting too few hits, you can pick the term least-often returned and exclude it from the terms of the search.

AltaVista offers several powerful ways to refine searches. For example, if you enclose a series of query terms within quotation marks, the results will only include sites where those words appear in the exact sequence you specify.

www.excite.com

Excite offers a feature that automatically evaluates your original question to determine its underlying principle. You will then see the suggestion that "related sites" be displayed. If you know exactly what you're looking for, such as one specific piece of data, this might not help, but if your question is still a little fuzzy, this is a good option.

■ **Hotbot is good** *for locating commercial products.*

www.hotbot.com

Hotbot is owned by the folks at Wired Digital, originators of the pioneering web site hotwired.com, which started out as the online cousin of the print magazine *Wired*. At one time it was considered to have the largest database of all the search engines, though this may not still be true as others expand their databases. Like AltaVista, Hotbot is better at locating commercial products and services than academic topics.

www.lycos.com

Lycos is one of the older search engines, and was once considered the premier database. Like its competitors, Lycos has introduced new and more advanced features, including an option called "SeeMore." This feature is supported by Microsoft Internet Explorer, and allows you to launch a search by right-clicking the mouse button on any word, term, or graphic that appears on any web page.

www.northernlight.com

Northern Light is known for a robust database, and for organizing query results into sets of folders as a way to break up large results lists into more manageable groups. Northern Light also offers premium services, including articles from newswires, periodicals, and proprietary databases.

www.infoseek.com

Infoseek has a smaller database but a much greater share from the .edu domain, so many users consider it a better place to turn with an academic topic. Infoseek is part of the "Go Network" of sites owned by Disney.

■ **Infoseek is** *good for researching academic topics.*

There are many more search engines, and we'll mention some of them in the next few chapters. Although most of them provide similar searching possibilities, each one also has unique features.

There is no one search engine that's always best for all purposes. You may find that you like one better than the others, but don't forget that in any particular case, another service might serve you better.

Sometimes, it's worth trying the same search in several different search engines, to help maximize your chances of finding the best sites.

Portals

■ **Portals are** *gateways into other "virtual" worlds.*

IN SCIENCE FICTION, *the term portal means a gateway to another dimension or time zone. In Internet terms, it has some of that same connotation. A web portal provides a gateway to the web, but it's also something like a general store.*

The term portal came into being as the major search engines realized that their visitors were often just running searches and then quickly clicking off to surf elsewhere.

To give their visitors reasons to stick around, search engine and directory sites began adding content, services, and community features, rapidly turning themselves into full-service portals. All the major search engines and directories have evolved in this direction.

The term portal is now used widely, for many types of sites. Portal publishers encourage web surfers to adopt the portal as their home page, and to visit frequently. Most portals include searching and directory tools, as well as "hot lists" of new and interesting web sites. There are "vertical" and demographic portals, such as Sonicnet (for music fans), Law.com (for people in the legal professions), NHL.com (hockey enthusiasts), and Bolt.com (for high school and college students). Geographic portals, such as NJ.com (New Jersey), and Sympatico.ca (Canada) have also gained popularity. Many ISPs, such as Earthlink (Earthlink.com), and ATT WorldNet (www.att.net), have turned their home pages into portals. Many news sites such as CNN.com, MercuryCenter.com, and Blomberg.com have also expanded their offerings into the portal arena. Our list of portals and types of portals could be much longer.

■ **Hockey fans** *should check out NHL.Com*

Just remember that, in general, a portal is a site with broad content and services, including "jumping off" points to other web sites, coupled with lots of features and benefits that entice you to linger, and to keep coming back.

Where to start

A web doesn't have any beginning or end, up or down – only round and round. There is literally no one right place to start a search, because you can ultimately get anywhere on the web from any starting point.

Hypertext links make it possible for any subject to be connected in any of a thousand directions to related subjects and to deeper levels of detail.

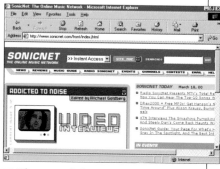

■ **The portal** *Sonicnet.com is aimed at music fans.*

For example, we once sought the original source of a literary quote that became a book title. We knew that *For Whom the Bell Tolls* was written by Ernest Hemingway, but we also knew he had created that title from a longer and much older quote: "Ask not for whom the bell tolls; it tolls for thee." Beginning with the AltaVista index, we entered Hemingway, Ernest. This produced lists of sites that discuss his works, including *For Whom the Bell Tolls*. Immediately, we began seeing bookstores where we could purchase that book. But after checking half a dozen hits, we found a site with information about the book, including the full quote from which the title came, and the original author – John Donne. Back at AltaVista, we entered John Donne, and soon arrived at a page devoted to this famous author of Renaissance England, complete with audio clips of some of the music of that historical period.

Be specific

If we had known that John Donne was the original author we could have started at the web site devoted to him. A search engine is a place to find the web sites most likely to be relevant, not the lodging place of the exact information needed. Even proper names can bring up false hits, so we probably should have first chosen the category closest to Literature, and specified the author Ernest Hemingway.

Say another Hemingway fan wanted to learn about the author's lifestyle rather than about one of his books. That person might have entered the same query, and received much the same collection of hits on Hemingway we did, but would have followed a different path. We did see biographies among that first list of hits (and were tempted to look at some of them), but this would have taken us away from the best path to our search goal. It can be difficult to keep a focused objective in mind and not be distracted by interesting things encountered along the way.

What to ask

A keyword is a word that plays a crucial part in the answer to your question, and that you believe is not too likely to pop up in unrelated contexts. Your selected keyword may need to change during the course of a search, as you find your way to specialized sites, where technical terms are recognized in their proper contexts. Sometimes, lack of success is caused by failure to respond to the hints given by the results returned by a search. For instance, if the keyword keeps bringing up lots of sites dealing with an irrelevant context instead of the one you want, it will help to exclude that context. There are a number of ways to do this, offered by virtually all search engines under a term like Advanced Search. These techniques are really exercises in the use of logical searching parameters, rather than computer skill.

Using advanced searching techniques, you'll usually be able to find exactly what you want.

Too much or too little

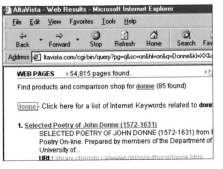

If there's anything more frustrating than seeing, "The search produced 0 results," it's probably, "The search produced 3,435,678 results." Either way, it's time to start over. In the case of too much, the search engine may suggest that you Refine the search. Click on this option to see some suggestions for focusing your query.

■ **The keyword search** *has yielded 54,815 matches, so it may need refining.*

For instance, we entered the word "fruit" in several search engines. Yahoo returned "25 categories and 1294 sites," and asked us to select a subcategory such as "fresh, dried, gourmet, etc." AltaVista returned 1,763,436 hits, and presented a list of Internet keywords related to fruit. Clicking on this, we saw fruit of the loom, fruitcake, fruit trees, fruit baskets, and more. Excite returned 282,464 hits, and asked, "Did you mean?" – suggesting that we specify whether we meant oranges, plums, or underwear. These results tell us that adding other words to the first keyword will help. You can do this simply by putting a plus (+) sign between words, or surrounding a phrase with quotation marks. If it's underwear we're looking for, we could just enter fruit+loom, or "fruit of the loom."

Options like Advanced Search, Power Search, or Search Help, available on all the major search services, enable many more refinements, requirements, and constraints. Some offer the power of Boolean techniques, discussed below.

New tools

As the web continues to grow, the problem of too many hits also grows. Several new types of search engines are now available to help search for words and information in more accurate and effective ways. Google.com measures web sites and ranks them in importance, according to how many other sites are linked to them. Google is fast, and very good at finding relevant sites. It even offers a button called I'm feeling lucky – which will automatically take you directly to the web site it judges most relevant to your query. Clever.com does an instant mathematical calculation of the sites most often linked to your keywords. On the assumption that popularity is usually earned, this "links analysis" ranks the hits in the order of their mathematical value.

DirectHit.com uses a model that analyzes the activity of Internet searchers to help rank the relevance of web sites in relation to search requests.

INTERNET

AskJeeves.com

This site employs a "natural language engine" that lets users simply type in their questions, and find the most useful page to answer those questions.

A result of zero hits generally means your original keywords were too general, and you need to enlarge the scope of your query. Take our search for fruit, for instance. If we had entered the botanical name of some rare species of persimmon, we might see "0 returns," and we'd then need to expand the search scope to persimmons in general. Zero results might also indicate a typo in your original query.

■ **The search word** *"fruit" could be a real lemon: you'd get far too many matches.*

Boolean logic

THIS OVERVIEW *of Boolean logic will prepare you for the more detailed description in Chapter 12. The word refers to the English mathematician and logician George Boole. It describes a logic for searching that uses inclusion and exclusion terms such as and, or, and not. Here's how it works. If our search for fruit was aimed at learning about fresh fruit only, we could enter fruit and fresh, or fruit, not dried, not frozen, not canned. The first entry would access web sites with both fruit and fresh in their titles. The second would access sites with fruit, but exclude sites that included the terms dried, frozen, or canned.*

■ **AskJeeves.com** has a *"natural language engine" which understands simple questions.*

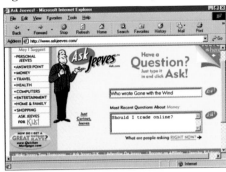

If we wanted to know about fresh fruit, but not citrus, we could enter fruit and fresh, not citrus. By combining these qualifiers or constraints, you can restrict the hits you get. From the smaller pool of relevant hits, you can introduce still other requirements and constraints to further narrow your search.

Association and relevance

The helpful tips search engines offer are based on a few important concepts. Intelligent concept extraction is the technique of determining the underlying concept upon which a query is based.

In this type of search, in addition to the specified query term, terms that are synonymous with, or semantically close to, the query term will be searched for as well.

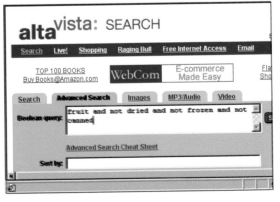

Relevance feedback is a means by which the search engine uses your response to the first round of a search to guide the second round, successively refining the search with each set of clues derived from your responses to the returned hits.

■ **Using Boolean logic** *really narrows your search.*

Even when you learn all about the search engines, the possibilities of Boolean logic, and the latest technological improvements in searching techniques, there may still be times when you can't find exactly what you want. This happens in libraries too. Sometimes, cataloguers have misunderstood something or confused its labeling, so that database searches don't find it. However, we believe that online resources, voluminous and unmapped as they are, still provide the best possible reservoir of information available.

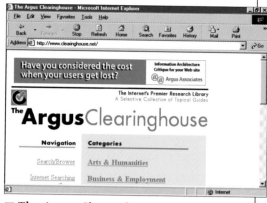

■ **The Argus** *Clearinghouse at www.clearinghouse.net is a top research site.*

Database skills

If you're not seeking the answer to a specific question, but rather gathering information on a topic, you may want to approach that topic in several different ways. In a library search, this would mean bringing home stacks of books with different call numbers, or compiling a bibliography and planning to do a lot of reading when time permits.

You can gather a bibliography of Internet resources in a bookmark or favorites list, and download web site pages into files on your computer.

True, you can't sit down in an easy chair and pet the dog quite as comfortably while reading online, but there are no due dates or late fines, either.

All the skills associated with library research apply online. In fact, the catalog of your favorite bricks-and-mortar library is probably online too. There are also thousands of complete books online, plus millions of reviews and articles, scholarly papers, and research findings. There is even the complete *Encyclopaedia Britannia* (Britannica.com). Authors now frequently publish literary and scientific materials online, using the Internet to make themselves and their work available to other writers and researchers more widely than they ever could before.

If you come to the Internet with a bibliographic entry, or even just an article title or author's name, there's an excellent chance that you'll find the material you want.

INTERNET

www.clearinghouse.net

A clearinghouse is like an online reference library, where a comprehensive directory cross-references many subjects, guiding the user to appropriate resources. There are numerous online clearinghouses devoted to specific subject fields. Then, there's Argus (www.clearinghouse.net) – the clearinghouse of clearinghouses.

In this chapter, we've introduced the subject of searching, and promised you much more in other chapters to come. After e-mail, searching is the most common online activity. We're certain you'll want to learn from experience how simple and effective online searching can be.

■ **Directories** *can be compared to the interlinked branches of a tree.*

A simple summary

✓ The major types of online searching tools are search engines and directories.

✓ Directories are organized in hierarchical "subject trees." You can browse and drill down through the trees to reach links to specific web sites and pages.

✓ Search engines are huge databases that can be searched via keyword queries.

✓ Directories and search engines do not and cannot encompass all the data available on the World Wide Web.

✓ Sometimes, it's quicker and more productive to conduct a search within one web site than through a general search engine.

✓ If a keyword query is too broad, a search will likely return too many hits; if it's too narrow, you may get no hits at all.

✓ There are many ways to improve your search results; search strategy help is available at the search engine sites.

✓ Boolean logic is a way to greatly increase the accuracy and specificity of a search.

✓ You can carry out extensive academic research online, using skills similar to those you'd use in a traditional library.

Chapter 12
Advanced Searching

I F ONLINE SEARCHING intrigues you, Chapter 11 may have just whetted your appetite. There is, indeed, a lot more to learn. This chapter is not so much advanced, as just more. There is, however, so much more to the subject of searching that all we can do here is introduce you to the most common avenues for finding on the web information and other things that may interest or benefit. In this chapter, we'll build on our learning from Chapter 11. Plus, we'll consider how and when to launch a "metasearch," look for ways to evaluate search engines, explore special criteria to sharpen a search's focus and filter out irrelevant sites, and talk about information reliability.

In this chapter...

✓ Search engine secrets

✓ Focusing and filtering

✓ Site searches

✓ Reliability

ADVANCED SEARCHING GIVES YOU POWER OVER THE WEB

Search engine secrets

BECAUSE OF INTENSE COMPETITION *among Internet services, good ideas that begin in one place nearly always quickly spread to competitors. Search engines that are contenders for popularity honors tend to offer what appear to be similar arrays of capabilities and services, although they may use slightly different terms to describe their functions. After a while, you'll recognize the functions, even if the names are slightly different. For instance, in the list of major search engines given in Chapter 11, most capabilities listed for any one of them are actually available at all of them.*

Metasearch engines

A metasearch engine is a service that will automatically submit a parallel query on several different search engines simultaneously, and then return a single list of results. Entering a query in many different search sites, one after another, one at a time, can be laborious. Metasearch engines shortcut the process.

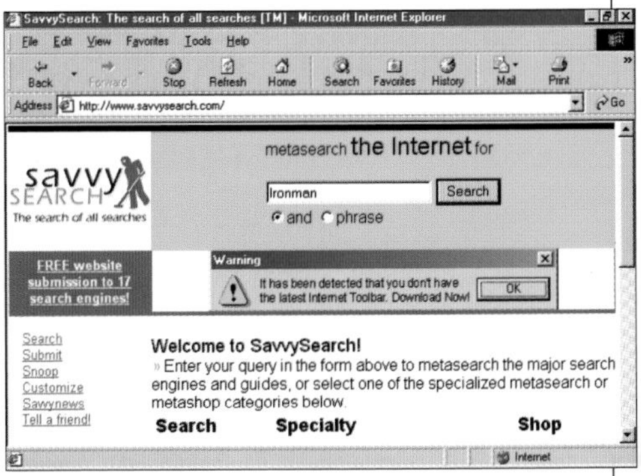

Some metasearch engines limit the number of keyword matches they list from each search engine, to avoid submerging you in floods of results.

■ **Meta-search engines** *let you search several search engines at the same time.*

Some metasearch tools rely exclusively on external databases, while others combine external querying with their own internal databases of web site listings. Others provide powerful options for narrowing the type of information you're looking for.

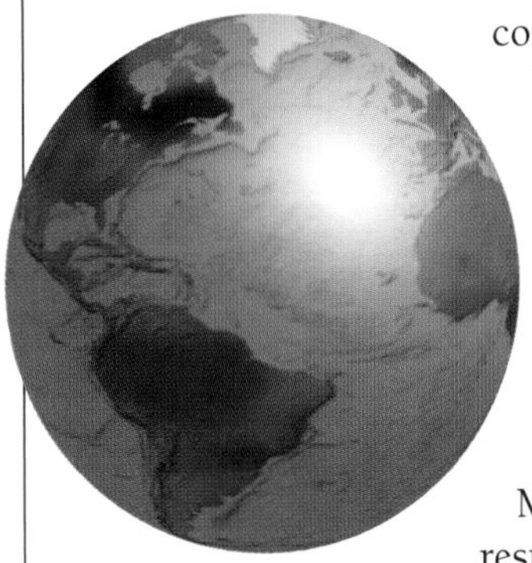

For instance, The Big Hub lets you click checkboxes to indicate which search engines you want included in your query. It also offers the convenience of choosing a time limit on waiting for responses from all the databases being queried, plus an extra level of specialty search. SavvySearch and C4 offer powerful customizing preferences. Mamma provides an internal ranking program logic that integrates results from multiple sources in order of relevance.

■ **A world of** *geographic information is at your fingertips.*

Dogpile offers access to more than a thousand different search engines, plus a robust geographic searching option.

Each metasearch engine has its own unique properties. We encourage you to try a few, explore their range of services and options, and bookmark the ones you like best. Here are just a few of the metasearch sites available on the web:

✓ The Big Hub: www.bighub.com
✓ SavvySearch: www.savvysearch.com
✓ C4: www.C4.com
✓ Mamma: www.mamma.com
✓ Dogpile: www.dogpile.com
✓ MetaCrawler: www.metacrawler.com
✓ ProFusion: www.profusion.com
✓ MatchSite: www.matchsite.com
✓ SearchRunner: www.searchrunner.com
✓ InferenceFind: www.infind.com

■ **Dogpile even** *found matches for Ironman+Hawaii+Results!*

To give metasearching a test, we went to Dogpile and entered Ironman+Hawaii. We wanted to find sites related to the famous Ironman triathlon event held in Hawaii each year. On the first results screen, Dogpile showed five hits from LookSmart, ten from GoTo, and ten from the Dogpile Web Catalog. It also offered the opportunity to see results from nine other search engines.

After scanning the initial results, we decided to focus on results from the most recent Ironman competition. So, we modified our search to Ironman+Hawaii +Results. In short order, we had several links to sites with detailed event results and coverage.

To some extent, a metasearch engine needs to take over the terms of the search, as it must often re-word your query to conform to the format required by the different search engines it calls upon. The metasearcher does this automatically. While you gain much from the ease and scope of the metasearch, therefore, you lose some control and some of your ability to refine terms. Another drawback is that many metasearch engines return only the top tier of matches from any specific search engine.

Sometimes, to find the best matches, you have to keep scanning deep into the query results, which you can do by searching directly on the individual search engine sites.

Many metasearch engines also help you find your "best bet" for some particular search among the great number of available search engines.

By following the subject tree, you can focus on the area of the search, note the one or two search engines recommended, and then conduct your search separately at those search engines. For instance, we clicked on the category "Arts" on Dogpile's subject tree, and found subcategories such as "Artists," "Humanities," "Arts Education," "Arts Advocacy," and so on. Each of these led to resources specific to that area, and to more promising places to search.

All-in-one pages

■ **Get arty** *on the web.*

An all-in-one page doesn't take over your search, but lets you retain control. It presents information about many search engines, letting you access any of them and submit searches – all without leaving the all-in-one page. You could, for example, enter one query and choose five or six different engines to send it to, choosing options for refining the query you know are supported by each engine. The all-in-one page sends the query to each search engine, complete with your customized search specifications.

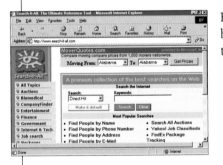

Here are a few popular all-in-one pages. The better acquainted you become with each of the search engines, the more effectively you can use this approach.

■ **All-in-one pages**
such as Search-It-All.com let you use several search engines at once.

✓ Search-It-All: www.search-it-all.com
✓ Skworm: www.skworm.com
✓ Proteus: www.proteus.com
✓ PureSearch: www.puresearch.com
✓ Better Brain: www.betterbrain.com

Reviews and ratings

For the guidance of online consumers and researchers, many magazines and services regularly review, evaluate, and report on the accuracy, relevance, and versatility of various search engines. One place to find a wealth of information about search engines, including reviews and reports, is at www.searchenginewatch.com. From there, you can link to some of the actual reviews, and read in-depth discussions of the strong points and limitations of a particular search engine.

Many of the leading Internet and computer industry news services pay intense attention to search engines, often evaluating new developments in each one. For instance, sites like CNet (home.cnet.com), ZDNet (www.zdnet.com), CMPNet (www.cmpnet.com), Web Reference (www.webreference.com), and InternetNews (www.internetnews.com)

provide archives of current and past articles and reviews. And you can follow their links to other sources, for closer examination.

Another way you can evaluate how well various search engines do their jobs is by checking out reviews of web pages. For example, you could begin a search with a general search engine, and then check the returned results against the information you find in an archive of web page reviews. This will help you determine both the overall quality of the hits, and which locations merit closer research. Newsletters such as Netsurfer Digest (www.netsurf.com), Your WebScout (www.webscout.com), and The Scout Report (www.signpost.org) take a quality control approach to describing and rating web sites.

If a search engine consistently returns highly-rated sites, it's probably a reliable resource, and one you'll find yourself using often.

Focusing and filtering

SEARCHING INVOLVES *keeping and eliminating, winnowing and filtering. We keep the leads that look promising, and eliminate those that are off-target. Most search engines let you use Boolean logic in your queries, to include or exclude certain kinds of information, or certain keywords. This helps increase the relevance of your search results. Some Internet experts say the term Boolean should be dropped because it sounds esoteric and tends to frighten newcomers away. The same processes of focusing and filtering, they contend, can be described without off-putting references to formal logic. In fact, many search engines provide help pages that describe using Boolean operators, but never actually get around to using the term. We're sticking with the word Boolean, though, primarily because it's a well-known, specific database searching methodology that many search engines use.*

■ Sites like WebScout.com
rate and review other web sites.

Learning a few basics of Boolean querying is really simple, and it's a very good way to improve your search success.

More Boolean

In Chapter 11, we outlined the use of the terms and, or, and not as basic elements of Boolean queries. Using and creates a "required term" in the search, while not creates a "prohibited term."

Here are some additional ways to sharpen the focus of your search and filter out false hits.

Each of these is an example of using "Boolean operators" to fine-tune a search query. After listing these, we'll describe how some of them worked for us during a real online search.

✓ Or: Placing the term or between keywords returns results that match any of the keywords.

✓ Exact phrase: Placing quotation marks around a key phrase requires that all returned search results include the entire phrase, exactly as worded within the quotes. Connecting two exact phrases with and tightens the focus still more.

✓ Near: Choosing this option means that hits will be returned if the specified words occur in proximity to each other. Some search engines decide what proximity means, and some allow you to set the distance to two, ten, or some other number of words apart.

✓ Wildcard: If you're not sure of the spelling of a name or word, the wildcard option will return the closest matches to your best guess of the spelling.

✓ Link search: This option restricts the search to sites that contain certain specified URLs as links.

✓ Search within results: A click on this particular option will restrict the search to the pool of hits returned in the previous round of searching.

✓ Results clustering: This option allows only one page per web site to show results, so you won't get tons of hits from pages at the same site. Turning off results clustering lets you receive more results from the same site.

■ **Boolean logic** *was created by George Boole.*

✓ Stemming: This particular option allows a search for a word in any form, or any word made from the keyword stem.

✓ Find similar, or "more like this": If, in the list of hits returned, you see one that seems really productive, highlight it and click on this term to find more similar sites, while excluding others.

✓ Sort by date: Sorting by date is useful if you know approximately when something happened. But be aware that dates are often not exact. Sometimes the date shown will not be when the event actually happened, but when a page was located by a spider, or added to the database.

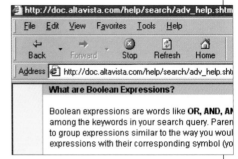

■ **Several sites** *explain how to use Boolean expressions in your searches.*

✓ Sort by domain: This is a useful option if you're getting a lot of false hits from an irrelevant area. For instance if you're looking for the history of the city of Hershey, Pennsylvania, you could avoid being inundated with candy sales outlets by excluding the .com domain.

When you combine these searching parameters into precise queries, you're using Boolean logic. It's usually not a good idea to combine more than three parameters, as this slows down the process. Also, keep in mind that not all search engines support all Boolean operators.

To be sure you make the most of each search engine's capacity, take a quick look at the Help or Advanced Search pages at each search engine, to discover which operators are allowed.

You probably won't be surprised to find that there are some wonderful web sites where you can learn more about Boolean searching. We suggest these excellent starting points, The Library at the State University of New York at Albany: www.albany.edu/library/internet/boolean.html and Searchability: www.searchability.com/boolean.htm

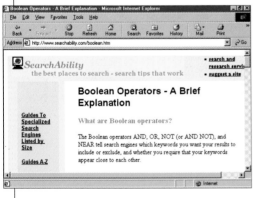

■ **SearchAbility**.*com is a good place to learn about Boolean searching.*

Real-life search

The following example isn't meant to show the only right way to conduct a search – there really is no one right way – but, rather, to share a real-life example of a web search, and some of the successes and failures you can expect along the way.

Narrowing it down

We decided to imagine we needed a watchdog, big and loud enough to scare off intruders, but gentle with children. We first went to AltaVista and entered the word dogs, with no other requirement except that reports come back in English. This brought over two million hits, along with a suggestion that we "click here for Internet keywords related to dogs." Among those first hits were a few that we thought might function like categories, leading to the subcategories of specific breeds – for instance, "Dogs Today Index Page," and dog categories such as "Working Dogs." But after checking a few of these, we could see we were on the wrong track.

Among the hits, we saw the web site for the American Kennel Club, so we clicked there and followed the lead "Breeds" to "Breeder's Education." Under "AKC Recognized Breeds," we found "Working Group." After reading about the various breeds, we decided that the strong, intelligent, good-natured Saint Bernard breed met our requirements.

We'd already decided a puppy would more readily bond with our family. So, back at the AKC home page, we clicked on "Buying a Puppy," then on "How to Find a Breeder," and then on "Breed Club Breeder Referral." Clicking on "Working Group," we found a link to the "Saint Bernard Club of America." But, for some reason, this link wasn't working. So before returning to AltaVista, we browsed further on the AKC site.

Refining the search

Back to the AltaVista home page, we entered Saint Bernard and puppy. This brought 173,625 hits. Among the first ten were The Saint Bernard Dog, The Saint Bernard Club of America, and dog.com. On the same page, under "Related Searches," there were two interesting options, "Saint Bernard Puppies," and "Saint Bernard Breeders." We clicked on the latter, and discovered sites listing breeders – including one called puppynet.com. Here, we found several breeders of Saint Bernard puppies. Continuing to refine this search, we certainly could have chosen "search within results," and focused on geographic areas, pedigrees, and, eventually, on individual puppies offered for sale.

We could then have chosen our puppy's gender, and finally located the one and only puppy exactly right for our family.

When searching the web, then, you have many options for narrowing down huge lists of potential matches to smaller, more manageable numbers that will eventually lead you to something useful. In the process, you'll undoubtedly alternate between searching and browsing – it's just too tempting. This is typical. So, enjoy it!

■ **Use the Net** *to find the perfect pet.*

Site searches

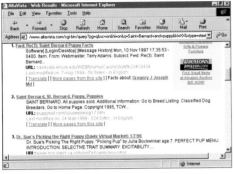

■ **Searching the** *results of searches can narrow down the list of matches.*

IF YOU'RE SEEKING *a specific piece or type of information from a specific web site, you may not want to spend a lot of time browsing from page to page. To help visitors find information faster, most large web sites now provide internal search engines that search only within that site. These services usually work much the same as the web search engines we've explored. And, like the web search engines,*

site searches often offer help pages, as well as tips for improving your results.

Searching and browsing

"A bird in the hand is worth two in the bush." If you've found a web site that deals with the right subject matter, don't be too quick to leave it, and don't fail to bookmark it.

Many searches will eventually call upon multiple sources, so even if you need to travel elsewhere to address some aspect of your question, you may want to return to this site for another part of the answer.

Skilled and experienced web site designers know that different kinds of people – some expert, others less comfortable or adept with search terminology and techniques – are

likely to search their sites. Well-constructed sites anticipate their visitors' needs and are set up to accommodate them. Not all of us speak English, so sites expecting multi-lingual visitors may provide language options. Not all of us understand arcane search languages, so many sites offer simple, "plain English" searching functions. When site architecture and searching functions are thoughtfully designed, finding what you're looking for is easy and pleasurable. Unfortunately, many sites – including some created by big names from whom you'd expect better – offer only poor navigation and very unsatisfactory searching tools.

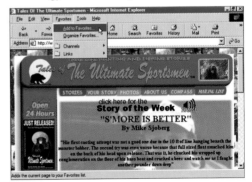

■ **When you find** *a web site you like, add it to your "Favorites" or "Bookmarks" list!*

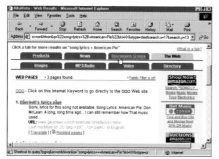

In short, never feel like an interloper just because you may be a novice at online searching. The best search engines make us feel at home, and make it easy for all of us, whatever our experience level or information needs, to find what we need. Are the searching directions at a site unclear or confusing? Look around a bit more carefully – it's possible that the information you need is there somewhere, expressed in understandable language for the convenience of ordinary users.

■ You can also *search for related discussion groups.*

If not, we suggest moving on quickly to another site — one that serves you better.

The search interface

Studies show that most Internet users now expect to find a search engine available on any large web site. Sometimes, it's easy to tell that one of the major search engines has provided a web site's search service, because the interface closely resembles the familiar home page of Excite, Lycos, or some other search engine you've used. In these cases, the web site's designers haven't fully integrated the search engine into their site, or bothered to customize its appearance. It may work perfectly well, but it may resemble its parent search engine so closely you might forget you're actually searching one site, not the whole web.

A web site's search interface should tell you exactly what's being searched – that is, full-text, indexing, or some selective version, and if so, what the selection criteria are. It will probably offer ideas and tips for searching techniques, similar to those provided on general search engines. Many web sites also let you ask for search help.

If your search isn't successful, there may be a message board, chat line, or e-mail address, to which you can direct questions about your search objectives, the organization of the site, or your need for technical assistance.

Reliability

■ Some sites *have message boards for posting your questions.*

HOW RELIABLE is the information retrieved on the World Wide Web? Issues of authenticity and accuracy are nothing new. The Internet is neither more nor less subject to the misleading statistics and errors of fact that creep into normally reliable sources than any other medium. In the U.S. today, poll results get prominent play in the news, and sports reports are filled with statistics from the past and present. News reporting is so immediate that facts and numbers describing events in progress are quite rightly assumed to be questionable. Careful observers find fault with many reporting methods, and question the reliability of much so-called factual information.

BIASED RESEARCH, BOGUS RESULTS

One of the best-known health information web sites recently came under fire when it was revealed that the site had praised several hospitals as among the nation's most innovative and advanced, without revealing that the site and the hospitals had a business relationship. Integrity of information has become a hot-button issue on many kinds of web sites.

■ **For major life** *decisions, don't just consult the Net.*

You may have a tendency to believe that books are quite reliable. If it's in the dictionary or the encyclopedia, it must be right. But in fact, the reference books now online, containing the same information, are actually more likely to be accurate than the print versions. Online references can be updated and corrected immediately as circumstances change, errors are detected, and the base of knowledge grows. Here are a few suggestions to help you evaluate sites and the information you find at them.

✓Use common sense. Evaluate information you find on the web exactly as you would evaluate information from any other source.

If the information is meant to help you make a major decision about your health, finances, or other important life issues, consult with other sources and trusted advisors such as your personal physician or financial advisor.

✓Consider the source. Have you ever heard of them? Are they known as reputable and trustworthy? Are they a company trying to motivate you to purchase their products or services? Are they an ideological organization promoting a possibly biased agenda?

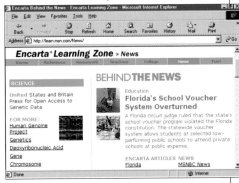

■ **Online reference** *sites can be updated when important events happen.*

✓ Beware of testimonials and anecdotes. Just because a person or two claims a baldness cure worked or a certain kind of investment made them rich doesn't mean you should whip out your checkbook.

✓ Question mystery sources. Claims like "according to experts" may not hold water. Who are the experts? How did they express their confidence in the product or information being discussed?

■ **Is the information fresh?**
Look for an article's publication date.

✓ Who stands behind the information? Is there an address and phone number for the company or organization? Is there at least an e-mail address? Is there any kind of organizational information, board of advisors, or credentials? What kind of site is the article or page a part of?

✓ Is the information fresh? Unlike journal articles or books in a library, information on the web often has no date on it. Some web sites contain text that hasn't been updated for years and may be out of date. Look for a publication or modification date – if none is provided, keep checking for another source.

✓ Is the site a "fake"? Some phony sites have been set up to look like they represent certain organizations or sources when, in fact, they don't. In some cases, this is illegal; in other cases it may be technically legal as "parody." Some disreputable groups use names very similar to credible organizations to lure the unsuspecting. People with an axe to grind will sometimes create look-alike sites with URLs and graphics similar to their target's web site.

Businesses, celebrities, politicians, and even ordinary individuals can find themselves targets. Make sure what you're looking at is the real McCoy!

✓ Keep printouts: If a web page has information you want to follow up on or double-check, print it out. Be sure to set your browser preferences so web page printouts include the URL and date. In Chapter 14, "Downloading," we'll give you more tips for successfully printing out web pages.

Imposters and traps

As in other areas of online activity we've looked at, searching is vulnerable to some abuses you should know about. Millions of

■ **You can print out** *web pages for further research.*

people are looking for many things with the help of search engines, and every online merchant wants to reach that huge audience. Therefore, there's fierce competition to be placed as one of the top hits on search result lists. As a searcher, you want to believe that the top hits returned by a search engine in response to your query are there only because they really are the best possible places to look for the information you want.

Unfortunately, search engines are subject to a variety of forms of manipulation that may tend to push some sites higher up in the list of query results than they should be.

Sometimes this occurs because of cheaters, called search jackers. These are people who try to "hijack" searches by playing tricks on the search engine. Spiders and web crawlers, you'll remember, are automated software applications used by search engines to index web sites. Search jackers employ tactics such as repeating one word hundreds of times, in hidden code that only spiders and crawlers can read, hoping to be indexed through that word – even though their business is totally unrelated. Others will spam the search engines with automated requests for some page as a way to affect a site's position. Some companies hide the names of their competitors in their page code, so, for example, if you search a company by name, their competitor's site will be listed first. In the ongoing war against sabotage, search engines are developing ways to overcome such devious search jacking strategies.

Be careful

In an even more malicious practice, popular among pornographers, a variety of tricky hidden codes divert surfers to pornography sites, for example, and then trap them there. New windows – but with yet more of the same material – keep popping up indefinitely. Redirecting traffic among online users is a dishonest practice that has been used for many purposes, but this recent practice is more technologically astute, and can actually bring your online activity to a complete standstill. Sometimes, the only way to get out of the site where you've been trapped is to exit your browser and then restart it.

One notorious sex site preys on careless surfers who think they're connecting to a government agency but forget to end the address with the correct suffix, .gov.

Another way you may stumble by accident onto salacious material is via a typographical error. Some triple-X sites have purchased domain names very similar to some of the more popular legitimate web site addresses – just to catch people who may transpose a couple of letters.

Track records

Over time, most web surfers come to depend on certain online information services. We learn that one place is usually the best place to turn for technical help, another for in-depth questions, another for quick answers, and another for the latest cutting-edge ideas. We learn when to consult the broadest possible sources, and when to save time and effort by sticking to a specific, familiar resource.

As you gain experience, your own online track record is certain to show increasing expertise, and more frequent success in searching.

Build on this knowledge base by staying abreast of new developments in searching. At some point, you might want to explore some of the search tools such as AskJeeves, Gurunet, Google, or any number of innovative search systems currently being developed. When new software first becomes available, it may be Beta software, which we don't recommend for most Internet users – only for experts. But usually, these applications are released to the general public as soon as the bugs are worked out. That's when you might want to check out some product reviews and consider using the tools yourself. Search engines will also establish their own track records with you, proving their worth over time by contributing the information you need.

Don't get in a rut, though – remember, there's no one service that's always best.

In this chapter, we've outlined more searching techniques, including metasearch sites and all-in-one pages. There's still much more to talk about. The coming chapters will cover specialized searches, downloading, and multimedia. For now, we've discovered some helpful techniques, and learned about some pitfalls to avoid.

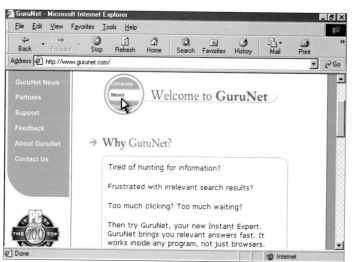

■ **Innovative search** *sites such as GuruNet.com are being developed all the time.*

A simple summary

✓ Metasearch engines send your query out to many search engines as one comprehensive search, but with some loss of control over the search parameters.

✓ All-in-one pages send your search query to selected services as multiple versions of the same search.

✓ Reviews of the accuracy and capabilities of different search engines are readily available.

✓ Boolean commands can help greatly in focusing a search and filtering out irrelevant material.

✓ Larger web sites generally provide their own internal search engines. These enable you to find things in that site without having to browse through all the pages.

✓ Issues of reliability are similar online to those that have always affected information providers in all media.

✓ Problems of misleading statistics, biased agendas, and other issues which may affect information integrity are common to all media.

✓ Competition among commercial interests for high visibility in search engine results has led to some abuses and "dirty tricks," intended to hijack the attention of online searchers.

✓ Over time, we all develop habits of searching, as we find services that we learn to depend on. No one way to search is right or wrong; the key is to develop and improve methods that work for you.

✓ When new software becomes available it could be beta software, which is suited most to expert internet users. However, these applications are usually released to the public when the bugs have been worked out. Then you may consider using the tools yourself.

Chapter 13

Specialized Searches

I N THIS CHAPTER, we'll review some of the areas available on the web for looking up news, people and businesses, jobs, places to go, things to do, local and national government sites, and international and foreign language search options. This chapter doesn't cover every type of narrowly focused web search; there are far too many options available. Rather, this chapter provides a tour of many common types of searching that may interest you.

In this chapter...

✓ News

✓ People and businesses

✓ Jobs

✓ Places to go and things to do

✓ Government

✓ International and non-English

News

■ **You should take** *regular breaks during extended sessions at your computer to avoid eye strain.*

YEARS AGO, SOME FUTURISTIC THINKERS

predicted that the more widely the Internet is used, the less attention the public will pay to newspapers and news magazines. Those predictions have not proven true. Print media have not gone away, and are not likely to disappear soon. In fact, because of the different experiences offered by various information sources, printed publications may never be replaced by computers. Today's computers require readers to gaze into a brightly lit monitor while leaning forward, typing on a keyboard, or clicking a mouse. In a word, it's work! Newspapers and books can be enjoyed on a comfy sofa, a breezy park bench, or aboard a commuter train on the way to work. And it's usually more enjoyable to read longer, in-depth stories from printed "hard copy" than from a glowing computer screen.

On the other hand, Internet news sites are thriving, and having a profound impact on the process of gathering and delivering news. Virtually all news organizations in the print or telecommunications realms have made major commitments to the Internet.

Many of the popular forms of online news are geared to time-sensitive "commodity" data that can be quickly updated and refreshed, for example, updates from financial markets, weather conditions, and sports scores. Also, many specialized online news outlets are feeding the interests of niche populations and communities.

The proliferation of web sites serving niche markets and specialized interest groups reflects a larger trend that was already in progress in the mass media many years before the Internet arrived as a consumer medium.

Magazines serving highly-targeted audiences have proliferated, as have cable television networks geared to topical or demographically specific programming. At the same time, the audiences of general interest outlets, such

■ **The web sites** *of major newspaper publishers are good sources for the latest information.*

as the major television networks, have become fragmented. There are a number of web sites dealing with media history; one fascinating collection is available at www.mediahistory.com.

Many people research topics in the news, looking for trends, or investigating the way a news story has been treated by the media. News report archives become a part of history, ending up in libraries and museums.

In the here and now, though, we're more likely to be searching for the details of some event – the correct names, quotes by those involved, or dates when the event occurred. The Internet lets us tap other media for that data, so a search may take us to newspaper web sites, television network web sites, the sites of independent online news providers, or directly to the home pages of the newsmakers themselves.

Wire services

As technology moved from teletype center to computer, and telegraph to satellite, the volume of news transmitted by AP and UPI grew rapidly. Today, the public expects instantaneous reporting and in-depth news analysis. The wire services provide millions of words each day to all forms of media. You can visit them yourself at www.associatedpress. com and www.upi.com.

For business and financial news, Reuters (www.reuters.com) is a good place to launch a search.

Major television networks are not dependent on wire services, as they deploy teams of reporters all over the world. You can find news reports on web sites provided by wire service news feeds, television news networks, and independent Internet news agencies. In addition, many web sites post up-to-the-minute news relating to their particular businesses.

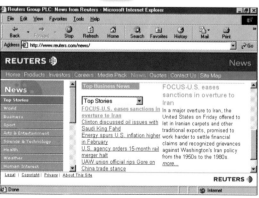

■ **Wire service** *news feeds provide up-to-the-minute reports.*

Network and portal sites

Sometimes, people want to get away from the pace of events and the flood of news (see Chapter 15 for some ideas on this). Usually, though, we appreciate the opportunity to catch the latest news in a few spare minutes during our busy days. If a particular breaking story, such as a local disaster or crisis, interests or concerns you personally, Internet news feeds can help keep you informed minute by minute.

■ **You can get** *online news customized to your interests.*

It's often easier to click into a news network to search for more information than to find a telephone and call for it.

In addition, many sites now offer customization tools that let you create personalized pages that automatically collect news of special interest to you. For example, Snap (www.snap.com), a leading web directory/portal, offers a service called "My Snap" that lets you construct a custom version of Snap with specific categories of news, local weather reports, scores for your favorite sports teams, updates on stocks in your portfolio, and even your horoscope.

The major news networks index their stories and transcripts of programs for their on-site search engines. After the death of NFL star Walter Payton, we heard that CNN had devoted its "Talkback Live" television program to live testimony from other famous football figures about their relationships with Payton. Not having seen the program, we wanted to hear the thoughts offered by Payton's former coach, Mike Ditka of the Chicago Bears. We entered the name Ditka on the CNN web site search engine, and the first hit returned was the transcript of that program.

■ **Did you miss** *the news last week? Search for it on the web.*

Push services are online news services that serve special audiences. Many of these offer subscriptions for e-mail newsletters that regularly deliver the latest news in your area of interest.

This kind of news delivery service saves you even more time, as the news of most interest to you is "pushed" via e-mail right into your Inbox, requiring no searching on your part.

Directories and search engines provide lists of such news services, listed by subject area. Beyond e-mail, there are several other technologies that let you automatically receive news and updates through the Internet. Some of the most popular are PointCast Connections, Microsoft's Active Desktop, and Netscape's Netcaster.

Local news

Even very small communities generally have online news outlets, maintained by local newspapers, broadcasters, libraries, or web portals. These sites generally provide reports of news from the immediate area. They offer a local slant on bigger stories, as well as providing local directory and calendar information. They also often provide site search engines, a service that's especially helpful to newly-arrived residents. But sometimes, these services are limited and inflexible. "Look it up" works well if your objective is simple, such as classified ads, schedules for community events, or birth and death notices – the kind of data important to local residents but of no interest to people outside the community. In large metropolitan areas, some people opt to read their city's major newspapers, while using the Internet web site of a local news outlet to find local information.

■ **Many community** *events are promoted online.*

People and businesses

■ **Guessing a** *corporate URL doesn't always work: the Associated Press is not ap.com, it's ap.org.*

YELLOW PAGES are a good way to find businesses, and white pages work fairly well for finding people. But this can take patience, and isn't always successful. It's also limited by the geographic scope of printed directories. Since most businesses have web sites, it can be easier to find a business online, even if you're not sure of their web site address. Trying to find the web site for a business? Try some version of their corporate name. For instance, we looked for the web site of Associated Press, first guessing at www.ap.com, but this turned out to be the address for a company called "Audio Precision." Our second guess was for www.associatedpress.com, which is correct.

If your search isn't for just one particular business, but for information about what businesses exist in a given locality, or where certain kinds of professionals can be found, try the online yellow pages. For instance, physicians are often listed in the yellow pages by specialty. So, if you're looking for an allergist with an office nearby, you'd start with yellow page listings of physicians, and then go on to the subcategory of allergy specialists.

Finding businesses and professionals

■ **Professionals** *such as dentists should be searched for by name.*

Let's say you visited an exceptionally interesting furniture store last summer while on vacation. You remember which city it was in, but can't remember the name of the store. Open a directory such as Yahoo, and click on yellow pages, city name, and category "furniture." If it's a big city, many categories of furniture will appear. Choose the one closest to the type of furniture you saw. The next screen will provide a list of stores in that city selling that kind of furniture. With luck, the name will be there, and you'll remember it when you see it.

Say you remember the name of the furniture store – but don't remember where it was. Just enter the store name in the directory search window, and you'll see a list of cities with stores with that name. We did this with the name "Ikea," knowing it was somewhere in the New York metropolitan area, and found several outlets, including the one we visited in Elizabeth, N.J. The yellow page listing gives address, phone number, and web site address, so you can then choose which way to make contact.

Some listings let you ask for a map of the store's surrounding highways and roads, an especially useful feature when visiting businesses in unfamiliar areas.

Doctors, lawyers, and other professionals don't always have yellow page listings, so you must search for them under their individual names – a potentially more difficult task, especially if the person has a common name. We'll talk more about that in the next section.

■ **Finding that store** *is easier with Yahoo! Yellow Pages.*

JIM'S FIREWOOD

When people live in remote locations, there may be no businesses nearby. We'd visited family members in a small town, enjoying the rustic environment, especially the big fireplace in their home. Wanting to send a thank you gift for their hospitality, we thought of ordering some firewood for delivery to their country home. In Yahoo's Yellow Pages, we entered the name of the nearest city (still pretty small), and the category "firewood." There was one listing – with no web site. But there was a phone number. We called Jim's Firewood and ordered half a cord of wood, which was delivered to our hosts the next day. The magic of the Internet!

Finding people

Most of the major search engines offer white page directories. E-mail addresses for individuals are collated, so your search will return a hit for any name you enter, with either a street address or an e-mail address.

One problem you might encounter in searching for individuals is the recurrence of the same name in different locations. It's much easier searching for distinctive names.

Looking for a particular "John Smith" somewhere in Utah will probably be an exercise in frustration, while looking for "Ichabod Crane" will yield very few hits. For instance, we entered an individual name we thought was fairly distinctive, complete with the city and state where we know that person lives. Yahoo's "people search" returned five hits with that name, none of which were the object of our search. In this case, we didn't know the name of the closest large city, and the very small town where this individual lives doesn't have its own directory.

In addition to the major search and directory sites, several other sites have become leaders in providing searchable, online directories of businesses and people. Here are a few of our favorite web sites:

✓ Switchboard: www.switchboard.com
✓ WhoWhere: www.whowhere.com
✓ SuperPages: www.superpages.com
✓ BigYellow: www.bigyellow.com
✓ InfoSpace: www.infospace.com
✓ Yahoo: www.people.yahoo.com

■ **You can search** *for people too – try whowhere.lycos.com.*

If all your initial attempts fail, directories and search engines offer other options. Many of these eventually lead to a search for a public record, for which there is a fee. The claim that anyone can be found may be true, but it may take time, money, and patience.

There are also many search tools available for specialized purposes, like directories of certain types of professionals or businesses. For example, most automobile manufacturers' web sites provide simple tools for finding local dealers. You can find medical professionals through services like Doctor Directory (www.doctordirectory.com) and The Health Pages (www.thehealthpages.com).

Often, the best way to start a specialized search is to locate a specialized search engine! There are lots of them. For example, Artcyclopedia (artcyclopedia.com) lets you search for artists; Lawyers.com offers an attorney search; and The National Association of Flight Instructors' web site (www.nafinet.org) provides a flight instructor lookup service.

Need an expert on wind energy? Try the American Wind Energy Association at www.awea.org. Cigar Shop? Try Cigar Aficionado, (www.cigaraficionado.com). Use your wits, and you'll be amazed what you can find on the web!

Jobs

■ **Find a vet** *on the Net.*

WHEN IT COMES TO *looking for job opportunities, traditional searching tools include classified ads in newspapers, employment agencies, personnel services, and placement offices maintained by colleges and professional organizations. The Internet has had an impact on all of these. Personnel recruitment and career counseling are two of the many areas where a shift in the national economy is occurring. As Internet services take over a greater share of this work, the workforce in these traditional services shrinks. For Internet personnel services, geography is not a problem. They can recruit from anywhere, and place workers anywhere. As the labor force of the U.S. has come to expect to be geographically mobile, employers and job-seekers alike have turned to the Internet as an indispensable resource.*

If you're looking for a job, or for new employees for your company, you overlook the Internet at your peril!

■ **You can net** *a new job on the web.*

Careers

Sampling the online employment services, we found two that help illustrate the myriad possibilities available. CareerMosaic (www.careermosaic.com) offers voluminous job listings in most occupational categories and most U.S. cities. The Tripod Career Center (www.tripod/explore/jobs_career/) provides career counseling and help in building résumés, as

well as job listings. And both these and similar sites offer a wide variety of services for job seekers and for recruiters. Many web sites do their own recruiting, posting positions available within their own businesses, and inviting applications.

CareerMosaic offers you a full range of searching options, including most Boolean commands, to help in your job search. You'll be invited to get very specific, picturing your dream job and describing it as accurately as you wish. If the search turns up some prospects you want to explore, you'll be invited to submit a résumé online, as well as given the names of individuals to contact personally.

It's very educational to spend some time at these web sites before beginning to submit résumés. Because jobs are listed by locality and by occupational category, the Internet offers excellent opportunities to learn about the job market in different geographic locations.

Just reading through some of the listings will give you a good sense of employers' needs and expectations — excellent preparation for your job search.

Along with CareerMosaic and Tripod, here are several other leading employment web sites:

✓ Career Path: www.new.careerpath.com
✓ HotJobs: www.hotjobs.com
✓ America's Job Bank: www.ajb.dni.us
✓ Monster Board: www.monster.com
✓ Career Builder: www.careerbuilder.com
✓ Headhunter Net: www.headhunter.net

■ **The Internet** *is a job hunter's paradise.*

Résumés and applications

Whether you've already built an impressive résumé, or have never prepared one before, you probably know what a crucial step this is in career planning. We can't fully address this complex subject here, but we do want to point you to some places to go for help in building, improving, and using your résumé. Look at web sites of professional organizations for advice pertinent to your particular occupation. Whether you want to move into a new career, or up the corporate ladder, expert evaluation of your résumé would be a good investment.

Tripod offers a basic résumé guide that's excellent for beginners. CareerMosaic includes detailed resources for improving your résumé, and step-by-step directions for putting it into the best format for use on the web, ready for transmission to potential employers. Once you follow these directions, your résumé will be ready to send to any platform or computer system.

Posting your résumé at these and other online employment sites is a good step to take. But for best results, take the initiative, go on searching, and actually send your résumé to appropriate potential employers. Remember that most corporate web sites include listings of positions within their own organizations, so if you're interested in a specific company or organization, their corporate web site may be a good place to start. Most of the major search engines also include classified ad banks.

For instance, Infoseek lists more than 350,000 jobs, and offers company profiles, career advice, and notices of job fairs.

Many of the sites listed above provide – along with hundreds of thousands of job openings – excellent resources, advice, and helpful information for job seekers. Here are a few additional sites for professionals looking to enhance their careers, and for job-seekers. And there are dozens of others.

✓Career Lab: www.careerlab.com
✓Career Magazine: www.careermag.com
✓The Riley Guide: www.rileyguide.com
✓Vault Reports: www.vault.com
✓Strive Online: www.strivemag.com
✓WetFeet: www.wetfeet.com
✓JobSmart: www.jobsmart.org
✓Minorities Job Bank: www.minorities-jb.com

■ **Some sites,** *wetfeet.com for example, offer career advice.*

Places to go and things to do

PEOPLE WORK HARD *and play hard. There is as much variety in our leisure pursuits as in our professional lives. Whatever your interest, Internet resources can help you plan. This section will look at some ways to search for help in travel planning, cultural opportunities, and just plain fun.*

■ **The web** *can be a new way to find undiscovered vistas.*

Travel

Let's say your family wants to have a reunion in a warm place, to escape the winter cold and just be together. You could go to some local travel agency and let their agents suggest vacation packages. You could go online, find major travel and airline web sites and check out their vacation offerings.

Or, you could find the online yellow pages, enter the place you're thinking of going, and check out family accommodations listed under resorts and hotels. You may already be thinking of still other ways you could use the Internet in this kind of search.

For instance, if you'd really like private accommodations, such as a whole residence to rent for your reunion, yellow pages can point you to real estate firms that handle rental property. In geographic areas with high tourist traffic, rental agents often post a lot of information on web sites, including pictures of properties available for, say, weekly rental. Resorts often load their web sites with tantalizing pictures of their lush grounds. And you can search cruise ship web sites for dates, destinations, and other details of planned cruises.

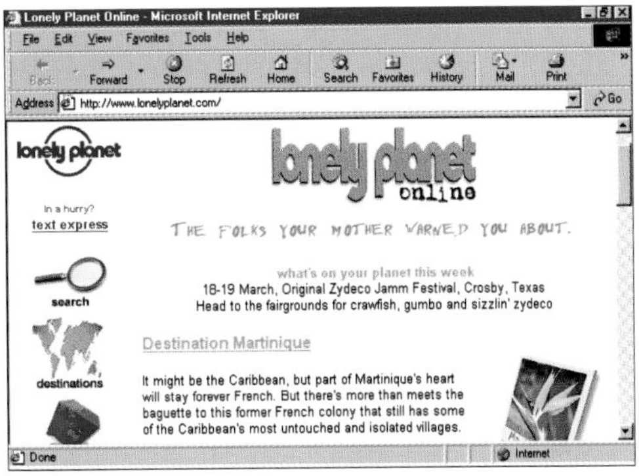

■ **Travel the world** *without leaving your chair at lonelyplanet.com.*

JUST MARRIED

We know an older couple who took a lot of time planning their wedding. Both working in high-level executive jobs, they knew it would be best to get away from it all. In their separate offices, they explored the Internet, searching for the perfect place. Separately, each came up with a certain feeling for the Virgin Islands.

With the help of Yahoo (where travel is a top-level category), a few tourism web sites, and airline reservations made through www.priceline.com, they put it all together and were married in a little white church in St. Croix.

Travel is one of the most popular subjects on the web. Here are a few URLs that provide just a taste of the fascinating, creative world of travel-oriented web sites. (We'll talk about shopping and buying things online, including travel services, in Chapter 21.)

✓ Virtual Tourist: www.vtourist.com
✓ MapQuest: www.mapquest.com
✓ Rand McNally: www.randmcnally.com
✓ Intellicast: www.intellicast.com
✓ Frommer's: www.frommers.com
✓ Fodor's: www.fodors.com
✓ Lonely Planet: www.lonelyplanet.com
✓ Concierge: www.concierge.com
✓ City Hunt: www.cityhunt.com
✓ Travelocity: www.travelocity.com
✓ Preview Travel: www.previewtravel.com
✓ Travelog: www.travelog.net
✓ Travel Channel: www.travel.discovery.com
✓ Trip.com: www.trip.com
✓ Adventurous Traveler Books:
   www.adventuroustraveler.com
✓ True Trip: www.truetrip.com
✓ About's Travel with Kids: www.travelwithkids.about.com
✓ BizTravel: www.biztravel.com
✓ Global Online Adventure Learning Site: www.goals.com

■ **The web can keep** *you in touch with the arts.*

Culture

The term "culture" covers everything from plays and art exhibits, to movies and pop concerts. In looking for cultural events, local community web sites can be invaluable. It might be worth bookmarking your local community site just so you can find out quickly what cultural events are taking place. In a small community, that bookmark may be enough.

But for a big city, you'll probably need a variety of bookmarks to keep track of all the different kinds of cultural information.

To get a taste of the diversity of cultural offerings in New York City, take a look at some of the web sites listed here.

■ **Many sites** *beat the drum for culture.*

✓ Movies: www.nyfilm.com, www.thescreeningroom.com
✓ Theatre: www.broadway.org
✓ Dance: www.abt.org, www.nycballet.com
✓ Music: www.nyphilharmonic.org
✓ Opera: www.metopera.org, www.nycopera.com
✓ Concerts: www.radiocity.org
✓ Art: www.metmuseum.org, www.moma.org

There are dozens of resources for finding guides to cultural events in the Big Apple, for example, www.nycvisit.com, www.nytoday.com, and newyork.citysearch.com. All this information is available to residents of New York City who might be planning an evening out, but also to Internet users anywhere. From the wilds of the boondocks, you could plan and schedule a cultural trip to the big city. In fact, many culture lovers do this, purchasing tickets and making travel arrangements months in advance.

In your search for art exhibits and other special cultural events, print media and the Internet can supplement each other. Art museums and galleries generally have web sites, and will post the same information there as in the major newspapers. And because they usually list events far in advance, it's often easier to get a long-range cultural overview online than any other way.

INTERNET

ny.yahoo.com

New York Metro Yahoo lists cultural events under subject categories such as music, dance, theater, and the like. Under those headings, you can search by title for specific movies, plays, and concerts; by location to find places within the metropolitan area; and by date.

Fun

The web sites of the NBA, NFL, and other sports leagues and teams are busy year around. Just to check this out, click on the site of World Series winners, the New York Yankees, at www.yankees.com.

Depending on the time of year, you might see a note stating that season tickets for the upcoming season will be available soon. If you follow horse racing, you probably know that you need to purchase your tickets for the Kentucky Derby at Churchill Downs in Louisville, Kentucky, at least a year in advance.

■ **Order your tickets**
online for a New York Yankees game.

At www.kentuckyderby.com, you may well see a note stating that all reserved seats are sold out, but that general admission tickets are available. These only allow entrance to the grounds, not seats. So, if you really want to see the greatest of all horse races, better get those tickets and arrive as early as possible on the first Saturday of May. If you really want seats, use the Internet to plan now for 2001, 2002, and beyond!

■ **Whatever your interest,** *it's catered for somewhere on the Net.*

Enjoy yourself on the Internet

Are we having fun yet? That question is not just an expression of boredom – it reflects a deep need for fun that leads people to many different diversions. There's summer fun and winter fun, family fun and singles fun, sports to see and sports to do, music, beaches, and so on.

The Internet not only helps in the search for things to do and fun places to go, but, as we've already pointed out, the Internet itself is fun.

ART AND CULTURE

An Internet auction recently gave web surfers the chance to bid on a very unusual collection – 350 items collected by a major art institution, the Whitney Museum of American Art in New York. Called "American Century: Art and Culture, 1900–2000," the collection included a number of banned books, a vintage issue of High Times, and a 1975 issue of Playgirl. These items had been gathered via the Internet, as the curator of the museum turned to eBay and other auction sites instead of more traditional sources. Maurice Berger of the Whitney commented that using the Internet was "more efficient, and saved on travel costs."

Online crossword puzzles, chess, and chat lines enhance leisure time for many people. In addition to games and contests, there are sites devoted to every hobby and collectible imaginable. You'll find much more about this in Chapter 19, "Special Interests."

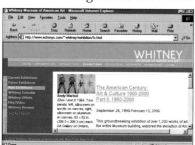

There's no category called fun on the search engines, because our definition of that word is so diverse. But however you define fun, the resources you want are there somewhere.

■ **These museum exhibit** *pages were tracked down via Internet auction sites.*

Government

SOONER OR LATER everybody *needs to contact their government. While stacks of snail mail still pour into the White House, Congress, the Internal Revenue Service, the FBI, and other offices in the U.S., e-mail has become a routine part of office procedure for all government services. Statistics show that the Internet has* increased citizen participation. People are more likely to communicate with their representatives when it takes just a few moments online, rather than requiring the expense and trouble of snail mail or the telephone. Search engines on many government sites can help you locate the agency, individual, form, or address that you need to enable you to contact them.

■ **Congress.org** *gives you information about the government.*

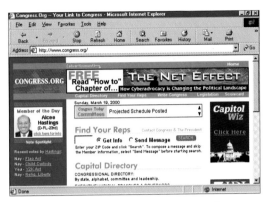

Some state and local governments are beginning to offer electronic government, or interactive web sites where citizens can pay parking tickets, complain about local problems, and access information of all kinds.

Some observers have expressed concerns about discrimination against the non-wired, but cities are finding they save money by using the Internet for a variety of purposes. If you live in a fair-sized city, there's a good chance that this option is available – check with city hall.

Here are some of the best starting points for finding U.S. government information on the web:

✓ Thomas: www.thomas.loc.gov
✓ FedStats: www.fedstats.gov
✓ U.S. Congress: www.congress.org
✓ WWW Virtual Law Library: www.law.indiana.edu/law/v-lib/states.html
✓ Council of State Governments: www.statesnews.org
✓ National Association of Counties: www.naco.org
✓ Official City Sites: www.officialcitysites.org

INTERNET

www.un.org

Your interests may extend beyond the U.S. borders. For information on things global, you can go to the United Nations' web site.

International and non-English

IF ENGLISH *isn't your native language, or if you're searching for sites and information from a specific country or region of the world, there are specialized search tools to meet your needs. More and more web sites are composed in languages other than English, or focus on specific countries or regions.*

Many of the primary search sites we've already talked about, such as AltaVista, Hotbot, Lycos, and Yahoo, offer options that support different languages, and focus on different world regions.

You can also look for practical help on international issues. Let's say you need information on currency exchange rates, but you speak Icelandic.

First, translate the search into your own language, and then access the subject area, such as "Banking," to bring up many currency exchange sites.

The international community is well represented on the Internet, participating in every aspect of online activity from cultural enrichment to shopping.

To find some of these international and multilingual search engines, check out some of the sites below. Remember that many languages use characters your computer may not be equipped to display. Special character sets are available for most languages; using them usually requires a quick download and installation.

- ✓ Euroseek: www.euroseek.com
- ✓ Yupi (Spanish): www.yupi.com
- ✓ Olé (Spanish): www.ole.com
- ✓ Ecila (French): www.ecila.fr
- ✓ Tapuz (Hebrew): www.tapuz.co.il
- ✓ Netfangaskrain (Icelandic): www.netfangaskra.is
- ✓ SearchDesk (Japanese): www.searchdesk.com
- ✓ Ayna (Arabic): www.ayna.com
- ✓ Ariana (Italian): arianna.iol.it
- ✓ Alles Klar (German): www.allesklar.de
- ✓ WhatSite (Chinese): www.whatsite.com
- ✓ Heureka (Hungarian): www.heureka.hu
- ✓ Onet (Polish): www.onet.pl
- ✓ WebIndex (Greek): www.webindex.gr
- ✓ @Rus (Russion): www.atrus.ru

■ **The Internet** *could help you learn Spanish!*

In this chapter, we've introduced a few special areas that may be of interest to you. If you want to keep up with news online, look up businesses and people, use the Internet in the development of your career, or use the "World Wide" part of the web, there are lots of ideas here. We also hope you've been motivated to surf ahead on your own, ferreting out whatever tickles your interest!

■ **Travel sites** *are great for vacation planning.*

A simple summary

✓ Online news services provide up-to-the-minute coverage of breaking news, "commodity" information such as weather, sports scores, and stock market prices, as well as in-depth coverage, especially of Internet-related stories.

✓ Online yellow pages can help you locate businesses, and you don't always have to know names and locations – a little information is often enough.

✓ Cultural and recreational planning can be short-range, such as an evening at the movies, or long-range, such as a trip to a major event planned well in advance.

✓ Finding individuals can be a little tougher, but there are several searchable databases available free on the web.

✓ Career planning, résumé building, and job hunting can be done online. Whatever your field or desired place to work, help is available on the web.

✓ The Internet has proven invaluable for travel planning, offering all the services found at travel agencies and airlines, as well as innovative ways to search for just the right vacation.

✓ Governments, federal, state, and local, are now using the Internet to improve services to citizens, and increase citizen involvement.

✓ Resources for persons from many cultures are available in native languages.

Chapter 14

Downloading and Printing

SUCCESS IN FINDING what you want online naturally increases with experience. Sometimes, you'll want to keep some of the materials you discover. This chapter is a kind of housekeeping, catch-up chapter about downloading – what it is, how to do it, and some things to watch out for. Even if you've already discovered how to download material from the web, we suggest you give this chapter a quick read anyway. You might find some additional ideas. You'll probably find it usually makes sense to save electronic copies of information, rather than printing it out. Generally, you'll find you print only those materials you need to share with other people, especially non-Internet users.

In this chapter...

✓ Which way is up

✓ Downloading

✓ Printing

✓ Downloading software

Which way is up?

WE REALIZE YOU PROBABLY already know this – but, just in case you're not quite sure, we'll answer the question. When you send files from your personal computer to another, usually bigger computer somewhere, you're uploading. This larger computer can then make the files accessible to the Internet.

To be specific, both uploading and downloading actually transfer a copy of an electronic file – the original document also remains in its original location.

Many people think of uploading as sending, and downloading as receiving. While that's certainly the right idea, it needs further explanation. Attaching a file to an e-mail you send is a form of uploading. In this case, your e-mail software functions as a file transfer application, and the file you attach is actually uploaded, right along with the e-mail message, to your ISP or online service. From there, it goes to the address you specified in the e-mail message. This is still a one-to-one transmission – the file you've attached is meant only for the e-mail destination you specify, and will be accessible only to that addressee. After the transmission is complete, the attached file is not online in a form available to anyone else.

■ **Have fun** *attaching a file to an e-mail.*

Another type of uploading involves transferring files to an Internet server. Once on the server, the files are accessible to others, in some cases to anyone online, and in other cases only to users with the proper ID and password access.

Those files will remain available until they're deliberately removed, or until the server is completely disconnected from the network.

■ **Craft designs** *and sewing patterns can be downloaded.*

A LITTLE REVIEW

Back in Chapter 6, when we talked about e-mail, we took a fairly detailed look at attachments. By now, maybe, you've become familiar with sending e-mail attachments. (If you haven't, you might want to quickly review Chapter 6.) As you recall, the simplest way to attach a file to an e-mail message is to click on Message on your e-mail toolbar, then click on Attach File, and then fill in the exact name of the file you want to attach. When you click on Send to start the message on its way, the file goes right along with it. We also talked about programs that compress files, making them smaller and easier to transfer. Some materials you download from the web may be sent to you compressed; you'll need to decompress them before you can use them on your own computer. When you're uploading or sending someone large amounts of data, or large files, compressing the files (with a compression tool like WinZip) will help your files travel more easily and rapidly across the Internet to their destination.

Your own web site

If you followed the steps outlined in Chapters 9 and 10 and created your own web site, you probably had to upload the site you designed and created to a host server, possibly at your ISP. You also probably had to find out how to make revisions and updates to your site, and to upload your new and improved version. But even if you don't have your own web site, it's still important and useful to learn how to upload data.

If your web site is really active and dynamic, you may be uploading new material frequently. For instance, writers who see the web as a primary avenue for publication are usually eager to post their latest poem or article for their online audience. Some web site publishers like to talk back to their visitors, describing the latest revisions and additions, and sharing the experiences that led to those changes. You can do this with e-mail, a message board or chat line, or even as an integral part of the web site.

This kind of regular, back-and-forth communication helps give your site an informal, personal, almost intimate, tone.

You can send almost any kind of file as an attachment to an e-mail message, including pictures and audio messages. There are some family-oriented web sites to which you can upload pictures and messages, making them available to family members for as long as you want to leave them there. For example, sites like www.superfamily.com, www.ecircles.com, and www.myfamily.com provide easy-to-use mechanisms that let you build a family photograph album – right online.

Browsers

Both Netscape Navigator and Microsoft Explorer provide versatile uploading and downloading capabilities. These may well be all you ever need. For more heavy-duty downloading and uploading, you'll use a utility called an FTP client. We'll describe FTP (File Transfer Protocol) below.

Downloading

■ **Store a small** *download on a floppy disk.*

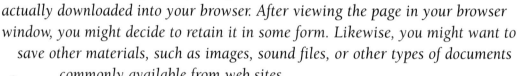

GENERALLY, THE TERM downloading means the transmission of data (files or applications) from some kind of server on the Internet to your own computer system. Every time you click on a URL, the web page you've asked to see (including its HTML, plus any images and other content), is actually downloaded into your browser. After viewing the page in your browser window, you might decide to retain it in some form. Likewise, you might want to save other materials, such as images, sound files, or other types of documents commonly available from web sites.

You can store the information, images and other data you download on your computer's hard drive, or on external storage media, such as a diskette. Or, you can print out a hard copy.

Downloading software

In addition to data files, you can also download software. We've mentioned freeware and shareware, software that's available in numerous locations on the web. Before you can try out a shareware or freeware program. you must download it from the web. You

can also purchase and then download many commercial software products, right from their designers' web sites. Many people first learn about downloading this way, when they go to acquire new shareware, freeware, or commercial software products. They soon realize they can use their newfound knowledge to download many other kinds of interesting things from the web.

■ **You have to** *download shareware before you can try it out.*

Whenever you're going to download something, we suggest following some of the basic "best practices" we've already discussed. These guidelines, as you recall, include being careful about beta or evaluation software, as well as not being too quick to devote storage space to anything you're not going to use.

Keep an eye on your storage space, and delete or remove things you no longer want.

FTP

■ **When you start** *to download, a dialog box will ask if you want to run the program directly or save it to disk.*

Remember when we talked about Internet protocols back in Chapter 3? File Transfer Protocol is yet another protocol, created just for the purpose of expediting file transfers from one computer to another over the Internet. After e-mail, FTP is usually the simplest way to transfer files between computers on the Internet. FTP is a powerful, flexible tool for transporting and managing all kinds of files.

The two major browsers have FTP capabilities built right in. You can usually tell when your browser's FTP capacity is being used. In Internet Explorer, a dialog box opens up, saying, "You have chosen to download a file, what would you like to do with this file?" If you choose "Save this program to disk," the browser will begin to download the file, using its built-in FTP. With the Netscape Navigator browser, you'll get a similar dialog, saying "You have started to download a file of type..." If you select "Save File," the FTP process begins.

If you're uploading your own web site files to your ISP, you may be able to use an FTP interface supplied by your online service.

There are also several FTP clients available that are handy for both uploading and downloading. Like many other types of software, each FTP client has its own interface, command names, and quirks. All of them, though, perform basically similar operations, sending and getting files. Some of the more popular FTP tools include WS_FTP from Ipswitch Software, CuteFTP from GlobalScape, FTP Voyager from Deerfield, BulletProof FTP from Bullet Proof Software, and Fetch, a Mac client from Dartmouth University.

FTP sites are online libraries and repositories that exist only to store and distribute files. FTP sites usually support shareware and freeware, long files such as dissertations, technical reports, and archives. FTP files can be shared by all kinds of computers – you simply enter the appropriate information about your operating platform at the FTP interface.

To access and download any file with FTP, you must know the name of the file you want, and its location. Usually, the reference that points you to a particular piece of software, or an online article you'd like to obtain, also includes the directory and host computer where it can be found. Once you have the file's location, your online service's FTP utility will download the file for you.

Logging in at an FTP site

If you're using an FTP program on your home computer, you'll need to log in at the FTP site. You can do this by using anonymous as your login name, and your e-mail address as the password. There's nothing sneaky or unusual about this arrangement. The "anonymous" option facilitates public access to FTP sites, and many users do this as a matter of course.

Once you log on, you'll see directories of the files available at that site. When you locate the file you want, and specify the location on your own computer where you want it to go, downloading is quick and easy.

FTP servers offer standard hierarchical folder menus and navigational systems. They're a bit arcane compared to web sites, but easy to use once you get the hang of it. Many have user-friendly welcome messages or README files at their entry points. ("user friendly" is a stretch – the U.S. Census Bureau FTP server greets visitors with this: "You have accessed a United States Government Computer. Mischievous/improper use of this computer is a violation of Federal law and can be punished with fines or imprisonment." Yikes!)

FTP server folders

Archives of information for public access are often located in FTP server folders called "Pub." There are lots of FTP sites, offering a myriad of shareware, documents, and other information. You can access some through "http" addresses, while others require that you use the "ftp" protocol. For example, here are the URLs for several publicly-accessible FTP servers. You can access these either through a web browser or an FTP client.

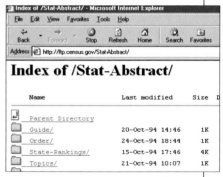

■ **Once you get** *the hang of them, folder menus on FTP servers are simple to use.*

✓The Oak Software Repository: ftp://oak.oakland.edu
✓UNC MetaLab: ftp://sunsite.unc.edu
✓Electronic Frontier Foundation: ftp://ftp.eff.org
✓National Technical Information Service: ftp://ftp.fedworld.com
✓U.S. Census Bureau: ftp://ftp.census.gov
✓CD Connection: ftp://ftp.cdconnection.com
✓Internet Chess Club: ftp://ftp.freechess.org

We offer two important cautions for using FTP sites. First, FTP sites are often heavily used by many people doing serious work, especially during normal business hours.

Therefore, it's best to conduct your FTP sessions in the off-hours. Secondly, when downloading software or unknown files, whatever their source, always take prudent precautions against viruses.

Some FTP sites are restricted and don't allow public access through the user name "anonymous." If you know that a file you want is available only on such a site, check with the site administrator to find if you qualify for access permission.

Downloading web pages

Downloading web pages for viewing in your browser is an active process. Whether you're surfing or searching, it's likely that you'll download one web site after another, not lingering long at any one site. If you regularly find certain sites useful, it's easy to bookmark them so you can easily return. Depending on how you use the Internet, there may or may not be times when you feel the need to save something from the web and store it in a file.

■ **A bookmark quickly** *returns you to a favorite site.*

Whatever you save from the web, and however you plan to use the materials, organization is very important. You can store a saved web page in a wide variety of places, just like any other type of file. But you should use care and logic in the decisions you make when selecting locations for your files. A logical, organized system will help you find the files you need, when you need them.

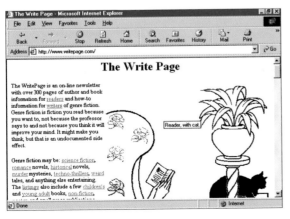

And you'll find that your day-to-day work will be much easier if you store all your files, whatever their source, in some kind of logical association with related files.

■ **The Write Page** *is a favorite of many creative writers.*

Saving a web page as a file is really just like storing an e-mail attachment. Click on File and Save As, enter your Save In location, click, and you're done. If a file transfer is ever interrupted for any reason, you may have to start at the beginning when you try again. This isn't always true, though – sometimes, you can begin right where you left off. Check to see if the file name appears at the location you specified. If not, you know you have to start over. You can also save a web page to your local system by selecting File, Print, and Print to File.

There are lots of advantages to saving a web page to your own computer. You can view the page later without going online, and you can study the page code to see how web page coding works. The disadvantages? Your saved version won't reflect any changes that may be made to the online page. And if you save only a copy of the HTML page, but not all the image files that go with it, you may see only text with "broken images" when you view your saved version of the page.

■ **If online** *browsing ties you in knots, try one of the offline browsers.*

Offline browsers

If you find you want to save copies of web sites for local viewing, an "offline browser" may prove helpful. There are several dozen offline browser products available, including ForeFront's WebWhacker, Web Buddy from DataViz, NetAttache from Tympani, and WebSnake from InterMark. Offline browsers can be tremendously helpful if you need to spend a lot of time at a particular web site but your web service is slow or the site is bogged down by heavy traffic. Good offline browsers let you check occasionally to see if the site has been updated, and will grab new content to update your local copy of the page.

Copying files from a web site to your local computer is generally OK if your purpose is purely your own personal use of that content. To avoid violating copyright law, never republish, copy, or distribute the material without checking with the site owners, or making sure the information is 100% free of any copyright protections.

■ **Saving a web page** *as a file is much like storing an email attachment.*

Portable media

Many newer computers come with a new type of drive that works like a floppy disk drive, but has enormous storage capacity. Products like Imation's SuperDisc and Iomega's Zip and Jaz drives give you the ability to store huge quantities of data without filling up your hard drive. You can get both external (standalone) and internal (installed right inside your computer's main cabinet) versions of these storage devices. The disks they use are more expensive than floppy disks, but hold vastly more data, and are small, light, and easily portable.

You can download a file to a high-capacity storage system drive in exactly the same way you download a file to your hard drive or to a standard floppy disk drive. But the name of the drive, or its "drive letter," will be different – perhaps "E" or "F."

The storage capacity of these devices is so great that you might find it handy to designate one for a particular use that calls for voluminous files, such as online books, games, music collections, software, or data archives.

Printing

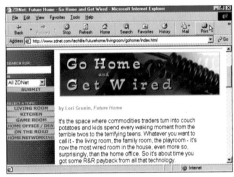

Printing a web *page is a mouse click away.*

AS THE ONLINE COMMUNITY *grows, more and more people are getting in the habit of printing e-mail messages and other material from the Internet to save or share with non-Internet users. You may have found yourself printing out things that just seemed too good to keep to yourself! Jokes, cartoons, fast-breaking news, and e-mail from far-off places are circulating in offices and social groups everywhere. This is great publicity for the Internet – the online folks get the message to those still offline. And the general public is getting used to the appearance of pages printed from the Internet.*

Remember the "paperless office?" The hope that the widespread use of electronic documents, as well as the advent of the Internet, would contribute to the reduction of the use of paper in offices has so far failed to materialize.

In fact, industry experts have noted that the popularity of e-mail has increased the importance of printed documents, as people print out electronic files, preferring to proofread hard copy; and print out e-mail messages to document important business communications.

The paper blizzard

Downloading to hard copy would seem to be a simple operation as long as you have a functioning printer. However, web pages often contain images, background patterns, and odd formats, lengths, and sizes that can make printing them out a bit dicey.

Hard copy or hard drive?

You might want to consider whether hard copy is really the best medium, or whether saving files to your hard drive or to floppy disks might not be more efficient. Also, if your objective is collaborative work for which people need to have access to the same documents, it's probably more efficient to share the materials on floppy disks or through e-mail. That way, if the material is edited or altered, the changes can be easily made on a computer file. And at some point, the changes made on hard copy will need to be coordinated and input on the computer anyway.

However, you'll surely encounter many occasions that do call for hard copies of such materials as recipes, coupons, owner's manuals, maps with step-by-step driving directions, hotel and travel reservations, and medical information. Here are a few hints to make printing easier.

■ **MapBlast** *offers printer-friendly versions of its maps.*

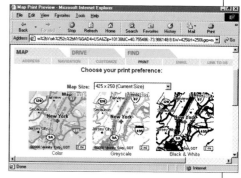

Printing

Color printers have become much less expensive for home use. If you expect to print out many web pages, color may help, not only to make the hard copies easier to read, but in capturing the look and feel of what you saw on the screen. Some web sites offer "printer-friendly" or "text-only" options to make it easier to send articles or other information to your printer. For example, at the Boston Globe's site (www.boston.com), there's an "Easy-print version" link at the foot of each article. Clicking it will bring up a simplified version of the story that's tailored for printing. MapBlast (www.mapblast.com) offers three choices for printer-friendly maps: color, gray-scale, and black and white.

You'll also see a few interesting variations on this idea, such as sites that let you click a button to e-mail a story to a friend, or to automatically fax it somewhere.

When you print a document from a web browser, take a look at the Page Setup command before you print. You can request that the printed page include the URL, date, and page title – useful bits of information to retain for yourself and anyone else who may see the printout. Page Setup also lets you eliminate the printing of web page backgrounds. This is useful when a busy background pattern makes the text hard to read when the page is printed. Your browser preferences also let you choose the font faces and sizes you want. Choose options that make the pages you print more readable. If you're trying to capture text from a web page but find printing is difficult, you can always copy and paste the text from the screen right into an ordinary word processing document, or even into a simple text editor file.

Always check where pages break; important lines of text sometimes get lost where page breaks fall.

Some web sites include formatted materials intended specifically to be printed. Many of these use a formatting technology called "Acrobat." The names of Acrobat files end with the extension "pdf," which stands for portable document format. To read Acrobat files, you need to download and install the free Acrobat reader. We recommend getting it the first time you encounter an Acrobat file. (Go to www.adobe.com, and follow the link to "Get free Acrobat reader.") We used Acrobat files when one of us needed a United States Passport Application. We found that the application form is published as a pdf file at the State Department's web site (www.state.gov).

Some cautions

Beware: Some files are incriminating. For instance, possessing child pornography is a felony. The FBI has been known to conduct sting operations on the Internet, trapping people who visit child pornography sites. Some files are valuable to someone else, and if you have no legitimate reason to download them, you could be accused of theft. If you're a worker using your employer's computer, or a student using a university computer, some files come from sites that you should not be visiting.

Downloading to a printer might seem like a risk-free way to keep something you found on the Internet. But it's seldom possible to keep those acts secret. Some files, especially pirated software, are often stolen property.

We mention these words of caution just to make you aware of the hazards – we believe it's very unlikely you would ever be affected by them. Again, always remember that the same courtesy, ethical conduct, and legal standards that apply elsewhere also apply on the Internet.

Downloading software

BACK IN CHAPTER 5, *we advised a conservative approach in downloading new software, and gave basic instructions about how to do it. In almost every intervening chapter, we've noted new software developments in each of the online activities we've described. New versions of established software, plus a dizzying array of completely new concepts, are constantly arriving on the Internet scene. We've tried not to throw too many new names at you. But we do want to let you in on some of the exciting new options we know of.*

Any new software tends to go through predictable stages of development. First, it is released as beta programs, usually by the developers, and is made available directly from the manufacturer's web site. After a trial period, the new software is released to the general public. By that time, similar or related software will generally emerge from some other developers, under different names. It may be a while before some of the more cutting edge applications become available as shareware through the online software libraries.

Virus protection

Virus protection software is one area where newer is virtually always better. We searched at an online software library (www.tucows.com) for anti-virus protection, or virus scanning software. The current listing for Windows 95 showed four possibilities: F-Secure, McAfee ViruScan, Norton Antivirus, and AVG Anti-Virus Guard.

But we can reliably assume that these versions of the applications don't protect against the latest virus we just heard about in the news, and that developers are hard at work developing updated forms of protection.

It's always a prudent practice to scan all files for viruses, before downloading them. It's especially vital when a file you're considering is a software program. It's also a good idea to periodically obtain the latest updates for the virus scanning application you use. If, at any time, you have reason to believe a virus has infected your computer, make careful notes about the symptoms and then shut down your system. There may be a cure; in any case, careful record keeping of what you downloaded when, from where, and what happened, will help you and others.

Please don't get spooked by all the talk about bugs and viruses. We actually don't know anyone who has ever lost anything major to a computer virus.

■ **Anti-virus programs** *should be used to scan downloaded programs.*

As quickly as new programs spring to life in the competitive atmosphere of the Internet, antidotes for the latest viruses also arrive. Be cautious, but don't get bogged down in the old for fear of the new.

Old dogs, new tricks

If you decide to download a major piece of new software, such as a different browser or e-mail program, give yourself plenty of time to learn how to use it. That learning will go much quicker than the initial learning when you were still a newcomer to the Internet, but it will still take time and practice.

If you decide to go for broadband (cable access) or DSL (Digital Subscriber Line), instead of a dial-up connection, be prepared to learn some very new tricks. Broadband-equipped software shoppers can try before they buy, using large programs and moving huge amounts of data very quickly. Broadband and DSL connections make easy, rapid downloading of the growing volumes of free digital content much more feasible, because they speed up information transfer so greatly. Look for much more about these issues in Chapter 15, "Multimedia."

A simple summary

✓ Uploading is like sending, and downloading is like receiving.

✓ Attaching a file to an e-mail message is a form of uploading.

✓ If you've created your own web pages upload that material to an ISP or other online host.

✓ Downloading material from the Internet is usually accomplished through FTP which can be done automatically by browsers.

✓ Anyone can download files from most FTP sites by entering the login "anonymous" and their own e-mail address as a password.

✓ Files can be downloaded to any location you specify within your own computer system's directory and file organization system.

✓ There are now new types of high-capacity portable storage media which work like floppy drives but can store massive amounts of data. New computers may have these systems built in.

✓ Downloading to printers is also an option, but hard copy can't be altered.

✓ Downloading Software carries risks. Anti-virus or file scanning programs should be used before downloading.

✓ Always look for the very latest virus protection.

✓ Exciting and powerful new software is constantly being developed. If you have, or decide to get, broadband or DSL, your possibilities are greatly enhanced.

Chapter 15

Multimedia

I<small>N THE WORLD</small> of computers and the Internet, "multimedia" refers to digital content, and to applications that combine different media, like text, pictures, audio, and video.

In this chapter...

✓ What is multimedia on the web?

✓ Download speed

✓ Multimedia players and formats

✓ Players

✓ MP3

✓ CDs and DVDs

✓ Convergence Finding multimedia

THE MILLENNIUM'S SOUNDS AND IMAGES ARE CAPTURED IN MULTIMEDIA

What is multimedia on the web?

■ **A multitude** *of umbrellas open in an international multimedia event.*

IN ITS EARLIEST DAYS, the Internet and the web offered text, but little else. New technologies led to the ability to transfer interactive software applications, pictures, animations, 2-D and 3-D environments, audio, and video. Many web sites now integrate many or all of these elements. These advances in technology, and the production of multimedia content, represent an explosive area of innovation and competition in the Internet realm.

On October 19, 1991 at sunrise, huge umbrellas were opened simultaneously in Japan and California, in the presence of artists Christo and Jeanne-Claude. In Japan there were 1340 blue umbrellas, and in California 1760 yellow umbrellas. They covered mountainsides in a random, whimsical pattern, like immense flowers blooming on the landscape. This was one in a series of artistic events conceived by the artists in which the earth itself became part of a multi-media artwork.

The problems with multimedia content on the web have always been that the content tends to take a long time to download, and that it often plays back poorly on the end user's computer.

The desire to overcome these technical barriers continues to spur intensive innovation. Read on, and we'll walk you through the various kinds of multimedia content you can find on the Internet, and how to get at it and use it.

Consider this

Many new Internet users avoid multimedia because of the slow-download problem, or because they say they don't care for "bells and whistles." If you feel this way, we won't take issue with you. However, some of us may have once felt a similar resistance to going online, and now we can hardly remember that time. Consider the current trend towards using multimedia resources in education.

Schools are usually conservative in adapting new technology. Now, they're starting to see technology-enhanced education as the wave of the future.

The benefits of new media

Traditionally, the audio-visual departments of schools, universities, and libraries gathered educational materials in the form of filmstrips, films, slide shows, audiotapes, and later, cassettes, CDs, and videos for use by teachers. Most of these media are still widely used in classrooms, and most school systems have a considerable investment in equipment for showing movies and playing audiotapes and videotapes. However, school budgets have increasingly reflected a reallocation of funds toward computers and Internet access, as teachers and administrators learn to harness the value and benefits of these new media. Billions of public and private dollars have been contributed to this redirection of technology in schools and libraries. You may find yourself following the schools' example, as your computer, and its connection to the world of cyberspace, becomes increasingly able to provide much of the information you used to get from other media.

If you're strictly a word person, with no great interest in audio and visual media, this chapter may not seem relevant. But even if your first thought is that you're doing fine without it, and you don't think you need access to multimedia content on the web, we strongly suggest that you read

■ **The Internet already** *gives you access to radio stations, webcasts and movies. The future will bring better systems for delivering such multimedia.*

on. We used to feel the same way, but we've gradually discovered the potential of this new universe. We've discovered the life-enhancing benefits of instant access to music archives and international radio stations; live "webcast" events with authors and health experts; footage from films, television, news, and sports; multimedia creations by digital artists; and online games and amusements. Even if you decide not to partake of multimedia content for now, remember that the future will certainly bring more and better systems to cure the slow-download problem, and make multimedia a routine part of Internet use for anyone who ventures online.

Eventually, you'll want to take the plunge. Think of this chapter as preparation for the future.

Download speed

NEWCOMERS TO THE ONLINE COMMUNITY *often marvel at the power of the modem to bring the web to their home computer. But after a while, we become aware of certain limitations, and begin to ask questions like: Why do web pages load so slowly?*

By experience, you learn that pages with large graphic images take a long time to load – and audio and video content dribbles in even more slowly.

This situation presents Internet users and publishers with a dilemma – one that technologists are striving mightily to eliminate. Enhancing a web page with rich content can provide a more desirable online experience, but the user has to wait longer for the page to download – so, that marvelous rich content can lead to frustration and inconvenience. In contrast, a plain-jane web page, without colorful graphics or audio or video enhancement, loads in a snap – but it might be boring, or less effective and interesting than it could be. Creative web publishers have developed many effective strategies for constructing attractive, well-designed pages that download quickly.

But no matter how clever the designers and HTML authors may be, when a site distributes multimedia content, the problem of slow downloading rears its ugly head.

Bandwidth and hardware

Therefore, before we tell you what kind of multimedia content is available on the web, where to find it, and how to experience it, we need to spend a few moments on the subjects of bandwidth and modem hardware.

Bandwidth is a measure of the frequency-response characteristics of a communications receiving system. It's directly proportional to the number of bytes required for data to be transmitted or received per unit of time, and is measured in bits per second.

It takes more bandwidth to download a picture than a snippet of text, and even more for audio-visual materials. Therefore, if you use a 56K modem, it may take what seems like a very long time to download multimedia material. In addition, download speed is affected not only by your own modem, but also by the capacity of the server from which the content is coming; the amount of traffic hitting at the same time; and by potential "latency" points on the Internet route between the server and your computer.

56K modems

Your modem's *lights may flicker during the download process.*

People who use the web primarily to view text, and who seldom attempt to download audio or video files, may feel perfectly content with a 56K modem. However, if your current modem is slower than 56K (such as 28.8 or 14.4), we recommend upgrading to 56K to avoid the problem one wag called the "World Wide Wait." If you really can't upgrade to 56K, we suggest that, for the most part, you forego multimedia content such as audio and video; it just isn't practical. One exception you might try is what's called "streaming media." We'll tell you more about that in a bit.

If you regularly request multimedia content from the Internet, the limitations of a 56K modem are likely to cause some frustration. Broadband Internet service is one answer that goes a long way towards eliminating the problem. However, at the time of this writing, 56K is the fastest available service for a large number of people, from the standpoint of availability and price. Fortunately, there's quite a bit of multimedia content you can enjoy fairly well at 56K – with a bit of patience.

The depth and variety of multimedia offerings on the Internet are increasing daily, and we believe most members of the online community (that includes you!) will find their lives enriched by taking advantage of some of these opportunities.

Broadband Internet service

Broadband access is available for home users mainly through cable service, and the Digital Subscriber Line (DSL). The monthly cost for broadband service varies, but is generally higher that the cost for a dial-up ISP. This also varies greatly, though, and the cost may well decrease as the pool of broadband users grows. You might also have to pay an installation fee, and buy a special new type of modem. Broadband service provides high-speed access, and is "always on" – that is, you don't need to dial up to log on to the Internet. As long as your computer is turned on, it's connected to the Internet. Download speeds with Broadband service can be hundreds of times faster than with a traditional analog modem.

Internet access via cable uses the same type of coaxial wiring that carries cable television signals. To use cable Internet service, you need a cable modem, which can be obtained from a cable ISP, such as Roadrunner or @Home. (By the way, even if you don't have cable television service, you can still get Broadband Internet service.)

Broadband Internet *services promise much greater speed.*

Digital subscriber line

DSL service requires a DSL modem, usually sold or leased by the telephone company, or by the Internet access service providing the DSL. DSL uses the existing copper wires that provide your voice telephone service, and allows a single line to provide both high-speed Internet service and regular voice telephone service. Many people who purchase DSL service are able to slightly offset the extra cost by canceling second phone lines they'd been using for Internet dial-up service. To use DSL, you must be close enough to the telephone center providing the service. However, the special telecommunications lines necessary for DSL are spreading rapidly, as telephone companies scramble to stay ahead of cable providers in answering the growing demand for high-speed Internet access.

It's best not to buy a DSL or cable modem until you've talked with your broadband service provider, just to make sure the equipment you're considering is compatible with their systems, as well as with your computer.

■ **More bandwidth** *means quicker downloads.*

Other contenders

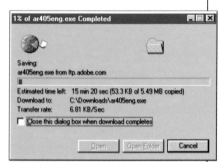

While cable and DSL are the two main competitors in the broadband arena, there are several other contenders. These include high-speed Internet service via satellite and wireless systems, Integrated Services Digital Network (ISDN), digital television (DTV), and T-carrier (T-1) lines. Most of these are either too new or too expensive to be viable options for private home users. However, there may be some areas where one of these options can be considered.

Broadband service is either "two-way" or "one-way." If you're shopping for broadband service, knowing this difference is very important, so be sure to find out!

Two-way broadband technologies let you send and receive information at high speeds over the same medium. One-way systems let you receive digital information at high speed, but rely on some other means (usually an old-fashioned modem, connected through a telephone line) for sending data. With a one-way broadband system, for example, you could enjoy rich media content like video with no problem, but you might be required to dial up your ISP through a modem to send an e-mail message. A person we know in a large city in the Midwest currently has one-way broadband service through his cable company. His costs include two phone lines, cable service, and two modems. But the speed at which he's able to send or upload anything is still 56K! Two-way service would clearly be a preferable option.

Greater bandwidth makes the downloading of multimedia faster, and much more feasible. The thirty minutes required to download a movie with a 56K modem, for instance, might be reduced to two or three minutes with broadband service. High-speed delivery also reduces the likelihood of interruptions occurring during the transmission, and can reduce the herky-jerky quality of audio and video transmitted through the web.

Multimedia players and formats

■ **Plug-in software** is *needed to play multimedia content from the web.*

TO EXPERIENCE *most types of multimedia content delivered over the web, you need to install special multimedia software. Often, the software products you need are free browser plug-ins. These products are called "players," because they play an audio or video file, much like a CD player, tape player, or (for those who remember) a record player. These players often have user interfaces inspired by physical audio and video equipment, with clickable graphics representing buttons for functions like fast forward, reverse, pause, mute, and play; and slider controls for volume and various playback levels. After you install such a player, you can generally configure it to launch automatically when you click or download the file types it plays.*

As with other software, these players usually offer a variety of preferences and display settings you can customize to your liking.

A few formats allow multimedia content to be played directly by your browser, or right in the browser window, without requiring a plug-in or separate player. These multimedia formats may use Java, a powerful programming language used to create applets. (Applets are Java programs embedded into web pages.) There are also a few proprietary technologies for delivering streaming media into your browser without plug-ins. For example, the Emblaze system, from Geo Interactive, activates a player right in your browser window. It plays audio, video, and sound synchronized with a series of slides.

The multimedia you're most likely to encounter on the web include audio, video, animation, and interactive content. You may run across others, such as virtual reality environments, as well. When you encounter a multimedia file, but don't have the software required to play it, your browser will usually display a message telling you that you need a plug-in, along with a link to a source for downloading it.

If you download the plug-in and follow the installation instructions, you should be able to go back to the file and play it. (Sometimes, you have to shut down and restart your browser or computer first.)

You'll then be able to play similar files anytime you encounter them, although you may occasionally have to upgrade the plug-in as newer versions, with enhanced functions, are released. You can also download many multimedia players independently of the browser, and experience rich media content without even having your browser open.

There are dozens of formats and software products for web multimedia. Some of the leading applications (audio and video) include:

✓ QuickTime from Apple
✓ RealPlayer from Real Networks
✓ Microsoft Windows Media Player
✓ Flash and Shockwave from Macromedia

There are many others as well, but these are the formats you're most likely to encounter.

■ **Netscape.com** *keeps a list of the multimedia plug-ins that work with Netscape Navigator.*

Use the Internet with confidence

In a moment, we'll take a tour of several multimedia players, but keep in mind that this is one of the fastest-growing areas on the Internet. Innovations appear rapidly. Old competitors merge, and new developers enter the fray. Many of the specific items covered in this chapter are sure to become outdated as technology evolves. Our point in reviewing these products is much like our underlying approach to this whole book. We want to provide basic understanding and knowledge that will put you in the driver's seat, so you can use the Internet with confidence and self-sufficiency, even as technologies change and develop.

Streaming versus "Download now and play later"

When multimedia files were first distributed via the web, you had to download a file in its entirety, decompress it (if it was delivered in "zipped," or archive, form), and then play it back with audio or video presentation software. This way, even though there might be a long wait to obtain the file, once you had it downloaded, playing it back on your own system wasn't affected by bandwidth constraints.

INTERNET

home.netscape. com/plugins

On this web page, Netscape maintains an excellent list of plug-ins for audio and video, as well as many other types of plug-ins.

In fact, you could play it back while disconnected from the Internet, and play it again anytime you wanted.

The down side of this process sounds familiar – downloading could take a very long time, and with long downloads, there's always a chance a glitch will cause the connection to drop, or the file to become corrupted, ruining the download. The quality of the multimedia, especially video, was often unsatisfactory. Often, you had to play downloaded videos in tiny little windows on your screen. And they tended to be low-quality, and very short. As HTML evolved and became more sophisticated, clever web authors learned to make short sound clips play automatically when pages were loaded, a practice still used on some web sites. Some users find this practice cute, while others find it annoying. One example is the New York Yankees home page (www.yankees.com), where visitors are greeted by the voice of Yankee Stadium's public-address announcer, Bob Sheppard.

■ **Hear the stadium's** *announcer, Bob Sheppard, on the Yankees' web site!*

Around 1995, a powerful new alternative for distributing and receiving multimedia content emerged and was quickly adopted by thousands of sites.

The process is called streaming media, a technique for transferring data as a continuous stream. In streaming, the plug-in begins playing or displaying the data before the entire file has been transmitted. Streaming media servers send packets of compressed content that are collected in a buffer. As the buffer fills, the software begins decompressing and playing the content, even as more content streams into the buffer.

■ **For many,** *"getting up and changing channels" is a distant memory.*

■ **The ".mov" format** *is for digital video.*

Streaming broadcasts of radio programming, and of long, extended music sets have become a popular part of web surfing for millions, including those on "slow" modems. However, streaming media files are not saved on your local drive, so to enjoy streaming content, you must remain connected to the Internet. And after you disconnect from a streaming media session, the audio or video isn't usually saved locally; therefore, you can't play it back later. Some of the leading streaming media software products, such as the RealPlayer, can play either streaming or downloaded files. Some web sites that distribute RealPlayer files give you the choice of either streaming or downloading the content.

Multimedia file types

■ **Musical Instrument Digital Interface (MIDI)** *was a common audio format for early Internet users.*

Several technologies have been commonly used for encryption and distribution of audio and video via the Internet. The formats used in the early days allowed for transmission of recorded sound and moving images, but each had drawbacks that limited large-scale use. As streaming formats and various proprietary tools, such as RealMedia and Shockwave, achieved better quality and allowed for greater accessibility via modems, audio and video distribution exploded.

Today, the MP3 format is the rage in digital audio. It's causing an uproar among copyright owners and the music industry, because of its high quality and the ease with which users can copy and distribute recordings. We'll talk more about MP3 shortly.

Several file types for audio and video were familiar to early Internet users. Common audio formats included Musical Instrument Digital Interface (.mid), Wave Form files (.wav), Sun Audio (.au), and Audio Interleaf File Format (.aif). These are still in use on many web sites. If you use your computer's microphone to record your own voice, chances are that the audio file you create will be a Wave file. Some of the familiar formats for digital video include QuickTime (.mov or .qt), Audio Video Interlaced (.avi), and RealMedia (.rm, .ra. or .ram). Several other formats are also used; wherever you come across them online, you'll usually find links to get whatever player you need.

Another important technology for multimedia encoding comes from an organization called the Motion Picture Experts Group. Their acronym, MPEG, is identified with a series of formats such as MPEG-1, MPEG-2, and MPEG-3 (commonly known as MP3). MPEG files usually have extensions such as ."mpeg" or ."mpg".

Players

EARLIER, WE MENTIONED *a list of multimedia players you may need in order to enjoy audio, video, and other rich media. Here's a quick tour of several leading applications.*

■ **With QuickTime** *software, you can watch movies on your computer.*

QuickTime from Apple

QuickTime comes from the Apple Computer Company, but is by no means limited to the Macintosh Operating System. In fact, QuickTime has become one of the dominant technologies across all platforms for multimedia content. Millions of users have installed the QuickTime player, and a large percentage of leading web sites use QuickTime.

You can download the player free from www.quicktime.com, and install it easily for use with either or both of the major browsers. In addition to playing high-quality multimedia content (it will play most audio and video file types), the interface offers several useful controls, such as time displays, bookmarks, and a "favorites" list.

When it launches, QuickTime sometimes functions externally to the web browser; it also may be displayed inline, within the web page shown in the browser window.

QuickTime also offers several powerful technologies for enhanced interactive multimedia. One example is called QuickTime VR. QuickTime VR (Virtual Reality) creates a 3-D effect, allowing you to change the perspective of an image with

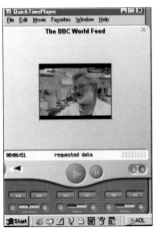

your mouse. For example, it can enable you to enjoy a complete 360-degree, panoramic view of an outdoor location, or a building interior. QuickTime movies can include embedded "hot spots," activated by mouse clicks; allow zooming in and out within images or 3-D environments; and incorporate interactivity, such as games. The QuickTime site points to showcase sites using QuickTime for a host of multimedia content. A survey of these sites will quickly convince most users that online multimedia offers features that "couch potato" television just can't match.

■ **With the QuickTimePlayer** *you can receive live feeds from news programs such as BBC World.*

Real Player from Real Networks

The RealPlayer was originally called RealAudio. RealAudio served as a major catalyst in the widespread development of streaming media. You can get RealPlayer software free at www.real.com.

Don't be confused by the heavy promotion of the commercial RealPlayer product on their web site. If you like the enhancements, you can choose to pay the fee for the commercial version, but try the free RealPlayer first. Look carefully — the free product really is there!

Like QuickTime, RealPlayer works with both Netscape Navigator and Internet Explorer, and should cause no trouble for AOL users. Also like QuickTime, RealPlayer can play either downloaded files or streaming media. RealPlayer usually launches externally from the browser, but sometimes launches as part of the web page, within the browser window. The RealPlayer, which plays both audio and video content, offers several user preferences and options that are worth exploring.

■ **The future of** *QuickTime could mean the days of your TV are numbered.*

The RealPlayer can play a wide variety of file and media types, though not as many as QuickTime. The manufacturer, RealNetworks, continually improves the product's ability to support high-quality transmission of both audio and video, under limited bandwidth conditions. Right now, there are probably more sites using RealPlayer than any other streaming multimedia format. RealPlayer includes a useful ability to bookmark streaming media sites you find online. The RealGuide, at www.realguide.com, provides a huge listing of such sites.

Microsoft Windows Media Player

Microsoft's streaming media player is a powerful addition to the array of tools available for Internet multimedia. You can download Microsoft Windows Media Player free from Microsoft's web site. Like other players we mention, it plays multiple audio and video file formats, including Windows Media Format files, AVI, QuickTime, MP3, MIDI, Wave, and many others. This player also provides a range of controls, bookmarking features, and links to outlets like online radio stations.

■ **The RealGuide** *offers listings of many online streaming media sites.*

In our experience, this player does a good job at maintaining the integrity of video resolution, even when you play a video at full screen size. Other players are improving in this, but the Microsoft player is the best we've seen so far.

Flash and Shockwave

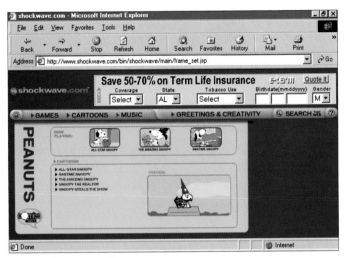

In the 1980s, a software application called Macromind Director became a leading authoring tool for multimedia content for distribution on Compact Disc (CD). In 1992, the company changed its name to Macromedia, and continued producing ever-better versions of Director, as well as several other software applications favored by top multimedia professionals. In 1995, Macromedia released Shockwave, a system

■ **Shockwave** *can be seen on the Macromedia web site, shockwave.com.*

for turning Director movies and applications into a format deliverable via the web. Shockwave quickly became, and remains, one of the hottest technologies for interactive, animated, sound-enhanced, live content on the web. Flash is another product from Macromedia; it lets graphic artists create animated, interactive, rich content.

QuickTime and RealPlayer provide channels for digitized versions of pre-existing music and video content. Shockwave and Flash are more geared toward new content, created on computers by digital artists and producers.

Both Flash and Shockwave operate as browser plug-ins, enhancing content within web pages. Once you install these products, they automatically play or display content. At this writing, it's estimated that more than 80 percent of installed web browsers are equipped with the Flash player, and more than 50 percent have Shockwave. Both players are free, and are available from www.macromedia.com. The Macromedia web site also includes links to galleries of Shockwave and Flash content.

Liquid audio's liquid player

Liquid Player is another contender providing multi-format audio support for streaming and local files. Liquid Player also plays back music that's been digitized with the Liquid Audio software. The player is a sleek application geared towards music producers and the music industry; it includes built-in buttons for displaying liner notes, lyrics, credits, and other information. We've found its playback quality excellent. Many music-oriented web sites use Liquid Audio files.

MP3

■ **MP3.com has** *become a major portal for ... MP3.*

WHEN MOVIES ON VIDEOTAPE *first became widely available, there were major battles over copyright ownership, as well as the residual rights of actors, directors, and others involved in the creation of films. These disputes have not yet been settled, as new aspects of the conflict continually crop up. But, for the most part, technology can't be denied, and Hollywood has had to find some accommodation with the videotape industry.*

MP3 has led a similar battle in the music industry. MP3 is a digital music format, offering quality equal to commercial CDs. Files can be delivered as downloads, or in streaming format.

This new technology has produced some fabulous new opportunities for musicians and others to overcome some of the financial and practical barriers to reaching audiences directly, with high-quality, original recordings. But MP3 has also created some major problems with copyright violations.

MP3 software, readily available on the Internet, allows most anyone with a computer to "rip" the contents of a commercial CD right off the disc, and then distribute the contents via the Internet. Unfortunately, this has been done on quite a large scale. The issue is becoming even more critical as portable MP3 players become available. Now, not only can you

■ **Not all** *digital recorded music available online is being distributed legally.*

go online and find free, downloadable, full copies of recordings you'd otherwise have to pay for, but you can also pop that music right into your portable MP3 player and listen while you go jogging.

The Recording Industry of America has undertaken a major initiative, the Secure Digital Music Initiative, to curb the problem of online music piracy. To learn more, visit www.sdmi.org.

We'll disclose our bias on this issue by observing that we wouldn't be happy if someone were to print unauthorized copies of this book and hand them out at the entrances to bookshops. Copying, distributing, and consuming copyrighted material without permission is illegal, and is a form of theft. We urge you not to do it.

On the other hand, MP3 has produced many benefits. These include a new, high-quality digital music format, and an explosion of online opportunities for artists to distribute their material online, thus reaching new audiences. There are now dozens of web sites where you can sample a rich variety of legal, high-quality MP3 music. Here are a few examples:

✓ Change Music: www.changemusic.com
✓ Shoutcast: www.shoutcast.com
✓ EMusic.com: www.emusic.com

MP3 players

There are dozens of MP3 players now available. We looked at several reviews, and then selected a player considered by many experts to be the best: a freeware product called Winamp. Through a dial-up connection and a 56K modem, we downloaded it in about thirty minutes. The program installed quickly and easily, and works very well.

■ **Winamp is** *a player of MP3, the new digital music format.*

INTERNET

www.mp3.com

One of the best-known new companies with a focus on MP3 is MP3.com. Their web site has become a major MP3 portal, where you can get a thorough introduction to the whole subject of Internet multimedia, especially music. There's a large list of MP3 players you can download, as well as many descriptions and product reviews.

In addition to the reviews at MP3.com, you can find reviews of MP3 players (both the software variety, and the portable MP3 devices) at Internet news sites like CNet and ZDNet; any of a multitude of MP3 sites such as MP3now.com, MP3 Nexus (www.bigg.net), and Riffage (www.riffage.com); and multimedia sites such as Scour (www.scour.net), and Vitaminic (www.vitaminic.co.uk).

Searching

There are search engines, such as Lycos MP3 at mp3.lycos.com, tailored specifically for MP3 searches. At these sites, you can enter the name of a song, artist, album, or composer, and get back a list of sites where you can download that music.

We decided to test the efficiency of these sites. We visited one and entered a search for "Mozart," wondering if there'd be any classical music there, or whether we'd find only modern music. The search returned a long list of the works of Mozart, including all our favorites. We were thrilled, but every link we clicked returned an invalid response.

At three other sites (www.musicgrab.com, www.audiofind.com, and www.jugalug.com), we fared much better. In short order, we were listening to beautiful Mozart recordings. We had no idea, however, whether the music had been copied legally.

At many sites that supply music and video, you'll see notes from the site designers, acknowledging that they realize many of us are still operating with 56K modems, and thus can't take complete advantage of all the multimedia opportunities. Some sites offer to provide estimated download times for various files.

CDs and DVDs

MOST COMPUTERS have CD-ROM drives, and more and more now come with DVD drives. CDs remain an important medium for distribution of many types of digital content but DVDs, Digital Versatile Discs, now offer the ability to play full-length feature films on your computer.

Physical storage formats for multimedia, such as CDs and DVDs, enjoy some powerful advantages over Internet distribution. When you load a disc into your computer locally, there's no bandwidth problem. Developers can use large graphics and rich media without worrying about modems or network traffic. The drawbacks of CDs, though, are also compelling. CDs cost money to produce and distribute. Also, after a CD is made, it can't be updated the way information on a web server can.

Physical media and internet distribution

Clever designers have discovered many ways to combine the advantages of physical media like CDs with the power of Internet distribution. For example, many companies who create computer-based games requiring graphically-intense, 3-D environments have developed combinations of local CD content with web content and interaction, allowing gamers to enjoy the benefits of both.

SYNERGY THEN AND NOW

Between 1870 and 1890, the most famous inventors in American history produced world-changing technology. Inventions in those years included the typewriter, telephone, phonograph, hearing aid, Kodak camera, escalator, internal combustion engine, incandescent light bulb, electric dental drill, and the submarine.

Great thinkers such as Thomas Alva Edison and Alexander Graham Bell built on one another's work in a flurry of synthesis and energy (which equals synergy).

A parallel might be drawn with the present time, as the developers of computer and telecommunications technologies spin off one another in the spiral of cooperation-competition that keeps bringing new inventions.

The Digital Versatile Disc (DVD) is bringing dramatic new multimedia capacity to the personal computer. A DVD has approximately twenty-six times the capacity of a CD, and the player hardware, or DVD-ROM drive, will also play CDs. Movie sales outlets still dominated by videocassettes are now seeing DVD sales increasing at a staggering rate. With over 6,000 movie titles now available on DVD, consumer demand is steadily increasing; predictions indicate an imminent, sharp increase in DVD production. And, in the not-too-distant future, virtually all movies will be produced digitally, requiring another major adjustment – in movie projection technology.

Some DVDs now include links to web sites. This allows the viewer to enjoy a full-length movie (an amount of content too big to conveniently transmit online) from the DVD, and also to experience related enhanced, dynamic content through a web site.

The web links create a connection between the static content on the disc, and the dynamic content on the web, which can include many types of related information, community, and commerce.

Finding multimedia

YOU'VE LEARNED *that multimedia isn't hard to find on the Internet. For example, almost any site with news offers rich media to enhance their information offerings. If you've visited some of the sites we mentioned in our discussion of multimedia players, such as the QuickTime site or the Shockwave home page, you've already seen lots of exciting and innovative multimedia.*

We've gathered a selection of a few more interesting and diverse multimedia content sites, just to give you a flavor of what's out there. We suggest surfing through them to get a feel for the many directions web-based multimedia are going.

✓ World Wide Internet TV (www.wwitv.com) is a directory of online broadcasting. There are links to a staggering variety of online television and radio signals around the world.

✓ Like Television (www.liketelevision.com) distributes digitized versions of classic television programs, movies, music performances, sports programming, and other material. We watched an episode of the old police show, Dragnet, digitized in black and white.

✓ MovieFlix (www.movieflix.com) delivers entire movies on demand, right to your computer via the web.

✓ Pseudo.com (www.pseudo.com) and Digital Entertainment Network (www.den.com) are two of many groups who are creating entirely new television and interactive programs for the Internet.

✓ HyperTV (www.hypertv.com) is a system that actually enhances existing television programming by coupling it with Internet content.

Convergence

CONVERGENCE MEANS *the merging of previously separate media – we've already talked about several examples. The telephone, previously a separate medium for audio communication, is merging with the Internet and may soon incorporate video. Sound technology, previously embodied in several separate media, now comes along with Internet and video components.*

Whether we find ourselves viewing DVDs on the computer, web sites on television, radio on the Internet, or e-mail on a cell phone, convergence is the wave of the future. Along with technological convergence, a kind of artistic convergence is also in the air.

Music, film, art, and literature are all finding themselves greatly influenced by the Internet. Digital convergence is the theory that all entertainment and communication devices will eventually merge into one digital appliance, and all content will be transmitted via a single information "pipe."

Just as the arrival of "talkies" changed the art of film making, convergence will change the nature of entertainment, communications, education, and the arts.

A simple summary

✓ Combining different media into one product is a technique long used in the fine arts.

✓ Music of any kind is available on web sites, but copyrights are a major concern.

✓ Streaming media is a technology that enables multimedia content to be played even as it continues to download.

✓ CDs and DVDs are digital-format recordings of audio and video. CDs and DVDs can offer multimedia without worries about bandwidth.

✓ Search engines and portals are available to find multimedia files.

✓ High-speed Internet access through broadband or DSL greatly facilitates the use of multimedia, but multimedia can be accessed with a 56k modem too.

✓ Sites offering rich media content for downloading and viewing are proliferating.

✓ Electronic multimedia have emerged as new possibilities for transmitting, downloading, and playing sound and video through computers and the Internet.

PART FOUR

THE INTERNET CAN BRING YOUR FAMILY CLOSER

THE INTERNET FOR FAMILIES

I N THE NEXT five chapters, we'll take a close look at some of the ways the Internet affects family life, and suggest ways to get the most from it. The family computer can become a place to *gather*, to play some games, work on homework assignments, or plan a family event. No matter the age or number of persons in the family, the Internet can offer another focus for family *togetherness*

Online resources can also help with parental concerns; health issues or special interests. Even very young children can learn how to use the computer. Guiding kids in their Internet use does call for parental supervision, but this can be time very well spent. Online opportunities can help families *maximize* their precious time together. We hope these chapters will prove useful for all families.

Chapter 16

The Wired Family

IN THIS HIGH-TECH ERA, often every family member, or at least every adult, has a television, telephone, and computer. Some household's family members might send e-mail messages to others under the same roof, across a home computer network. In other households, where the whole family may share a single computer, competition for computer time may arise frequently. There's also sure to be competition for the shared telephone line, with someone wanting to make calls when somebody else is online. A bit of sensible, thoughtful organization – along with a few basic ground rules – can assure peace and success.

In this chapter...

✓ System care guidelines

✓ User-friendly computing

✓ Sharing the surf

✓ Privacy issues

✓ Signing-up for things

System care guidelines

BACK IN CHAPTER 5, *we listed some basics of computer care – use surge protectors, don't block the air vents, avoid extremes of temperature and moisture, don't put other appliances with magnetic fields too close, and don't let a furry pet sleep on the equipment. Use antivirus software. Avoid loading up the system with beta or evaluation software. Don't let the hard drive get more than 90% full. Then, there are some obvious precautions. If you must have a cup of coffee or a soda while online, place it as far as possible from the keyboard; don't drip while you sip. Enforce handwashing for children before using the computer, to keep peanut butter off the keys and greasy fingerprints off the screen. Maintain well-organized and thoughtfully-named directories and folders. In short, everyone in the family must use the system safely and responsibly.*

■ **Dog fur can** *seriously damage your computer's health.*

Computer know-how

You don't have to be an expert to go online, but if you happen to have a computer expert in the family, it makes sense to designate that person as "family computer wizard," responsible for system care, software, and troubleshooting. (You might do the same thing with cars, with one family member responsible for oil changes, repairs, and the like.)

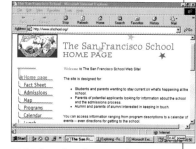

■ **U.S. schools** *provide extensive information about themselves on the Internet. Many have their own home pages, like this one.*

Your designated wizard need not be an adult; many young people know more about computers and the Internet than their elders. Current figures show that at least ten million children between 2 and 17 are using the Internet – six million at home, and four million at school.

At least forty percent of U.S. schools now provide Internet access for students, and that number is increasing rapidly. Today's teenagers have often been computer literate most of their lives, and have much to teach others.

Do's and don'ts

Whenever a computer is shared, it makes sense to agree on a few important ground rules, write them down, and post them at the work station. These rules should include the practices and cautions we listed above. Whether or not your household includes children, it's important that everyone who uses your home computer system is aware of these simple guidelines, for both safety and efficiency.

1 Any user who notices a system malfunction, of any kind at all, should promptly alert the primary owner and caretaker of the computer, to assure that the problem is taken care of and not allowed to get worse.
2 All new software and hardware should be licensed and registered.
3 If there are special pieces of gear used by some individuals, don't leave them laying around – put them in a safe storage place except while in use.
4 Label floppy disks and other portable data storage media such as CDs or Zip disks, and store them properly. Don't use or remove someone else's CD or disk.
5 Don't start a download that will take a long time without checking with others.

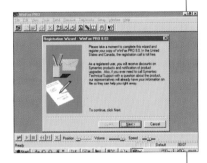

The rest of this Chapter covers additional guidelines for smooth online sailing, some geared to families with children, and some to adults sharing an Internet computer.

■ **You can register** *software when you install it. This is often completed online and many applications provide a registration wizard.*

User-friendly computing

POSTURE MATTERS AS much when you're at your computer as anywhere else, so ergonomic furniture design is important. Your chair should be comfortable, keeping your back straight and your weight centered. Specially-designed chairs, as well as additional cushions, are fine if they help you maintain comfort and good posture. If you have a history of back problems, we recommend consulting your doctor about the merits and dangers of different types of chairs. For ideas about computer furniture for children, see Chapter 17.

It's not a good idea to rest your wrists or the heels of your hands on the table below the keyboard. Maintaining a "typist's position," with your elbows up and your hands parallel to the keyboard, is much healthier, and more comfortable. (Back in the days of manual typewriters, it took a lot of force to strike the keys, so typists had to use their upper arm strength, not just their hands.)

HEALTH HABITS

Head movement

Your computer monitor (display screen) should be approximately 20 to 26 inches (50 to 65 centimeters) from your eyes, with the top of the screen at about eye level, so you can look at the screen without tilting your head upwards. If you'll be looking at reference documents, such as books or papers, while using the computer, you should arrange some way to position those

■ **While on the Net**, *think carefully about your posture.*

documents so you can view them without repeatedly tilting your head or bending your neck. Office supply and computer equipment dealers offer a variety of special document holders made for computer work stations.

Comfort

Your feet should rest, comfortably flat, on the floor. Your mouse pad and keyboard should be within easy range; you shouldn't have to reach out, up, or in an awkward direction to use them. Test a couple of the new "natural" keyboards; you may find such designs easier on your arms and hands. If clicking a traditional mouse causes you discomfort, there are several alternatives, including specially-shaped mice, as well as other types of pointing devices such as trackballs, touchpads, joysticks, pen tablets, and even foot pedal controls.

Protect your eyes

To prevent eyestrain, your monitor shouldn't reflect glare from light coming in a window, or from artificial light. Curtains or shades may be an easy solution to glare from outside, but different members of the family may have different preferences for indoor lighting. Take time to discover what works best for you. Adjust screen brightness and contrast, font sizes, and screen resolution for comfort and clarity. Keep the screen clean, free of smudges and fingerprints. If, despite wearing the right eyeglasses and taking these other steps, you find yourself squinting and leaning forward, you might want to consider a magnifying device.

By now, you've doubtless heard about carpal tunnel syndrome. This ailment, which can cause crippling pain in the arm, hand and wrist, may have existed before the computer era, but it's now primarily identified with those who spend many hours a day at a computer keyboard. We believe the health habits we're mentioning here can help prevent such ailments.

Computer sharing

You might be wondering why a lengthy discussion of healthy, safe computing is in this chapter on the online family. We've mentioned some of these issues elsewhere, but the full discussion is here because of the ramifications of having more than one person sharing a single computer. Think about the automobile analogy. If you share a car, you've probably adjusted the driver's seat and mirrors more than a few times. Like the car, your computer station should allow different drivers to make appropriate adjustments. If the people who use the computer have very different needs, this might be more complicated – for example, if one user is right-handed and another left-handed, or if one user is 30 inches taller than another.

■ **A comfortable chair** *and correctly positioned monitor are vital. In this illustration the monitor is too low.*

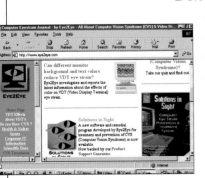

■ **Eye2eye.com** *provides help with eye problems.*

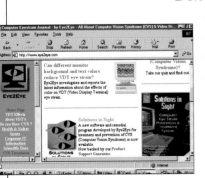

INTERNET

www.aoanet.org

At the American Optometric Association web site, you can learn more about protecting your eyesight while using a computer. You can also check out the Computer Eyestrain Journal at www.eye2eye.com.

Trivia...

We're not just talking about height differences between adults and children. We know a couple who are 22 inches (56 cm) different in height. At six feet ten inches (2.08 m), he pushes the car seat back as far as it will go; at just five feet (1.52 mm), she pushes it all the way forward. When purchasing a vehicle, their height difference is a major factor. We're not sure how they manage their shared computer!

Don't just jump in and start using the computer after the previous user. Take good care of yourself – always take time to arrange and customize your work environment. Encourage other family members to do the same. Failure to take these small but important precautions can result in headaches, eyestrain, aches and pains, and other physical problems.

Ergonomics is a field of study concerned with designing and configuring things people use in a way that's most usable, efficient, and safe for the human body and mind. Ergonomic researchers have devoted a lot of attention to the design of offices and computer stations. Here are five web sites with useful information about ergonomics:

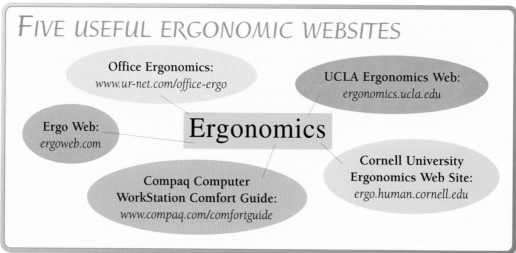

FIVE USEFUL ERGONOMIC WEBSITES

Office Ergonomics:
www.ur-net.com/office-ergo

UCLA Ergonomics Web:
ergonomics.ucla.edu

Ergo Web:
ergoweb.com

Ergonomics

Cornell University Ergonomics Web Site:
ergo.human.cornell.edu

Compaq Computer WorkStation Comfort Guide:
www.compaq.com/comfortguide

Sharing the surf

WE GENERALLY think of web surfing as a solitary occupation, shared only with other people out there in cyberspace. But today, corporations and Internet companies have conference rooms with projection screens and giant monitors set up so groups can view web content together. These systems are too bulky and expensive for most people to install at home, but there are options available for shared family viewing at home.

Owners of WebTV, and other systems that display web content on a television screen, are one step closer to an environment where users can share web experiences together.

More and more families want to surf together for all kinds of reasons – including just for the fun of it. Studies show that surfing with Mom or Dad enhances the educational value of the Internet, especially for younger children.

Be considerate

Some people find it annoying to watch television when one person monopolizes the remote control, especially if that person is a frequent channel-switcher. Likewise, when two people surf together, the person who controls the mouse might tend to follow his own interests and preferences, perhaps mentally wandering away from the original shared purpose. There's a world of difference between two people surfing together, and one person watching another person surf.

Many so-called power users lose patience quickly when sitting with a novice surfer who may need to go slower, or who isn't familiar with all the shortcuts and quickest ways to do things. If the power user keeps wresting the mouse and keyboard away from the novice, the novice might well feel less motivated to learn. We recommend taking turns controlling the mouse, and sharing the experience of becoming an expert on the web. If you're the power user, you'll have plenty of time to put the pedal to the metal when you're online alone. We want to help people new to the Internet, and perhaps even fairly new to computers, become skilled and effective Internet surfers. From our standpoint, everyone gets to surf, and everyone should have their turn "at the wheel."

If your family includes multiple Internet users, we suggest planning the work area so at least two posture-healthy chairs can be placed in front of the screen. Position the mouse within comfortable reach of both users. Whoever is "driving" should let the other person request certain pages or sites, or ask to stay longer on particular pages. As you surf together, share your reactions to what you see. Surf cooperatively!

Surfing with children can be very rewarding. There are many wonderful children's books online, which a parent can read to a child right off the screen.

Sharing web sites

Sharing a computer presents certain privacy challenges, but it also presents opportunities for fun. For example, there are several online "sticky notes" (like electronic Post-It(tm) notes) applications that let you leave notes for one another – right on the computer screen. Some of these products let you place clickable web page links on the notes, and others actually let you place a note at a web page, so another person will see it when viewing that page. Some of these products provide enhancements, for example, including multimedia information with the note, and having scheduled reminders pop up for events like birthdays. Some of these products include Memo4U from Protech Information Systems, Sticky from Maintree Systems, and Post-It Software Notes from 3M.

Scheduling

If your family is as busy as we think you probably are, we suggest using a calendar system for scheduling time at your Internet station. When you get to this point, its likely you'll start considering an extra phone line, so your family isn't cut off from telephone contact for long periods while someone's online.

You can check out some of the services and alternatives for Internet users with only one telephone line. These include Pagoo from pagoo.com, Callwave from ActionTec, Call Waiting Modems, the Call Pending Indicator from NetSense, and HotCall from Command-Comm. These services function like an answering machine. You're notified online, and can listen to the recording right on your PC, without going offline.

Privacy issues

Remember that *your work e-mails can be read by others.*

Trivia...

"Hello mudda, hello fadda" – those letters kids send home in the summer when they're away at camp still travel, for the most part, by snail mail. E-mail would seem like a good alternative, but many camps forbid e-mail from kids to home, and put restrictions on the amount parents can send kids. A camp web site is another option – parents can download pictures of camp activities and reports of their children's achievements.

YOUR INTERNET USAGE

may include information and activities that are private and personal. Private and personal does not mean secret or shameful, only that your Internet usage may reflect what you read, think, do, or buy, who you correspond with and what you say to them or hear from them. Shared computers create the potential for these private matters becoming "public," or at least revealed to others, deliberately or accidentally. Below, we'll review a few areas where this issue may arise, and offer some ideas for addressing it.

We also have to remind you, however, that you can't expect privacy regarding your computer and Internet activities at work. Employers can check up on you, read your e-mail, review web sites you visit, and oversee and measure your online activities. In most workplaces, these oversight activities are the employer's right. Wherever you work, make your behavior decisions as an employee with full knowledge that your computer activities may be monitored.

E-mail

E-mail is important in all wired households, with or without children. Shared e-mail addresses work well for some families, but it's generally impossible to maintain much personal privacy, and inevitable that some confusion will result. Especially if someone receives business e-mail at home, we suggest having separate e-mail addresses. Some ISPs allow multiple addresses for a single monthly fee, while others don't.

■ **Pagoo takes voice** *messages and instantly plays them for you on your computer – all while you're still on the Internet.*

When setting up personal e-mail accounts for additional family members, consider some of the free e-mail services available on the web.

Whatever solution you decide on, keep in mind that e-mail is mail. It should be treated with the same respect as postal mail. If your family members don't open and read one another's letters, they shouldn't look at one another's e-mail, either. E-mail, though, is just a click away, awfully tempting for the "inquiring mind." We suggest making an explicit rule about family e-mail privacy. And if you really want total privacy, use a web-based e-mail account and keep your password to yourself.

The two writers of this book live in different cities, and use different ISPs. One ISP charges an extra fee for each additional e-mail address. The other provides up to five e-mail addresses as part of the basic service package. These variations are not unusual. Check out your ISP's policy before assuming you only get one address; you may be able to get one for each family member at no extra cost.

Bookmarks

If more than on person begins saving bookmarks with a web browser, the bookmarks list can quickly become a colossal mess – unless it's well organized. We suggest setting up a bookmark folder for each family member, and keeping them separate. Each user can then add or delete personal bookmarks, leaving the common pool of bookmarks clean and easy to use for everyone. And to keep your own bookmarks better organized, create additional folders within your personal folder.

■ **Many sites,** *such as Lycos's Free Internet Access, offer a free e-mail account, personalized web pages and much more.*

Footprints

Web surfing leaves tracks. These include cookies left by sites visited, history lists, links whose colors changed because they were clicked, welcome messages for logging users, and back buttons. This means that people sharing a computer can usually see what others have been up to online. Some people are quite savvy about erasing their footprints; we won't address how to do it here, but a quick search online will yield several methods. However, be aware that these techniques are not foolproof.

■ **Bear in mind** *you leave a trail of footprints behind you as you browse the web.*

We believe that where someone surfs (unless it's your child) should be considered private information. However, if you're sharing a computer, you can't really expect complete privacy. As they surf, your fellow users will probably notice hints that reveal where you've been surfing. We've seen a number of minor unfortunate revelations, such as the time someone's birthday surprise was spoiled because she stumbled onto the web page displaying confirmation of an online gift purchase. We suggest you remain aware that some occasional breaches of privacy are likely. When it comes to the privacy of web footprints, our policy is that each user should keep his or her nose out of other peoples' web-surfing habits, unless some extraordinary situation requires violating the normal bounds of privacy.

Trivia...

Certain sophisticated programs maintain detailed databases of clickstreams and preferences of browsers. These are used to target both content and advertising. For example, a person who visits a lot of sites related to fishing or hunting may see more advertisements for fishing and hunting products than someone who hasn't visited such sites. The effectiveness of this is dampened when several people share a single computer. After Dad finishes planning his latest fishing trip, such a targeting system might show fishing gear ads to a youngster, who's more interested in looking for Bert and Ernie.

Signing-up for things

WEB SITES WITH *membership, user ID and passwords, log in and log out options, lots of customization and preferences, and personal records such as account information or investment portfolios, are becoming more and more common. When a computer is shared, using these sites becomes slightly more complicated.*

■ **You may have** *to log on to pages where your personal data is stored, such as this online banking site.*

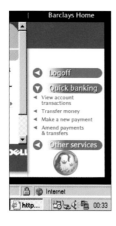

■ **Remember: log off** *when you leave a site where your personal data is stored, otherwise another user may view.*

When you leave a site that you've logged into with a user name and password, there are three ways to exit. Two of them are very bad ideas! (This is especially important if you've used a computer strangers have access to, such as in a library, airport, or Internet café.) What you should never do is just close the browser, or just go to a different web site. Always log out first from the site you logged into, then close the browser or move to another web site. If you simply quit the browser or go to some other site without logging out, another user may be able to return to your user session at the site. If you had been using your web-based e-mail account, for example, someone could read your mail and send mail in your name. If you had been reviewing your brokerage account, someone else could review it as well. Logging out closes your session, and removes your user name and password. Always log out!

■ **An e-mail message** *should be treated with the same respect as snail mail.*

Password organizers

We're in a world of too many passwords, PINs (personal identification numbers), secret codes, and account numbers. Managing all these is a challenge for anyone, and it becomes even more complicated with a shared Internet computer. There are various software products available, but we do it the old-fashioned way – on paper.

Here are a few products you might investigate to assist in keeping User IDs and passwords organized: Password Power by WorldStart, Darn! Passwords! from EmmaSoft, Password Plus from Author Direct, Password Manager from Celerity, and WebMining's WMVault. If they're to be shared, these applications require multi-user functions.

Electronic wallets

Similar to password manager software, but with a slightly different twist, is a new breed of software called Electronic Wallets, or Personal Information Managers. This kind of software promises to automatically fill in registration form information with a click or keystroke, so you don't have to type the same information over and over into online forms.

Here are a few examples of contenders in this arena: Gator from Gator.com, Obongo from Obongo.com, eWallet from Launchpad Technologies, and RoboForm from Rudenko Software. Like password managers, these products require multi-user capacity if you're using them on a shared computer. If you plan to save sensitive information, like credit card numbers, with these types of products, be sure to look for, and use, security and password protection features.

Communication

■ *In the same way as you would lock up when leaving home, it is important to log off before leaving.*

Families are often very busy. People come and go at different times, get interrupted in the middle of online work, and forget to come back to it. Someone may log onto a site that requires a password and then leave, forgetting to log out. If another family member then comes to the computer, he or she may be quite confused by the message "Welcome back!" on the screen. Some of the hyperlinks on that site may show (by their color) that they've been clicked, when in fact you know you haven't visited those links.

Sometimes, a family member will sign up somewhere without telling anyone else. Someone might even visit a shopping site and use a family credit card number to make purchases, and forget to share that information. One family member might request an e-mail newsletter that another person sees as obnoxious spam.

We all have different notions of what should be communicated and what's private, but most families work best with a steady flow of communication. Whatever your method, it's important to keep one another informed and updated, to avoid misunderstandings and problems.

Sometimes, something happens and you just can't get back to the computer to log out of a site you'd logged into. If you have only one telephone line and you leave the Internet station without disconnecting, you might cause a major problem for the whole family. And what if you happen upon a screen filled with personal information?

You need to decide whether to try to save it, or to contact the last person who used the computer and remind him or her of the transaction they abandoned midstream. Remember, communication and personal responsibility are key in shared-computer households.

■ **This online demo** *at Gator.com shows how Gator's electronic wallet automatically submits your details in registration and billing forms.*

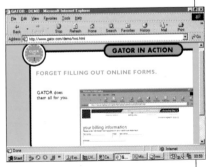

Security

Most people really don't want to violate one another's privacy. You'll usually be fine if you take a reasonable amount of care. Close programs when you go offline; put away personal information and avoid leaving it displayed on a shared computer; and respect the privacy of others. If you really don't want your children to go online when you're not there, invest in one of the security software applications we've already mentioned in this chapter. The ultimate in security, though, is the total lockdown, which will prevent access to the Internet.

In this chapter, we introduced the subject of a household computer shared by multiple users, and offered ideas for ground rules and good practices. Communication and respect for privacy are most important.

A simple summary

✓ Computers need care to protect them from damage.

✓ The computer work station should be safe and protect users' health.

✓ Basic rules for using the Internet and the computer should be clear to all users.

✓ Surfing together can be rewarding and productive.

✓ E-mail is private correspondence, and each family member should have a separate e-mail address.

✓ Keep each family member's bookmarks in a separate folder.

✓ Keeping track of accounts and passwords is important. Consider using electronic wallet software.

✓ Shared web browsers may display evidence of "footprints," revealing where you've surfed.

✓ Users with online memberships, passwords, account information, and other personal information should take care to assure the security of their data.

✓ Communication and responsibility are the keys to overcoming confusion and avoiding violations of privacy.

Chapter 17

Children Online

W E'VE ALL SEEN news reports about the dangers people can encounter on the Internet. We understand your feelings and concerns! For lots of reasons, the world can be a scary place these days. We strongly support your efforts to get up to speed about the Internet, and helping you get there is one of the reasons we wanted to write this book. One place to turn for help with potential Internet pitfalls is a site called GetNetWise.

In this chapter...

✓ Essential rules for kids

✓ Child-friendly gear

✓ Parents and kids online

✓ Fun and learning

✓ Searching and researching

✓ Communities and pen pals

✓ Teens online

THERE IS A LOT OF EDUCATIONAL MATERIAL FOR CHILDREN ON THE INTERNET

Essential rules for kids

✓ Kids, if you've met someone through the Internet, never meet that someone in person without your parents' knowledge and permission.

✓ Never provide your name, address, phone number, user name or password, credit card number, name of the school you attend, or any other specific information without your parents' permission.

✓ Never send pictures of yourself, your house, your family, friends, or anything else of a personal nature over the Internet without discussing it with your parents first.

✓ Don't go into an online area that costs money without getting your parents' permission.

✓ If you ever receive offensive, threatening, or scary messages via e-mail, chat, or any other online communications, tell your parents or another adult you trust (such as a teacher) immediately!

■ **Rules are not** *confined only to the classroom. The Internet has many rules that your child should learn before she begins to "surf."*

Just as a child too young to drive would not be given the car keys, no child should venture online until he or she understands the basic rules for Internet safety and security. And just as a parent might take away a teenager's car keys if the teen breaks rules about no beer in the car, a parent may have to rescind Internet privileges if a child breaks important safety rules.

We can't tell you how to parent. But we feel strongly that when it comes to the Internet, the best way to keep your child safe is to be actively and knowledgeably involved.

Back in Chapter 4, we mentioned a few rules that we believe should always govern the interaction of children with the Internet. At this point we want to supplement those, and emphasize their importance. Kids, read these rules carefully!

■ **This is the** *web site eleven-year-old Christopher produced for the church of his local pastor, Rev. John E. McKnight.*

Child-friendly gear

AN ENRICHED LEARNING environment, with age-appropriate equipment, enhances children's physical and mental development. Dr. Maria Montessori, one of the best-known authorities in early childhood development, says that children shouldn't be presented with environmental challenges that lead to failure, and that they thrive best in an environment conducive to success. Attempting new achievements in a supportive environment leads to increasing self-confidence.

Hardware

Educational toys now include a wide array of "kids' computers," developed by a number of established toy manufacturers. For example, VTech (www.vtech.com) markets at least a dozen models, from the simplest "laptop" (designed for kids nine months to thirty-six months), up through a model called "The Equalizer," which looks an awful lot like a real computer. We'll mention certain toy manufacturers as examples, but that doesn't mean we recommend their products over others. In fact, we've not done enough research to fairly compare and rate similar products. We know that Fisher-Price, Mattel, and others market products similar to the VTech line. These age-appropriate keyboards provide children with all kinds of basic learning, as well as a good introduction to the world of computers.

We believe the average child who's introduced to computers, either through these toys or just by observing family members using a home computer, will be ready to make the transition to the real thing by age four or five.

At about that point, most children realize the real computer is more than a toy. That's a good time to introduce them to a component like the Kidboard, a colorful, simplified keyboard you can connect to your computer. With the Kidboard, children can surf the Internet, discovering the many sites created just for them; play online games; and gradually learn computer skills as well as benefit from the educational content offered at those sites. You can get more information about the Kidboard at www.kidboard.com or www.kidswonders.com.

■ **VTech produce** *a wide range of kids computers and educational aids from infant and pre-school electronic toys to "The Equalizer."*

INTERNET

www.kinderlink.com

At the Kinderlink web site, you can see, read about and buy special, child-size computer tables and other furniture. These wood products come in several different heights. If your family includes more than one growing child, your investment in this ergonomically-engineered, child-friendly furniture might well be justified.

Software

There's an ocean of software just for children. In fact, there's so much we can't even survey the possibilities. For example, look into www.kidsdomain.com to see software arranged by age bracket (2-5, 4-8, 8+ and grown-ups), and by subject area. We opened the age 4-8 bracket, called "Web Workshop," and found a list of software to teach kids of that age about simple things to do on the web. This is only an example; similar sites are common and easy to find through any general search engine or through the special children's searching services. (See "Searching and researching," later in this chapter.)

While children's software will never have explicit sexual content, there can be a lot of violence. This particular problem is very troubling to some parents. Keep this in mind when shopping online or in stores for any software your kids will be using. It may be great fun, but parents should know what's there.

Software and department stores stock a large inventory of children's software and programs on CD-ROMs. Most of these same items are available online from such e-commerce sites as www.officedepot.com, www.valueamerica.com, and www.ecost.com. Just to give you a hint of the influence of the web on shopping habits among the younger generation, figures show that 72% of kids from age 5 to 12 are influenced in offline buying by their online browsing.

■ **SuperKids** *(www.superkids.com) provides news and reviews of educational software for parents and teachers as well as online and offline tools.*

Parents and kids online

AT WWW.DEARPARENTS.COM, you'll find a wealth of information about all kinds of family issues, including the debunking of some myths about children and computers. For instance, it's not true that small children can easily learn to use a mouse – many actually have a tough time, even with a kid-sized mouse. And it's certainly not true that boys naturally have more interest in computers than girls. Studies in schools have shown that boys are more aggressive than girls, though, and will tend to take over the computers. When girls are given equal opportunity, they demonstrate equal interest.

Here are some sites we recommend for learning about kids and the Internet.

✓ CTW Family Workshop Parents Toolbox: www.ctw.org/parents
✓ America Links Up: www.netparents.org
✓ American Library Association: www.ala.org/parentspage
✓ Cybersmart!: www.cybersmart.org
✓ Net-mom: www.netmom.com
✓ ZDNet Family PC: familypc.zdnet.com
✓ familyeducation.com

These sites are invaluable in parental learning, checking out your hunches, and getting new ideas for helping your kids learn and grow. There's information here for almost any topic, problem, or special interest. Many parents still rely on books, and there are plenty of those available in bookstores, but you'll find many of the leading parenting advisors on web sites too. These have the advantage of being constantly updated – plus, they're often interactive.

Parental supervision

How young is too young to use a computer? Early childhood education experts agree that every child is unique – so no rule applies to every kid. (By the way, when it comes to kids and computers, we'd rather listen to childhood development and educational experts than to computer experts.) Some parents don't have the time or patience to work at the computer with very young children, so it's safer to make a rule your family can live with. If there's a parent available who has the time, patience, and computer skills, even preschoolers can get started on the computer. And this can be much more conducive to their development than time in front of the TV.

We suggest that preschoolers not use the computer without parental supervision, and that parents remain accessible when elementary school-age children are online. Keep at least two (ergonomically correct) chairs near the computer, to foster the atmosphere of shared discovery.

If the Internet has proven stimulating to us, our excitement about the wonders of the web can entice a child into a lifelong habit of intellectual curiosity and development.

Many of the web sites created for parents to use in teaching their children about the Internet were designed by teachers. These often reflect a high level of expertise in child development and parenting skills. You'll also find chat rooms where parents can talk to one another, and "ask the experts" options where you can enter questions and get answers by e-mail or message board. For example, check out www.parenting-qa.com and www.parents-talk.com.

Blocking and filtering

"Family filter" tools and options are now part of many search engines, online services, and ISPs. These are designed to automatically filter out objectionable material. AOL, for instance, offers parents the ability to filter out specified URLs or keywords; the filter can be set to exclude sex, hate, violence, illegal activities, and other undesirable material.

■ **As with gold panning,** *the material available on the Net needs careful filtering in order to shield your children from unsuitable information*

Children surfing

In our view, the use of filtering software that's primarily intended to block undesirable content implies the expectation that the child may be surfing the web alone. If the parent is surfing with the child, the parent can quickly steer away from inappropriate material without the need for any additional software.

Software which automatically blocks preselected sites is bound to have several serious shortcomings, such as the accidental blocking of valuable sites. We know a few parents who've disabled filtering systems after learning that the software blocked sites they didn't consider inappropriate at all. Another shortcoming is the inability of software to completely block out all the undesirable stuff. (You'd be amazed how quickly an enterprising teenager can find and access exactly the stuff that filtering systems are supposed to screen out.)

An even more troubling facet of filtering systems is the potential harm that could come from the misuse of content blocking. Human judgment must be involved in deciding what to screen out, and those judgments may be made by individuals with hidden agendas. For instance, reports have emerged about filtering systems being used by companies and even governments to prevent people from seeing material considered critical or undesirable.

Unsuitable material

Both authors of this book are parents. Naturally, we're concerned about access the Internet provides to materials we'd rather our children weren't exposed to. Considering the options, however,

■ **Smartparent.com** *can offer words of wisdom..*

INTERNET

www.smartparent.com

At SmartParent.com, you can see a long list of available filtering and blocking software. But be aware that there are controversies swirling about this subject. SmartParent.com also provides a list of organizations concerned with these topics, and you can read some of the arguments advanced on both sides.

we both feel more comfortable exercising our responsibilities as parents by supervising and teaching values to our children, rather than by relying on software, or on the information-blocking decisions of strangers. Playing an active role in our children's developing lives is more difficult than simply installing a software package, but we feel it's still the best way to direct them away from inappropriate content (on the Internet, television, and elsewhere).

Underlying our position is the principle that the computer and the Internet shouldn't be used just to keep children quiet and occupied, as television has often been used. In addition to the blocking and filtering issues, there are a host of other reasons for us to say that, when your young children are online, you, or another adult whose judgment you trust, should be there too.

Parents can take control

One simple but powerful measure parents can take is to maintain control of passwords. Then, a parent must be present for the kids to log on to the Internet, or even on to the computer itself. Another way to exert some control is to use monitoring software that compiles a log of web sites visited. Several of the "filtering" products offer this capability. There are also many other applications that monitor online and computer activity. Check out Spector from SpectorSoft, Investigator from WinWhatWhere.com, and Kid Control from Tybee Software. Using this power regularly could certainly be seen as an unwarranted invasion of privacy, like listening in on a child's telephone calls. Use it carefully, respectfully, and when you have sound justification.

It helps to place the computer in a public area of the house, such as the family room, so users aren't off in some dark corner where they could carry out untoward activities in secret.

Regardless of your point of view or level of concern about blocking content and monitoring your child's activity, we urge you not to obsess about it. Many family-oriented web sites we've already mentioned provide excellent help for parents whose kids use the Internet. Here are two more we suggest you visit and bookmark. The New York Public Library has a wonderful resource for parents at www.nypl.org/branch/safety.html. The United States Department of Education has also created a well-recommended site at www.ed.gov/Technology/intsaf.html.

■ **Spector secretly** *takes hundreds of snapshots every hour, like a surveillance camera, to show what's being accessed online and offline.*

Fun and learning

INITIALLY, WE PLANNED *separate sections in this chapter, on fun and on learning – then we realized that the two really go together. It's not only that the same web sites offer fun and games, along with information and discovery, it's also that kids just naturally learn while playing, and play while learning. Designers of web sites for children obviously know this, and there are some really exciting, colorful, stimulating places for kids to go on the Internet.*

Digital playgrounds

At one point, the most popular web site for kids age 5-12 was www.Nick.com, the online version of the Nickelodeon cable television network. This site is a true digital playground, showcasing all the familiar TV shows, and offering games associated with each one. Kids can download these games, or play them right online. (These online games usually require a plug-in, such as Shockwave.)

■ **The Cartoon Network**
TV channel's web site showcases their wall-to-wall schedule of toons from the Flintstones to Scooby Doo.

Similar content can be found at the following locations (and many more!):
✓ www.disney.com
✓ www.pokemon.com
✓ www.cartoonnetwork.com
✓ www.warnerbros.com
✓ www.mamamedia.com

■ **The Net can**
be a "virtual" playground for kids across the globe.

Many of these digital playgrounds require signing in and picking a password. After entering that information, your child will be greeted by name when returning to the site – like meeting friends at the playground. New games appear fairly often; the web site providers are mindful of the attention span of their young audience.

Homework

A child in our extended family is now in the fifth grade. She recently called to ask for our help in doing a homework assignment called "football geography." The teacher had given the kids a questionnaire about the geography of cities with NFL football teams, such as "what NFL city has a bird for its team emblem, and is called 'the emerald city'?" Why did she call us for help? Because it was nine o'clock in the evening (her bedtime), the assignment was due next day, and she knew "you know how to help me find this stuff on the Internet!"

We went over to her house and sat down with her at the family computer. Starting with Yahoo, we tried several approaches, explaining what we were doing, and why. Our first few efforts failed, but this seemed like a good part of the lesson – adults don't always get it right the first time either! It was when we entered the word "emerald" that we finally got our answer (Seattle). Simple searching is possible even for kids her age (eleven) and also younger kids too.

Clicking on any choice from that list takes you to child-friendly sites where you can find material about that subject. Selecting "reference" from the home page brings up choices of encyclopedias, dictionaries, and other places to look for the needed material. If they were doing their assignments at the library, older children might be using Encyclopaedia Britannica, World Book Encyclopedia, or similar reference works.

Those resources are also online now – see www.britannica.com, www.worldbook.com, or related sites.

Searching and researching

SEARCHOPOLIS *is one example of the child-oriented search engines now online. Other significant sites are Yahooligans (www.yahooligans.com), Ask Jeeves for Kids (www.ajkids.com), AOL Netfind/Kids Only, and Go Kids (kids.go.com).*

Yahooligans

The kids' version of Yahoo (www.yahooligans.com) is organized in the same way as Yahoo itself, with subject trees and search options. You can access it from the Yahoo home page. But it's different from the parent site in several important ways. First, it has an automatic filtering system that removes all references to sites related to sex, and secondly, it's designed and organized specifically for children.

Searchopolis

Designed for children ages 10 to 18, Searchopolis (www.searchopolis.com) operates just like Lycos, AltaVista, and other general search engines. It uses the same powerful tools, and accesses 90 percent of the same databases accessed by the major searching services.

All web sites are reviewed by real live editors before being approved or filtered out. This site boasts child-friendly how-to instructions, and emphasizes information of special interest to kids.

Other options

Two other good sites for kids are Ask Jeeves for Kids (www.ajkids.com), and AOL Netfind/Kids Only. Ask Jeeves is organized differently, inviting kids to ask questions, and providing answers from a preselected archive of answers. Some children prefer this approach, as asking questions is so natural to them. The AOL site is so simple even a beginner can easily navigate it. It's aimed at children ages 6 to 12, and is used in many schools.

■ **With the help** *of the Internet, you don't need to live next door to your friends in order to communicate with them.*

Communities and pen pals

WITH ONE-ON-ONE *communications, children can not only learn a lot, but also gain a sense of community with their peers in other places. Schools have traditionally encouraged pen pal arrangements with children in other parts of the world, and that tradition continues now via the Internet.*

Online friends

We went to Searchopolis and entered "pen pals," which brought up a list of several web sites offering pen pal arrangements, but most of these turned out to be for adults. So we tried again, with "pen pals kids," and got a list that included sites such as iConnect-Kid Connect (www.iconn.com.ph/subcat.kids), and MVLA Kids (www.mvla.org/kids). MVLA links with Keypals Club International (www.worldkids.net), where you'll find a detailed description of the safety features of their service. We suggest you look for this kind of information on any site where kids are put in touch with other kids as potential pen pals. Be sure to follow the instructions listed in the safety features.

Special needs

Virtually any kind of special need is addressed somewhere on the web. One excellent resource is www.wemedia.com, dedicated to making the Internet fully accessible to people with disabilities. At www.adoptionscentrum.se/barn/pen friends, adopted kids can communicate with one another and share their special concerns. Parents of children with special needs can find resources on most of the parental guidance sites.

■ **World Kids Network** *(www.worldkids.net) has the look and feel of a fun kids site but includes safety features.*

Teens online

WEB SITES ESPECIALLY *for teenagers seem to be dominated by chatting!* *This comes as no surprise to parents, who often put in extra phone lines rather than battle the insatiable teenage appetite for talking with friends. However, there's also evidence online to support the idea that teenagers care about the state of the world, and are educating one another on some important issues of the day, including religion, health, and the environment.*

Bad news involving teenagers often seems to implicate the Internet. A completely different picture emerges if you spend some time surfing web sites created by and for teenagers. Oh, you'll find some undesirable material, too, but you'll also discover lots of enlightening discussion.

Religious Communities

Many families are actively involved in religious communities, where children have the opportunity to learn about the family's faith, and also make friends with other kids. Other families do care about this side of children's development but find it hard to participate in religious organizations. In addition, check the home page of any faith community to see if they provide special pages for children. These resources provide kids the opportunity to get acquainted with children who share their faith. They also offer proof that the Internet can be a wholesome and constructive influence in the lives of children of all ages.

SOFTWARE REVIEWS

The Internet provides many excellent web sites where kids can find religious knowledge, as well as friendship with other kids. Here are a few such sites:

✓ Guideposts for Kids (www.gp4k.com): a non-denominational resource featuring Wally's World, a small town kids can explore.

✓ Network for Jewish Youth (www.anjy.ort.org): a site offering The Ultimate Jewish Youth Guide, chat rooms, and pen pals.

✓ Catholic Youth Online (www.catholicyouth.com): a developing site designed for Catholic kids.

Hanging out

One place where teens hang out on the web is at teens.liv4now.com. The message boards and chat rooms are very busy there. There are also newsgroups and mailing lists just for teenagers, to whom the technology of navigating the Internet is not usually a challenge. Other hangouts include www.snowball.com, www.bolt.com, www.thedigs.com, and www.mtv.com. Parents can go to these sites to learn about their policies for monitoring, and for blocking inappropriate content.

Music

If your computer station isn't equipped for multimedia, the kids will start clamoring for it, probably even before the teen years, and certainly by the time they're entering junior high school. Music can be a controversial topic in the family, but there's no denying that most teens want to hear a lot of it.

As we said back in Chapter 15, we suggest you download MP3 software. But do try to keep control over the type and amount of music your teens choose.

Trivia...

That same eleven-year-old who called for help with her homework is wild about The Backstreet Boys. Her parents haven't equipped their computer for multimedia, nor do they have high-speed Internet access. We're now waiting for the other shoe to drop – that is, for another phone call, this time asking if she can use our multimedia computer!

Shopping

Next to homework, chatting, and music, teenagers most love to spend their Internet time at shopping sites.

■ **Multimedia software** *can be educational as well as entertaining.*

Figures are just approximate, but it appears that the average online teen spends at least $300 a year on the Internet. And trends indicate a rapid escalation. When asked why

they like shopping online, teens say it's easier, prices are better, and that they trust the Internet!

In this chapter, we've discussed a few of the big issues affecting kids online, and surveyed the offerings of the Internet for kids of different ages. We've expressed our belief that there's no substitute for regular, ongoing parental involvement in supervising younger children online. But we've also encouraged

■ **Internet shopping** *may someday overtake the traditional method.*

you to start your kids off on Internet exploration early, as soon as they express interest. And we've noted that teenagers are usually doing online what they love to do in every setting and with every available means – talking to one another.

■ **As the name implies,** *teenagers use The Digs as a place to store stuff – music, files, whatever – and drop in to chat.*

A simple summary

✓ Pre-schoolers can get started learning about computers with educational toys .

✓ Software for kids is plentiful, and much of it is of good quality. Parents can obtain lots of this good software as freeware and shareware.

✓ Software and services to block and filter undesirable material away from children comes in many varieties.

✓ Digital playgrounds offer fun for kids of all ages.

✓ Some parents feel that supervision and guidance, rather then blocking systems, are the best means to control the online experiences of children.

✓ Sites that provide resources for learning and help with homework are also plentiful and easy to navigate.

✓ Special search engines are available for children of all ages.

✓ Kids can easily find pen pals, nearby or far away, right online.

✓ Children with special needs can find others with the same needs to share with, and parents can find help for dealing with those special needs.

✓ Teenagers love chatting and messaging on the web, but also use the Internet to do homework, to access music, and to shop.

Chapter 18

Health and the Internet

HEALTH IS AMONG the most popular subjects on the web. Millions of people visit health sites every day. Tens of thousands of web sites addressing health are now available online, with more appearing rapidly. With new information about diseases, drugs, and prevention, the Internet allows quick distribution of up-to-date knowledge.

In this chapter...

✓ Reliability

✓ Consumer protection

✓ Standards

✓ Health web sites

✓ Health and e-commerce

✓ Aging

✓ Electronic medical records

IF YOU WANT TO KEEP FIT, YOU WILL FIND MANY HEALTH-RELATED WEB SITES TO HELP YOU

Reliability

■ **Beware, not everyone** *who puts things on the web is an expert in their field.*

THE VAST POOLS *of information readily accessible on the Internet can be empowering, but it's important to keep in mind that not all information on the web is accurate or trustworthy. Several detailed reviews have found web sites with inaccurate, outdated, and in some cases, potentially dangerous information. Simply clicking from one site to another, or entering a term in a search engine and getting back a list of web sites, doesn't provide any filtering for credibility or validity.*

We recommend always reviewing health decisions, and sorting out conflicting information, with a competent, trusted family physician or health care professional.

We also suggest a strong dose of common sense, as well as keeping an eye out for reports from independent reviewers and consumer advocates on the relative accuracy of health sites. Claims of miracle cures, especially if you haven't heard of them anywhere else, or if the purveyor of the claim wants your money, are probably dubious.

Never take online suggestions that contradict your physician's advice, for example, "Throw away your prescription medications and buy our miracle potion."

Many health information sites mention well-established brands, or names of institutions or individuals who lend credibility, but those trustworthy names are not always closely involved with the management of the site, or its content. We recommend checking out the "About Us" page on any health site you visit. Look for editorial policies, advisory boards, medical review guidelines, and the credentials and expertise of the people who actually operate the site,

■ **Remember, there is** *usually a profit motive behind an online business even if it is not immediately apparent.*

Profit motive

Many web users have come to enjoy and expect free information and service online, sometimes failing to understand or consider the underlying profit motive of most online businesses. In the web environment, advertising, merchandising, and editorial content are blended in new ways, making it more difficult for a consumer to know if information is coming from independent reporting, or from a commercial sponsor.

Several health web sites have been criticized for failing to disclose relationships with companies such as hospitals and pharmaceutical companies. These kinds of relationships create potential conflicts of interest in the presentation of information. While commercial relationships are not inherently bad, and do not necessarily result in misleading information, it makes sense to be alert to the underlying sources and purposes of messages you read online.

Links

Health web sites often contain many links to other sites, including some found in advertising banners and on bulletin boards, where individuals are free to post web site links. Even if a site maintains high standards for reliable articles, it's easy to click on a link, and the transition from a reliable site to one not so reliable may not always be clear to consumers. Some people may assume a credible site would only have links to other reliable sites. We suggest keeping an eye on exactly where you are any time you click from one web site to another. And always read and heed the disclaimers connected with message boards and chats.

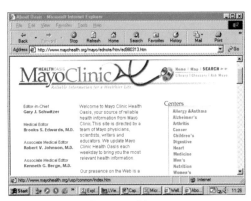

■ **The Mayo Clinic** *Health Oasis's "About Us" page includes their editorial policy and the credentials and expertise of their editorial board.*

Attribution of sources

Many health web sites have been criticized for publishing articles without naming the writers, reviewers, or publication dates. We believe an article or resource on a health site should indicate who authored the material, and when it was created or last modified. This helps readers evaluate the information and place it in proper context. If you see an unattributed article that seems interesting or useful, try contacting the site publishers to request the source reference. Again, we also recommend that you consult with your physician before acting on any health care decision for yourself or a loved one.

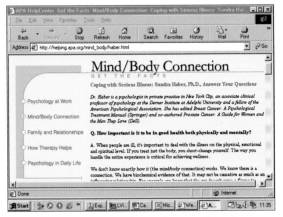

■ **Psychologist** *Dr Sandra Haber's credentials preface her article on coping with serious illness.*

Consumer protection

CONSUMER PROTECTION is important in every arena, but nowhere is it more crucial than when our health is at stake. Here are some of the hazards consumers should know about in evaluating and utilizing health-oriented web sites.

■ **Consumer protection** is an important issue on the web, especially in the field of health.

Bias

It's relatively easy to create a web site that looks very professional and official, even if the publisher is an individual or small group. Many sites have been set up to promote strong opinions or biases about health-related subjects, rather than balanced, researched information. We know a physician who has several patients who routinely bring web site printouts with them to their appointments. Sometimes, the articles are from sites published by people with "axes to grind" – these articles sometimes make wild claims, or raise premature hopes about miracle cures.

If you really want to evaluate the material, and have checked out the source, then it's a good idea to consult with your health care professional to get an educated and balanced view.

Confidentiality

Personalization provides clear benefits, but many privacy advocates have pointed out that it can also potentially result in the unauthorized use or sharing of sensitive personal information. Be sure to review privacy policies at health sites; oversee any activity by children; and look for privacy seals from such industry groups as Trust-E, BBB Online, and HON (Health On the Net Foundation).

■ **As in other arenas,** it's easy to be fleeced on the Internet.

Redress processes

If a consumer acts on faulty information obtained from a web site, and some kind of harm results, what redress is available? The answer is unclear.

Our suggestion is to use the Internet to gather information, support, and resources, but to make decisions in consultation with your own health professional, who works in an environment with professional oversight and procedures for redress.

Access

The Internet is clearly the new frontier for empowering consumers, and increasing their access to health information and services. What effect, then, will this have on those who can't afford the costs of computers and Internet service? Will their health care begin to decline as more resources are shifted to the online world? Will people who aren't aboard the Internet be left behind? If you're reading this book, or you're already connected to the Internet, this problem probably doesn't affect you. It is, however, an important issue we believe must be addressed at the public policy level.

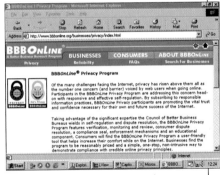

■ **The BBB OnLine** *Privacy Program enables webmasters to include a privacy seal that establishes compliance with credible online privacy principles.*

Standards

INTERNET

www.ihc.net
www.hon.ch

Several initiatives are underway to create standards, guidelines, and perhaps even accreditation for health web sites. Two organizations working in this area are the Internet Health Coalition (www.ihc.net), and the Health On the Net Foundation (www.hon.ch). Their web sites provide useful news and updates.

INVESTMENTS IN ONLINE HEALTH *ventures are so significant that issues like information reliability, conflicts of interest, and privacy are a high priority for industry leaders.*

The Federal Trade Commission in the U.S. has published a useful resource, filled with suggestions and ideas for avoiding unscrupulous and fraudulent marketers in the Internet. We urge you to check it out at (www.ftc.gov/bcp/conline/edcams/miracle/). We also encourage you to visit The National Organization for Reliable Health Information (www.ncrhi.org), and QuackWatch (www.quackwatch.com).

Some people over-react to suspected fraud, and some under-react. We urge you to be alert, refuse to be victimized, and if you have reason to suspect abuse, report it. As good citizens of the online community, people help one another by using all means available to weed out abuses.

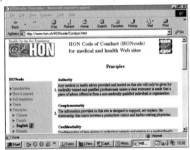

■ **The Health On the Net Foundation's** *Code of Conduct clearly states principles and standards for online medical publication at their site.*

Health web sites

MANY TYPES *of health-related web sites are competing for the attention of consumers and healthcare professionals. Online health sites include "pure-plays" created specifically for the Internet, along with sites launched by "landed" organizations that existed before the web, and whose web sites are closely integrated with their traditional activities or business. This section surveys representative sites in several categories. Lists of web sites in this chapter, as in most sections of this book, are not intended to be comprehensive, but only to point you to a selection of industry leaders, useful examples, and resources.*

■ **Useful medical** *advice can be found online as well as at the doctor's office.*

Consumer health information sites

Consumer "health portals," rich with information, news, services, and links, have proliferated on the Internet. These sites are often structured into broad categories, geared to certain groups of people or subject areas, and augmented with reference databases, message boards, and various services. For example, several of the sites are organized around subjects like "nutrition" and "fitness," while others have sections like "family health" which lead to subcategories for children, women, and men.

USEFUL HEALTH SITES

General consumer health information sites include:
- ✓ WebMD: my.webmd.com
- ✓ OnHealth: www.onhealth.com
- ✓ Mediconsult:: www.mediconsult.com
- ✓ DrKoop: www.drkoop.com
- ✓ Adam: www.adam.com
- ✓ Health Central: www.healthcentral.com
- ✓ Intellihealth: www.intelihealth.com
- ✓ Mayo Health: www.mayohealth.org
- ✓ Thrive: www.thriveonline.com
- ✓ AllHealth: www.allhealth.com
- ✓ Health Gate: www.healthgate.com
- ✓ HealthAnswers: www.healthanswers.com

■ **Johns Hopkins Health Information** *at InteliHealth is organized into medical zones, health centers, featured areas and breaking news articles.*

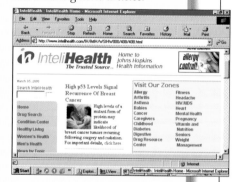

Several media companies that operate magazines or television programs with health coverage have also launched health sites. These sites often involve partnerships between traditional media companies and "dot.coms." Examples include:

✓ Reader's Digest: www.readersdigesthealth.com
✓ CondeNast: www.phys.com
✓ Discovery Health: www.discoveryhealth.com
✓ Prevention: www.prevention.com
✓ CBS HealthWatch: cbs.healthwatch.com.

More sites like these are on the way; for example, News Corporation, parent of Fox, and the America's Health Network cable network (www.ahn.com) recently announced a strategic relationship in WebMD. Consumer health information web sites have many similarities, as well as distinctions. Most have a unique tone and target audience; for example some are more youth-oriented, while others give more prominence to topics of interest to older people. Some share the same medical information sources, news feeds, and databases. Most have advertising and links to online stores selling medication, personal care products, books, and other merchandise.

We suggest you visit a few of these sites, compare their usefulness and relevance to your needs, and then bookmark your favorites.

Directories

There are several types of online health directory sites, including indexes of health web sites, services for looking up physicians and other health care providers, hospital and health care facility databases, directories of health insurance plans, and other directory services.

Examples of sites which aspire to be indexes of online health include Achoo (www.achoo.com), Stay Healthy (www.stayhealthy.com), and MedExplorer (www.medexplorer.com).

■ **Health advice** for *all ages can be found on the web.*

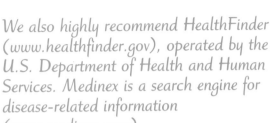

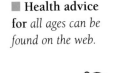

We also highly recommend HealthFinder (www.healthfinder.gov), operated by the U.S. Department of Health and Human Services. Medinex is a search engine for disease-related information (www.medinex.com).

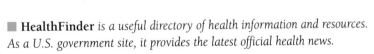

■ **HealthFinder** *is a useful directory of health information and resources. As a U.S. government site, it provides the latest official health news.*

There are many sites offering up-to-date and breaking health news. 48Hours (www.48hours.net), and Health News Directory (www.healthnewsdirectory.com), are directories of health news. Reuter's Health Information Service (www.reutershealth.com), Medcast (www.medcast.com), and Ivanhoe (www.ivanhoe.com) are health news services. HealthScout (www.healthscout.com) lets you create a personalized health news page. Most of the major general health sites listed near the beginning of this chapter include medical news sections, and many of the general news sites such as CNN.com, MSNBC.com, and ABCNews.com also carry significant health news sections.

There are several directories of physicians, other health professionals, hospitals, and clinics:

✓ HealthStreet: www.healthstreet.com
✓ The Health Pages: www.thehealthpages.com

And check out PRNewswire's list of health organizations at www.prnewswire.com/health/healthcare_assc.html.

■ **Advice for new parents** *is plentiful on the Net.*

Subject-specific sites

Many web sites target specific audiences or medical conditions. These types of sites can easily be found through search engines and directories, or through health portals such as StayHealthy.com

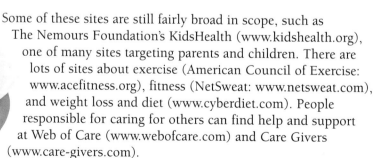

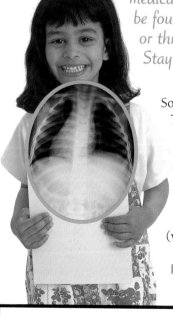

Some of these sites are still fairly broad in scope, such as The Nemours Foundation's KidsHealth (www.kidshealth.org), one of many sites targeting parents and children. There are lots of sites about exercise (American Council of Exercise: www.acefitness.org), fitness (NetSweat: www.netsweat.com), and weight loss and diet (www.cyberdiet.com). People responsible for caring for others can find help and support at Web of Care (www.webofcare.com) and Care Givers (www.care-givers.com).

■ **Pediatric medicine** *is covered in some web site.*

Specific conditions

There are also many web sites for specific diseases and conditions. The Comprensive Cancer Center (www.cancer.med.umich.edu) is just one of many sites focused on cancer. Diabetes.com (www.diabetes.com) is a portal for diabetics. HIV InSite (hivinsite.ucsf.edu) and the AIDS Research and Information Center (www.critpath. org/aric) are examples of sites devoted to HIV and AIDS. Muscular dystrophy is the subject at the Muscular Dystrophy Association (www.mdausa.org); multiple sclerosis is the topic at the National Multiple Sclerosis Society (www.nmss.org).

■ **As well as** *providing health tools and up-to-date news, HealthScout allows you to create a personalized health news page.*

For anorexia, we found the American Anorexia Bulimia Association (www.aabainc. org) and an organization called Anorexia Nervosa and Related Eating Disorders (www.anred.com). Allergy, Asthma, and Immunology Online can be found at allergy.mcg.edu. Brain Diseases are covered at the Dana Alliance's Brainweb (www.dana. org/brainweb). Lupus resources are available at lupus.miningco.com. Sufferers of herpes can find resources and information at Café Herpe (www.cafeherpe.com). The Urology Channel (www.urologychannel.com) covers a range of urological conditions.

LITTLE ANNIE

Back in the sixties, the drug thalidomide took a terrible toll among newborns. Children whose mothers had taken this drug were born with stunted limbs. Little Annie's parents were both physicians, and they blamed themselves when she was born with tiny, stunted arms. She was happy and bright, but her mother had a hard time with her sense of guilt. This was long before the web existed.

Thalidomide was banned, so this tragedy is not happening anymore, but there's now an organization called the Thalidomide Victims Association of Canada at www.thalidomide.ca (Annie is Canadian and used to live in Nova Scotia).

The web site carries several pictures of these men and women, now mostly in their thirties, who have found one another through the Internet.

Support groups

Discussion groups, mailing lists, and chat rooms for many aspects of medical problems and family health are easy to find. For instance, we went to AltaVista, clicked on the health category, then clicked on "women's health, discussions." We found a hundred discussions underway on such topics as infertility, pregnancy, and menopause.

If you've never had any interest in message boards or chat groups before, the chance to share important personal concerns might prove to you the worth of online group communication.

There are also newsgroups discussing many specific medical issues; you can find these via Deja (www.deja.com) and the various other newsgroup searching tools we talked about in Chapter 7. Most of the major consumer health sites also have community areas and topical message boards.

■ **Why not go** *online and chat about about your pregnancy concerns?*

Many sites devoted to specific diseases or conditions have links to online support groups, as well as listings of support group meetings in your local area. This kind of communication and support is not only informative, but also helps build a sense of community among people facing similar problems.

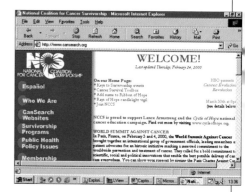

■ **Support for cancer** *patients at the National Society for Cancer Survivorship's web site comes in many forms including a Survival Toolbox.*

Clinical trials

Many web sites provide information about medical research and clinical trials. Some of these sites help researchers get in touch with patients interested in participating in upcoming clinical trials. We'll list a few, but we also recommend you use some of the online searching tools we've already talked about if you're interested in additional sources of information about clinical trials.

✓ Understanding Clinical Trials from the FDA: www.fda.gov/oashi/cancer/pdart.html
✓ Cancer Treatment Studies: www.clinicaltrials.org
✓ NIAID Clinical Trials Database: www.niaid.nih.gov/clintrials
✓ AIDS Clinical Trials Information Service: www.actis.org
✓ CenterWatch: www.centerwatch.com
✓ MedTrials: www.medtrial.com
✓ About Clinical Trials:: act.musc.edu
✓ National Eye Institute Clinical Trials: www.nei.nih.gov/neitrials

Health and e-commerce

IN CHAPTER 21, we'll talk more about shopping online, and about ordering products from web sites using your credit card. However, because this section is about health, it makes sense to review online pharmacies and other health-related e-commerce here. We'll talk about the mechanics of buying things online, as well as touch on related topics, such as credit card security.

■ **Drugstore.com** *is one of the newer online pharmacies. Features include an index of drugs and a page where prescriptions are written.*

Before pointing the way to these sites, we repeat some basic advice: consult with your health care provider to determine which drugs, remedies, or other personal health products are appropriate for you, when and how to use them, and what combinations of drugs to watch out for.

Online pharmacies

The online pharmacy and drugstore business has become an increasingly crowded market. Some of these services accept insurance coverage for prescriptions, while others don't; some deliver through the mail, while others offer in-store pick-up.

Levels of service, as well as products offered online, vary from site to site.

Several Internet drugstores, such as Drugstore.com, PlanetRX.com, Soma.com, RX.com, and More.com are brand-new companies. Also competing are the new online outposts of the larger traditional "brick and mortar" retail drugstores and mail order prescription-fillers. These include Eckerd (www.e-pharmacy.com), Drug Emporium (www.drugemporium.com), Walgreen's (www.walgreens.com), RiteAid (www.riteaid.com), and CVS (www.cvs.com). Many other contenders are entering this business, including new pharmaceutical offshoots of organizations with large existing customer bases, such as the American Association of Retired Persons and Reader's Digest.

Web sites selling vitamins, herbs, supplements, and alternative medicines have also proliferated on the Internet. Here are a few examples:

✓ Mother Nature: www.mothernature.com
✓ Vitamins.com: www.vitamins.com
✓ GreenTree Nutrition: www.greentree.com
✓ ENutrition: www.enutrution.com

■ **Medicinal herbs** *and other alternative medicines can be purchased on the Internet.*

Many online pharmacies are more than just simple, mechanical prescription-fillers. To prevent their customers from suffering from any harmful interactions among different drugs, these pharmacies (like traditional pharmacies) maintain detailed databases on each customer's prescriptions and purchases.

Some even employ physicians, who examine customer records and keep a lookout for possible problems. We feel that this extremely important service represents professionalism and bespeaks medical responsibility. Wherever you purchase prescription drugs, be sure that someone with pharmaceutical expertise is paying attention to prevent potentially dangerous interactions among drugs. The best policy is to check out all drugs (including supplements and over-the-counter remedies), whether obtained online or from other sources, with your own doctor.

Manufacturer sites

Most makers of pharmaceuticals, over-the-counter drugs, and other personal care products publish web sites filled with information about their products. Many also pay for the placement of banners, sponsorships, and other advertising messages on other health and consumer sites. The Virtual Pharmaceutical Library (www.pharmacy.org) provides a directory of pharmaceutical companies, as well as other resources. Other industry and trade resources include the American Pharmaceutical Association (www.aphanet.org), the Health Industry Manufacturers Association (www.himanet.com), and the Consumer Healthcare Products Association (ndmainfo.org).

■ **MotherNature.com** *offers a guided tour of their virtual store, which sells vitamins, minerals, herbal medicines, and other natural products.*

Health insurance programs

Health insurance, HMO, and managed care program web sites provide varying levels of information, service, customer support, and marketing through the web. Some offer provider directories, appointment scheduling, prescription refill ordering, online claims lookup for members, health reference archives, and policy and application information. Examples include Aetna U.S. Healthcare (www.aetnaushc.com), Blue Cross Blue Shield Association (www.bluecares.com), Kaiser Permanente (www.kaiserpermanente.org), and Cigna (www.cigna.com).

Several new companies have set up shop to broker insurance polices via the Internet, promising consumers better access to plan research and comparison, greater choices, and cost savings.

Examples include InsWeb (www.insweb.com), EhealthInsurance (www.ehealthinsurance.com), HealthAxis (www.healthaxis.com), and QuoteSmith (www.quotesmith.com). Channel Point (www.channelpoint.com) is positioned to assist insurance brokers in moving their business processes online.

Aging

MANY SENIOR CITIZENS are well educated about health concerns, and senior citizen organizations keep tabs on issues of special relevance to them. Dr. C. Everett Koop, former U. S. Surgeon General, is a senior citizen himself, so we clicked on the tab at his drkoop site that says, "Aging Healthy." We found articles about diet and nutrition, fitness and disease prevention, mind and body changes, and much more.

> **Trivia…**
>
> *Under "mind and body," we looked at an article called "Outsmarting Forgetfulness," and found an upbeat list of things you can do to outsmart forgetfulness, such as writing things down, staying involved, not drinking too much, and adopting "kick-start" habits, or what psychologists call mnemonics.*

In the senior years, the interrelationship between mind and body becomes particularly obvious. One person might be burdened with serious physical ailments and disabilities, yet still cope very effectively by staying mentally healthy; while another person's physical health might be severely degraded by a loss of zest for living. This reality is reflected in many web resources about aging.

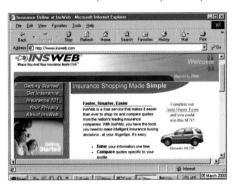

■ **At InsWeb** *you can shop for insurance by entering your information, comparing quotes, and choosing from the most trusted companies.*

Support groups and discussions for seniors and their families provide lots of health information. In addition, many sites for seniors also address their avocations, hobbies, volunteer work, politics, and social activities such as dating. Travel planning sites are popular among seniors, who move back and forth seeking warmer climates, and discuss the health benefits of particular climates, regions and lifestyles.

■ **Seniors can organize** *their sporting activities over the web.*

THE GRAY PANTHERS

The Gray Panthers is an organization only indirectly related to the health of the aging, but we can't resist mentioning it here. It was founded in Berkeley by Maggie Kuhn, who, when in her seventies, caught the spirit of social activism and spoke up for the rights of senior citizens.

Her organization has been advocating for seniors ever since, and in fact, has been consistently militant and fiercely political in lobbying and in organizing protests.

While the Gray Panthers has never been a very large group, its uppity attitude has clearly influenced more mainstream senior citizens advocacy groups. Health is always a political issue for the aging, as health care costs consume huge amounts of the limited income on which many seniors must live. Visit The Gray Panthers at www.graypanthers.org.

■ **You can contact** *other seniors with similar interests on the Internet.*

Trivia...

Many track and field events now include "masters" categories, with entries and finish records broken out by age groupings. Several organizations, such as The Fifty-Plus Fitness Association (www.50plus.org), have developed programs to help mature people practice regular exercise routines and stay fit.

At www.aarp.org you can find links to advocacy groups, as well as articles about Medicare, nursing homes, wellness research, health insurance options, and other important topics for seniors and their families. Family members, if you want to help preserve the health of your seniors, educate yourself on their issues and needs by checking into these web sites now and then.

Body and soul

At marathons and other races and sports contests, participants are generally divided by gender and age into separate classes. "Over 60" is usually the oldest group, but sometimes there's an "over 70" class, too. Men and women in that age bracket often finish well ahead of many

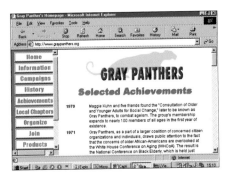

■ **Although a** *relatively small organization, the Gray Panthers has had a major impact in combating ageism and advocating rights for senior citizens.*

younger athletes. Some of these are people who run regularly, maintaining cardiovascular and muscular fitness through the aerobic activity of daily exercise. They tend to keep tabs on themselves, comparing their time on different days for running the same distance, and keeping log books of their daily activity.

Physicians who specialize in health care for the aged are called gerontologists. We're not sure when that word came into the vocabulary of the American Medical Association, and it's not yet a recognized field of specialization, nor have formal medical residencies been established to prepare doctors for it. However, many medical schools are starting to give this subject special treatment in coursework. And some arrange for new doctors to care for the elderly in Veterans Administration hospitals, or in "swing-bed" wards in hospitals, where elderly patients are waiting for placement in nursing homes.

INTERNET

www.medicare.gov

Visit this web site for information about Medicare.

As the numbers of elderly Americans grow, more physicians may be drawn into this specialty. We can expect to see many more web sites dedicated primarily to the health concerns of seniors.

Seniors on the net

There are now computers in many nursing homes, usually owned by individual patients but sometimes provided by the institution.

The joys of surfing and e-mail are helping many seniors stay abreast of the news, and feel connected to their families and to the world.

In this sense, the Internet does more than just inform people about health care issues, it becomes an integral part of their efforts to stay healthy in body and soul. Actually, we hope this group of Internet newcomers is a part of our readership – and we hope this book will provide many seniors with a bridge into the online community.

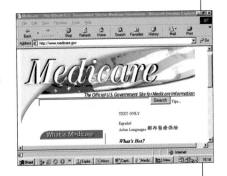

■ **The not surprisingly** *comprehensive web site of Medicare, the largest U.S. health insurance program, includes information on fraud and abuse.*

337

Hospitals and nursing homes often have their own web sites, offering information about their facilities and services, as well as access to social workers who can help families make suitable arrangements for the care of their seniors.

Online research and negotiation may help save families money, time, worry, and expense, and serve as an alternative to telephone calls. However, when selecting care facilities for your senior family members, we recommend always visiting any facility in person if possible, and checking its references before making any decision.

LONG-TERM CARE SITES

Here are some useful online resources for researching options for long-term care:

✓ Health Care Financing Administration: www.medicare.gov/nursing/home.asp.
✓ American Association of Homes and Services for the Aging: www.aahsa.org/public/sh.htm
✓ SeniorCare Nursing Home Reporter: www.seniorcarehelp.com
✓ Benjamin Rose Institute: www.benrose.org/aging/nursehome.asp
✓ Nursing Home Information: www.nursinghomeinfo.com
✓ ElderCare Consulting: www.jeffdanger.com
✓ Nursing Home Visitor Exchange: www.members.tripod.com/~tbohacek

Electronic medical records

THE ELECTRONIC MEDICAL RECORD (EMR) is considered one of the most important lifesaving innovations in the developing field of health care and the Internet. Imagine that a car accident victim is rushed to an emergency room, unconscious. An Emergency Medical Technician finds a bracelet with a web site address and password, and calls in to the ER. The doctors there have instant access to the patient's name, physician, and medical file – even before the ambulance arrives.

Many people in the health care and Internet industries envision a day when paper medical files have become a thing of the past. Patients, physicians, pharmacies, hospitals, and insurers will all transmit information into a single digital file.

Naturally, privacy advocates are concerned about privacy safeguards, and about maintaining individuals' confidentiality and personal control over such online records.

Assuring needed levels of data security is a key part of the challenge for companies developing EMR applications, such as WellMed, MedicaLogic, MedicalRecord.com, Healtheon, Elixis, and PersonalMD.

In this chapter, we've surveyed online health and medicine resources. We've reviewed a variety of sites, including general consumer health resources, directories, subject-focused sites, health organizations online, support groups, online drugstores and pharmacy services, and other e-commerce operations. We've surveyed a tiny number of the many thousands of health-related web sites, and learned that there are many kinds of sites for many kinds of health needs and issues. We learned there are many benefits and advantages to accessing health information and services online, but several pitfalls as well, including the risk of inaccurate or unreliable information, and a lack of clear distinctions between commercially influenced and independent reports.

A simple summary

✓ Web sites devoted to health and medicine include many resources.

✓ General health reference sites are a good place to start for many medical subjects.

✓ There are many web sites that will help you locate appropriate medical insurance.

✓ Many online pharmacy services and other health-related e-commerce operations are now open for business.

✓ Health concerns of senior citizens.

✓ Many sites offer help in locating nursing homes and other long-term care.

✓ You can easily find online support groups, where you can share your particular medical interests.

✓ The Electronic Medical Record is considered a major new innovation that will be widely used in coming years.

Chapter 19

Special Interests

THE VARIETY of possible interest areas is endless – for instance, we could write a whole book on sports-oriented families, music makers, automobile enthusiasts, model shipbuilders, or teddy-bear collectors. There are shelves full of books on any one of these topics. So in this chapter, we'll just touch on major categories of special interests, pointing out that you can find sites for virtually any avocation, hobby, or specialty, somewhere on the Internet. If you're a family of one, this chapter applies to you as much as any other family.

In this chapter...

✓ Culture

✓ Hobbies and collectibles

✓ Games and recreation

✓ News and politics

✓ Genealogy

FAMILY INTERESTS ARE WIDELY CATERED FOR ON MANY WEB SITES

Culture

■ **Whatever your** *interest you will find it featured on the Net.*

BACK IN CHAPTER 13, *the subject of culture arose in the discussion of searching for entertainment online. Now, we're going to go a little deeper, and consider those who aren't just spectators, but performers or students of culture – not just of the fine arts, but of popular culture, too. If you've already done some searching into your personal interest areas, you've probably noticed that the Internet always invites active participation. Along with the information we find online, there are lots of invitations to jump in and play.*

Many teachers of English and literature are also writers; many music teachers, at all levels, are also performers; and many teachers of painting and sculpture would really rather be in their studios, creating. They teach to make a living, but live for the times when they can pursue their art, and talk about it with fellow artists.

The Internet provides a new outlet for creative people of all kinds. Many of the most interesting web sites are published not by big-name companies, but by individuals, small groups and organizations.

Part of the fun and reward of delving into a niche online is finding these gems of high-quality information, created for the sheer love of a subject, rather than purely for profit.

Book lovers

There are so many resources on the web for book lovers, fans of particular authors, and amateur writers that it's almost a web within the web. Bookstores, publishers, magazines, newspapers, writing workshops, book reviews, online books, in-progress collaborative writing, specific author discussion groups, classes and reading groups – there are endless resources, much too numerous to list. Dozens, if not hundreds, of USENET newsgroups host discussions of various authors, books, literary genres, and other topics of interest to book lovers. If you happen to be a fan of a particular writer, but haven't found any web sites devoted to your favorite, you might well find fellow devotees in a newsgroup. And if not, you can start your own group.

INTERNET

www.well.com

One online community of book lovers gathers at The Well. Subscribers to The Well can join literary conferences that often include well-established writers. The conversation is sophisticated and witty, and anyone in the conference can participate. Subscriptions aren't expensive, and the Well's resources are well worth the modest cost.

■ **An online resource** *for book lovers, The Well site features annual writing awards, witty literary conversation, and a book store.*

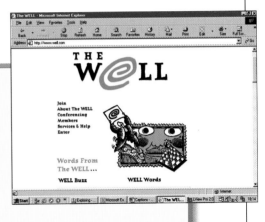

LITERATURE SITES

Here are a few web sites of interest to lovers of literature. Most of these also provide links to related sites.

✓ Atlantic Unbound: www.theatlantic.com
✓ Poets & Writers: www.pw.org
✓ BookWire: www.bookwire.com
✓ LitLine: www.litline.org
✓ Bookspot: www.bookspot.com
✓ Zuzu's Petals Literary Resource: www.zuzu.com
✓ Overbooked: www.freenet.vcu.edu/education/literature/bklink.html
✓ The Literary Web: www.people.virginia.edu/~jbh/litweb.html
✓ Literary Resources on the Net: www.andromeda.rutgers.edu/~jlynch/Lit
✓ New Fiction Project: www.newfiction.org

Libraries are also important for book lovers. If you teach, write, or do literary research, you probably already have many connections to useful libraries. A good place to find others is the American Library Association at www.ala.org. If you're an aspiring writer, good places to find practical information about publishing are www.booktalk.com and www.inkspot.com.

And of course, don't forget that publishing your own work on the Internet is simple, and will likely put you in contact with potential readers, other book lovers, and fellow writers.

Music lovers

If you've read Chapter 15, on multimedia, you know how to find the music of your choice online, and how to download, play, or purchase it on CD. So we won't talk about music retrieval sites here. Instead, we'll concentrate on online musical information and interactive opportunities. We went to Yahoo and entered a search for music, beginning with "jazz." Just that one word returned a list of categories that led to a steady stream of promising web sites. For instance, we found sites devoted to jazz artist John Coltrane and looked at a number of these, learning about his life and why he had such a great influence on the music world. In a sidebar, we noticed the entry, "Y Clubs for Music." A click on that spot brought choices of Yahoo clubs for different interests. We clicked on "for musicians."

For musicians

Here, we were asked to choose from a list including instruments, conductors, singers, songwriters, and other groups. We clicked on "view most popular clubs." This brought a long list of music clubs with anywhere from thirty to five hundred members, along the comment, "clubs created today will appear in the directory within 24 hours." By this time, it was clear that there's lots of interaction among musicians happening online. And this is only one avenue to make contact. Back at Yahoo, we tried the same process with classical music, starting our search with "Beethoven." From the pool of returns, we selected the Beethoven IRC channel, a very busy IRC chat channel dedicated to Beethoven. Visitors are urged to get an IRC client if they don't have one, and to submit brief bios and photos for the guest book.

DEFINITION

International Relay Chat (IRC) is one of the older communications methods, predating the World Wide Web. It requires special software, and enables real time communication with others who also have IRC software installed.

We then decided to look for sites on country music, and decided Willie Nelson would be a great starting point. His name brought several returns, and another link to music clubs; that path eventually took us to www.gentleman-jim.com.

At this site, devoted to Jim Reeves and many other country music stars, fans of Willie Nelson and many other artists can read biographies of their favorites, and find links to many other sites.

■ **Why not go** *online to find out more about your musical interests.*

Repeatedly during this process, we were given the option to choose regional web sites, which would let us know where musicians in a particular geographic area get together to make music. Local community networks would also be helpful. Other options might include sites like the American Society of Composers and Performers (ASCAP) at www.ascap.com, and the American Federation of Musicians at www.afm.org. ASCAP is a society of professional songwriters, lyricists, and music publishers that helps protect the rights of members by licensing and distributing royalties for public performances of copyrighted works. ASCAP also provides a wide variety of resources for every kind of music lover, especially performers and composers. The American Federation of Musicians is the union of professional musicians. Members support one another, and work cooperatively for the common good.

■ **Searching for** *"Beethoven" at Yahoo yields tens of thousands of possible pages.*

Are you really interested in a particular subject? Keep in mind that neither the major search engines, nor the directory sites, nor any single list of links, no matter how comprehensive, can possible keep up with the universe of related sites.

Keep on surfing from site to site, and from list of links to list, and you're sure to uncover a few gems. If not, chances are you'll find yourself practicing HTML so you can fill the need for a truly great web site about whatever your passion may be! Also, try multiple searching strategies – for example, if your passion is coins, try general search terms like "coin collecting" and "numismatics," but also some more specific queries, such as "1943 pennies" (the ones made of steel during wartime).

Art lovers

New York City is arguably the center of the art world in the United States, so we began this subject at www.nycvisit.com, where you'll finds lists of all the museums and galleries in the Big Apple. The official site of the city itself, www.ci.nyc.ny.us, has a site search engine where the word "art" brings a long list of arts programs the city currently supports. If you live in any major city, it's likely that similar resources are available. Approaching local opportunities through local web networks is one way to contact the arts community wherever you live.

For people who live in small towns, it's often more difficult to experience and discuss art with others, so online resources can be a rewarding alternative. Infoseek is a good place to start a search for art and artists. Start with any well-known name, and you're likely to find lots of information about that artist and his work. These sites will often lead to other information and sites.

R.S.V.P.

Art is one of the categories in trivia games, and it often appears on TV game shows. Real art lovers may groan when contestants fail to recognize the world's great art works, or are totally clueless on art-oriented questions. Book lovers and music lovers are numerous, but art lovers seem to form small, elite communities in most locations. Internet groups devoted to specific artists, or to discussions of the world of art, can often be doubly important to those who live outside metropolitan areas. The best gathering place for the arts community in a small town may be one mini-gallery or an artist's studio. There may be more blue jeans than tuxedos, but the spirit is the same as in the big city. Small art communities exist all over the web as well, but in these settings, the participants can live anywhere on the planet!

Contacting individuals interested in art in chat rooms or on message boards is a little harder than finding folks who want to talk about music, sports or politics, but it can be done. For example, it didn't take long to find a few sites like ArtSpeak (www.artspeak. com), Artists Corner (www.artistcorner.com), Arts Wire (www.artswire.org), and Artists Exchange (www.artistexchange.about.com), which include message boards and chat rooms.

ARTS DIRECTORIES AND PORTALS

There are also several arts directories and portals, such as:
✓ Culture Finder: www.culturefinder.com
✓ ADAM: www.adam.ac.uk
✓ Artcyclopedia: www.artcyclopedia.com
✓ Gallery Guide: www.gallery-guide.com
✓ Visual Arts Network: www.visualartsnetwork.com

Thousands of artists have painstakingly created digital images of their work for display on the web. When seeking images of paintings, photographs, sculpture, drawings, and other visual art, the issues of downloading and monitor resolution take on special importance. Web images that offer high resolution take longer to download. But if you're looking at art, your patience will be rewarded. If an image of an artwork takes a while to download, that's so it will look good when you see it! Also, many people who publish art online have carefully tailored their web sites to look best at specific monitor settings.

Sometimes, the opening screens of these sites will suggest monitor resolution settings that will give you the best look at the art displayed there. For example, you may see a message like, "best viewed at 1024 x 768." While changing your screen resolution may be slightly inconvenient, we suggest giving it a try.

Hobbies and collectibles

WHEN IT COMES *to hobbies, the Internet is like a continuous convention, offering collectors endless opportunities to talk, buy, sell, and trade. There are so many places to do this it's pointless for us to spend much time listing sites – just a few examples will give you an entry point into the world online community for hobbyists. You can take it from there!*

Stamps, memorabilia, and collectibles

At the American Numismatic Association web site (www.money.org), we found club listings, links to online exhibits, and lots of other resources and news about coins and paper money. Other sites for coin collectors include www.heritagecoin.com, and www.greysheet.com, the coin dealers' newsletter.

At the HotBot search engine, we entered "stamp collecting," and got a wonderful list of web sites.

Exploring a few links, we found the Junior Philatelists of America (www.jpastamps.org), with informative articles, educational resources, and lots of links.

Other interesting sites we explored include the American Philatelic Society web site at www.stamps.org, Linn's Stamp News at www.linns.com, the U.S. Postal Service's stamp collecting site at www.stampsonline.com, and Stamp Link at www.stamplink.com.

Thousands of sites are devoted to all kinds of memorabilia and collectibles. Comic Book Link (www.comicbooklink.com) is a directory of comic book sites. CurioScape (www.curioscape.com) is a directory of antique sites.

Hard-boiled bargain hunters might turn up something at Yard Sale Search (www.yardsalesearch.com). For the vehicular collector, sites include the Antique Automobile Club of America, on the web at www.aaca.org. Yesterday's Tractor plows a furrow online at www.ytmag.com. RailServe at www.railserve.com is a directory of Railroad sites. Autographs are the focus at Autograph Collector (www.odysseygroup.com).

If the Great Teddy Bear Hug is your cup of tea, go to www.teddybears.com. Perhaps your cup of tea is tea – try Tea Masters at www.tea-masters.org. For serious map collecting, one launching point might be Mercator's World at www.mercatormag.com. Pin collectors might enjoy PinTraders at www.pintraders.net. Vintage computer enthusiasts will enjoy the Computer History Association of California at www.chac.org. The Lunch Box Pad is devoted to lunch box fever – click over to www.echoroom.com/lunchbox. If you're an Abe Lincoln nut, you've got to visit the Rail Splitter site at www.railsplitter.com. An all-hobbies type of resource is found at www.krause.com.

Many of the sites we visited link to online auctions. We'll talk a bit about this now. Later, in Chapter 21, we'll consider more about how web auctions work, both for buying and selling things online.

Trading, buying and selling

Serious collectors generally have detailed knowledge of the current market value of whatever they collect. Sometimes, your particular collection is lacking a certain item, so you're willing to spend more for it than the going rate – in order to fill in that hole in your collection, or to complete a set or series. Sometimes, you have many more than you want of some item, and selling or trading is the way to get something better, or get some cash to buy something you really want. You can easily find lots of web sites where you can do this.

Auctions are another avenue to consider, but require that you keep some important cautions in mind. At a live auction, you can see and handle the items you bid on.

■ **The Internet provides** *an exciting opportunity to purchase collectables, such as antiques at a live auction*

Internet auction sites try to provide the best possible descriptions, pictures, and guarantees, but it's not quite the same. So, be careful where you do business. The number one rule is probably, "If it seems too good to be true, it probably is."

Message boards and newsgroups can help you find other collectors, and track down specific or unusual items. We know a man who has a collection of antique paperbacks called Ace D – these were printed during the Forties and Fifties, and some are now extremely valuable. His collection is almost complete, and he's constantly searching for the few remaining volumes, identified by number. Message boards at web sites have put him in touch with a few people who've provided some of those missing volumes.

Games and recreation

GAMES FOR ONE *or two people are plentiful on the Internet – there may be more varieties of solitaire than you ever heard of. In gaming, your mouse can become a lion, as you click your way to the winner's circle. Games for all age brackets are also available on CD-ROMs; if you're an avid gamer, you may already have an inventory of these. We won't discuss CD-based games here – just games you play online. In addition, we'll have a bit to say to sports fans and animal lovers.*

Chess and other games

You can play chess online at a number of sites, including www.chess.net, www.chessmasternetwork.com, and www.chessclub.com. You can also get chess software from these sites, or from general libraries of shareware. Chess clubs are often regional; live tournaments in each region are announced on the club web sites. One listing of these opportunities is found at www.uschess.org.

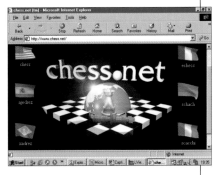

■ **Play chess online** at Chess.net either by purchasing the software on CD or downloading free versions for Windows, Java, or Telnet.

There are also many resources with archives of famous or historic chess games, information about great names in chess, and educational opportunities.

Interactive chess sites work much like chat lines, where you can enter a room, select one name from among the players present, and engage that person in a game of regular or speed chess.

Playing online

Of all the games people play, chess has by far the greatest body of history, so it's not surprising that its presence on the Internet is strong. Use any search engine to locate chess sites. Look under the subject heading "games" on the search engines, and at countless other sites, large and small, for other games such as solitaire, crossword puzzles, board games, strategy games, bingo, card games, trivia games, online versions of television game shows, and numerous other possibilities. Online games include single player and multi-player games, sometimes with simultaneous chat rooms. When we checked the Lycos gaming message board, it showed almost a hundred discussions underway about different aspects of game-playing. The vast majority of the specific games we looked into turned out to be sites for playing online, or for downloading freeware or shareware versions of specific games.

This will be no scoop for veteran game players, but parents should know that many of the gaming sites are also gambling sites. This is another place where kids may need ground rules and parental supervision.

■ **A search for** *"Beanie" at eBay's auction site finds 33,836 Beanie Babies auctions. Sorry – Batty the Tan Bat Ty Beanie's just been sold!*

Sports

Sports fans can find pretty much anything they want on the Internet, from detailed information on any professional or collegiate team sport, to sites covering individual sports, to audio broadcasts of games and matches. Streaming video of many games from the NFL, NBA, NHL, and Major League Baseball and other sports and leagues is often available. When you create a customized page at a web portal, search engine, or news site, you can usually ask that your home page show current information about your favorite teams. In short, the web is as sports-crazed as the rest of U.S. society. Chat with other fans, shop for sports memorabilia, buy tickets to games, and read up on individual players – it's all there.

■ **Baseball fans,** *the net should be your first port of call for information and tickets.*

CNNSI: *www.cnnsi.com*

ESPN: *www.espn.com*

Live Sports Action

SportsLine: *www.sportsline.com*
Sporting News: *www.sportingnews.com*

Reporting of live sports action is one of the things the Internet does best. Just check, for instance, at any of the following sites and you'll see the current scores of games underway all over the country, with running commentary as the scores change.

Whether you have time for a lengthy online session, or just a moment to check the action, such rapid news reporting can't be beat.

These are just a few of the sports sites available. As with the other subjects we discuss in this chapter, there are thousands of others, ranging from large business and media sites, to sites created by individual fans and athletes.

■ **CNN Sports Illustrated**
(www.cnnsi.com) is one of many web sites offering full sports coverage including live action with running commentary.

Animals

Animal lovers come in many varieties. Some are devotees of one particular type of animal, some are avid animal-rights advocates, and some just want to learn more about their own pets. The web has lots of resources for all these folks. For instance, we thought about horse lovers, and without even looking anything up, took a try at www.equestrian.com. This turned out to be the web site of the Internet Horse Breeders Association.

In the major web directories, from the search category of animals come lists of subcategories, where you can pick types of animals, pets, wildlife, or animal protection groups.

■ **Horse lovers!**
Why not contact your local riding club on the Net to find out about upcoming events?

These include People for the Ethical Treatment of Animals (www.peta.com), and the American Society for the Prevention of Cruelty to Animals (www.aspca.org). The category of horses leads to subcategories for various breeds, riding, shopping for saddlery and riding accessories, and many local riding clubs and associations, complete with message boards and notices of upcoming events. We even found a couple of animal lovers' pen pal sites.

Please keep your guidelines for children on the Internet in mind! Pen pal relationships are a longstanding and rewarding part of many children's lives, but before letting your youngster begin a pen pal relationship, we urge parents to check references, and make sure the pal on the other side of the pen is exactly who it should be.

■ **The American Society** *for the Prevention of Cruelty to Animals pioneered animal protection in 1866 and continues doing so at www.aspca.org.*

News and politics

MOST OF US *have more than a passing interest in the news, but some people follow the news much more closely than others. Politics gets mixed reviews, as some people pay very close attention, while others try to avoid the subject entirely. For instance, telecasts of election results have become steadily less popular over the past decade. Back in Chapter 13, we described the many options the Internet offers for customizing your personal news feed, and getting the news you really care about delivered directly to you.*

Issues

■ **Keep up to date** *with news as it happens.*

Subscribe to an online news source like the New York Times (www.nytimes.com – online registration is free) if you really want to stay abreast of breaking news. But if your interest in the news centers on a few specific issues, the best place to connect with the latest developments may be the web site of some organization or news service set up specifically to address those issues. All the major questions of the day, from health care to environmental concerns to Internet regulation, are represented by such organizations.

Not only will these sites provide more content about your issues of concern, but they'll approach their reporting with a slightly different attitude, assuming that their audience expects them to give the subject in-depth attention.

Find the groups most concerned with issues you care about, and bookmark their sites. If different members of your family have different interests, set up a common bookmark folder called News, and list those sites together.

■ **Access to the** *New York Times on the web is free.*

Parties and people

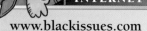

INTERNET

www.blackissues.com

Just as an example, check the coverage of news for African-Americans at www.blackissues.com, the web site of Black Issues in Higher Education. You'll find news briefs similar to those at CNN and other general news sites, but also articles about careers for black Americans, as well as related topics that won't appear in the general news.

What if you live in the United States and your family included Republicans, Democrats and Independents? As elections draw near, will there be heated debates at the dinner table? Some families face a generation gap when it comes to politics, with the younger members voting differently than their parents. Sometimes, it's a gender gap. On the web, you'll find ample ammunition for all sides of any debate about candidates, issues, or political parties. Visiting the home pages of the two major parties, you'll find both of them set up to encourage local participation.

Both Democrats and Republicans are organized at local, county, and state levels, and many of these organizations have their own web sites. For instance, New York Democrats are found at www.nydems.org, and Illinois Republicans at www.ilgop.org. These sites provide a wealth of information, as well as the opportunity to contribute money or opinions, right online. Directories of such sites can be found at the Democratic National Committee site (www.democrats.org), and the Republican National Committee site (www.rnc.org).

POLITICAL WEB SITES

Directories of politically oriented web sites are available at several sites, such as:

✓ ePolitics: www.epolitics.org
✓ Policy.com: www.policy.com
✓ Politics1: www.politics1.com

■ **Soon you may** *be able to vote over the Internet.*

Observers say we'll soon be voting via the Internet. The first official public vote using the Internet recently took place in Alaska, when the Republican party conducted their straw poll Presidential primary online. During the Alaskan winter, daylight is limited to four hours, as darkness prevails for twenty hours. Using computers enabled greater participation in the election. The election was conducted by VoteHere (www.votehere.com), a company that now has a patent pending for secure online elections.

Genealogy

WE SAVED THIS *section for last in this chapter because it's the one special interest activity that may be avidly pursued by just one family member, but that directly affects the whole family. Genealogy is very popular among Americans these days, as the old melting-pot metaphor for the United States has been replaced by multiculturalism and the desire to know more about your family's background and roots. Genealogy research is complicated enough that many community colleges offer courses on the subject.*

Research

One excellent web site to begin exploring genealogy resources on the web is www.cyndislist.com. There are several indexes to this site, each with a different focus.

The "topical index" led us to a number of topics, from which we chose "research tools." This opened a long list of resources, from sites within countries of origin, to religions, locations, and many other options.

A click on one of these took us to yet another list of archives and information resources, where we could have continued the quest and been asked more specific questions. The web offers tremendous possibilities for genealogical research.

■ **At JewishGen** *you can talk to other Jews all over the world.*

If you're new to genealogical research, we recommend that you spend some time studying the methodologies outlined at such sites as www.rootsweb.com, www.genhomepage.com, and www.familytreemaker.com.

Once you have an idea of how to proceed, you might want to visit www.ancestry.com, where thousands of family names are listed.

If you're of Jewish extraction, a good place to begin is at JewishGen (www.jewishgen.org). For many reasons, genealogical research may be more fully developed among Jewish citizens than in any other group. At JewishGen, you'll find links to archives, descriptions of ongoing research work, and discussion groups all over the world. A special box invites input from any visitor to the Holocaust research and records.

Genealogy is an undertaking that requires patience. Don't get discouraged if you encounter many dead ends.

Finding your roots often takes patient detective work over a long period of time. Leaving your name and contact information in relevant places will help other genealogists to find you, when their own research brings them to a point where your search and theirs connect.

Family history

Other family members may or may not have expressed interest in the work of the family historian, but when your work produces significant results, they'll probably take notice. Particularly at family reunions, which often take place in the summer, a well-organized family history will be the center of attention.

At www.familytreemaker.com, you can download a software program that provides access to voluminous records, plus a format for constructing your family tree, designed for major computer platforms.

Genealogy is a long-term project. You can go back as many generations as you wish, and even create a complete history, right back to the origin of your family name. Through one of the family-oriented web sites such as www.myfamily.com, you can gather more recent information to bring your family's history up to the present. This type of Internet connection also enables the family historian to keep everyone informed about the progress of genealogical work.

You may encounter branches of your family tree that aren't online. That's where Internet yellow pages come in handy. Or, you might consider a public records search to get telephone numbers and addresses for contacts. In short, the Internet has made genealogical research much easier than it ever was before, which has probably contributed to its increasing popularity.

■ **Music lovers can** *find kindred spirits on the web.*

A simple summary

✓ Book lovers, music lovers, and art lovers can find many web sites that will put them in touch with kindred souls, as well as offer information about their interests.

✓ Collectors can buy, sell, and trade online, as well as contact fellow collectors, locally and around the world.

✓ You can play lots of single-player and multi-player games, right online. Be aware that some include opportunities for gambling.

✓ Lots of sites are devoted to hobbies, memorabilia, and collectibles.

✓ Web sites devoted to sports are very busy, providing up-to-the-minute reports of ongoing games, in-depth information about teams and individual players, and the opportunity to communicate with other fans through message boards and chat rooms.

✓ Animal lovers can contact one another via the web, finding specific local organizations as well as animal rights groups.

✓ Those with special interest in the news, particularly on important issues, can get in-depth reporting and commentary on those issues from the web sites of relevant organizations.

✓ Political parties, organizations, and causes have established online presences.

✓ Many families are interested in exploring their roots and doing genealogical research. The web offers many easy-to-find resources.

Chapter 20

Net Education

WE CONCLUDE this Part of the book about the Internet and the family with a chapter on education – because we believe the Internet experience usually stimulates curiosity to know more about many topics. When they first go online, people often think of the Internet as just a convenience, or a nice little addition to everyday life. After delving into the online world, though, most users come to realize that it's really much more than that. Whatever your age, the Internet encourages you to expand your horizons and enrich your personal world. Just about any time you're surfing the web, you're really engaged in informal learning.

In this chapter...

✓ Distance learning

✓ Support traditional education

✓ Continuing education

✓ Internet skills

✓ Impacting the family

THE INTERNET OFTEN STIMULATES LEARNING

Distance learning

IN THIS CHAPTER, *we'll talk about distance learning at every level. Well start with online degree programs, set up by universities, that enable students to progress through all the steps involved in earning a college degree. You can earn bachelor's degrees and graduate degrees this way, doing everything necessary right from your computer. In most cases, these degrees carry the names of well-known, respected, traditional educational institutions that have expanded into distance learning. We'll also mention some "virtual universities" that are accredited to grant degrees.*

■ **It is possible** *to apply and study for a degree online.*

If you never finished an earlier degree program, or think that a graduate degree might now be worth working for, online study might be your answer. If a traditional college experience is what you have in mind, there are many resources online to help you prepare for college entrance exams (SAT or ACT), and graduate school exams (GRE, LSAT, and MCAT.) Check web directories or search engine sites to find them, or check higher learning sites such as:

✓ College Board: www.collegeboard.org
✓ Educational Testing Service Network: www.eds.org
✓ American College Entrance Directory: www.aaced.com

At these sites, you can find schedules for where and when these exams are given, along with all necessary information and applications. (These traditional kinds of tests are usually not required for online degree programs.) If you never finished high school, you can prepare to take the GED (general equivalency diploma) test through online study. You can learn English as a second language, study a foreign language, or pursue

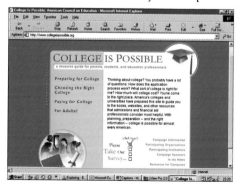

■ **College Is Possible** *is a useful starting point for would-be students, guiding them through the complexities of course selection and application.*

continuing education to strengthen your professional skills. In short, the Internet has become an extension of traditional education, and can now supplement, support, or even replace many of the more familiar forms of learning.

College level

Distance learning programs use both synchronous and asynchronous technologies. Synchronous methods require real-time participation of both student and teacher. These include computer conferencing, audiographics, and interactive TV. Asynchronous methods include e-mail, listservs (e-mail-based lists, that we talked about back in Chapter 6), videotaped courses, and web-based courses.

There are a number of steps involved in formally enrolling in any college or university. The same steps, from seeking financial aid, to contacting the admissions office, to registering for courses, also apply to online study. You can find applications for admission, student information, FAQ lists, and avenues for submitting questions at the web sites of participating institutions.

Among the institutions that currently offer full degree programs online are Baker College, Boise State University, Embry-Riddle Aeronautical University, Rochester Institute of Technology, the University of Phoenix Online, and many others.

At eCollege.com, we were invited to choose a type of degree and a particular field, and search for courses currently available online. We entered "Masters degree in Humanities," and received a list of two hundred courses, covering every aspect of the Humanities, from religion to music appreciation, offered all over the country – including Denver, Chicago, and cities in California and Connecticut.

■ **At eCollege.com** *students can seek courses or learn online. There are facilities for teachers and for higher education in companies.*

Another useful web site to visit for complete information about these opportunities is Peterson's Education Supersite (www.petersons.com.) Navigating through this site, we found that bachelor's degrees are offered in more than 80 different fields. We checked a few and found most traditional college subject areas, ranging from communications to animal science. Another useful site is www.intered.com. And alt.education.distance is a newsgroup for distance learning students.

At www.pbs.org/netlearning, we opened the FAQ and found the question, "Do students just view web pages in online learning, or is there human contact?" The site provided this answer, "Some courses simply require students to browse lecture notes, but the dominant method is for communication between students, their peers, and the instructor." Online discussions, virtual bulletin boards, and conversation and debate are all part of the learning process, with two-way interactive audio and video the primary technologies.

■ **Online discussions** *are a part of many courses of study on the Net.*

Human contact is becoming a scarce commodity in traditional education. Classes in major universities are often too large to allow for much student participation. Professors sometimes turn over their teaching duties to graduate assistants, while exams are graded by computer. Even though students and teacher are in the same place at the same time, active involvement may actually be less than an online student can enjoy.

The online classroom

We were invited to visit a sample online classroom. Here, we found that software tools make the online classroom tick. The professor's office has unlimited office hours, because the Internet never sleeps. We learned that approximately thirteen million students are now attending classes in traditional classrooms, while one million attend school online. About a third of U. S. institutions of higher learning offer courses online; dollars spent on distance learning total one billion.

■ **Western Governors** *University is a virtual university, created for online teaching. Degrees include Learning and Technology and Associate of Arts.*

It's estimated that about fifty-five percent of the faculties of existing educational institutions are resistant to the idea of online and distance learning. Nevertheless, statistics gathered by the National Center for Education Statistics (www.nces.ed.gov) indicate that three-quarters of the nation's colleges and universities plan to increase their distance education programs. The Distance Education Training Council (www.detc.org), in Washington, D.C., supervises accreditation for distance learning programs.

A virtual university is an institution created specifically for online or distance learning. One example is the Western Governors University (www.wgu.edu), which incorporates into its offerings a number of means for distance learning, from the old methods of snail mail correspondence, to the latest telecommunications technology. A virtual university classroom exists wherever the student may be, working by whatever means the student chooses. Web-based courses are the most popular among the forms of technology offered.

Financial aid is available for students in distance learning programs, but exactly what kind, and how to get it, depends on a great number of variables. The financial aid office of the program you select will patiently work through your particular situation. They may want you to begin with the traditional federal student aid application, which you can find and complete online.

If you believe you might want to pursue a college degree through distance learning, start by seeking the same kind of information you'd look for in a more traditional setting – what will it cost, how long will it take, what advantages will this degree give me, and so on. The web sites of the institutions you choose will often have all the information you need to make your decisions. The Internet references we mention in this chapter are only examples of the many resources available. Any one of them will link to many others, and you can get lists of even more resources from any search engine.

Campus outreach

We wanted to see if some well-known universities offer distance learning courses, so, we visited the web sites of several major universities. We found that online learning is a growing part of the academic program at these revered institutions. For example, we went to the web site of the University of Notre Dame at www.nd.edu, and entered "distance learning" in the site search engine. We found that Notre Dame offers a videoconference MBA program, conducted right at the headquarters of several corporations in their region. The synchronous technology supporting this program is quite sophisticated, involving two-way audio and compressed digital video, spanning the distance between on-campus classrooms and the business location conference rooms. Workers can participate in real-time cyber courses leading to the MBA degree, right from their own work locations.

INTERNET

**www.mcli.dist.
maricopa.edu/tl**

Alan Levine is an "Instructional Technologist," a professional devoted to the use of technology in education. Mr. Levine, who works at the Maricopa Center For Learning and Instruction in California, maintains a diverse and fascinating list of educational uses of the Internet.

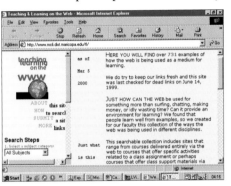

■ **The Maricopa Center** *for Learning and Instruction lists "over 731 examples of how the web is being used as a medium for learning."*

Many enterprising businesses support such programs to help their employees maintain and upgrade their skills. Other corporations and institutions provide financial support for graduate education – including online degree programs – that individual students pursue on their own.

If you're not interested in a degree program, but would like to pick up some advanced training through one or two courses, check with eCollege.com, www.embark.com, or www.usdla.org – chances are, the very course you want is available.

High schools

Distance education is being used in a number of ways for high school students. These programs are generally developed within a particular city or state, often by a local university's department of education. For instance, the Indiana Academy Office of Ball State University (www.bsu.edu) conducts distance learning programs for small high schools through interactive telecasts, along with supplementary web sites and e-mail.

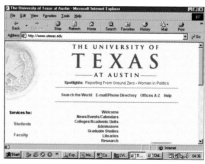

■ **The University of Texas** *at Austin provides web-based distance learning courses for high schools.*

One of the most exciting and enterprising developments in high school distance learning is the virtual high school (VHS) – a consortium of high schools all over the country that greatly expands course offerings in large and small schools. To belong to the VHS, a school must donate some staff time (to coordinate the program within that school), and teacher time for at least one or two courses. The VHS (vhs.concord.org) provides software, training for participating teachers, and technical support. With the VHS, even very small schools can greatly enlarge their effective teaching staffs, as all the resources of all the participating schools are available to any. Sponsors of the VHS include Compaq, Lotus, Interliant, American Power Conversion, the 3Com Corporation, and Fitchburg State College.

The National PTA (Parent-Teacher Association) is on record as supporting distance learning. Their advocacy of electronic technologies often takes them to Washington, D.C. The PTA has made this official statement: "The National PTA opposes any Federal requirement that will infringe on schools' and students' ability to access information on the World Wide Web." The National PTA web site (www.pta.org) is a source for a variety of information and resource links.

INTERNET

www.utexas.edu

The University of Texas (www.utexas.edu) provides web-based high school courses that any school can take advantage of. These are just examples of programs that can be found all over the country, in conjunction with colleges and universities. And because many of these distance learning programs also serve as training modules for future teachers, they also help enhance teacher education.

In fact, the PTA reports that these programs increase parental involvement in education, sometimes as much as 80 percent.

We've already talked about how students at every level use the Internet for help with homework. Many high schools now encourage this web-assisted study by putting computers in libraries and study halls, and scheduling time for students to do homework assignments there. This helps span the digital divide between homes with computers and homes without.

Primary schools

Elementary schools have also embraced the principle of pooling resources to expand their capabilities through the Internet. Child U (www.childu.com) is an all-purpose resource for schools and homes, offering everything from curriculum materials to teacher support suggestions and assigned tutoring. Similar online resources are easy to find, and very plentiful, on the web. The full effectiveness of these tremendously helpful classroom aids depends on the level of technology available in each classroom. Local schools are generally dependent on federal and state funding for classroom technology.

All fifty states and the District of Columbia are part of a federal program called Star Schools. This federally-funded effort targets children in disadvantaged, illiterate, and limited-English families, as well as children with disabilities and those living in areas of greatest poverty, including children served by Bureau of Indian Affairs schools. In many of these areas, few qualified teachers are available, and online resources supplement traditional classroom methods.

Star Schools, serving 1.6 million children, are located in big cities and rural areas, wherever there's an appropriate group of children. The funds come directly from the federal government, and are administered locally.

Star School funds supply the computer technology that enables distance learning. Star School programs employ a variety of technologies, depending on what kind of equipment is available. If the computers being used are old, or have severely limited capabilities, web-based technologies aren't always the best choice. Look for more details about Star Schools at www.ed.gov and www.wested.org.

■ **Child U's all-purpose resource** *for schools and homes, The Learning Odyssey, includes curriculum materials and assigned tutoring.*

In addition to the Star School program, traditional schools supplement their classroom teaching with distance education, especially for courses – such as foreign languages – that interest only a few students. Synchronous technology fits well into many elementary schools, where many students can share a presentation. Asynchronous technology is replacing the special teachers who used to help with home-bound students. To find out about local elementary school programs, check with your city or state department of education.

In addition to the ones we've mentioned, three other Federal programs supporting online access in elementary education are Technology Innovation Challenge grants, Education Technology, and Original Technology in Education Consortia.

All of these provide training for teachers in the effective use of technology in the classroom. If you're a teacher or parent, you might want to investigate the possibilities of these programs at www.ed.gov.

Home schooling

■ **Parents!** *The net can help your child learn at home.*

Some parents choose to educate their children at home. Best estimates from the U.S. Department of Education, and the National Home Education Research Institute, indicate that more than a million children from pre-school age through sixth grade are being educated at home in the U.S. There are home schools in all fifty states. The National Homeschool Association (www.nha.org) states, "Parents have the right to educate their children." Purposes of this organization include advocacy, communications, networking, and support.

It's hard to find data about use of the Internet in home schooling. The home setting, and the small number of students, seem to invite use of online resources, but some advocates of home schooling are somewhat anti-technology. Others, though, are very Internet-wise, have well organized web sites, and are in touch with other home schoolers all over the world. Examples of such sites include the HomeSchoolZone (www.homeschoolzone), and A-Z Home School, at www.gomilpitas.com/homeschooling. At these sites, you'll find links to curricula for teachers in home schools, as well as many other resources.

Private online classrooms sometimes use programs and services created to support online teaching and learning. For example, www.blackboard.com provides interactive

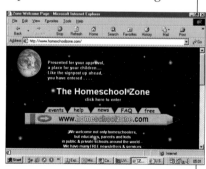

■ **The HomeSchool Zone** *is a well organized web site reaching out to home schoolers across the world through newsletters and services.*

tools you can downloaded and use to place customized course materials online. For more online information about home schooling, look at Homeschool.com, Home Educator (www.homeeducator.com), and Home Study International (www.hsi.edu), a Christian-oriented resource.

Blackboard.com uses both synchronous and asynchronous technologies, allowing teachers to specify course method and content.

Support traditional education

THE FEDERAL GOVERNMENT'S *Department of Education (www.ed.gov) offers many resources for schools and teachers, including publications and products, programs and services, and local success stories. However, state departments of education must follow a number of guidelines to keep their school systems eligible for federal help. There continues to be much disparity between more and less prosperous states.*

Use of telecommunications and computer technology is growing everywhere, and commercial interests are now providing many support services for the traditional classroom, through the Internet.

PARTNERSHIP ARRANGEMENTS

Electronic technology first made its way into college life quite soon after the computer networks of the academic community came into being. At first, there were computer centers on campus, but gradually, the electronic presence made its way into individual libraries, offices, and classrooms. Filtering down into secondary, and, finally, elementary schools, took some time, and was resisted by many teachers and parents. These protectors of the welfare of children worried that introducing technology into classrooms, especially at the elementary level, would degrade and depersonalize the quality of education. They assumed that instruction by real teachers was always superior to instruction through computers. That tension hardly exists anymore, as the partnership of live teachers and Internet teachers clearly benefits children.

■ **The net will not** *replace human interaction in the classroom.*

Teachers are often overworked, and need all the help they can get! Staying abreast of Internet developments has become just another job – in addition to the many they already do. High school teachers, in particular, are confronted with a student body of young people who are very savvy about electronic resources. It can be tough for a teacher to stay ahead of them! Teachers must continually learn not only how to use the Internet itself, but also how to tap into its vast resources for new and interesting course content.

A teacher's computer can become a valuable professional partner, replete with bookmarks for useful web sites, mailing lists, newsfeeds, and other customized services.

In addition, savvy teachers surf the web for lesson plans, and for supplementary materials for any and every subject area and grade level. We don't have any figures to support this contention, but it seems likely to us that the average teacher – especially elementary school teacher – also does a fair amount of teaching of basic computer skills. There are numerous sites set up primarily to help educators. The Educational Resources Information Center (Eric), at www.gwu.com, is a database of 950,000 articles about education.

Classroom resources

Often, personal resources belonging to individual teachers find their way into classrooms for use by students. If the school hasn't provided the technology a teacher needs to present a particular lesson, the teacher will often wind up bringing personal possessions to school – whether it's a CD or DVD player, floppy disks or CDs made at home of Internet-based material, or printouts of web site content.

It's probably not a good idea to go too far with this – not only because it seems above and beyond the call of duty for a teacher's personal resources to be used, but also because students who come from homes that aren't online may not relate quite as well to the web-based materials. Teachers: Don't make assignments that require students to use the Internet unless there are ample resources available in the school or library, as this may put the offline children and families at an unfair disadvantage.

■ **Teachers can download** *lesson information and record on CD.*

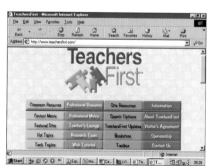

■ *TeachersFirst.com has a weekly Brain Twister (for students), and a fast multiple-choice quiz.*

Continuing education

ALL THE REFERENCES *we mentioned in the first part of this chapter, about college-level distance learning, are also relevant to continuing education. Not just teachers, but almost any professional, can find appropriate opportunities online to satisfy the continuing education requirements for professional credentialing or certification. You can also update your skills through short-term workshops and seminars. Many of these are also available online, generally from professional organizations, or centers for post-graduate education.*

Sites for teachers

Continuing education is a necessity for teachers; in the past, teachers often sacrificed their summer vacations to this need for professional upgrading. Teachers, especially in small, single-school towns, often had little opportunity to interact with their professional peers. The Internet offers teachers numerous avenues to continuing education, professional enrichment, and constructive sharing with their colleagues. Teachers use virtually every group communications resource the Internet provides.

One excellent resource for teachers is the National Education Association site at www.nea.org. This site is filled with news of special relevance to teachers, postings of job openings, ideas, references, and continuing education offerings. The NEA offers a weekly e-mail letter with all these same resources. In addition, state departments of education, and state universities with teacher training programs, plan, conduct, and publicize continuing education opportunities for teachers.

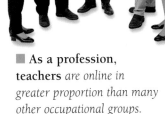

■ **As a profession, teachers** *are online in greater proportion than many other occupational groups.*

SOFTWARE REVIEWS

If you're a teacher, we recommend exploring the host of sites by and for educators; a few examples include:
✓ The Busy Teacher: www.ceismc.gatech.edu/busyt
✓ TeacherFirst: www.teacherfirst.com
✓ TeachWeb: www.teachweb.com

Internet skills

TEACHERS CAN *also tap into any of the several online education sites that teach Internet and computer skills. One example is SmartPlanet, at www.smartplanet.com. SmartPlanet also offers courses on many other topics, such as finance, business, health, and science. Other techie learning sites include:*

✓ CyberStateU: www.cyberstateu.com
✓ Learn2: www.learn2.com
✓ Technology Education Network: www.tentv.com.

In addition, mini-courses that simply hone and update skills, without offering college credit, are widely available at almost any major site focused on Internet technology. Search engines will help you find many of these opportunities. To get started, check out www.telecampus.edu or www.free-ed.net.

The horse's mouth

In this book, we've talked a lot about new and innovative forms of software. Repeatedly, we've commented that installing new software generally involves a learning process, and that you should allow some time for it. There's no better place to turn for that kind of learning than the web site of the software's manufacturer. When you begin thinking seriously about adding software, especially if it's completely new, and not just a new version of something you already use, take time to visit the web sites of competing manufacturers. Look for detailed tutorials. For example, Netscape and Microsoft offer many online training and learning opportunities through their web sites.

■ **Straight from** *the horse's mouth...*

Impacting the family

IN A FAMILY *where almost everyone is using the Internet, there may be a kind of natural sharing of experiences. Children tell parents, and spouses tell each other, about online discoveries. We know one family where Grandma is online every day, especially for e-mail. She's always forwarding family messages to other family members who live elsewhere. And she often comes to family* *gatherings with printouts of things she's found on the web. This is a mutual education process, in which all family members are both teachers and students.*

As the PTA says, parental participation in their children's education is increased when some of that education happens at home. An atmosphere of rising expectations can create a heightened awareness of education within the whole family, so it's less likely than anyone will ever forget about the joy of learning.

This chapter has summed up the family Part of this book, with a look at how a family's view of education is affected by their Internet experience. We've considered formal and informal education, discovered distance learning, and looked at the importance of education for individuals, and for the family.

A simple summary

✓ Distance learning programs in higher education offer bachelor's degrees and advanced degrees, in almost any field.

✓ Continuing to refine Internet skills is always possible, as the web provides ample material.

✓ A virtual university, or a virtual high school, is a distance learning opportunity set up specifically for the Internet.

✓ High schools are providing online technology, partly to supplement their traditional classrooms with courses they couldn't otherwise provide.

✓ Elementary schools also use online resources, both in the classroom, and as background support for teachers.

✓ About a third of all the nation's colleges and universities are already offering distance learning, and many more plan to do so.

✓ Continuing education opportunities for professionals, available online.

PART FIVE

SPECULATE TO ACCUMULATE ON THE NET

THE INTERNET AND YOUR MONEY

HERE AND NOW, we have some pressing questions about how the Internet can help us manage our funds more wisely and *effectively*. We'll see that the Internet offers endless opportunities to further your financial education — as well as to spend your money.

There are powerful software tools to help you organize and constantly update your personal

balancesheets. Millions of people are now shopping, banking, investing, and researching financial subjects online. The Internet not only greatly *simplifies* record-keeping, it enables you to see an up-to-the-minute picture of your financial condition — any time.

Chapter 21

Online Shopping

THERE ARE TWO ASPECTS to online shopping: the shopping, and the actual buying. Whether you're looking to buy, or just looking, the Internet has placed a huge and growing array of shopping possibilities right at your finger tips.

In this chapter...

✓ What is e-commerce?

✓ Product research

✓ Buying and selling

✓ Giving gifts online

✓ Digital money

✓ Consumer protection

GO SHOPPING WITH A FRIEND ONLINE

What is e-commerce?

E-COMMERCE *is the buying and selling of products and services online. Many people who've never bought anything online find this concept very foreign, complex, and perhaps unpleasant. If you're one of those folks who prefers buying from a live person in a retail store – where you can handle the merchandise, and bring it back for return or servicing – you probably won't find the Internet your favorite place to buy things.*

If you're nodding your head and thinking, "I like to buy from a real person I can see, so e-commerce is not for me," think for a moment. Have you ever bought anything by mail order or by telephone? Have you ever planned a trip and then called an airline to order tickets? Have you looked at pictures in a catalog, and then wrote a check or called a toll-free number to order? If the answer is yes, you've already proved you don't require the personal presence of a clerk ringing up your purchase at a cash register in order to buy something.

The Internet is just another channel for buying and selling, one that lets you peruse and shop at thousands of stores and product databases, 24 hours a day, right at home.

UPS AND THE DOWNS

A recent survey of online shoppers found a variety of reasons for using the Internet. Some examples: It saves time; traditional stores and malls are too crowded; the Internet is never closed; it reduces driving; there are lots of bargains online; you can shop earlier in the season; no haggling with salespeople; no sales tax; better selection than store shelves; and better availability of merchandise. The same survey also asked online shoppers their biggest peeves with e-commerce. Some answers? The shipping costs are too high; prices are too high; you can't try things on; not appropriate for bulky items; not appropriate for luxury items; and, it's nice to see and feel an item before buying it.

■ **Despite the advantages** *of online shopping, some people dislike not being able to feel an item before buying it.*

What can you buy online?

When e-commerce was new, one of the most popular types of transactions was the buying and selling of software. This worked well, because buyers could download the product and get instant satisfaction. Software sellers liked it, too, because downloads reduced their distribution costs dramatically. (However, many software companies still prefer to distribute boxed copies of their products on CD-ROMs with installers, to prevent unauthorized copies from floating around online too readily.)

■ **Online shoppers** *get their own "shopping cart" to gather items, before proceeding to the "checkout."*

In the mid-1990s, online retail businesses like Amazon.com and CDNow.com began operating in earnest. The number of people using the Internet now formed a potentially lucrative customer base, and thousands of entrepreneurs started offering e-commerce opportunities. Because of security concerns, ordinary consumers initially resisted online shopping, but these fears gradually eased, as big names in consumer banking, credit, and the computer industry came aboard and helped establish standards for credit card security. This brought consumers a greater comfort level with online buying.

Online retail sales now cover the gamut of consumer products, with intense competition in almost every product category.

Online shopping is simple – you click around the store until you see something you want, and then follow the directions to make the purchase. If you want more than one item, there's usually a "shopping cart" or "basket" in which you can gather multiple items before "checking out."

Some stores have express buying – if you want just one item, the process is speedier. To check out, you usually need to fill in two or three screens of information – specifying your name and address, credit card number, shipping method, and so on.

Often, doing this registers you at the site, so future purchases won't require as many forms. You'll generally see a confirmation page you can print out, and you'll often get a confirming e-mail as well. Some sites offer online order status lookup services, and various other customer services.

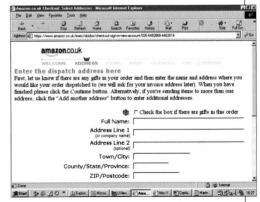

■ **After filling** *your "shopping basket," check out by completing a form like this.*

375

Online stores typically provide order confirmation numbers on the screen at the end of a purchase. Always print out the confirmation page, or write down the number, in case you need customer service or have a problem with the order.

Often these pages can't be bookmarked (for security reasons), so don't try to save the confirmation by adding the page to your bookmarks! Just print it out or save a copy of the page to your hard disc.

■ **Wearisome shopping** *lists are a thing of the past.*

SOME ONLINE STORES

✓ Books: Amazon.com (www.amazon.com), Barnes and Noble (www.bn.com), Borders (www.borders.com), FatBrain (www.fatbrain.com)

✓ Music: CDNow (www.cdnow.com), Tower Records (www.towerrecords.com), CD Universe (www.cduniverse.com), MusicMaker (www.musicmaker.com)

✓ Movies: Bigstar (www.bigstar.com), Reel.com (www.reel.com), TotalE (www.totale.com), BlockBuster (www.blockbuster.com), DVDExpress (www.dvdexpress.com)

✓ Toys: Etoys (www.etoys.com), FAO Schwartz (www.fao.com), Toys R Us (www.toysrus.com), Zany Brainy (www.zanybrainy.com)

✓ Sporting Goods: FogDog (www.fogdog.com), The Sports Store (www.thesportsstore.com), Gear (www.gear.com), ChipShot (www.chipshot.com)

✓ Outdoor products: Recreational Equipment Inc. (www.rei.com), Planet Outdoors (www.planetoutdoors.com), AdventureGear.com (www.adventuregear.com), and Eastern Mountain Sports (www.emsshop.com)

✓ Pet Products: Pets.com (www.pets.com), PetSmart (www.petsmart.com), Petopia (www.petopia.com), PETCO (www.petco.com)

✓ Flowers: 1-800 Flowers (www.1800flowers.com), ProFlowers (www.proflowers.com), PC Flowers (www.pcflowers.com)

✓ Clothing: The Gap (www.gap.com), BlueFly (www.bluefly.com), J Jill (www.jjill.com), Land's End (www.landsend.com), Eddie Bauer (www.eddiebauer.com), Underneath (www.underneath.com)

✓ Software: EggHead (www.egghead.com), Outpost (www.outpost.com), humbo (www.chumbo.com), Beyond.com (www.beyond.com), CDW (www.cdw.com)

✓ Computers: Gateway (www.gateway.com), Dell (www.dell.com), Compaq (www.compaq.com), Apple (www.apple.com)

✓ Gifts: Gifts.com (www.gifts.com), Red Envelope (www.redevelope.com), Present Picker (www.presentpicker.com)

Stores on the web

Online stores in most categories include "pure play" Internet companies, as well as traditional "brick and mortar" companies that have launched online businesses. There are many sellers blending the expertise of Internet companies with the established networks and business processes of traditional companies. We've already covered a few examples of online stores in earlier chapters; for example, in Chapter 18, we reviewed online pharmacies.

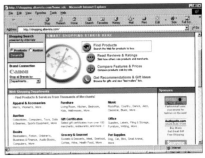

■ **Shopping.com**, *now part of Alta Vista, is a premier virtual mall.*

Finding online stores is easy. To get you started, here are several in popular categories. (Most of these stores actually carry many product categories; read the headings below as "category listed plus lots more.") These lists only scratch the surface, and may or may not be the best stores for you.

Remember that many narrowly-focused online merchants may offer deeper resources on specific subjects of interest than a larger, more broadly focused store.

Virtual malls and department stores

Another increasingly popular type of online shopping environment is the "virtual mall." These malls vary in how they work and what they offer. Some allow you to collect items in a single "shopping cart" from multiple vendors. Slow to catch on at first, these malls are becoming more and more popular with consumers.

SOME VIRTUAL MALLS

Check out a few at places like:

✓ Shopping.com: www.shopping.com
✓ CyberShop: www.cybershop.com
✓ Yahoo Shopping: www.shopping.yahoo.com
✓ Value America: www.valueamerica.com
✓ Lycos Shop: www.shop.lycos.com
✓ Mall.com: www.mall.com
✓ NetMarket: www.netmarket.com
✓ Buy.com: www.buy.com

■ **Feeling tired?** *No need to visit your local mall, visit the web instead.*

There are also several category-specific online malls, such as fashionMall (www.fashionmall.com). Most of the well-known "brick and mortar" department stores, all across the price spectrum, are also now online. Examples include: Macy's (www.macys.com), Nordstrom's (www.nordstrom.com), Nieman Marcus (www.neimanmarcus.com), Dillard's (www.dillards.com), Sears (www.sears.com), Target (www.target.com), and Kmart (www.bluelight.com).

Most major international department stores have also colonized cyberspace. Because of shipping costs, these outlets, while interesting, may be impractical for many shoppers (except for unique or special items).

■ **Your every fashion** *need can be met at sites such as www.fashionmall.com.*

We'll give you a few examples of international department stores online in English: Harrod's of the U.K. (www.harrodsonline.com), Arnott's of Ireland (www.arnotts.ie), Galeries Lafayette of France (www.galerieslafayette.com), and Germany's Karstadt (www.karstadt.de).

Tickets and delivery services

A host of sites sell tickets for events and travel, and another whole crop have sprung up to provide convenient delivery services, bringing food, videotapes, and other products right to your door. Most sites advertising movies now provide links to buy movie tickets; you can also buy tickets online from Moviefone (www.777film.com).

Most sports arenas, cultural institutions, night clubs, and other event venues offer either direct sales through their web sites, or links to other sites that handle online ticket selling for them.

Sites specializing in online tickets include CultureFinder (www.culturefinder.com), Ticketmaster (www.ticketmaster.co), TicketWeb (www.ticketweb.com), and Tickets.com (www.tickets.com). WebTix (www.tixs.com) includes online classified ads for tickets. Guess what goes on at Ticket Auction (www. ticketauction.com)? Most airlines have web sites where you can order tickets; many other travel-related sites sell tickets online as well.

Online home delivery services have also come into vogue, spurred along by companies like Kozmo (www.kozmo.com) and StreamLine (www.streamline.com), who bring items such as food and videotapes right to people's homes. Many of these services are available only in certain areas, so you'll have to do

INTERNET

www.bbbonline.org/con sumers/safesurfing.html

The Better Business Bureau's guidelines for safe surfing and online shopping contain a wealth of good advice. We suggest printing them out and keeping them near your computer.

Trivia...

Before the supermarket era, neighborhood grocery stores took orders by telephone, and delivered groceries – a service especially helpful to the elderly and homebound. That practice disappeared as Mom and Pop stores lost out to the supermarkets, except for a few isolated spots where small-town grocers continued to deliver within their immediate areas. Internet grocery shopping and home delivery services represent a restoration of that convenience, made possible through technology.

a bit of footwork to find out who offers delivery service in your neck of the woods. And if your area doesn't yet have such a service, you might consider pursuing this idea when you get to Chapter 24, "Making Money Online."

There are lots of online grocery shopping sites, including Home Grocer (www.homegrocer.com), PeaPod (www.peapod.com), NetGrocer (www.netgrocer.com), and WebVan (www.webvan.com). At many sites, you can order restaurant food and have it delivered; check out Food.com (www.food.com). At still other sites, you can order home delivery of health items, laundry service, and photo processing.

■ **Make your weekly shopping** *easier by getting food delivered to your door.*

Product research

PEOPLE CONSIDERING *a purchase often do several types of research before making a decision about whether, what, when, where, and how to buy – and how much to*

pay. *Research can include learning detailed information about a product, such as features, functions and construction, and options such as color and size. Buyers often want to compare similar products, read product reviews, evaluate the quality and durability of the item, and hear from people who own the product. Then there's*

■ **Most of the** *well-known department stores and mail order companies are now online.*

customer service. If the potential purchase is a home, the prospective buyer might want to know about the local community, schools, and environment. Some buyers are concerned with product safety and appropriateness for children. Let's surf through some of the online resources available to people researching a product or service.

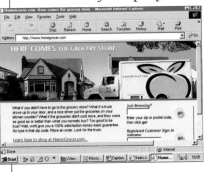

■ **There are many** *grocery shopping sites, such as Home Grocer at www.homegrocer.com.*

Price comparisons and bargain hunting

Several services are available to help consumers compare prices for various products at different web sites. These services, sometimes called comparison "bots" (after "robots"), are increasingly more refined, sophisticated, and powerful. You can download price-comparison software; or tell the "bot" to automatically trawl the web, find the lowest price for a particular product, and notify you via e-mail. These services can help short-cut the process of searching many sites, though you'll probably still want to visit individual sites to check out policies, inventory, and the like.

INTERNET

(www.dealpilot.com)

Deal Pilot searches for prices on books, music, and video products.

MySimon (www.mysimon.com), Dealtime (www.dealtime.com), Jango (www.jango.com), PriceWonders (www.pricewonders.com), and Ecompare (www.ecompare.com) let you search and compare prices for a wide range of products. BargainDog (www.bargaindog.com), Deal Finder (www.deal-finder.com), and SmartLiving (www.smartliving.com) are focused on alerting you to discounts and sales on items or shops you designate. There are many other shopping agents and comparison tools available, with more arriving frequently.

Online ratings and reviews

You can find product reviews online through several different avenues. General searching techniques are helpful for many niche subjects; the search engines and directories may help you find small but interesting sites that writers or site visitors have found useful. There's also been growth in sites devoted to consumer ratings of specific products, and of online stores. Take a look at Epinions (www.epinions.com), Shop Serve (www.shopserve.com), and Productopia (www.productopia.com).

Newsgroups and message boards are sometimes useful for hearing about the e-commerce experiences of others. But keep in mind that you never really know who's posted a negative or positive comment

You can find even more information and ratings for online stores at sites like BizRate (www.bizrate.com), Gomez (www.gomez.com), and Ratings Wonders (www.ratingswonders.com).The lines between independent editorial information, and commercially-driven advertisements, can be awfully fine online. Are online product recommendations independent – or paid for?

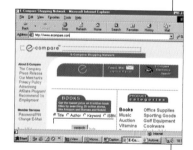

■ **E-Compare** *does your comparison shopping for you in a range of online stores.*

The distinction should always be made clear to consumers. However, there have been a number of high-profile cases where it was revealed that sponsors were paying for the right to be featured or recommended on web sites in ways that gave the false appearance of independent recommendations.

For example, one of the web's biggest booksellers had to change its business practices when the public learned the company was accepting payments from publishers for featuring certain books and authors "recommended by editors."

High ticket items

There are few products you can't buy on the Internet. However, there are many types of businesses who expect consumers to use the web more for research than for actual purchasing. For example, car buyers use the Internet heavily for research about new and used vehicles. Most

■ **The Internet can** *help you buy the right car.*

car dealers have web sites, and auto manufacturers publish robust, multimedia sites about new cars and their various features. A whole industry of automotive web sites has sprung up; many buyers and sellers of vehicles now make their initial contacts online. Some car manufacturers let you specify the model and options you want, then point you to a dealer who has such a model in stock.

Examples of "car shopping portals" include: AutoVantage (www.autovantage.com), Autoweb (www.autoweb.com), Cars.com (www.cars.com), AutoByTel (www.autobytel.com), and CarPoint (www.carpoint.msn.com). Car shoppers also can access other useful resources such as the Kelly Blue Book (www.kbb.com), and Edmund's Auto Buying Guide (www.edmunds.com).

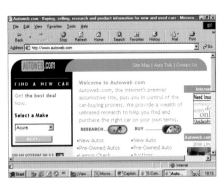

■ **Autoweb.com,** *one of many automobile sites, offers deals, auctions, and financing.*

Lots of magazine sites also contain helpful research, such as Auto News (www.usautonews.com), Motor Trend (www.motortrend.com), and Popular Mechanics (www.popularmechanics.com).

Potential buyers can also go online to gather information about other high-ticket items, like appliances, fine art, boats, aircraft, jewelry, furniture, and all kinds of electronics. Sellers of these higher-priced products are often equipped to accommodate online sales, but, in this arena, the web is more often a research and communication medium than a venue for transactions.

Home-buying

For most of us, the highest-ticket purchase we ever make is our home. House shoppers can do lots of research online. Many web sites offer help to folks preparing to buy a new home, perhaps in another part of the country. In Chapter 22, we'll point out several sites that offer online mortgage processing; most of them also have links to resources for prospective home-buyers. Likewise, many sites geared to home-buyers provide information on mortgages.

Sellers who don't want to use real estate agents can list their homes for sale online at a number of sites. Examples include Owners.com (www.oweners.com), and PrivateFor Sale (www.privateforsale.com). HomeGain (www.home gain.com) is a service site for people selling a home.

INTERNET

www.consumerreports.org

Consumer's Union, the venerable publisher of Consumer Reports, has a rich, useful site with a section called "E-Ratings" that addresses online stores, as well as offering helpful tips and forums for members. Many sections of the site are accessible only to subscribers; CU is practicing some e-commerce of their own by offering online subscriptions.

SITES FOR HOMEBUYERS

Sites for home-buyers include searchable databases of property listings, as well as research services about communities, schools, and costs of living in various areas. Here are just a few examples:

✓ Homefair: www.homefair.com
✓ Realtor.com: www.realtor.com
✓ Cyberhomes: www.cyberhomes.com
✓ Homes.com: www.homes.com
✓ Wall Street Journal Homes Center: www.homes.wsj.com
✓ The New Homes Directory: www.newhomebuysell.com
✓ Home Advisor: www.homeadvisor.msn.com

■ **Whether you're buying** *a home in the country or an apartment in the city, you should be able to find useful information online.*

Buying and selling

THE INTERNET *continues to spawn creative ways to buy and sell things that offer alternatives to the traditional retail model.*

Auctions

Online auctions are extremely popular, having taken off like wildfire after eBay (www.ebay.com) led the way. eBay remains a hugely popular auction site, where an amazing variety of collectibles and other items are bought and sold every day. There are lots of other auction sites, some focusing on specific product categories or special interests. Examples include uBid (www.ubid.com), and boxLot (www.boxlot.com). Auction portals worth visiting include Bidder's Edge (www.biddersedge.com), and AuctionWatch (www.auctionwatch.com).

■ **At Cyberhomes** *your house search begins by clicking on a state and then going down to street level.*

According to the Internet Fraud Watch (www.fraud.org), travel tickets and packages sold through auction sites are among the most common types of scams being perpetrated on the web. One scam involves the sale of an airline ticket, voucher, or frequent flyer award. The seller collects a payment from the highest bidder, and then sends a ticket or voucher of no value – or nothing at all.

We recommend reviewing the Internet Fraud Watch site to learn more about potential red flags, and learn how to use due diligence before buying anything (especially travel tickets) through an auction site.

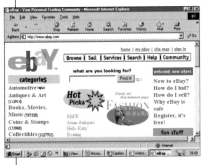

Cooperative buying

Cooperative buying, also known as buying clubs or group buying, is a concept that lets consumers reduce the prices they pay for products and services by pooling their purchases, thus driving down prices. Several players are operating in this area. Look at Mercata (www.mercata.com), Accompany (www.accompany.com), IPool (www.ipool.com), Act Big (www.actbig.com), and Zwirl (www.zwirl.com).

■ **eBay was the first** *of the big auction sites, and is arguably still one of the best.*

Name-your-own-price sites

Another innovative and highly successful type of e-commerce site serves as an intermediary between consumers, and sellers of goods and services. Priceline (www.priceline.com) is perhaps the best-known of these sites – sometimes called "reverse auction" businesses.

■ **Try bargaining** *for your airline ticket on the web.*

At Priceline, you can select from several types of services and products, including airline flight tickets, hotel rooms, automobiles, home mortgages, and groceries, and propose your own prices.

Priceline then offers your bid to sellers of the service or product you've named, and lets you know if you get any takers. If not, you can try increasing your bid. A variety of sites allow you to "negotiate" prices through various mechanisms. Priceline is one good example; you also might check out:

✓ NexTag: www.nextag.com
✓ Reverse Auction: www.reverseauction.com
✓ eWanted: www.ewanted.com
✓ The Haggle Zone: www.hagglezone.com
✓ Make Us an Offer: www.makeusanoffer.com
✓ Respond: www.respond.com

Memberships and registration are often required before you can take advantage of the services offered at most of these sites . So, when you're finished bargaining, don't forget to log out of the site. Failing to log out could mean that someone else could access the site — and conduct transactions through your membership.

■ **"Name your own price and save"** *is the motto at Priceline, one of the best-known "reverse auction" sites.*

Giving gifts online

SOFTWARE IS JUST ONE *type of electronic product that can be delivered online. Digital music is already being delivered via MP3, and it's likely that retail music stores will eventually be in jeopardy as people become equipped to* *create custom CDs online, or download them directly from music labels or distributors. Video may also go a similar route in the future. Right now, though, there several forms of online shopping that take place without anything physical being shipped.*

■ **You can shop** *for gift certificates at GiftPoint.com.*

Gift certificates

Online stores, like those we've visited along the way in this chapter, often sell gift certificates. Sometimes, a paper gift certificate is mailed to your recipient, who can then redeem it at an ordinary retail store.

Many online stores also sell electronic gift certificates. When you buy one, your credit card is charged for the amount of the certificate, and an e-mail is sent to the recipient. There's usually a personal message from you, redemption instructions, and a special code. Sometimes, the e-mail contains a hot link to a customized web page with a picture of a gift certificate. In addition to being cute and high-tech, online gift certificates generally reach your recipient in minutes. This is great for busy people who've forgotten an important birthday or other occasion until the last minute!

GIFT CERTIFICATE PORTALS

In addition to gift certificates available from individual stores, there are several "gift certificate portals." Such as:

GiftPoint.com: www.giftpoint.com
Gift Spot: www.giftspot.com
Flooz: www.flooz.com
GiftCertificates.com: www.giftcertificates.com

If the person redeeming the gift certificate buys something that costs more than the face value of the certificate, he or she must use a credit card to make up the difference. If they buy something less expensive, the online merchant generally holds the unused portion in an online account so that it can be on another occasion The site requires a subscription, not a magazine subscription, but rather an online subscription.

Online registries

The Internet is ideally suited to provide gift registries, and lots of them have been created. Online registries let people from far and wide register any time, and can coordinate purchases among buyers to avoid duplicate gifts. Online registries are provided by many retailers, such as Crate and Barrel (www.crateandbarrel.com), JC Penney (www.penneys.com), Service Merchandise (www.servicemerchandise.com), and Fortunoff (www.fortunoff.com).

As you might guess, a batch of companies also have creative, special-purpose online gift registries. These include wedding registries, as well as general "here's what I want" lists.

You can create your own wish list, and then have the registry send e-mails to your friends, telling them where to find your list online. We've used wedding registry services on the Internet several times, and enjoyed them.

Digital money

WHILE IT HASN'T *yet caught on in a big way yet, there are lots of efforts afoot to create "e-cash" – digital money you can "spend" on the web. Several technologies have been introduced, encompassing several different models. With "prepaid" systems, you deposit funds into an account. You can then spend those funds online, automatically debiting your account as you make purchases – no credit card required. "Aggregation" services let you combine several online purchases into a single charge, which can then be billed in any number of*

■ **Cash and credit card** *sales on the web may soon become a thing of the past with "digital" money.*

ways. Possibly most intriguing are the so-called micropayment schemes. These would let you "pay-as-you-click," paying small amounts, incrementally for games, pay-per-view web content, and other services – rather like dropping digital coins into a jukebox. Several of these systems are under development.

Consumer protection

SCAMS AND CUSTOMER *abuse occasionally occur online. We've already talked about legal protections, and how to reach your state attorney general.*

If you think you've been scammed, or you've had some kind of e-commerce misadventure, take the same steps you'd take if something went wrong in any other commerce setting. You can also look in at any of several sites devoted to assisting consumers who've experienced problems with e-commerce.

■ **The Knot lets** *couples post their wish list of wedding presents to friends and relatives.*

Online shopping has become a mass, mainstream retail channel that offers convenience and new opportunities, for both consumers and merchants. Small merchants can reach people all over the world, and customers can find a vastly greater array of goods and services through the web. Online shoppers can research and buy all kinds of services and commodities, from tickets and groceries, to home mortgages.

A simple summary

✓ Technology assures credit card security.

✓ Buying online is easy.

✓ You can find a vast array of products and services on the web.

✓ Bargain hunters can take advantage of automated price comparison tools and search engines.

✓ Auctions, group buying arrangements and reverse auction sites are an option.

✓ Electronic gift certificates and online gift registries are popular.

✓ Methods are being developed to create a system for "electronic cash" for the Internet.

✓ Consumer protection organizations help consumers avoid scams and problems.

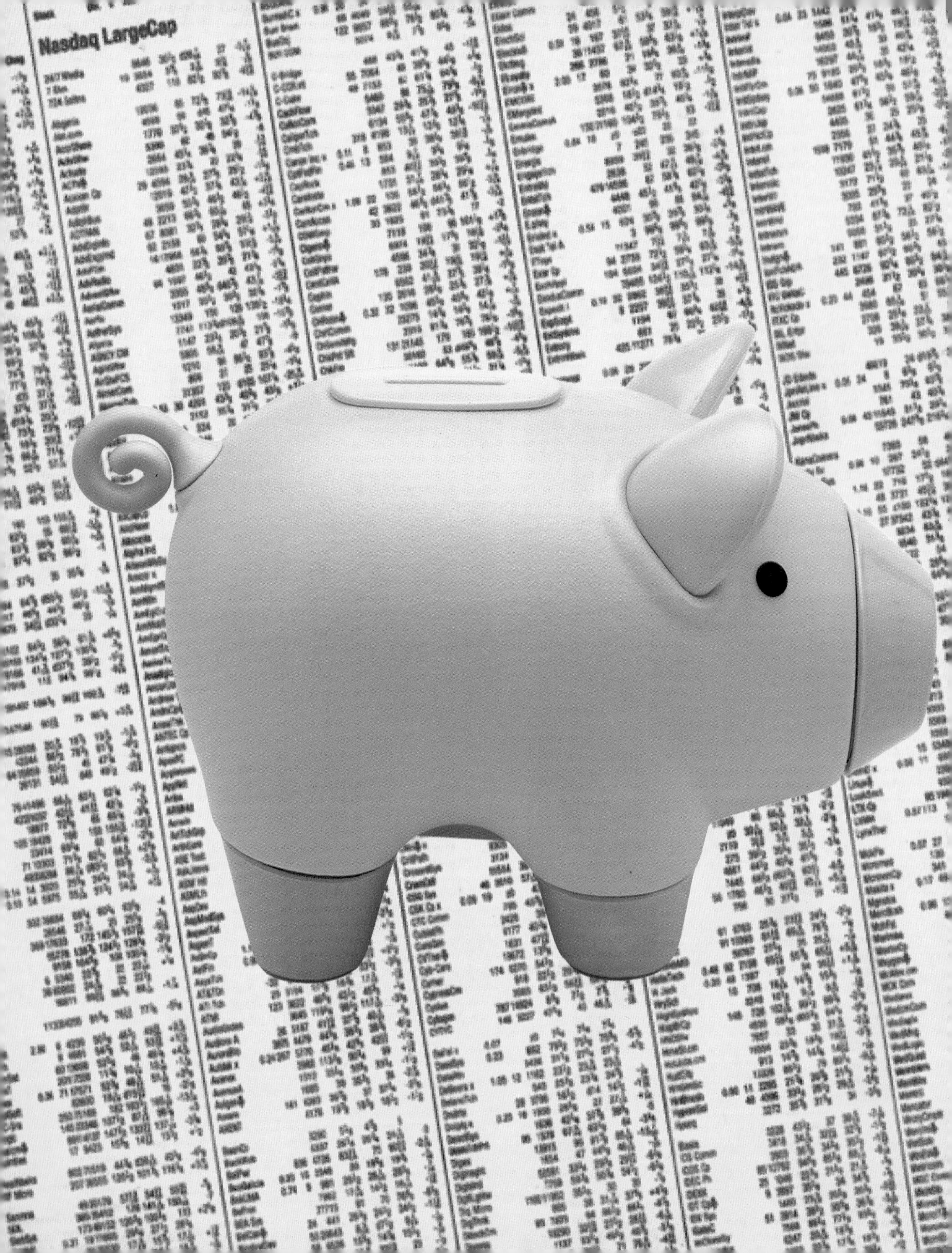
Nasdaq LargeCap

Chapter 22

Managing Your Money

WHATEVER YOUR FEELINGS about money, we hope to outline ways the Internet can help you. You'll notice that this chapter isn't called "Managing Your Investments." (Chapter 23 will discuss investments, and Chapter 24 is about making money online.) Rather, this chapter is about keeping on top of your cash flow, bookkeeping, planning for a rainy day with online tools and experts, and using the Internet to help you lower costs and save money.

In this chapter...

✓ Banks and bills

✓ Insurance

✓ Retirement planning

✓ Saving money online

Banks and bills

THE DEVELOPMENT OF PAYMENT *and exchange systems, forms of currency, and channels for transferring and storing money, makes a fascinating history. The Internet and telecommunications technologies, along with many other international trends, are bringing about significant shifts and innovations in this arena. Many experts believe that the Internet's capacity to enable rapid exchange of goods and services, even across international boundaries, will have profound effects on traditional currency, taxation, regulation, and law enforcement. The new forms of "digital money" we talked about in the last chapter will bring yet more profound changes in the 21st century. This chapter is mostly about how the web can help you, right now, with all those routine, but vital, household financial tasks.*

■ **A Polish Active Media Group** *survey found that 90 percent of Polish businesses questioned have web sites.*

Today's senior citizens may be the only ones who remember a time when most people paid bills with cash. Everybody carried cash, purchases were paid for in cash, and bills were paid in person at the offices of utility companies, doctors, and dentists. Businesses such as insurance companies, whose headquarters were far from most of their customers, sent collectors out to customers' homes to collect payments – which were often made in cash. Bank accounts, especially checking accounts, were used mostly by the affluent minority until after World War II, when post-war prosperity generated a wave of growth in banking. Consumers were attracted by easy, inexpensive checking accounts, millions of people made a lifestyle adjustment, and merchants started accepting personal checks.

OTHER LIFESTYLES

Many communities, industries, and even nations still have a "cash economy," where most transactions still involve actual, physical money – coins and currency. In such environments, the Internet isn't very useful for buying, selling, or financial management. One area experiencing rapid change is Eastern Europe, where economic systems have undergone radical changes. In Poland, for example, credit wasn't introduced until the 1990s. Internet activity in Poland has risen steadily since; a survey by the Polish firm Active Media Group (www.amg.net.pl) found that almost 90% of Polish businesses surveyed are operating web sites.

Then came credit cards, now the medium of most online shopping. Between credit cards, automatic teller machines, debit cards, electronic checks, and the like, sometimes it's tough to keep track of where our money goes.

We still have to pay bills, and we still need banks, but the paperwork and bookkeeping takes a lot of time. But now, we have another resource — the Internet.

Software

Financial management software programs has been in use for years, and two packages in particular are very popular for personal bookkeeping: Quicken, and Microsoft Money. Each of these comes in different versions, from simple to more powerful, depending on your need.

To enable either of these packages to do what it's meant to do, you must first enter a lot of basic information — like the account numbers and current balances of every credit card and charge account, and every monthly commitment you have.

Once you have patiently entered the data, the program will update everything automatically, checking figures and giving you a running balance sheet. At any time, you can get a complete, up-to-the-minute accounting of exactly where you stand with bank accounts, credit card balances, and other information. When they set up these tracking procedures, people discover interesting things about their spending habits, resulting in a feeling of, Wow – I didn't realize I spent so much on that kind of thing!

Choose carefully

Before choosing one of these software applications, check them both out at their respective web sites. If you expect to begin an investment portfolio, look at how Quicken (www.quicken.com) and Microsoft Money (www.microsoft.com/money) handle that part of the financial picture as well.

You should also find out if your bank offers online banking, and if they recommend a particular software application. Microsoft Money developed a feature called "what if," to show you the effect on your financial situation of theoretical changes, such as a new mortgage or a job change. Quicken has now incorporated that feature, too. Quicken provides tax planning and tax prediction features, review of tax returns, alerts about new tax issues, and year-round tax planning. Microsoft Money has now also incorporated most of these features. These software helpers can take over your ordinary daily finances – if you keep them current. You can even pay your bills online; reminders will pop up when bills come due. Like any other record-keeping system, it works better if you work with it.

Financial management software can be a wonderful help for customers of traditional banks, but its greatest potential is realized when people switch to online banking. Figures show that the numbers of Americans using online banking rose from 1.4 million in 1996, to 12.4 million in 1999.

Online banking

Online banking is sometimes done directly through the Internet. In other cases, your bank may provide a special software kit, along with a private dial-up network, for its customers. If your bank uses its own dial-up network, your modem can be configured to connect directly to the bank's network.

With the rapid growth of the Internet, most banks have set up at least some kind of online service. But there are also a host of new companies called "Internet banks." Finding traditional banks online, as well as the new Internet banks, is easy – try any search engine, or use a web site with financial institution directories, such as:

✓ bankonline.com: www.bankonline.com
✓ electronicbanker: www.electronicbanker.com
✓ bankweb: www.bankweb.com
✓ MyBank: www.mybank.com
✓ The Credit Union Home Page: www.cu.org

> **DEFINITION**
>
> *The term* online banking *means systems that let you perform standard banking activities like getting checking account balances and activity histories, transferring funds, reconciling accounts, and applying for accounts, online. Some banks have also moved their credit and lending businesses online. Exactly which banking activities are available online depends on the financial institutions you use.*

A recent survey conducted by www.efunds.com reported that 80 percent of U.S. consumers using online banking were happier online than with their old, traditional banks. However, 90 percent of these are doing business with banks that also have bricks-and-mortar establishments, as opposed to the online-only banks.

The survey showed that the one area with the most customer complaints is account opening, which was said to be very cumbersome and difficult.

Bill-paying

Most banks have offered automatic payment plans for years, and sometimes loans for major purchases are approved on the condition that payments be made by the bank. Each month, the bank would make this automatic payment, listing it on the customer's printed monthly statement, along with an accounting of all the checks the customer wrote that month.

■ **Bankonline.com** *helps you find online banks and offers other financial services.*

Automatic bill-paying, through banks, or through any one of the new personal bill-management services, can now be set up and managed online.

You can have bank statements delivered on request; and have your bills paid either automatically on their due dates, or upon your request. Account activity records are updated daily. Once you set up this kind of system, writing a check will become a rare event.

ONLINE BANKING PROGRAM

Check to see if your bank offers bill-paying as part of its online banking program, and compare their services and prices to some of the online bill management companies, such as:

✓ PayTrust: www.paytrust.com
✓ TransPoint: www.transpoint.com
✓ PayMyBills: www.paymybills.com
✓ Check Free: www.checkfree.com
✓ Status Factory: www.statusfactory.com

Many of these services can send you your bills right online – no more paper bills to get lost in the mail. And with many services, record-keeping tools let you download your transaction information, and import it into software such as Quicken.

As you peruse web sites addressing online banking and bill payment, you'll quickly discover how fast this area is growing. Several companies are developing services that let you manage multiple accounts at different institutions – with a single tool.

PayPal (www.paypal.com) offers you the opportunity to "beam yourself" money via e-mail. RocketCash (www.rocketcash.com) and DoughNet (www.doughnet.com) are sites where parents can set up ways for their teenagers to shop online without credit cards.

Innovation and competition are intense, and the consumer has ever-growing options. These services and features can bring refreshing convenience and simplicity to your day-to-day financial tasks.

■ **Paying your bills** *through online bill management companies such as PayMyBills.com may be cheaper.*

Hints and tips

The full impact of online banking is greater than you may realize at first. Imagine being liberated from those long sessions at your desk, piled with statements and bills; writing checks; licking envelopes; hunting for the stamps; and hoping you don't get fined for overdue payments. It's a tempting prospect. But there are a few things to consider before you make a decision to take your banking online.

■ **Long lines could** *be a thing of the past thanks to online banking.*

As with other Internet activities, we suggest you pay careful attention to the privacy policies of any company you're considering for online banking or bill-paying. Look for privacy seals, such as TrustE or BBB Online.

ONLINE BANKING TIPS

✓ You must have your own computer. It would be foolhardy to attempt online banking if your only computer access is at work.

✓ How fast is your Internet access, and how fast is your bank's online system? Check both sides of this equation before taking the plunge – you might be better off for now using the phone.

✓ Having both checking and savings, and possibly investment funds, makes online banking more flexible and helpful. (We'll talk about that part of the picture in Chapter 23.)

✓ If you do decide to open Internet accounts, have your password mailed to you by regular mail, not e-mail, for security purposes. Never share your password with anyone on the Internet!

✓ Be sure to include accurate account numbers with every regular payment, especially if you have more than one account with the same creditor.

✓ Learn about the differences electronic transfer of funds may cause in your bill-paying and spending habits. If you're in the habit of writing a check on Friday, assuming it won't be presented for payment until Monday or Tuesday, that may change!

Bankers use the term float to describe the period between the time you write a check, and the time the money becomes available to the recipient. When funds are electronically transferred from your bank to another electronically-equipped bank, the transfer of funds can be immediate.

This power can come in handy if you've forgotten to send a check, and realize it's almost the end of business on the day the check is due. You can send it at one minute to five – and still make the deadline.

If your check must cross state lines, and the recipient is not electronically equipped, several days of float time may pass before your check is credited. As the pool of Internet banking customers grows, this will happen less often. But it's important to remember that your bank posted a debit to your account as soon as you hit the Send button on your computer screen.

Mortgages

You can arrange for loans for the purchase or refinancing of a home, as well as obtain home equity loans, through the Internet. In fact, just to get a quick picture of how many lenders are available for mortgages and loans, go to any major search engine and enter the word "mortgage." Most of the results will be for national lenders who are making such loans daily, all over the country, and have perfected their online application and credit check processes. Their web sites are usually user-friendly and informative. A few of these are:

■ **Online mortgage brokers** *such as E-Loan have a high profile on the web and are opening up international sites.*

✓ iOwn.com: www.iown.com
✓ E-LOAN: www.eloan.com
✓ financenter.com: www.financenter.com
✓ Lending Tree: www.lendingtree.com
✓ MortgageQuotes.com: www.mortgagequotes.com
✓ QuickenMortgage: www.quicken.com/mortgage
✓ Upland Mortgages: www.uplandmortgage.com/mortgages/
✓ National Association of Mortgage Brokers: www.namb.org.

Don't get discouraged if you don't succeed right away in getting a mortgage. Lenders make it sound easy at first, but when they spot potential problems, such as questionable credit ratings or inadequate income levels, they may hand down rejections.

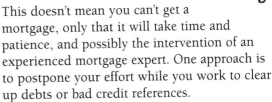

This doesn't mean you can't get a mortgage, only that it will take time and patience, and possibly the intervention of an experienced mortgage expert. One approach is to postpone your effort while you work to clear up debts or bad credit references.

■ **The National Association of Mortgage Brokers** *offers impartial advice and information on mortgages.*

Potential lenders

Since there are so many potential lenders, interest rates tend to be much the same across the board, although some special circumstances can affect this. So-called jumbo loans (over $240,000) often involve higher interest. Special circumstances in an individual borrower's background, or factors about a particular property, can also affect rates. All these mortgage-finding services supply information and advice about rates and trends, even as rates change. The differences usually involve payment arrangements, where you must consider fixed rate, adjustable rate, balloon payments, and other options.

We checked at www.mortgagequotes.com to see how to find potential lenders for property in different parts of the country. We found a list of all fifty states. When we clicked on one state, we expected to see lists of lenders located in that state, but that's not what we found. The mortgage finder makes appropriate contacts with potential lenders online, rather than referring you directly to them.

We believe one such comparison experience would show that the online services are real step-savers, producing results as good as, or better, than you could find yourself.

Priceline

INTERNET

priceline.com

You could also try Priceline, mentioned in Chapter 21. There, you'll be invited to propose your own terms – what size mortgage you need, what interest rate you're willing to pay, and other details, such as the length of the loan you want.

Priceline will send your request to several mortgage lenders. If one of them agrees to your terms, you'll be notified within hours. If no one accepts, the lenders have two days to offer competitive bids that you may consider, but are not obliged to take. This service is free. If you do secure a mortgage, you'll probably end up paying a relatively nominal fee to Priceline ($200 at the time of this writing). This process cuts out some of the middlemen usually involved in home purchases. This can be a mixed bag. It saves some trouble and some money, but eliminates the relationship some home buyers have with intermediaries, who do a lot of little things to help.

A real estate agent may still be involved – for example, the one who helped you find the property you decide to buy. Some people come to think of the online lender in a very friendly way, but others miss human input.

■ **Protect your** *family abroad with holiday insurance bought on the web.*

Insurance

INSURANCE PROVIDERS *are often experts in financial planning, and their representatives are generally ready with lots of information. However, they are also salespeople, out to convince you of your need for their products. This is one place where we believe the Internet offers an invaluable service that can benefit almost anyone. All the background, definitions,*

■ **Mortgagequotes.com** *compares quotes from different lenders, saving you time and possibly money.*

statistical analyses, and insurance coverage options are clearly laid out on the web. You can peruse it at your leisure – without any pressure from salespeople.

Insurance planning

We've already visited some insurance-related web sites in Chapter 18, while discussing online health care. Web sites that offer insurance information include Quicken's wwws.insuremarket.com, www.insweb.com, and www.4freequotes.com. At any of these sites, you'll be invited to create a personal portfolio, but it's also possible to do a "trial walk" through the evaluation and planning process, without creating a portfolio, leaving no personal information behind.

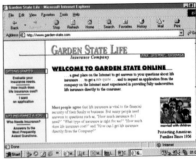

■ **Online insurance** *planning companies like Garden State Online walk you through your insurance requirements.*

The online application will ask about your age, profession, health, family history, lifestyle, assets, and existing coverage. You'll get a profile of your insurance needs, suggesting coverage you're missing and may need in the future. If you wish, the planner will tell you how to meet the identified need, and what it might cost.

We know that the one type of insurance we don't have, and probably should consider, is long-term care insurance. So, we put online insurance planning to the test by walking through an analysis of our own situation. When the analysis was returned, it showed a pressing need for exactly that type of coverage. We could then have turned to search engines for a fresh approach to locating insurance providers. One search brought www.travelers.com, www.budgetlife.com, www.garden-state.com, and many others. Each of these web sites is filled with information similar to the kind that insurance representatives give in their presentations, and that many people use to decide which policies to purchase.

Insurance decisions are extremely personal. The experts know about the wisdom of good coverage, but they can't know the many personal factors that enter into your decisions. Being heavily insured brings some people a sense of security, while others see it as money down the drain.

Life, property, and the rest

We've already discussed health insurance. The details of life, auto, long-term care, property, and other categories of insurance aren't really the business of this chapter. We just want to point out that you can thoroughly research the insurance component of your overall financial planning right on the Internet. You don't have to immediately construct the perfect insurance portfolio as soon as you install financial management software, or switch to online banking. But a better picture of your situation will show more plainly what you're actually spending on insurance, what those dollars are buying, and where the gaps are in your coverage.

■ **Find the right** *insurance for your family possessions.*

We suggest devoting plenty of time to an assessment of your present coverage, and to an investigation of possible changes and additions.

Retirement planning

IF YOU'RE OVER FORTY, *you may have done some thinking about retirement. Mandatory retirement at age sixty-five is not quite as common as it once was, and many factors have influenced this change. Events that tend to delay retirement include an expanding economy, low unemployment rates, the difficulty of replacing highly-skilled workers, and the planned raising of the eligibility age for Social Security benefits. Other factors encourage some people to take retirement as early as financially possible.*

■ **Insure.com provides** *insurance-related news, especially relating to disputes or fraud.*

SOME WEB SITES

Many of the web sites mentioned here as resources for insurance and general financial planning also provide retirement planning. Here are a few more:

✓ SaveWealth.com: www.savewealth.com
✓ financenter.com: www.financenter.com
✓ Capital Management Group: www.capitalmgt.com
✓ eStrong.com: www.strong-funds.com
✓ Guardian Retirement Planning:
www.guardianretirement.com

■ **Retirement planning** *is easy on the web.*

Pensions, social security, and savings

Many companies and employee benefits programs offer pre-retirement seminars to anyone over fifty. These can be very informative, and fit right in with all your other financial planning efforts, including those we've discussed in this chapter. See if your employer offers such seminars; if not, you can locate similar events online.

Financial information sites, and general interest sites for seniors and retirees, also publish useful articles and guides. For example, see:

✓ AARP: www.aarp.org
✓ senior.com: www.senior.com
✓ New Choices: www.newchoices.com
✓ ThirdAge: www.thirdage.com

■ **Get advice on** *saving, tax reduction, and retirement planning at SaveWealth.com.*

Many of these sites provide tools where you can enter information (as you did for the insurance analysis), and get a prospectus of your financial readiness for retirement, as well as ideas for improving your situation.

If you're enrolled in a pension plan through your employer, find and bookmark the web site for that plan. Check frequently to see where you stand with regard to your potential retirement income.

The same is true for Social Security. The government's web site (www.ssa.gov) will tell you how to get your personal account data. If you've never gotten a full accounting from Social Security, ask for one. Sometimes, there are record-keeping errors or discrepancies, and it can take time to clear up mistakes.

TAX RETURNS

After attending a pre-retirement seminar some years ago, this author decided to check with Social Security to see if my records were correct. I learned that tax returns are the primary basis for Social Security records. I found that they had totally skipped the year 1982, as if no tax return had come in that year. Fortunately, I had a copy of the return in my files, but sending it to them didn't solve the discrepancy. I had to find copies of the actual checks for tax I paid that year before they acknowledged and corrected the mistake. This took several months. You wouldn't want to wait until the day before retirement, and then discover such a glitch.

People who switch to online tax payments might find it easier to correct such mistakes in the future, but it's still always a good idea to keep a paper trail.

This applies to Internet transactions as much as to any other financial transaction. And with regard to "non-paper" transactions, don't forget, we already do lots of these, such as buying airline ticket by telephone. Your banks and other financial institutions should provide written monthly account statements (even for online accounts), and you should always have the right to question a bill.

Even if Social Security doesn't play a big part in your retirement picture, the Social Security Administration's site is a good place to visit. It's full of information, including the latest news, statistics, and many excellent articles. There's some overlap between this site and the Medicare site (www.medicare.gov), as health coverage is available to all Social Security recipients via Medicare.

Consultants and helpers

Where do you turn for advice and guidance on financial planning questions? Some of us have bankers we know and trust, some have financial consultants, brokers, accountants, or attorneys who can help manage and advise. But many people don't have any of these consultants and helpers. When you consult any of the

■ **Your financial** *planning queries can be e-mailed to trained consultants during chat sessions.*

■ **The Social Security**
Administration's web site at
www.ssa.gov could play a big
part in your retirement planning.

web sites we mention in this Chapter, your responses usually come from automated systems. These resources are very helpful, but not very personal.

Most of the major sites we've mentioned, such as www.strongfunds.com, have chat options, and occasionally conduct organized, topical chat sessions. The times and topics of these sessions are announced in advance, and you'll be invited to submit your personal questions for real-time answers during the chat session. You can find other interactive opportunities in newsgroups and on mailing lists. Financial-planning web sites get many e-mailed questions; the answers generally come from consultants on staff with the planning service represented by that site. For the ease, cost, and savings, of online consulting, you give up some of the personal attention of a hired consultant.

But even if you do hire someone, or use an expert hired by your employer or employee benefits program, we suggest that using online resources as well provides a supplement, and a valuable basis for comparison in making financial decisions.

Saving money online

■ **With a little** *patience, the web can save you money.*

WHILE INTERNET SURFING, *you may have noticed contests, games, and offers of prizes, free or in return for completing surveys. You may have wondered if these are legitimate. Usually, the web site providers are promoting some product, or just keeping you at their site longer than you might have remained otherwise. But some of the advertising gimmicks can result in savings – if you're willing to give up some of your time.*

Coupon-clippers should know that coupons – as good as, or better, than the ones you find in newspaper ads – are available in many places on the web.

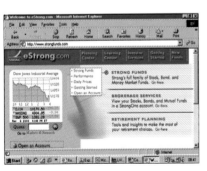

■ **eStrong.com** *provides real-time answers to financial planning questions in chat sessions.*

Shoppers' helpers

Online coupons are not negotiable everywhere in the U.S., but the practice is becoming more widespread. FamilyTime (www.familytime.com) maintains a list of online coupon opportunities.

SOFTWARE REVIEWS

Here are several more sources on the web where you can find and print out coupons to use in purchasing all kinds of products (not just groceries):
✓ ValuPage: www.valupage.com
✓ The Internet Coupon Directory: www.coupondirectory.com
✓ CentsOff: www.centsoff.com
✓ coolsavings.com: www.coolsavings.com

These sites often provide maps showing which states and cities are participating in their web coupon offerings. Even if your area isn't included, though, you can still use some coupons printed from the web. For instance, national brands that issue coupons to newspapers for general publication sometimes provide online versions of the same coupons, with the same bar codes and conditions. Presenting these at your local grocery is worth a try. If they're not yet prepared to accept online coupons, it's probably just a matter of time until they get used to it. In addition, some coupon web sites will e-mail you information about new coupon offers, if you give them your e-mail address.

National manufacturers and distributors also post coupon offers on their web sites. For instance, we checked www.jollytime.com and found some tempting offers to help us buy popcorn.

Rebates and free stuff

Rebates involve getting money back after a purchase, rather than getting a discount at the time of purchase. Rebates are very popular, and many are available at the same sites that provide coupons. You can get e-rebates at e-coupons, for example. Depending on the purchase price of the product, these rebates are sometimes substantial.

You can also easily find totally free services and products on the web. Many of these, such as teacher aids and materials for classroom use, are designed to be downloaded to files or printers. The shoppers' helper sites listed above may supply links to other sites, like www.freebies.about.com, where free stuff is available.

Sites for kids

■ **Children can learn** *about money from a range of fun sites.*

The Internet has some really wonderful sites specifically designed to help children learn about money. Here are a few of these resources – valuable for learning, and a lot of fun:

✓ Treasury's Page for Kids: www.ustreas.gov/kids
✓ Moneyopolis: www.moneyopolis.com
✓ Kids' Money: www.kidsmoney.org
✓ The Young Investor Web Site: www.younginvestor.com

We've skimmed along the top of some very big subjects! In this chapter, we've advocated sound financial planning, and suggested software to help accomplish it. We've noted how important the financial realm is to many readers, and outlined some of the Internet resources that can help you manage your money. While web sites can't replace human consultants, they offer distinct advantages of ease and flexibility, a wealth of information available whenever and for as long as you wish, and freedom from sales pressure.

A simple summary

✓ Online banking and bill-payment sites manage your money.

✓ Quicken and Microsoft Money can help organize your family's day-to-day financial tasks.

✓ Research home mortgages and home equity loans online.

✓ Getting an accurate assessment of where you stand in regard to various kinds of insurance coverage is important.

✓ Looking ahead to make sensible plans can be easier with the help of online resources.

✓ Most people find their spending habits are not changed by financial aspects of Internet use.

✓ Online coupons can be a way to save money.

✓ Web sites especially for children are a good way to teach kids about money.

Chapter 23

Investing in the Stock Market

THE INTERNET has made tracking, buying, and selling stocks easier than ever. In just a few minutes, you can log on, ante up some money, and start buying and selling shares. In this chapter, we'll focus mostly on two subjects. Investing online and the subject of investing prudently and sensibly. The numbers of Americans who have joined the investment community by putting their savings to work, joining mutual funds, or purchasing stocks and bonds, has grown by leaps and bounds. An initial search for "investing" at Northern Light brought us 13,517,610 returns.

In this chapter...

✓ Financial planning

✓ Investing

✓ Financial research

✓ Taxation

INVESTING IN THE STOCK MARKET IS EASY ONLINE

Financial planning

IRONICALLY, MANY OF *those who go it alone in the investments world by using online brokerage services are the very people who most ought to be consulting in person with a financial advisor or stockbroker. The professionals can provide information and advice to novice investors that simply can't be found online. They can assist in deciding on the best course when problems occur with investments, and in creating a plan and a portfolio in line with your assets, needs, and future plans.*

Financial advisors will often help you evaluate, before you start investing, whether changes in your current money management practices might increase your assets or curb needless losses. For example, an advisor may help you compare the interest rates you're earning on savings to the rates you're paying against debts, and to analyze whether paying off the debt with the savings would increase your cumulative assets.

Some of the web sites of financial planning firms contain useful information about financial planning and financial advisors. For example, see Paine Webber (www.painewebber.com), Merrill Lynch (www.ml.com), and Fidelity Investments (www.fidelity.com). An advisor will help you think ahead to when, and why, you'll need to use your assets, and to plan a range of investments in line with those needs. Sound investment portfolios usually include short-term, mid-term, and long-term investments, encompassing several different strategies and types of investments. A financial advisor can help you put yourself and your family on a sensible and disciplined financial foundation. They'll probably advise you to view online investing not as a way to generate quick riches, but, rather, as a high-risk endeavor. Maybe this doesn't sound like as much fun as putting funds into the stock market, and sitting at your computer waiting for the price to move up so you can make a quick killing.

■ **Like a slot machine,** *the stock market is a gamble.*

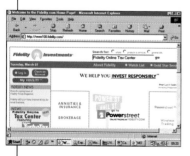

All too often, this process is not far removed from playing a slot machine (which you can also do online), except that it costs a lot more than quarters to play in the stock market.

■ **Web sites like** *Fidelity Investments contain useful information about financial planning and financial advisors.*

Here are a few links that can help you find a qualified, professional financial advisor:

✓ Certified Financial Planner Board of Standards: www.cfp-board.org
✓ Institute of Certified Financial Planners, Consumer Division: www.icfp.org
✓ International Association of Financial Planners: www.planningpaysoff.org

With or without a financial advisor's help, we recommend that you first create a personal financial plan that addresses your financial needs and goals, before putting your funds into new investments. Several sites we've already discussed in previous chapters offer resources that can help with personal financial planning.

PERSONAL FINANCIAL PLANNING

Here are a few more sites worth exploring:
✓ American Association of Individual Investors: www.aaii.org
✓ Motley Fool: www.fool.com
✓ Money Magazine: www.money.com
✓ Invest-FAQ: www.invest-faq.com
✓ Investor Protection Trust: www.investorprotection.org
✓ Real Life Investing Guide: www.rlig.com

■ **Money Magazine**
(www.money.com) offers many resources for financial planning.

Investing

JUST IN CASE *it isn't already clear, if you're new to investing and financial planning, we recommend that you have a minimum of one meeting with a financial planner. Or, spend as much time as you need, before investing, charting a personal financial plan that includes investments in line with your overall needs and resources.*

Investing is a broad subject. It can include buying and selling shares of publicly-owned companies, real estate, bonds, currency, and many other types of investments.
In the rest of this chapter, we'll address stock market investing because it's by far the most common online activity. We'll then briefly address mutual funds, commodities, and tax issues. Other types of investing also can be done online, but are outside the scope of this book.

■ **It is very important** *to meet with a financial planner before investing on the Internet.*

Getting the lingo down pat

Many of the web sites we mention in this chapter offer information for newcomers to the world of investing. It's probably a good idea to read a few of them, just to get comfortable with the language, the process, and some of the unique variables you need to understand as an online investor. Most online brokers require certain minimum deposit levels, and charge fees for trading. Many offer premium services, including research, for additional fees, or for customers whose volume or account balances reach higher levels. Comparing service levels is very important if you expect more than minimal service.

We also suggest doing some reading and comparing before deciding on a broker. Don't base your decision solely on price, but also on customer service.

For example, you might try the company's telephone support line to ask a question or two, and see how well they respond to your call. This, too, will help you quickly get past any jargon or mysterious terminology.

Selecting a broker

These days, online trading has become so popular that many of the names you're familiar with in the investment industry, such as Donaldson, Lufkin, and Jenrette (www.dljdirect.com), and T. Rowe Price (www.troweprice.com), are now doing business online. There are also several Internet-based brokerages, such as ETrade (www.etrade.com), and Ameritrade (www.ameritrade.com).

INTERNET

www.gomezadvisors.com

You also might check a few message boards, as well as online review sites, such as Gomez, to help make an informed decision. You also might find it useful to try an online "broker finder" such as Money Magazine's (www.pathfinder. com/money/broker).

Some people base their choice on reputation or past experience with a company. Others use different criteria. We have no recommendation for who you should use. We do suggest you spend some time comparing prices, services, reputations, and impressions from people whose judgement you trust before deciding. Directories of brokers can be found at any major search engine; just enter a term like "online brokers."

Opening an account

Many online brokerage services offer online applications; some provide almost real-time approval. Others may require you to fill out an applications and return it by mail. One of the authors of this book opened an account with one of the well-known services; the process took about 60 seconds.

Once your account is open and contains the minimum deposit, you can access the information through the web site with a user name and password. Normally, you'll have access to account information like balances, pending orders, and

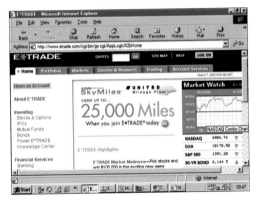

history. You may also have various service options, such as receiving alerts. You'll probably also get occasional correspondence and account information by mail. Your computer lets you conduct transactions from the comfort of home, or even in transit – a great advantage for frequent travelers.

However, don't forget to always log out of your account fully before leaving any computer where you've been logged in.

■ **ETrade offers** *Internet-based brokering and many other financial services.*

Transferring existing stocks

If you already own stocks, transferring your portfolio to an online brokerage service, and learning to manage your investments via the web, may be much simpler than you think. It depends on where your stocks are held, and where you want to put them.

We suggest calling the customer service support line at the online broker you're considering. The broker you choose can usually accomplish the transfer as soon as you provide the needed information.

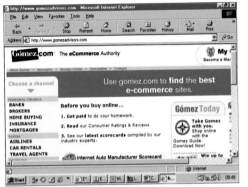

Buying or selling

Executing a trade is normally also a simple process of clicking through a few screens to indicate what stocks you want to trade, how many, whether you want to buy or sell, and your conditions.

Normally, you'll get confirmation when the transaction has been made, along with an update to your account holdings and balance.

■ **Gomez.com** *is one of several sites that provide reviews and ratings of online brokers and other e-commerce sites.*

Even the Internet can't eliminate the lag time involved in stock trading. Between the time when the investor puts in an order with his broker, and the time when the transaction is fulfilled, the price may change.

This is nothing new to experienced investors, and your online broker will probably alert you to the fact that no transaction can be instantaneous. Part of the great success of online trading is that lag time is generally reduced. But in a volatile market, even those present on the floor of the stock exchange can't make guarantees.

Financial research

INVESTING IS A TOP-LEVEL category at most major search engines. The Internet is filled with information about this subject. If you're looking for investment information, it's just a matter of where to ask the type of question you have. At first, looking through some of the financial web sites, it may seem that everybody is busy doing it, and the sites are for those who already know what they're doing. But just a little more investigation will show that some sites do a good job of helping beginners get started. Like most of the categories we've covered, there are lots of choices; we suggest trying several sites until you find one, or a few, you feel most comfortable using.

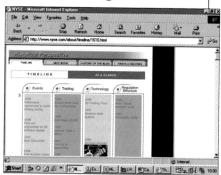

■ **The New York** *Stock Exchange's Timeline page shows the history of the stock market.*

Deciding what to buy or sell

The authors of this book aren't professional investment advisors, and we caution you not to interpret our mention of specific web sites here as recommendations upon which you should base investment decisions.

We've mentioned the increasing amounts of attention paid to financial news by general news providers, such as newspaper and television. In addition, almost every web site we mention in this chapter also includes financial and business news. Paying regular attention to the news is another way to educate yourself.

There are many kinds on online news sources. For instance, check:

✓ CNN financial network: www.cnnfn.com
✓ CBS Marketwatch.com: www.cbs.marketwatch.com
✓ The Street: www.thestreet.com
✓ Bloomberg News: www.bloomberg.com
✓ Barron's: www.barrons.com

Bookmark one of the financial news sites, and check it every day for a while, paying special attention to the terminology and subjects covered. If you have a customizable home page, set it up to give you a few daily financial reports. After a while, you'll find it all begins to make

■ **Online news** *sources provide an alternative to traditional financial publications – for keeping up with market trends.*

sense. You can also use newsletters for investors as sources of education and insight. For example, take a look at www.tulipsandbears.com, a newsletter with live chat rooms and busy message boards.

Just reading articles and postings can be informational, and when you feel a little more comfortable with the terminology, you might elect to try one of their interactive seminars.

Brokerage sites generally offer both general news, and specific news about companies. Usually, you can enter a company name or ticker symbol, get a quote for the latest reported price of a share, and then click to see news about the company, recent announcements, annual reports, descriptions, and lots more.

On the message boards of major financial web sites, you may see many requests for investment money, with promises of tremendous returns, "getting in on the ground floor," and so on.

We suggest you avoid all these offers, at least until you have extensive investing experience. Lots of these notices are from "lone ranger" types, who have unusual ideas they want to test with someone else's money. Even if your funds were unlimited, it takes an awful lot of experience and skill to figure out whether these schemes are legitimate. There have been several sad stories on the Internet of, for example, a message board post starting a rush on a particular stock, pushing up the price per share. The rush attracted lots of unwary buyers, who then lost their money when the over-valued stock price dropped back down again.

Getting good information

In all the news, talk, and theorizing on financial web sites, the art and science of buying and selling stocks is probably the number-one issue. Open any of the references in this chapter, or consult:

✓ BusinessWeek Online: www.businessweek.com
✓ InvestorLinks: www.investorlinks.com

You're sure to find articles about what's hot and what's not, as well as the overall mood of the market at any given time. *Bears and bulls* are a daily fact of life for brokers, so they generally know which are likely to dominate the market.

It's simple to buy and sell online from an active portfolio. Advertisements for commercial brokers on the Internet often emphasize the convenience of being able to conduct business at any hour of the day or night.

What happens when a request comes in during the wee hours of the morning? A worker in the broker's office opens that message at the beginning of the work day, and sends your request to buy or sell straight to the floor broker who represents that firm on the stock exchange floor. Your transaction may be the first thing done by the floor broker that morning, as soon as the opening bell sounds.

We know an advisor who publishes stock tips at a web site, and charges $169 a month for access to his tips. He has a loyal, growing base of subscribers in several countries who love his service and pay the fee gladly, because of the valuable tips they get from his site.

■ **Bear investors** *hope to profit from a downturn in the market.*

You may not want to pay that much for stock information, but if you do find a solid, knowledgeable source of information and help (online or offline), you may find you're willing to pay.

Mutual funds

A mutual fund is like a group portfolio. If you have limited funds to invest, but want a diversified holding, a mutual fund is a good option. Take a look, for example, at www.pioneerfunds.com. Investing in a mutual fund means purchasing shares of the fund, which are put into the pool of available investment money. Each share of the fund represents a mini-version of the entire portfolio. Mutual funds are administered by banks, brokers, and other investment firms.

Before joining a mutual fund, consider asking a few questions. Does it have active management, or indexing?

■ **Check out** *BusinessWeek Online for tips on buying and selling stocks and shares.*

Active management means that a fund manager decides what stocks and bonds will be purchased for the fund portfolio; while indexing ties the decisions to some formula, such as devoting a percentage of available funds to the top stocks in a given industry. How successful has this particular mutual fund been? Compare its performance record to similar funds. How risky is the fund? Are the investments relatively low-risk, or is there a more adventurous component? What does it cost to join? Mutual fund members pay a fee to maintain and administer the fund.

For online information about mutual funds, check out:

✓ Wiesenberger: www.wiesenberger.com
✓ Morningstar: www.morningstar.net
✓ Value Line: www.valueline.com

Commodities

Trading stocks via the Internet has skyrocketed during the past few years, and some observers believe the same growth spurt is set to happen in commodities trading. E-trading of commodities enables farmers and traders to place orders to commission merchants dealing in futures; they then complete transactions on the floor of the Chicago Board of Trade, or other markets.

■ **Morningstar** *has many financial reports, tools, and products including advice and information on mutual funds.*

Trivia...

An investor in our family holds stock in U.S. Sprint. One day, he got a phone call from a friend, asking if he'd heard about "the pending merger of Sprint and GTE," which might greatly increase the value of his stock. He had heard the rumor, and if he'd had an online account, he probably would've looked it up immediately. Since he doesn't do business online, though, the rumor wasn't confirmed for him until a few days later. This is just one example of the convenience of the Internet.

Commodities trading carries a slightly higher risk than trading stocks and bonds. Therefore, it tends to attract a specialized group of investors – those with personal interest in commodities futures, such as farmers, food processing industries, and others who deal in the end products. Major brokers generally offer commodity trading. There are also specialized web sites such as:

✓ Commodities.com: www.commodities.com
✓ Progressive Ag Marketing: www.progressiveag.com

Taxation

■ **Farmers may be** *more likely to deal and invest in commodities.*

PEOPLE WHOSE INCOME *is entirely from wages have it easy when April 15 rolls around, but most of those who have to file the long form, and possibly even quarterly estimated tax payments, often need tax help. The manufacturers of Quicken seemed to see this as a very big issue, and their software is designed to provide a lot of help with tax preparation. Microsoft Money also provides the means to help prepare for tax time, and to make sure your tax bill isn't bigger than it needs to be.*

General tax help

At the U.S. government's own tax site, www.irs.gov, you can access and download tax forms and publications. You can also file your return online; more taxpayers do this each year. Once you file an online return, the IRS makes it easier for you to do it again by contacting you online the next year, when they mail out forms. But even if you prepare a traditional tax return, the ability to get less-common tax forms and full information right online can make life a little easier.

While online filing of tax returns is a great help, it doesn't mean you can wait until April 15 to start preparing. Traditionally, post offices stay open late on that date, as the regulations specify that, if your mailed return is postmarked before midnight, you're not late. The same deadline applies to online returns – the difference is that putting information on paper and making copies takes enough time that nobody waits until the last minute to start.

We may think a few minutes at the computer is all it takes. But there are always potential problems such as an equipment breakdown or software glitch. If you made no plans for a traditional return, sat down at your computer at a quarter to twelve on April 15, and found your ISP was down, it would be too late to go to Plan B.

Capital gains and other special issues

For detailed answers and expertise, visit the tax pages of financial web sites. How to minimize the impact of capital gains tax, for instance, falls within the bigger picture of financial planning and portfolio management.

We went to www.quicken.com, and selected "Turbotax," which activated a link to www.turbotax.com. There were options for doing taxes right on the web, for tips and quick answers to tax questions, for an investor tax center, and other pages.

Under tips and quick answers, we opened this question: "When should you roll over your traditional IRA to a Roth?" Answer: "When the market is down – you'll pay less in taxes, because your IRA is worth less then." Selecting the investor tax center opened a link to the brokerage house Morgan Stanley Dean Witter (www.msdw.com), where capital gains taxes were a major category. These are just examples of the tax questions investors ask. If you don't want to get deeply involved in the subject, but prefer to leave it to a hired tax consultant, look for these services online, too, at such sites as www.securetax.com.

■ **SecureTax.com** *operates an online automated tax consultancy service.*

In addition to the tax features of Quicken and Microsoft Money, you can also get tax preparation software, such as Turbotax. Because taxes are so variable, and each individual situation is unique, we question the worth of online discussion and chat. But e-mailing tax questions, and getting answers from the experts, can be a big help. Anyone who's ever tried to get an answer on the phone from the IRS can testify to the frustration of that method. We believe the services of the IRS are probably improving as a result of Internet alternatives, which provide much better service to customers – as well as some relief for over-worked IRS employees.

■ **TaxWeb** *gives general information and help on tax for consumers.*

Day trading

Many Americans first heard about day trading in 1999, when a man in Atlanta walked into a broker's office and shot several people to death. The media soon discovered that he had lost a lot of money day trading; that misfortune, combined with other problems in his life, proved too much for him. Day trading? We said, "What's that?"

Day trading is the activity of an individual investor who buys and sells stocks and bonds completely alone, unaided by any intermediaries except fellow day traders and observers of the scene at stock trading web sites. Some day traders monitor sites such as Career Day Trader (www.careerdaytrader.com) and Raging Bull (www.ragingbull.com).

These sites keep a very close watch on the markets, provide advice online to day traders, and encourage a tolerance for high risk in the hope of exorbitant profits.

At Career Day Trader is this disclaimer: "There is a very high degree of risk involved in day trading." This site includes a "tradeometer," which supposedly gives a reading of the expected performance of any given stock. Our caution is, go ahead only if you can afford to lose your money.

These statements are found at LoneWolf Systems (www.lonewolf.com): "Trading offers an opportunity to make a lot of money fast." And, "If you know how to trade you can make your own hours, live and work wherever you please, and be your own boss." This may have happened to some day traders, as it has occasionally happened for people who think they can make a lot of money gambling.

But for the vast majority, it's a recipe for bankruptcy or worse, and disaster comes, not because traders were not smart enough, but because disaster is the expected result of delusionary thinking.

Every responsible financial advisor will say that long-term investment yields the greatest returns. Make wise, informed investments and leave them alone. If you can't resist the siren's call, day trade only with money you can afford to lose. We mention day trading in this chapter only because you may have wondered about it, but it's much more closely related to gambling than to serious investing.

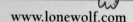

INTERNET

www.lonewolf.com

The ultimate in day trading philosophy is found at LoneWolf Systems, where trading stocks is described as "stalking prey." We suggest you not go there except to get the flavor of day trading in its purest essence.

■ **The stock market** *creates both winners and losers.*

In this chapter, we've taken a look at many aspects of investing, and provided an orientation to the subject for new investors. We've also introduced the online arena to those familiar with investing, but not with the Internet. We've sampled just a taste of the great variety of online resources, and have seen how much more is out there on the World Wide Web.

■ **Career Day Trader's** *site includes a "tradeometer," which claims to predict stock performances.*

A simple summary

✓ Thoughtful financial planning is the starting point for any investment decision.

✓ Investing in the stock market calls for getting acquainted with the language used in this arena, selecting a broker, opening an account, possibly transferring existing stocks, and learning the ins and outs of buying and selling.

✓ For those who are just getting started as investors, research and self-education must come first. Beginning with the basics, the newcomer can graduate to the more detailed information available at financial resource web sites.

✓ Creating a portfolio calls for deciding what to buy; gathering reliable information; and looking into the option of investing in mutual funds.

✓ Commodity trading is becoming more popular, but carries a slightly higher risk than stock trading.

✓ Taxation is a demanding subject for investors, but there's a great deal of help online. You can file your tax returns online, as well as download forms and publications. You can also get answers to many questions about tax law at many web sites.

✓ Day trading is a very high-risk venture, more like gambling than legitimate investing. We don't recommend it for anyone.

Chapter 24

Making Money Online

NOW THAT YOU'VE BECOME a full member of the online community, you might be wondering if there's a way to make a little money on the Internet. This book is not a business book, and shouldn't be used as a reference for setting up a business – we just want to point you toward some some resources you might need to pursue your ideas.

When it comes to profiting from the Internet, there are, as usual, loads of resources online. We'll talk about starting a new online business, putting an existing business online, and using the Internet to earn supplemental income.

In this chapter...

✓ Setting up a new online business

✓ Marketing your online business

✓ Other money makers

✓ Other dollars

YOU CAN TOAST IN ADVANCE IF STARTING A BUSINESS ON THE INTERNET IS YOUR PLAN

On the web, you'll see lots of talk about "get rich quick" schemes. Many of the ideas that are supposed to make money for you begin by requiring that you give money to someone else, helping them out along their path to getting rich quick. A few of these opportunities are legitimate (if risky), but others are dubious at best, and fraudulent at worst.

We recommend a conservative and wary approach. If you're considering an investment or business venture, we encourage you to use due diligence, check references, consult with trusted advisors, and use the consumer protection sites and organizations, such as www.fraud.org, we've already mentioned.

We'll suggest a few ideas you can explore as ways to make money via the Internet. We'll also look at what it takes to start a new online business, how to use the Internet to grow revenues for existing small businesses, and then consider a few ways to utilize Internet opportunities to supplement your income.

Setting up a new online business

THE INTERNET HAS *increased the opportunities for small businesses, partly because the initial investment required for start-up can be relatively small, as compared with the cost of establishing a bricks-and-mortar business. But the necessary planning is the same as for any small business. Market research, competitive analyses, operational plans, staffing support requirements, bank accounts, insurance, credit card merchant accounts, and many other factors are all part of that planning for small businesses.*

If you're thinking of starting a new business, start from the ground up with the traditional processes required to start any small business: writing a solid business plan; covering legal bases such as incorporating and obtaining licenses; and getting your finances in order.

■ **The official** *Small Business Administration site at www.sba.gov is a good place to begin research on setting up an online business.*

The Small Business Administration's (www.sba.gov) site provides links to SBA offices all over the country, as well as over 3,000 outside resources. There are lots of other web sites addressing issues like forming a new business, writing a business plan, obtaining capital, and marketing. For example, try:

✓ Online Women's Business Center: www.onlinewbc.org
✓ Yahoo's Small Business Center: www.smallbusiness.yahoo.com
✓ American Express Small Business Exchange:
    home3.americanexpress.com/smallbusiness

■ **If your** *cyberbusiness involves products, such as books, then shipping costs must be taken into account.*

Cyberbusiness

Many small online businesses have relatively few overhead expenses. Conducted from someone's kitchen or den, they can access the global marketplace, sometimes providing services or products that can be delivered online. For instance, a résumé writing service, or a web design service, produces income for the business owner – even though nothing is ever boxed and mailed. If there's an actual product involved, the operation becomes more complicated, requiring the storage and monitoring of inventory, shipping, and receiving. These operations have to be either set up, or outsourced.

Whatever the product or service, online businesses have real-world needs. Your business may require professional service providers like attorneys, accountants, bankers, designers, and technology providers. The ramifications of your business will probably turn out to be more far-reaching than you first thought. Take time to think it through and get well organized.

Accepting credit cards

Almost any successful web-based business needs to accept credit card payments. To do this, you'll need a "merchant account." Most banks can grant this, but some banks are reluctant to do so. Many banks impose restrictive policies – requirements such as a certain amount of capital reserve, or length of time in business. But your own bank might be more receptive, especially if you've done business with them for a while. Rather than risk losing you as a customer, they may accommodate your request for a merchant account. If not, you'll have to seek merchant account services elsewhere.

There are some alternatives to the customary merchant account. Sometimes, an intermediary, such as an ISP, can hold the merchant account, allowing you to do business by renting their services. You can also secure, from some Internet services, non-merchant accounts that will process payments for you, for a fee (although some of these are expensive).

Sites to check for these possibilities include www.bigstep.com and www.econgo.com. There are also methods being developed to take online payments without credit cards.

Putting a business online

WHAT IF YOU OPERATE a business, but don't yet have a web site? In this book, you've already learned that creating one is simple. If your business sells products that can be shipped, the Internet is an obvious vehicle for reaching millions of potential customers. We've already listed sites that can help you set up e-commerce. Creating an online store is more than child's play, but it's within reach for most businesses.

No matter what your business, before forging ahead with site-building, we suggest you address a few key questions. How will a web site benefit your business? How will you maintain it, and measure its return on investment? What kind of web site is best suited to your business? How much will it cost, and how you promote it? Are there other online marketing strategies that would be more useful than a web site? Answers to these questions vary for every business. Here are a few basic ideas being used by lots of businesses.

Promotion

■ **Why not advertise** *your service on the Net?*

If your business provides a service, like house painting, interior design, hairstyling, or plumbing, you might think a web site makes no sense. After all, why bother advertising to people all over the world, when all your business takes place within a ten-mile radius? Are there local web sites or directories that serve your community? How about getting listed there?

Perhaps you could get links to a site where you can display examples of your work, and generate leads by inviting e-mailed requests for estimates.

Or perhaps you could promote your landscaping business by writing an "ask the expert" column about lawn and garden care for the local portal site. Do you have loyal customers? Why not post your schedule online, and offer news and sales promotions, such as "refer-a-friend" programs? In our experience, the key to leveraging the online sphere is to be creative and purposeful. As usual, the Internet itself is rich with marketing tips and examples. See what people in your business – and other businesses – are doing, and be inspired!

■ **You can buy** *home improvement tools online.*

Selling advertising

If you've created an attractive and effective web site that generates lots of traffic, offering advertising space to others may be a good way to earn extra income. If your site is devoted to a particular subject, advertisers of related products (that aren't in direct competition with you) may want to advertise their messages to your visitors. Advertising can include banners, tiles, special offers, section sponsorships, and many other options.

Reducing costs

We heard about one company whose first web site resulted from an analysis of the costs of distributing daily lunchroom menus. Posting their cafeteria menu each day on their web site made it unnecessary to photocopy the paper version and have someone carry it to all the employee work stations in the building. The site paid for itself quickly. There are lots of ways the Internet can reduce shipping, printing, and distribution costs.

Other ways the Internet can save you money include streamlining internal communications, and shortening the RFP (request for proposal) and purchasing cycles.

Many professional organizations and journals are addressing ways to help their members and industries benefit from the Internet. We can't tell you what will work for your business, but we do suggest that cost reduction be on your radar, along with e-commerce, advertising, and generating leads.

Customer service

Online customer service can be a powerful communication tool between a company and its customers and prospects. This encompasses customer retention, marketing and sales, and cost reduction.

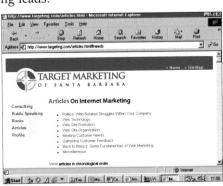

■ **Intriguing articles** *on online customer services can be found at Target Marketing.*

Famous examples like Federal Express' success with online package tracking have often been cited in web business courses. Jim Sterne of Target Marketing has published several insightful articles on this subject at www.targeting.com/articles.

Don't make the mistake of creating a web site for your business, publishing it, and then just thinking of it as self-sustaining. Building the site is just the beginning.

Someone must be responsible for retrieving and answering e-mail every day, attending to technical issues, posting new information, checking links, and continually updating and improving the site's appearance and content. A site with out-of-date information is a sure way to turn customers away. And, updating your web site encourages potential customers to keep coming back, to check out what's new, or what's on sale.

Marketing your online business

ONCE YOU'VE INVESTED *your effort and financial resources in a web site, you'll want to generate visibility and traffic. There are lots of methods. If you've been watching television lately, you've noticed that "dot.coms" are clamoring for attention. Your business doesn't necessarily have to buy a slot during halftime at the Super Bowl to create awareness. There are lots of less expensive means. We urge you to gather ideas online.*

■ **Check out** *Search Engine Watch for advice on getting listed in search engines.*

Search engines

Research into online shopping habits shows that search engines and directories are among the chief drivers of site traffic. Getting top positions with search engines is a highly-competitive arena, requiring lots of energy, strategy, technique, and a bit of luck. Unfortunately, it's also an area that can prove frustrating for a combination of reasons, including technical limitations of giant online databases, as well as the underhanded practices of some search engine spammers. The major search engine and directory sites offer links (sometimes hard to find, but they're there) that allow you to submit your web site's URL to their databases.

Each search site has its own requirements, procedures, and processes for incorporating your URL into its index — sometimes it takes as long as two months for a site to begin showing up. Optimizing the value of search engines requires the use of "meta tags" in your HTML documents.

We recommend you not to rush out to hire one of the services that claim they'll submit your site to lots of search engines, for a fee. Rather, take time to learn about the subject first, so you can make an informed judgement about your most effective course of action.

Online public relations

Public relations online is all about getting your business mentioned in a positive light on other web sites, and in the media, without paying for it. Editorial offices receive a staggering volume of faxed and e-mailed press releases. However, editors do cull through them, looking for noteworthy items. If your site is mentioned as a "hot site" by one of the major portals, or on a television broadcast, you may well see a big jump in traffic. If you're planning a marketing program, make public relations and online publicity part of the mix. Here are a few web sites with helpful information:

✓ Publicity.com: www.publicity.com
✓ Online Public Relations: www.online-pr.com
✓ Tenagra's Internet Marketing Center: www.marketing.tenagra.com/imr.html

Advertising

If you're serious about promoting your online business, there's a good chance your media budget will dwarf any other expense you incur. Even at a more modest level, advertising may be a good idea. If done well, it can contribute greatly to your success.

ADVERTISING SITES

You can find useful information about online advertising at many web sites:

✓ Advertising Age: www.adage.com
✓ Ad Guide: www.ad-guide.com
✓ AdMedia: www.admedia.com

■ **There are online** *advertising ideas at many web sites including Internet.com's Ad Resource.*

Adauction (www.adauction.com) is a site where advertising space is auctioned. Some sites use a type of free advertising called a banner exchange. Banner exchanges let sites trade ad banners.

You can set up such an arrangement with just an electronic handshake between your site and another, or through any one of numerous banner exchange service sites.

E-mail marketing

Well-executed e-mail marketing can be one of your most effective tools in bringing traffic to your web site, and generating sales and relationships with customers. If done poorly, though, it can turn off potential customers and tarnish your company's reputation. The web has many sites devoted to e-mail marketing. Some of them take rather extreme positions, for example, using terminology like "kill the spammers." We find the extremism distasteful, but understand the frustration with excessive commercial e-mail, especially the more offensive varieties. We suggest that e-mail marketing programs follow these guidelines:

✓ Send e-mail only to people who have granted you permission to do so.

✓ Always honor requests not to receive e-mail.

✓ Publish a clear and easy-to-find privacy policy, preferably with an online privacy seal such as BBB Online or eTrust. By the way, don't just publish a policy; follow it, and be sure everyone in your organization who might send e-mail understands it!

✓ Reply to e-mail messages promptly.

✓ Work hard to make any e-mail messages you send truly relevant, useful, and informative.

✓ Don't overwhelm your customers with frequent e-mails.

✓ Be extremely selective before renting e-mail lists; rent lists only of people who've specifically stated they want e-mail on the subject you address, and who've granted permission for others to send them such messages.

Due to abuse, e-mail marketing has come under the regulation of several state laws, and may eventually be covered by federal laws as well. These laws specify that certain techniques used by spammers can result in heavy fines and penalties. When sending commercial e-mail, always use a valid return e-mail address the recipient can reply to.

Never fake, or try to obscure, the header information that shows where the message originated, and don't use deliberately-misleading subject lines designed to get the recipient to open the e-mail under false pretenses. Not only are these maneuvers bad business practices; in some places, they're illegal.

Site performance, design, and maintenance

Always offer relevance, freshness, speedy service, ease-of-use, and up-to-date content. Impatient surfers with trigger fingers will inevitably compare your site to others. Your site must perform well and look good. Your content must be clear and current. Would you come back to an online store you saw advertising a holiday promotion a month after the holiday has passed? Marketing will translate into sales only if visitors can be converted into customers. This requires attractive, informative style and content.

Other money makers

ASIDE FROM ONLINE *businesses, there are many opportunities for alert, innovative minds to earn money on the Internet. This section doesn't claim to cover them all – you may discover additional creative options we never imagined! But here are just a few tips you might want to follow up.*

Selling at auctions

Online auction sites are very popular. To list items for sale, you must register, give the auction site a credit card number, and then submit items according to the site's selling rules. These rules always include attaching an item number distinguishing each item from all others. Sometimes, after bids come in, the seller and buyer communicate directly to complete the transaction. More often now, though, the auction sites provide credit card payment options and electronic payment transfers. Once a bid is accepted and payment made, the seller's account is credited. The seller is then notified by e-mail, and must forward the item to the buyer.

■ **The Yahoo Store** *is a shopping mall that can have the feel of a flea market.*

Accounts at eBay, Yahoo, and other auction sites are generally very effective ways to sell desirable merchandise. After you've done this a few times, you'll be familiar with the various techniques of describing items for sale, and picking the best times to market different things. Some people become quite expert in finding articles for almost nothing at rummage sales and flea markets, and then making a profit by selling them at auction online.

FIFTY CENTS?

People who conduct annual rummage sales for charities or institutions learn how to spot the dealers. As soon as a sale opens, the first customers in the door will include some of these apparently nonchalant, unhurried shoppers who browse the tables of old clothes and junk, picking up an item here and an item there. If the item is marked a dollar, they'll offer fifty cents. Later on, these rummage sale purchases will appear in shops for ten or twenty times what the dealer paid for them. And now, they may well show up online for even more. Is this taking advantage of the uninformed, or is it good business? Depends on your outlook!

Flea market sites

The Yahoo Store is like a shopping mall with many small merchants, but it can also seem more like a consignment shop, a craft show, or even a flea market. A seller can set up shop within the Yahoo Store, and all transactions take place there. You need a merchant account to sell things, but Yahoo will help you acquire one.

■ **If people collect it,** *you'll find it on the Net. A search for "rosemaling" (a Scandinavian decorative art) led to this page.*

The ins and outs of marketing crafts and collectibles are best known to in-groups of artisans and collectors. Opportunities to work together with others to market similar products, and to exchange information and ideas, are available on the web – most often under the subject headings of the particular craft or collection involved. For instance, we entered the word "rosemaling" in a major search engine. (Rosemaling is a Scandinavian decorative art, popular among Norwegian communities.) One return among the first list was the Norskland Discussion Forum (www.Norskland.com).

We believe there are similar locations online for every kind of handicraft and collection, and that much of the discussion at such sites involves the sale of creations and collectibles.

The unintentional business

Sometimes, people create personal web sites, not intending them to be income-producers. The online world beats a path to their door, though, and eventually some visitor will ask if they can buy whatever is the focus of that web site – a cookbook, a joke book, a collection of poetry, or a sample of your handicrafts. This is a real invitation to set up shop. Many well-known, web sites started that way.

Other dollars

THERE ARE OTHER *legitimate ways to make a little money on the Internet. Prizes for "catching the monkey," winning some online game or completing some survey are not what we mean by legitimate ways! Don't believe such offers of incredible giveaways they are usually not all that they seem. We did talk, back in Chapter 22, about some of the free materials available on the Internet, but the ones we mentioned are reasonable offers that generate good will for the providers, or help promote products.*

Associate, affiliate, and referral programs

Associate, affiliate, and referral programs are arrangements with e-commerce sites in which you agree to sell or advertise their product through your own web site. These deals are something like commission or revenue-sharing agreements, where the amount you earn is dependent upon the volume of sales generated by your site. Or, you can be paid a standard fee, rather like a rental.

■ **Clickrewards is** *one of the sites that rewards Internet shoppers by giving them points that can be redeemed online.*

A simple summary

✓ Setting up a new business should be well thought out before you execute plans for putting the business online.

✓ Accepting credit card payments is important for e-commerce.

✓ Putting an existing business online calls for deciding on a business approach, establishing a web site, and maintaining it, promoting it, and marketing it.

✓ Advertising on your own web site can also be a source of revenue.

✓ Those with collectibles, can often find buyers at auction sites.

✓ Sometimes a business develops unintentionally, out of a particularly attractive web site, or one with an unusual focus.

✓ There are many opportunities to earn money through associate and affiliate relationships, where products or services of one web site are offered for sale by another.

Conclusion

AT THE BEGINNING *of this book we sought to overcome the trepidations of people who wanted to get online but had been discouraged by unhelpful books and discourteous computer experts. You have come a long way with us now, and we hope that all our readers have the same respect and appreciation for the Internet that motivated this writing.*

You're reading about the Internet from a book made of paper and ink. We think that is a significant fact. We like books, magazines, and newspapers and believe they'll always be here. Lots of people think the Internet is eventually going to "save a lot of trees," which would be good for the forests, but would mean fewer paper and ink publications. That may happen, but we believe online resources will continue to supplement and expand our horizons, and will not replace other media.

Prognosticators agree that the Internet will continue to grow, they only differ as to how big and how fast. There seems little doubt, however, that immense growth will take place in numbers of users, international reach, economic might, cultural and political impact, technological breadth, and in its presence in our daily lives. We believe new technologies will continue to refine and expand existing capabilities, making Internet operations faster, easier, and more diverse. Finally we want to express our faith in the Internet as an influence for good in the world.

The Internet is much more than a huge database, a technological achievement, and a convenience for improving life. We believe it is a powerful influence in shaping society, and as historically significant as the industrial revolution. That social movement forever altered the relationships between employment and homes, impacted the family, and enabled the economic development of the industrialized nations. The influence of the electronic revolution also continues to spread throughout society, and it may be another generation or two before its impact is revealed and social scientists begin to consider how the Internet has altered economic, social, and personal relationships.

We see the Internet as a gateway to a richer life and more opportunities for all the things we want to do, from finding better jobs, to finding toys at Christmas, to finding help for staying healthy, and all the things we've touched on in this book. If it seemed that we brushed by too quickly some of the things you wanted to know more about, we knew that would happen because the subject is just too big to put between book covers.

Additional resources

Bookmarks of Interest

Here are a few web sites you might find helpful and enjoyable.

www.aim.aol.com
Download the AOL Instant Messenger.

www.aixs.net
Aixs.net can help shield your identity in Internet activity.

www.aladdin.com
Stuffit explains about transmission of files and offers compression utility for Macintosh systems.

www.albion.com/netiquette
Good educational content about netiquette.

www.allcam.com
AllCam's webcam.

www.ancestry.com
Thousands of family names are listed at this site.

www.anexa.com
A web site that represents a virtual community.

www.anonymizer.com
On the home page you surf the net anonymously.

www.aoanet.org
The American Optometric Association has advice on how to avoid eyestrain.

www.aqualink.com
Aqualink is a a web site for fishkeepers.

www.army.net
A site with mail forwarding and other helpful services for members of the U.S. armed forces.

www.associatedpress.com
The news wire service.

www.av.ibm.com
You will find a lot of background information on the subject of viruses, current concerns, and anti-virus protection.

www.bankweb.com
A directory of online financial institutions.

www.bankonline.com
A directory of online financial institutions.

www.bbbonline.com
A traditional guardian of consumer protection is the Better Business Bureau.

www.BET.com
The home page of Black Educational Television.

www.betterbrain.com
A useful all-in-one page.

www.bettycrocker.com
Check out Betty Crocker to find great recipes on line.

www.bigfoot.com
A site with mail forwarding and other helpful services.

www.blooberry.com/indexdot/html/index.html
Index Dot HTML will lead you to information about cutting-edge extensions to basic HTML.

www.britannica.com
Encyclopaedia Britannica is a good general reference site.

www.budgetweb.com/
BudgetWeb has listings you can search for web site hosts.

www.builder.com
Web Builder is one of our favorites pages on HTML and web site design.

www.cammunity.com
Cammunity's webcam.

www.cast.org/bobby
Bobby helps in ensuring the quality of your site.

www.cdt.org
The Center for Democracy and Technology, a resource for information about the latest in Internet law.

www.clipart.com
Clipart.com is an online image archive where you can access and download graphics.

www.clipartconnection.com
An online image archive where you can access and download graphics.

www.clubs.yahoo.com
A web site that represents a virtual community.

www.compaq.com/comfortguide
Compaq Computer WorkStation Comfort Guide has ergonomic information about computer use.

www.computerprivacy.org
Americans for Computer Privacy has information about privacy issues and policies on the Internet.

www.congress.org
Congress.org is one of the best starting points for finding government information on the web.

www.consumer.gov
The Federal Consumer Information Gateway is one web resource for consumers.

www.consumerreports.org
You'll find a rich, useful site with a section called E-Ratings that addresses online stores, plus offering helpful tips and forums for members.

www.consumersunion.org
Find Consumer's Union (publishers of Consumer Reports) at this site.

www.coollist.com
This site offers help in starting new mailing lists.

www.cpsc.gov
The Consumer Products Safety Commission is one web resource for consumers.

www.cu.org
A directory of online credit unions.

www.culinary.com
Check out Culinary.com to find great recipes on line.

www.cwrl.utexas.edu/moo
At this site you can access the Multiple User type game.

www.cyberfiber.com
Look at Cyberfiber to find newsgroups organized within USENET.

www.cyber.findlaw.com
A resource for information about the latest in Internet law.

www.datafellows.com/virus-info
You will find a lot of background information on the subject of viruses, current concerns, and anti-virus protection at Data Fellows.

www.deja.com
Enables you to search or browse either to find newsgroups dealing with specific subjects or to find postings containing specific keywords.

www.desktoppublishing.com/cliplist.html
Image Paradise is an online image archive where you can access and download graphics.

www.discovery.com/cams/cams.html
The Discovery Channel's Live Cams page.

www.drsolomon.com/vircen
You will find a lot of background information on the subject of viruses, current concerns, and anti-virus protection at Dr. Solomon's Virus Central.

www.dvdresources.com
Check this site out for current information about DVDs.

www.earthcam.com
Earthcam's webcam.

www.ebbs.english.vt.edu/moo.html
Find MOO links here.

www.eff.org
Electronic Frontier Foundation has information about privacy issues and policies on the Internet.

www.efuse.com
Efuse is devoted to promoting top-quality web design.

www.egroups.com
This site offers help in starting new mailing lists.

www.electronicbanker.com
A directory of online financial institutions.

www.encarta.msn.com
Encarta is a good general reference site.

www.encyclopedia.com
Columbia Electronic Encyclopedia is a good general reference site.

engage.webpromote.com
This site offers help in starting new mailing lists.

www.epic.org
The Electronic Privacy Information Center is a civil liberties protection group.

www.epicurious.com
Find great recipes on line.

www.ergo.human.cornell.edu
Cornell University Ergonomics web site has ergonomic information about computer use.

www.ergoweb.com
Ergonomic information about computer use.

www.escribe.com
A catalog of mailing lists can be found at eScribe.

www.eye2eye.com
Advice on how to avoid eyestrain.

www.familypoint.com
A web site that represents a virtual community.

www.familytreemaker.com
A site for beginning geneaologists.

www.fedstats.gov
FedStats is one of the best starting points for finding government information on the web.

www.forumone.com/build.htm
A web site that represents a virtual community.

www.FTC.gov/privacy/protection.htm
The Federal Trade Commission is the governmental agency with authority to regulate communications media.

www.funkandwagnalls.com
Funk and Wagnalls is a good general reference site.

www.Gardentown.com
A web site devoted to gardeners.

www.genhomepage.com
A site for beginning geneaologists.

www.getmessage.com
Getmessage.com provides information about telephony.

www.getnetwise.org
Get NetWise is a user advocacy organization.

www.gettingstarted.net/
Getting Started is one of our favorites pages on HTML and web site design.

www.gooey.com
Roaming chat tools are made available at Gooey.

www.helping.org
Helping.org provides useful resources for assistance for non-profit organizations seeking to use the Internet to further their cause.

www.highfive.com
HighFive.com is one of our favorite web sites devoted to promoting web design.

www.home.netscape.com/security
A good site for more information about SSL and other security topics.

hometown.aol.com/sjastroc/index.html
A web site with audio messaging.

www.hon.ch
The Health On the Net Foundation is working to create standards and guidelines for health web sites.

www.htmlgoodies.com
HTML Goodies will lead you to information about cutting-edge extensions to basic HTML.

www.htmlhelp.com
HTML Help is one of our favorite pages on HTML and web site design.

www.hwg.org
HTML Writer's Guild has very good information on HTML and web site design.

www.iana.org/cctld.html
Here's a web site to find out more about registering international TLDs.

www.iconbazaar.com
Icon Bazaar is an online image archive where you can access and download graphics.

www.icq.com
Download the ICQ Instant Messenger.

www.idealist.org
Action Without Borders provides useful resources for non-profit organizations seeking to use the Internet to further their cause.

www.ihc.net
The Internet Health Coalition is working to create standards, guidelines, and perhaps even accreditation for health web sites.

www.imagiware.com/RxHTML
Dr. HTML provides help in ensuring the quality of your site.

www.infi.net/wwwimages/colorindex.html
You can look up and learn more about color and hexidecimal values at this site.

www.infohiway.com/faster
Bandwidth Conservation Society is one of our favorite web sites devoted to promoting top-quality web design.

www.info.med.yale.edu/caim/manual
The Yale Web Style Guide is impressive and is devoted to promoting top-quality web design.

www.infoplease.com
Information Please is a good general reference site.

www.jade.wabash.edu/wabnet/info/netiquet.htm
Good educational content about netiquette.

www.jurist.law.pitt.edu
The Law Professor's Network Cyberspace Law Guide, a resource for information about the latest in Internet law.

www.latinolink.com
Latino Link, a site of special interest to Hispanics.

www.law.indiana.edu/law/v-lib/states.html
The Virtual law Library is one of the best starting points for finding government information on the web.

www.lcweb.loc.gov/global/html.html
Library of Congress HTML page will lead you to information about cutting-edge extensions to basic HTML, including JavaScript, Dynamic HTML, Cascading Style Sheets, and XML.

www.lightsphere.com/colors
You can look up and learn more about color on the web and hexidecimal values at this site.

www.lissaexplains.com/
A web site with audio messaging.

www.Liszt.com
Mailing lists are catalogued at Liszt, currently with almost 100,000 different lists.

www.livewebcam.com
Web Cams of the World's webcam.

www.lonewolf.com
The ultimate in day trading philosophy is found at this site. We suggest you go there only to get the flavor of day trading.

www.lynda.com/hex.html
You can look up and learn more about color and hexidecimal values at this site.

www.mcafee.com/centers/anti-virus
You will find a lot of background information on the subject of viruses, current concerns, and anti-virus protection at McAfee's Anti-Virus Center.

www.mcli.dist.maricopa.edu/tl
Alan Levine is an Instructional Technologist who works at the Maricopa Center For Learning and Instruction in California, maintains a diverse and

fascinating list of educational uses of the Internet.

www.mediametrix.com/TopRankings/TopRankings.html
Media Metrix, provides the latest rankings of top web sites.

www.medicare.gov
The web site for information about Medicare.

www.messenger.msn.com
Download the Microsoft Instant Messenger.

MetaSearchEngines.com
A directory of meta search sites, is worth checking out.

www.microsoft.com
Microsoft home page for Internet Explorer.

www.moo.mud.org/moo-faq/
Find MOO Cows FAQ here.

www.mpeg.org
Check this site out for current information about DVDs.

www.mp3.com
This web site has become an MP3 portal where you can get a thorough introduction to the whole subject of Internet multimedia, especially music.

www.mudcentral.com
Find MUD Central here.

www.mudconnector.com
Find a MUD Connector here.

www.m-w.com
Mirriam Webster is a good general reference site.

www.mybank.com
A directory of online financial institutions.

www.my.deja.com
A web site that represents a virtual community.

www.myfamily.com
A web site that represents a virtual community.

www.my-meals.com
Check out My Meals to find great recipes on line.

www.mytalk.com
MyTalk provides information about telephony.

www.naco.org
National Association of Counties is one of the best

starting points for finding government information on the web.

www.nashville.net/~carl/htmlguide/index.html
How do they do that with HTML? will lead you to information about cutting-edge extensions to basic HTML, including JavaScript, Dynamic HTML, Cascading Style Sheets, and XML.

www.netmechanic.com
Net Mechanic provides help in ensuring the quality of your site.

www.netnoir.com
Net Noir is a site of special interest to African-Americans.

www.home.netscape.com
Netscape maintains an excellent list of plug-ins available for audio and video as well as many other purposes at home.netscape.com/plugins.

www.net2phone.com
Net2Phone provides information about telephony.

www.nielsen-netratings.com/hot_off.htm
Nielson/Netratings search to find out the latest rankings of top web sites.

www.nonags.com
A library of shareware and freeware.

www.nonprofit.gov
Non-Profit Gateway provides useful resources for non-profit organizations seeking to use the Internet to further their cause.

www.nonprofits.org
Internet Non-Profit Center provides useful information for non-profit organizations to further their cause.

www3.ns.sympatico.ca/thekarls/
A web site with audio messaging.

www.odigo.com
Roaming chat tools are described and made available at Odigo.

www.oed.com
Oxford English Dictionary is a good general reference site.

officialcitysites.org
Official City Sites is one of the best starting points for finding government information on the web.

www.onebox.com
OneBox provides information about telephony.

www.onelist.com
This site offers help in starting new mailing lists.

www.ontap.com/spy-cams
OnTap's SpyCams's webcam.

www.pager.yahoo.com
Download the Yahoo pager Instant Messenger.

www.pagoo.com
Pagoo provides information about telephony.

www.pal.excite.com
Download the Excite Instant Messenger.

www.pcwebopaedia.com
There are lots of web sites to visit if you want more knowledge about technical matters like screen resolution.

www.pkware.com
Pkzip explains about transmission of files.

www.pobox.com
A site with mail forwarding and other helpful services.

www.privacyalliance.org
Online Privacy Alliance has information about privacy issues and policies on the Internet.

www.privacyrights.org
Privacy Rights Clearinghouse has information about privacy and policies on the Internet.

www.projectcool.com/developer/
Project Cool Developer's Zone will lead you to information about cutting-edge extensions to basic HTML, including JavaScript, Dynamic HTML, Cascading Style Sheets, and XML.

www.proteus.com
A useful all-in-one page.

www.proxymate.com
ProxyMate can help shield your identity in Internet activity.

www.puresearch.com
A useful all-in-one page.

www.radsci.ucla.edu/telemed/zhuling/index.html
A web site with audio messaging.

www.refdesk.com
Internet Reference Desk is a good general reference site.

www.relaymail.net
A site with mail forwarding and other helpful services.

www.reuters.com
Reuters, the news wire service.

www.rewebber.de
Rewebber can help shield your identity in Internet activity.

www.rootsweb.com
A site for beginning geneaologists.

www.rr.gmcs.k12.nm.us/staff.htm
A web site with audio messaging.

www.scambusters.org
General security issues are discussed here.

www.searchenginewatch.com
Several sites offer excellent information and guides to getting listed in search engines.

www.search-it-all.com
A useful all-in-one page.

www.shareware.com
A library of shareware and freeware.

www.shockzone.com
The ShockZone is an online image archive where you can access and download graphics.

www.shoutmail.com
ShoutMail provides information about telephony.

www.skworm.com
A useful all-in-one page.

www.startribune.com
The Minneapolis Star-Tribune newspaper web site provides a message board entitled Talk.

www.state.gov
The U.S. State Department web site distributes passport applications as pdf files.

www.statesnews.org
Council of State Governments is one of the best starting points for finding government information on the web.

www.sun.com/styleguide
Sun Computer's Style Guide is devoted to promoting top-quality web design.

www.sunsite.unc.edu/usenet-i
Begin with the Usenet Info Center Launch Pad to find newsgroups organized within USENET.

www.symantec.com/avcenter
You will find a lot of background information on the subject of viruses, current concerns, and anti-virus protection.

thelist.internet.com
The List has useful listings where you can search for web site hosts.

www.thirdage.com
At Third Age, a web site for active older adults, the link called Community leads you to message boards.

www.thirdvoice.com
Roaming chat tools are described and made available at ThirdVoice.

thomas.loc.gov
Thomas is one of the best starting points for finding government information on the web.

www.tile.net
Go to Tile Net to find newsgroups organized within USENET.

www.tips-tricks.com
HTML Tips & Tricks will lead you to information about cutting-edge extensions to basic HTML.

www.tophosts.com
Top Hosts has useful listings where you can search for web site hosts.

www.topica.com/
This site offers help in starting new mailing lists.

www.TRUSTe.org
TRUSTe is dedicated to three main purposes: to educate Internet users about ways to protect their privac; to encourage businesses to post privacy statements; and to serve as a liaison between consumers and TRUSTe's licensees.

www.tucows.com
A library of shareware and freeware.

www.ucook.com
Check out UCook to find great recipes on line.

www.upenn.edu/computing/group/dmp/technical/colors/curious.html
You can look up and learn more about color on the web and hexidecimal values at this site.

www.upi.com
United Press International, the news wire service.

www.ureach.com
UReach provides information about telephony.

www.ur-net.com/office-ergo
Office Ergonomics has ergonomic information about computer use.

www.use.ergonomics.ucla.edu
UCLA Ergonomics web site has ergonomic information about computer

www.users.erols.com/seyfritp/index.htm
A web site with audio messaging.

www.utok.com works
Utok is like a roaming message board, overlaid on web sites as you visit them.

www.veg.org/
A web site with audio messaging.

www.virtual-voice.com
Virtual Voice provides information about telephony.

www.vocaltec.com
VocalTec gives telephony information.

www.watson.addy.com
Dr. Watson provides help in ensuring the quality of your site.

www.wcom.com/cerfsup
This fascinating web page provides information about the project in space technology created by Vinton Cerf.

www.webclipart.about.com
About.com's Clip Art list is an online image archive where you can access and download graphics for your own personal web site.

www.webdeveloper.com
Web Developer is one of our favorites pages on HTML and web site design.

www.websitegarage.netscape.com
Web Site Garage provides help in ensuring the quality of your site.

www.weblint.org
WebLint provides help in ensuring the quality of your site.

www.webmonkey.com
WebMonkey will lead you to information about cutting-edge extensions to basic HTML.

www.webphone.com
WebPhone provides information about telephony.

www.websitesthatsuck.com
Web Sites That Suck is an impressive web site devoted to promoting top-quality web design.

www.whatis.com
What Is has lots of information about technical aspects of the web.

www.winsite.com
A library of shareware and freeware.

www.winzip.com
Winzip explains about transmission of files and offers compression utility for PC systems.

www.wm.edu/law/publications/jol
The Journal of Online Law provides abstracts of its articles about Internet law and invites you to download the articles if you wish.

women.com/foodchannel
This provides great recipes on line.

www.wpdfd.com
Design for Designers is devoted to promoting top-quality web design.

www.w3.org/WAI/References/Browsing
This site is designed to provide special help to persons with disabilities.

www.w3c.org/Markup
W3C is one of our favorite pages on HTML and web site design.

www.xoom.com/clipart
Xoom ClipArt Archive is an online image archive where you can access and download graphics.

www.yuri.org/webable/index.html
This site is designed to provide special help to persons with disabilities.

www.zeldman.com/askdrweb/
Ask Dr. Web will lead you to information about cutting-edge extensions to basic HTML.

www.zipmagic.com
ZipMagic explains about transmission of files.